The Last Poems of Ovid

Mark Bear Akrigg

The Last Poems of Ovid

ISBN/EAN: 9783337555573

Printed in Europe, USA, Canada, Australia, Japan

Cover: Foto ©Thomas Meinert / pixelio.de

More available books at **www.hansebooks.com**

by Mark Bear Akrigg, Ph.D.

This edition and commentary are dedicated to
ROB MORROW

"quo non mihi carior alter"

TABLE OF CONTENTS

ACKNOWLEDGEMENTS

The Editor gratefully acknowledges the permission of the Herzog August Bibliothek for the use of Herzog August Bibliothek Wolfenbüttel: Cod. Guelf. 13.11 Aug. 4° (fragmentum Guelferbytanum).

PREFACE

It is a pleasure to present to the public this digital edition, with commentary, of *Ex Ponto* IV, the final poems written by the Roman poet Ovid, published after his death as a posthumous collection quite separate from the earlier *Ex Ponto* I-III.

These poems have a special place among Ovid's works, but have not received the attention which they deserve. In particular, there has been no full modern commentary on these poems.

This text presented in this edition is based on my personal examination of ten manuscripts. I have also restored to the text certain readings commonly accepted by editors until the nineteenth century. Finally, the edition contains several dozen new textual conjectures by myself and others.

The intended audience of this edition

This edition is intended to serve as a guide to the poems for intermediate and advanced students of Latin poetry. However, I have deliberately made it as straightforward as possible, and my hope is that even a beginning student of Latin poetry embarking on the study of these poems will find the commentary helpful.

This edition is also directed towards present and future Latin textual critics.

My expectation when starting my research for this edition was that I would be presenting a text that differed little from that to be found in current editions. However, I made two discoveries during my research into the text.

The first discovery was that many important textual corrections generally accepted in the seventeenth and eighteenth centuries had been suppressed by editors in the course of the nineteenth century. I have restored many of these readings to the text, and others will be found in the textual apparatus.

The second discovery was that there was a surprisingly large number of passages which appeared to be corrupt and for which it was possible to suggest corrections. Given the long history of Latin textual criticism, and Ovid's central position in Roman literary history, it was surprising to find that so much remained to be done. Yet such was the case.

Nothing is more certain than that this book of poems as well as the three earlier books of the *Ex Ponto* represent an outstanding opportunity for future editors and commentators to contribute to the progress of Latin scholarship.

History of this edition

I originally prepared this edition and commentary during my time as a graduate student at the University of Toronto. Upon its completion (and my graduation) in 1985, a copy was deposited at the National Library of Canada.

Had I followed a university teaching career after graduation, I would undoubtedly have taken the necessary steps to publish the edition, if only in pursuit of academic promotion. But I instead chose a career in the software industry, which both removed the external incentive to publish the edition, and denied me the time that I would have needed to prepare it for publication.

However, I wished to ensure that future editors and commentators were aware of the edition and would be able to make use of it. I therefore decided to publish two short articles drawn from the edition. These articles were intended to make generally available two textual conjectures which I considered likely to be correct. But the articles were also intended to make future editors aware that I had worked on the text of Ovid, so that they would seek out my unpublished edition.

The first article ("An Intrusive Gloss in Ovid *Ex Ponto* 4.13") appeared in *Phoenix* (vol. 40, p. 322) in 1986: it reported the restoration of IV xiii 45 discussed at page 408 of the commentary. *Phoenix* is published by the Classical Association of Canada, and since my own training in the classical languages had taken place almost entirely in Canada, it seemed appropriate that my first publication should be in a Canadian journal.

To my surprise and pleasure, my short article attracted a critique by Professor Allan Kershaw ("*Ex Ponto* 4.13: A Reply", *Phoenix*, vol. 42, p. 176), followed by a learned defense of my conjecture by Professor James Butrica ("Taking Enemies for Chains: Ovid *Ex Ponto* 4.13.45 Again", *Phoenix*, vol. 43, pp. 258-59).

Four years later, I published a second article ("A Palaeographical Corruption in Ovid, *Ex Ponto* 4.6"), which appeared in the May 1990 issue of the *Classical Quarterly* (pp. 283-84). This article reported the restoration of IV vi 38 discussed at pages 240-41 of the commentary. I selected the *Classical Quarterly* because of its prominence within the world of classical scholarship, and in particular because of its close association with the modern history of Latin textual criticism: it was in the *Classical Quarterly* that many of the learned articles of A. E. Housman first appeared.

My hope had been that these two articles would serve as a signpost that would lead editors to my edition. The publication of J. A. Richmond's Teubner edition of the *Ex Ponto* in 1990 proved that this plan was inadequate. Professor Richmond had indeed discovered the existence of my edition: it received a prominent and flattering mention at the end of his preface. However, he stated that he received the microfilm of the edition too late for use in his edition!

In his review of Richmond's Teubner edition in the *Classical Review* (n.s. 42, 2 [1992], pp. 305-06), Professor James Butrica highlighted a number of proposed emendations from my edition.

It had become clear there was considerable outside interest in the work that I had done, and that simply having a copy of an unpublished edition on deposit at the National

Library of Canada was not a sufficient means of making the edition available to the public, so over the years that followed I gave some consideration to how I might publish the edition so that it would be conveniently available to students of Latin poetry.

Early in 2006, I was working as a volunteer proofreader for the Project Gutenberg digital library: I noticed that the Project Gutenberg library included some public domain classical editions comparable in scope to my own. Prompted by this, I decided that I would publish my edition online in order to make it instantly accessible free of charge to anyone wishing to use it. This seemed in every way preferable to seeking out a university press, going through the time-consuming process of seeking the necessary grants to subsidize publication, in order to produce a printed book so expensive that no student and not many libraries could afford to purchase a copy.

Nature of this edition

In essence, this is a corrected version of the original typescript. Typing errors have been corrected, and minor errors have been set right.

All statements made and conjectures proposed should be considered to have been made in 1985.

The HTML and Text versions of this edition

This digital edition is being made available in two versions.

The *HTML version* takes advantage of the Unicode character set to present Greek passages using the Greek alphabet, and to present certain other special characters, such as the macron. It also offers hyperlinks from the table of contents and from the indices to the relevant sections of the edition.

Popular and useful as HTML is, it does not offer the universality of ASCII text. Essentially every computer can display plain ASCII text correctly. The *Text version* is presented so that the edition can be read on any computer, large or small, new or old. However, this portability comes at a price. The ISO 8859-1 ASCII character set does not include the Greek alphabet, nor does it include certain special characters which form part of this edition.

Therefore, the Text version of this edition presents Greek passages transliterated into the Latin alphabet. Similarly, in the textual apparatus any capital letter occurring in the report of a manuscript should be considered to be that letter in lower case, with a macron (dash) above.

When the textual apparatus reports a manuscript correction where the original reading is no longer legible, the HTML version underlines the corrected letters, but the Text version uses capitalization. For example, the Text version reports "facTisque _B2c_" at iii 25: a later hand in B has erased the original fourth letter, and has replaced it with "t".

In the commentary, when metre is being discussed and a Latin word is quoted, any vowel in that word which is capitalized is long, and any vowel which is not capitalized is short. I have occasionally pointed out explicitly that a word is metrically inconvenient because it has a series of short vowels: in the HTML edition, because the actual letters are marked short, these statements will appear to be redundant.

In the Latin text, the start and end of passages which are deeply corrupt and therefore difficult to correct are indicated by an asterisk, instead of the usual dagger (obelus).

Finally, in the critical apparatus, 'æ' is used where a manuscript has 'e' with a cedilla.

Enhancements made: the indices

In order to make the digital edition as useful as possible, I have added this preface, a full table of contents, and two indices.

The first index (starting on page 477) is an index of *topics discussed*. It is a selective rather than an exhaustive index for the following two reasons:

(1) A commentary is already in effect indexed by the text it is linked to. If, for instance, readers wish to find what the commentary has to say about a certain passage, all they need do is turn to the part of the commentary dealing with that passage.

(2) A digital edition can be searched online very quickly and easily. A reader wishing to find any mention of the eminent Dutch textual critic Nicolaus Heinsius could find every mention of Heinsius in the edition simply by using "Heinsius" as a search argument.

However, some of the discussions in the commentary do not have an obvious link to the text, nor would they necessarily be found quickly by an electronic search. An example would be the discussion of "Simple verbs used for compound ones" at page 281.

Also, there were some parts of the introduction and commentary which I wanted to highlight to the reader as being of possible interest: including references to these in the index would serve this purpose.

For similar reasons, I have included (starting on page 489) an index of textual emendations first proposed in this edition. Some of these emendations involve works other than *Ex Ponto* IV, and authors other than Ovid. The index of textual emendations makes these corrections easy to find.

The debt I owe to others

I was able to create this edition only because of the help that I have received over the years from others.

My basic training in the classical languages took place at the University of British Columbia, where I completed my B.A. in 1974, and my M.A. in 1977. It is impossible to repay the debt I owe to every single member of the Classics Department at that time.

Professor Charles Murgia of the University of California (Berkeley) initiated me into the mysteries of Latin palaeography and textual criticism.

I created this edition while a Ph.D. candidate at the Department of Classics at the University of Toronto. I owe an enormous debt of gratitude to Professor Richard Tarrant, who encouraged me to undertake the edition, posed many excellent questions, and offered many excellent suggestions.

I owe a similar debt to Professor Alexander Dalzell, Professor Elaine Fantham, Professor J. N. Grant, and Professor C. P. Jones, all of them members of the Graduate Department of Classics at the University of Toronto when I was creating the edition.

I have known Rob Morrow for twenty-one years, and he has touched every aspect of my life. The study of Latin poetry is a field of endeavour far removed from his usual interests: but even here he has made an important contribution in the work he did in scanning the original typescript, and in his continuing encouragement and support during the months I worked on creating this digital edition. It is to him, with deep affection and gratitude, that I dedicate this edition.

INTRODUCTION

In AD 8, when he was fifty years of age, Ovid was abruptly banished from Rome to Tomis, an exile from which he never returned. In his poetry from exile, he gives two reasons for the banishment: the publication of the *Ars Amatoria*, and an unnamed error (*Tr* II 207; *EP* III iii 71-72)[1]. The *Ars Amatoria* had been published some years previously, being generally dated on the basis of *AA* I 171-72 to 2 BC or shortly thereafter; compare *Tr* II 545-46. The error was clearly the real cause of the banishment; what precisely this *error* was Ovid does not reveal, but it appears from *Tr* II 103-4 and *Tr* III v 49-50 to have been the witnessing of some action that was embarrassing to the imperial family. Beyond this nothing is known, for Ovid was careful to avoid compounding his original mistake by mentioning what it consisted of.

The catastrophe which befell Ovid did not put an end to his poetic activity; from the eight or nine years of his exile we possess a corpus of elegiac verse that substantially exceeds in bulk the combined production of Tibullus and Propertius.

The first work produced by Ovid was book I of the *Tristia*. Although it is perhaps not literally true that Ovid wrote much of the poetry on shipboard (*Tr* I xi 3-10), all of the poems are directly related to the circumstances of his downfall and his journey to exile; and it is reasonable to suppose that the book was published shortly after Ovid's arrival in Tomis.

In his first poems from exile, Ovid had attempted to engage the sympathy of the public on his behalf; his next production was a direct appeal to Augustus in the 578-line elegiac poem that comprises the second book of the *Tristia*. The poem is written with Ovid's usual clarity and elegance, but its failure to secure his recall is not surprising. The poem deals only with the publication of the *Ars Amatoria*, which was not the true cause of the exile; and rather than admitting his guilt and appealing to Augustus' clemency, Ovid tactlessly argues that Augustus had been wrong to exile him.

The years 10, 11, and 12 saw the publication of the final three books of the *Tristia*. The charge of monotony that is generally brought against Ovid's poetry from exile (and was brought by his friends at the time; Ovid makes his defence in *EP* III ix) is most nearly true of these three books of verse. He was unable to name his correspondents and vary his poetry with personal references as he was to do in the *Ex Ponto*; and the pain of exile was so fresh as to exclude other topics.

Not all of Ovid's literary efforts in exile were devoted to his letters. It appears from *Fast* IV 81-82 and VI 666, as well as from the dedication to Germanicus at the start of the first book (at *Tr* II 551 Ovid says he dedicated the work to Augustus) that the *Fasti* in the edition we possess is a revision produced by Ovid in exile after the death of Augustus.

In AD 12 Ovid produced the *Ibis*. The greater part of the poem is a series of curses showing such minute mythological learning that many of them have not been explained; but the poem's lengthy exordium is a powerful treatment of Ovid's circumstances and Ibis's perfidy that has been considered Ovid's most perfect literary creation (Housman 1041).

Many scholars also ascribe the composition of the final six *Heroides* to the period of Ovid's exile; but although the literary appeal of these three sets of double epistles is considerable, I believe that their comparative diffuseness of manner indicates that Ovid was not their author. They are, however, clearly modelled on the *Heroides* written by Ovid, and I have frequently quoted from them in the commentary.

In AD 12 Ovid must have received some indication that it was safe for him to name his correspondents. He took full advantage of this new opportunity to induce his friends to work on his behalf; it is clear from Ovid's references to his fourth year of exile (I ii 26, I viii 28) and to Tiberius' triumph of 23 October AD 12 (II i 1 & 46, II ii 75-76, II v 27-28, III i 136, III iii 86, III iv 3)[2] that all three books were written within the space of a single year: as fast a rate of composition as can be proved for any part of Ovid's life. The three books were published as a unit: the opening poem of the first book and the closing poem of the last are addressed to Brutus, who was therefore the dedicatee of the collection; both poems are apologies for Ovid's verse. No such framing poems are found at the start of books II or III, or at the end of books I and II, although the addressees of II i and III i, Germanicus and Ovid's wife, were clearly chosen for their respective importance and closeness to Ovid.

Ex Ponto IV

The fourth book of the *Ex Ponto* constitutes a work separate from the three books composed in AD 12. The earliest datable poem in the book is the fourth, written shortly before Sextus Pompeius' consulship in AD 14; the latest is the ninth, written in honour of Graecinus' becoming suffect consul in AD 16. Of the books of Ovid's verse which are collections of individual poems, the fourth book of the *Ex Ponto* is the longest, being some 926 lines in length (excluding the probably spurious distichs xv 25-26 and xvi 51-52). The mean average length of such books is 764 lines; and the next longest after *Ex Ponto* IV is *Am* III, with 824 lines (excluding the spurious fifth poem). I take the length of the book as an indication that in its present form it is probably a posthumous collection: Ovid's editor either gathered the individual poems to form a single book that was unusually long, or added a few later poems to a book previously assembled by Ovid[3].

Syme (*HO* 156) argues that the order of the poems indicates that Ovid survived to publish or at least to arrange the book: the fact that the first and penultimate poems are addressed to Sextus Pompeius indicates that Ovid dedicated the book to him. Professor R. J. Tarrant points out to me correspondences of structure between *EP* IV and some of Ovid's earlier books. If the sixteenth and final poem of *EP* IV is considered a *sphragis*-poem, as is indicated by *Nasonis* in the opening line, we are left with a fifteen-poem book of which the first and last poems are addressed to Sextus Pompeius, and in which the middle poem is addressed to Germanicus through his client Suillius[4]. The same structural outline of 1-8-15 appears in *Amores* I and III—the opening and closing poems of both books are concerned with Ovid's verse, while the eighth poem of each book stands somewhat apart from the other poems: *Am* I viii is about the procuress Dipsas, while III ix (the eighth poem in the book after the removal of the spurious fifth poem) is the elegy on the death of Tibullus.

Ovid's addressees in *Ex Ponto* IV

Sextus Pompeius, *consul ordinarius* in 14, and himself a relative of Augustus, is the recipient of no less than four letters in *EP* IV[5]. It is significant that he is not the recipient of any of Ovid's earlier letters from exile; this is discussed in the next section.

In the attention Ovid gives Sextus Pompeius there can be seen, according to Syme (*HO* 156), a deliberate attempt to gain the favour of Germanicus, who is mentioned in connection with Sextus Pompeius at v 25. It is interesting that in viii Ovid addresses Germanicus' quaestor Suillius (and in the course of the poem addresses Germanicus), and that the recipient of xiii is Carus, the tutor of Germanicus' sons. But it is only natural that Ovid, when at last permitted, should address so influential a man as his benefactor Sextus Pompeius; and it does not seem strange that he should address his fellow poet Carus, still less that he should send a letter to Suillius, husband of his stepdaughter Perilla.

C. Pomponius Graecinus, the recipient of ix, must have had some political influence, since the poem is in celebration of his becoming suffect consul in 16. But he probably owed this influence to his brother Flaccus, a close friend of Tiberius who succeeded Graecinus as *consul ordinarius* for 17, and whom Ovid gives prominent mention at ix 57 ff. Graecinus must have been an old associate of Ovid, since he has the rare distinction of being mentioned by name in a poem written by Ovid before his exile (*Am* II x 1).

Two of Ovid's correspondents were orators. Gallio, the addressee of the eleventh poem, is frequently quoted by the elder Seneca. He was a senator; both Tacitus and Dio give accounts of how he fell into disfavour with Tiberius for proposing that ex-members of the Praetorian guard be granted the privilege of using the theatre seats reserved for members of the equestrian order (*Ann* VI 3; LVIII 18 4). Brutus, the recipient of the sixth poem and dedicatee of the first three books of the *Ex Ponto*, is not mentioned by other writers, but it appears from vi 29-38 that he had a considerable reputation as a forensic orator, although some allowance must be made for possible exaggeration in Ovid's description of his close friend. The poem contains six lines on the death of Fabius Maximus, to whom Ovid had addressed *EP* I ii and III iii; perhaps he and Brutus had been associates.

Five epistles are addressed to Ovid's fellow poets. Cornelius Severus, the recipient of the second poem, was one of the most famous epic poets of the day; he is mentioned by Quintilian (X i 89), and the elder Seneca preserves his lines on the death of Cicero (*Suas* VI 26), Albinovanus Pedo, the recipient of the tenth epistle, was known as a writer of hexameter verse and of epigram. He served in Germanicus' campaign of AD 15 (Tac *Ann* I 60 2), and the elder Seneca preserves a fragment of his poem on Germanicus' campaigns (*Suas* I 15). It might be argued that in addressing him Ovid is once again trying to win Germanicus' favour. But in view of his intimacy with Ovid (mentioned at Sen *Cont* II 2 12), Albinovanus seems a natural choice to receive one of Ovid's letters. Tuticanus, the recipient of the twelfth and fourteenth poems and author of a *Phaeacid* based on Homer (mentioned at xii 27 and again in the catalogue of poets at xvi 29), is known only through the *Ex Ponto*; the same is true of Carus, author of a poem on Hercules and, as already mentioned, tutor of the sons of Germanicus.

Vestalis, the recipient of the seventh poem, is in a class separate from the other recipients of Ovid's verse epistles. As *primipilaris* of the legion stationed in the vicinity, he would of course have been without influence at Rome, but as (apparently) the prefect of the region around Tomis, he presumably had some control over Ovid's circumstances.

The traitorous friend to whom the third poem is addressed was a real person, for Ovid is quite explicit when speaking of their past together and of the friend's perfidy towards him; the same cannot be said of the *inuidus* to whom is addressed the concluding poem of the book, a defence of Ovid's reputation as a poet.

Cotta Maximus, the younger son of Tibullus' patron Messalla, is prominently mentioned at xvi 41-44 as an unpublished poet of outstanding excellence. He is the recipient of six letters in the earlier books of the *Ex Ponto*. Syme finds it significant that there is no poem in *EP* IV addressed to Cotta: 'Ovid ... was now concentrating his efforts elsewhere: Germanicus, the friends of Germanicus, Sextus Pompeius ... The tardy tribute may perhaps be interpreted as a veiled reproach' (*HO* 128). But arguments from silence are dangerous; and Ovid's mention of Cotta seems flattering enough.

It is perhaps safer to postulate a change in Ovid's feelings towards his wife. She is never mentioned in *EP* IV, although she had been the recipient of some eight earlier letters from exile (*Tr* I vi, III iii, IV iii, V ii, xi, xiv, *EP* I iv, III i; *Tr* V v was written in honour of her birthday). At *EP* III vii 11-12 Ovid indicates that his wife's efforts on his behalf had not matched his hopes:

> nec grauis uxori dicar, quae scilicet in
> me
> quam proba tam timida est
> experiensque parum.

The fact that Ovid chose not to address any verse epistle to his wife during his final years at Tomis may well reflect a cooling in his attitude towards her.

Differences between *Ex Ponto* IV and the earlier poetry from exile

The criticism most often made of Ovid's poems from exile is that they are repetitive and therefore monotonous. *EP* III ix 1-4 shows that the same criticism was made while Ovid was still alive:

> Quod sit in his eadem sententia, Brute,
> libellis,
> carmina nescio quem carpere nostra
> refers:
> nil nisi me terra fruar ut propiore
> rogare,
> et quam sim denso cinctus ab hoste
> loqui.

Ovid does not attempt to deny the criticism, but explains that he wished to obtain the assistance of as many people as possible:

> et tamen haec eadem cum sint, non
> scripsimus isdem,
> unaque per plures uox mea temptat
> opem.

> *(41-42)*

nec liber ut fieret, sed uti sua cuique
daretur
littera, propositum curaque nostra
fuit.
postmodo collectas utcumque sine
ordine iunxi:
hoc opus electum ne mihi forte putes.
da ueniam scriptis, quorum non gloria
nobis
causa, sed utilitas officiumque fuit.

(51-56)

Ovid's explanation is reasonable enough, and is confirmed by the speed with which he composed the first three books of the *Ex Ponto* once he knew that it was safe to name people in his verse. The first three books of the *Ex Ponto*, like the *Tristia*, were written with the single objective of securing Ovid's recall, and this naturally caused a certain repetition of subject-matter.

By the time Ovid wrote the poems that would form the fourth book of the *Ex Ponto*, he had lived in Tomis for six or more years, and it must have been clear to him that his chances of recall were slight. The result of this is a diminished use of his personal situation as a theme for his verse. Often he introduces his plight in only one or two distichs of a poem, subordinating the topic to the poem's main theme. The result of this technique can be seen in such extended passages as the descriptions of the investiture of the new consul (iv & ix), the address to Germanicus on the power of poetry (viii), or the catalogue of poets that concludes the book. In all of these passages Ovid's desire for recall is only a secondary theme.

The mixing of levels of diction

As well as variety of subject, the fourth book of the *Ex Ponto* shows a variation in style that is typical of Ovid's letters from exile. The poems use the metre and language of elegiac

20

verse. But at the same time they are *letters*, and are strongly influenced by the structure and vocabulary of prose epistles. This influence is naturally more obvious at some points than at others; and even within a single poem there can be a surprising degree of variation in the different sections of the poem.

Some poems tend more to one extreme than the other. The eleventh poem, a letter of commiseration to Gallio on the death of his wife, is extensively indebted to the genre of the prose letter of consolation; this prose influence is evident in such passages as:

> finitumque tuum, si non ratione,
> dolorem
> ipsa iam pridem suspicor esse mora

(13-14)

At the opposite extreme is the final poem of the book, a defence of Ovid's poetry; as this was a traditional poetic subject, the level of diction throughout the poem is extremely high, particularly in the catalogue of poets that forms the main body of the poem.

An interesting result of the mixture of styles is the presence in the poems of exile of words and expressions which belong essentially to prose, being otherwise rarely or never found in verse. Some instances from *Ex Ponto* IV are *ad summam* (i 15), *conuictor* (iii 15), *abunde* (viii 37), *ex toto* (viii 72), *di faciant* (ix 3), *secreto* (ix 31), *respectu* (ix 100), *quominus* (xii 1), *praefrigidus* (xii 35), and *tantummodo* (xvi 49).

Both in subject and style the sixteen poems of *Ex Ponto* IV show a wide variety, worthy of the creator of the *Metamorphoses*. The following section examines the special characteristics of each of the poems.

The letters to Sextus Pompeius

Sextus Pompeius is the recipient of poems i, iv, v, and xv; only Cotta Maximus and Ovid's wife have more letters from exile addressed to them. It is clear from the opening of IV i that Pompeius had himself prohibited Ovid from addressing him; and Ovid is careful to present himself as a client rather than a friend; the tone is of almost abject humility, and he shows circumspection in his requests for assistance.

In the opening of the first poem, Ovid describes how difficult it had been to prevent himself from naming Pompeius in his verse; in the climactic ten lines he declares that he is entirely Pompeius' creation. Only in the transition between the topics does he refer to future help from Pompeius, linking it with the assistance he is already providing:

> nunc quoque nil subitis clementia
>   territa fatis
> auxilium uitae fertque feretque meae.

(25-26)

The fourth poem is a description of how Fama came to Ovid and told him of Pompeius' election to the consulship; Ovid then pictures the joyous scene of the accession. At the end of the poem he indirectly asks for Pompeius' assistance, praying that at some point he may remember him in exile. The device of having Fama report Pompeius' accession to the consulship serves to emphasize the importance of the event and raise the tone of the poem. Ovid had earlier used Fama as the formal addressee of *EP* II i, which described his reaction to the news of Germanicus' triumph. In the fifth poem Ovid achieves a similar effect through the device of addressing the poem itself, giving it directions on where it will find Pompeius and what consular duties he might be performing[6]. Only in the concluding distich does Ovid direct the poem to ask for his assistance.

The fifteenth poem contains Ovid's most forceful appeal for Pompeius' assistance. It is interesting to observe the techniques Ovid uses to avoid offending Pompeius. The first part of the poem is a metaphorical description of how Ovid is as much Pompeius' property as his many estates or his house in Rome. This leads to Ovid's request:

atque utinam possis, et detur amicius
aruum,
remque tuam ponas in meliore loco!
quod quoniam in dis est, tempta lenire
precando
numina perpetua quae pietate colis.

(21-24)

He then attempts to compensate for the boldness of his
request. First he says that his appeal is unnecessary:

nec dubitans oro; sed flumine saepe
secundo
augetur remis cursus euntis aquae.

(27-38)

Then he apologizes for making such constant requests:

et pudet et metuo semperque
eademque precari
ne subeant animo taedia iusta tuo

(29-30)

He ends the poem with a return to the topic of the benefits
Pompeius has already rendered him.

The letter to Suillius addressing Germanicus

No poem in the fourth book of the *Ex Ponto* is addressed to a
member of the imperial family, but the greater part of IV viii,
nominally addressed to Suillius, is in fact directed to his
patron Germanicus. Suillius' family ties with Ovid and his
influential position would have made it natural for Ovid to
address him in the earlier books of the *Ex Ponto* or even in
the *Tristia*; and it is clear from the opening of the poem that
Suillius must have distanced himself from Ovid:

23

Littera sera quidem, studiis exculte
Suilli,
huc tua peruenit, sed mihi grata
tamen

In the section that follows, Ovid asks for Suillius' assistance, rather strangely setting forth his own impeccable family background and moral purity; then he moves to the topic of Suillius' piety towards Germanicus, and in line 31 begins to address Germanicus with a direct request for his assistance. In the fifty-eight lines that follow he develops the argument that Germanicus should accept the verse Ovid offers him for two reasons: poetry grants immortality to the subjects it describes; and Germanicus is himself a poet. In this passage Ovid allows himself a very high level of diction; as the topic was congenial to him, the result is perhaps the finest extended passage of verse in the book[7].

Ovid ends his address to Germanicus by asking for his assistance; only in the final distich of the poem does he return to Suillius.

The letters to Brutus and Graecinus

Only two of the ten addressees named by Ovid in *EP* IV were recipients of earlier letters from him. Brutus, to whom IV vi is addressed, was also the addressee of *EP* I i and III ix, while Graecinus, to whom IV ix is addressed, was the recipient of *EP* I vi and II vi.

There is some difference between Ovid's treatment of Brutus and Graecinus in *EP* IV and in the earlier poems. *EP* IV vi is highly personal, being mostly devoted to a lengthy description of Brutus' apparently conflicting but in fact complementary qualities of tenacity as a prosecuting advocate and of kindness towards those in need; no poem in the fourth book of the *Ex Ponto* is more completely concerned with the addressee as a person. In contrast, nothing is said of Brutus in *EP* I i, where he acts as the mere recipient of the plea that he protect Ovid's poems, or in III ix, where Brutus is the reporter of another's remarks on the monotony of Ovid's subject-matter. The address to Graecinus in IV ix, on the other hand, is much less personal than in I vi and II vi. The part of *EP* IV ix concerned with Graecinus describes his elevation to the consulship, and was clearly written (in some haste) to celebrate the event. The earlier poems are more concerned with Graecinus as an individual: in *EP* I vi Ovid describes at length Graecinus' kindliness of spirit and his closeness to his exiled friend, while in II vi Ovid admits the justice of the criticism Graecinus makes of the conduct which led to his exile, but thanks him for his support and asks for its continuance.

The letters to Tuticanus

The two letters to Tuticanus show a similar dichotomy.

Of the two poems, xii is more personal and more concerned with poetry. The first eighteen lines are a witty demonstration of the impossibility of using Tuticanus' name in elegiac verse, while the twelve verses that follow recall their poetic apprenticeship together. In the final twelve lines, referring to Tuticanus' senatorial career, Ovid asks him to help his cause in any way possible.

Poem xiv is far less personal than the earlier epistle. The only mention of Tuticanus is at the poem's beginning:

> Haec tibi mittuntur quem sum modo
> carmine questus
> non aptum numeris nomen habere
> meis,
> in quibus, excepto quod adhuc
> utcumque ualemus,
> nil te praeterea quod iuuet inuenies.

The bulk of the poem is a defense against charges raised by some of the Tomitans that he has defamed them in his verse. Ovid answers that he was complaining about the physical conditions at Tomis, not the people, to whom he owes a great debt. It is characteristic of the fourth book of the *Ex*

Ponto that Ovid complains less of his exile than in his earlier verse from exile; this poem furnishes the most explicit demonstration that the years spent in exile and the dwindling likelihood of recall has made Ovid reach an accommodation with his new conditions of life.

The topic of the poem clearly has no relation to Tuticanus; Professor R. J. Tarrant points out to me Ovid's use of the same technique in some of the *Amores*, such as I ix (*Militat omnis amans*), and II x, to Graecinus on loving two women at once, where there is no apparent connection between the addressee and the subject of the poem. Professor E. Fantham notes that the bulk of xiv could even have been written before Ovid chose Tuticanus as its addressee.

Other letters to poets

Three other poems in the book are addressed to poets. In all of them poetry itself is a primary subject.

The letter to Severus

The second poem in the book, addressed to the epic poet Severus, opens with a contrast of the situations of the two poets. The main body of the poem is concerned with the difficulty of composing under the conditions Ovid endures at Tomis, and the comfort that he even so derives from pursuing his old calling. The poem is well constructed and the language vivid. A particularly fine example of the use Ovid makes of differing levels of diction is found at 35-38:

> excitat auditor studium, laudataque
> uirtus
> crescit, et immensum gloria calcar
> habet.
> hic mea cui recitem nisi flauis scripta
> Corallis,
> quasque alias gentes barbarus Hister
> obit?

The emotional height of the tricolon, where Ovid describes poetic inspiration, gives way to a comparatively prosaic distich where he explains that the conditions necessary for inspiration do not exist at Tomis.

At the poem's conclusion Ovid reverts to Severus, asking that he send Ovid some recent piece of work.

The letter to Albinovanus Pedo

In the tenth poem of the book, poetry is not the main subject; instead, Ovid describes the hardships he endures at Tomis, and then describes at length the reasons the Black Sea freezes over. Towards the end of the letter, however, he explains why he is writing a poem to Albinovanus on this seemingly irrelevant topic[8]. The language recalls the poem to Severus:

> 'detinui' dicam 'tempus, curasque
>   fefelli;
>   hunc fructum praesens attulit hora
>   mihi.
> abfuimus solito dum scribimus ista
>   dolore,
>   in mediis nec nos sensimus esse
>   Getis.'

(67-70)

In the poem's concluding lines he links his own situation with the *Theseid* Albinovanus is engaged on: just as Theseus was faithful, so Albinovanus should be faithful to Ovid.

The letter to Gallio

This letter is remarkable for its economy of structure, and indeed is so short as to seem rather perfunctory. Only twenty-two lines in length, it is a letter of consolation addressed to Gallio on the death of his wife. In the first four lines Ovid apologizes for not having written to him earlier.

27

Ovid's exile serves as a bridge to the main topic of the poem:

atque utinam rapti iactura laesus amici
sensisses ultra quod quererere nihil

(5-6)

The remainder of the poem consists of the ingenious interweaving of various commonplaces of consolation. The poem is a good illustration of the secondary importance Ovid often gives his own misfortune in the fourth book of the *Ex Ponto*.

The letter to Carus

The thirteenth poem, like the second letter to Tuticanus, shows Ovid's acceptance of his life in Tomis. In it he tells Carus of the favourable reception given a poem he had written in Getic on the apotheosis of Augustus. The poem's opening is of interest as showing Ovid's consciousness of verbal wit as a special characteristic of his verse. He starts the poem with a play on the meaning of Carus' name, then tells him that the opening will by itself tell him who his correspondent is. In the lines that follow he discusses the individuality of his own style and that of Carus; this serves to introduce the subject of his Getic verse.

The letter to Vestalis

The subordination of the topic of Ovid's exile to another subject can be clearly seen in the seventh poem of the book, addressed to Vestalis, *primipilaris* of a legion stationed in the area of Tomis. As in the letter to Gallio, mention of Ovid's personal misfortune is confined to one short passage near the start of the poem:

aspicis en praesens quali iaceamus in
aruo,
nec me testis eris falsa solere queri

The descriptions that follow of wine freezing solid in the cold and of the Sarmatian herdsman driving his wagon across the frozen Danube are so picturesque that the reader's attention is drawn away from Ovid's personal situation. Ovid describes the poisoned arrows used in the region; then, in language recalling his letter to Gallio, expresses his regret that Vestalis has had personal experience of these weapons:

> atque utinam pars haec tantum
> spectata fuisset,
> non etiam proprio cognita Marte tibi!

(13-14)

The remainder of the poem is a description of Vestalis' capture of Aegissos. The description is conventional and unfelt; Ovid seems merely to have assembled a few standard topics of military panegyric.

The third poem

Poem iii, addressed to an unidentified friend who had proved faithless, is a well-crafted but not particularly original warning that Fortune is a changeable goddess, and his friend might well find find himself one day in Ovid's position. The familiar examples of Croesus, Pompey, and Marius are used; as the last and therefore most important example Ovid uses his own catastrophe. The device recalls the *Ibis*, where Ovid's final curse is to wish his enemy's exile to Tomis.

Poem xvi

The concluding poem of the book is a defence of Ovid's poetry. The poem's argument is that poets generally become famous only after their death, but that Ovid gained his reputation while still alive. The greater part of the poem is a catalogue of Ovid's contemporary poets, the argument being that even in such company he was illustrious.

As elsewhere he equates his exile with death; the defence of his poetry therefore includes only the poetry that he wrote before his exile.

TEXTUAL INTRODUCTION

The Manuscripts

The manuscript authority for the text of the fourth book of the *Ex Ponto* is significantly poorer than for the earlier books because of the absence of *A, Hamburgensis scrin. 52 F*. This ninth-century manuscript has been recognized since the time of Heinsius as the most important witness for the text of the *Ex Ponto*; it breaks off, however, at III ii 67.

The manuscript authorities for the fourth book can be placed in three categories. The fragmentary *G* is from a different tradition than the other manuscripts. *B* and *C* are closely related, and offer the best witness to the main tradition. The other manuscripts I have collated are more greatly affected by contamination and interpolation; of them *M* and *F* show some independence, while no subclassification can be made of *H, I, L,* or *T*.

G

The *fragmentum Guelferbytanum, Cod. Guelf. 13.11 Aug. 4°*, generally dated to the fifth or sixth century, is the oldest manuscript witness to any of Ovid's poems. Part of the collection of the Herzog August Bibliothek in Wolfenbüttel, it was discovered by Carl Schoenemann, who published his discovery in 1829; details of his monograph will be found in the bibliography. The two pieces of parchment are a palimpsest, having been reused in the eighth century for a text of Augustine; later they were incorporated into a bookbinding. As a result of this treatment they are in extremely poor condition.

G contains all or part of ix 101-8, ix 127-33, xii 15-19, and xii 41-44. To make it perfectly clear when *G* is a witness to the text, I have not grouped it with other manuscripts, but have always specified it by name. If *G* is not mentioned in an apparatus entry, it is not extant for the text concerned.

G is written in uncial script, with no division between words but with indentation of the pentameters. Its one contribution to the establishment of the text is at ix 103, where it reads *quamquam ... sit* instead of the more usual *quamquam ... est* found in the other manuscripts. In general, the text offered by *G* is surprisingly poor. At ix 108 it reads *fato* for *facto*, at ix 130 it has the false and unmetrical spelling *praeces*, at ix 132 it has *misscelite* for *misi caelite*, at xii 17 it reads *lati* for *dilati*, and at xii 19 *naia* for *nota*. These errors demonstrate that the rest of the tradition does not descend from *G*.

Korn gives an accurate transcription of the fragment in the introduction to his edition; photographs of parts of the fragment can be found at Chatelain, *Paléographie des classiques latins*, tab. xcix, 2 and E. A. Lowe, *Codices Latini Antiquiores*, vol. IX, p. 40, no. 1377.

B and C

Monacensis latinus 384 and *Mon. lat. 19476*, both dated by editors to the twelfth century, are descended from a common ancestor. This is easily demonstrated by the large number of shared errors not found in other manuscripts[9]. At iv 36 *B* and *C* have *intendunt* for the correct *intendent*, at viii 6 *uolo* for *uoco*, at viii 18 *perueniemus* for *inueniemur* (*-ntur,-mus*), at viii 44 *illa* for *ulla*, at viii 89 *cara* for *care*, at ix 44 *fingit* for *finget*, at ix 71 *quod* for *cum* (*FILT*) and *ut* (*HM*), at ix 92 *praestat* for *perstat*, at ix 97 *et* for *ut*, at xiii 5 *certe est* for *certe*, and at xiv 30 *culpatus* for *culpatis*. In some of these passages *B*'s still visible original reading has been corrected by a later hand. In other passages it is clear from the signs of correction that *B* originally agreed with *C* in distinctive readings now preserved in *C* alone: *subito* for *sed et* (iii 27), *erat* for *eras* (vi 9), *occidit* for *occidis* (vi 11), *suspicit* for *suscipit* (ix 90), *parent* for *darent* (xvi 31).

B and *C* on the whole offer a better text than any other manuscript. At iii 44 B^1 and *C* omit the lost pentameter, where the other manuscripts offer interpolations. At iv 11 they alone give the probably correct *solus* for *tristis*, at xii 3 *aut* for *ast*, and at xvi 31 *tyrannis* (conjectured by Heinsius) for *tyranni*. At v 40 C and B^2 alone have the correct *mancipii ... tui* for *mancipium ... tuum*.

Both manuscripts naturally have readings peculiar to themselves. B has about fifty unique readings. It places iii 11-12 after 13-14, omits v 37-40, and interchanges viii 49-50 and 51-52. At iv 34 B alone has *erunt* (for *erit*), conjectured by Heinsius; C omits the word. Similarly, at xi 21 B and F^1 have *mihi*, omitted by C; the other manuscripts have *tibi*. B has *ab* at i 9 for the other manuscripts' *in*; *ab* is possibly the true reading.

Under the influence of Ehwald, modern editors have wrongly taken some of B's other readings to be correct, placing *aspicerem* in the text for *prospicerem* at ix 23, *ara* for *ora* at ix 115, and *illi* for *illum* at ix 126. At ix 73 editors print B and T's *quem*, which is clearly an interpolation for the awkward transmitted reading *qua*.

Unlike C, B has been quite heavily corrected by later hands.

C has more than one hundred readings peculiar to itself. Two of them I have accepted as correct: *summo* (for *summum*; H has *mundum*) at iii 32, and *horas* (that is, *oras*) at vii 1; the reading is also given by I. It is possible that C's *correptior* should be read at xii 13 for *correptius*. At xiv 38 C's *sceptius* is the manuscript reading closest to the correct *Scepsius* restored by Scaliger.

Most of C's errors are trivial, but at some points it departs widely from the usual text. It omits ix 47 and xiv 37, and interchanges the second hemistichs of iii 26 and 28; xvi 30 is inserted by a later hand, perhaps in an erasure. At viii 43 it has *in uita* for *officio*, at xiii 12 *contra uiam* for *nouimus*, at xiv 36 *in* for *loci*, and at xv 31 *colloquio* for *uerum quid*.

C also contains a greater number of purely palaeographical errors than any other manuscript: *hunc* for *nunc* (i 25), *humeris* for *numeris* (ii 30), *hec* for *nec* (ix 30), *lucos* for *sucos* (x 19), *hasto* for *horto* (xv 7), *ueiiuolique* for *ueliuolique* (xvi 21), *pretia* for *pr(o)elia* (xvi 23).

B and *C* sporadically offer the third declension accusative plural ending *-is* (ix 4 *fascis C*, ix 7 *partis C*, ix 73 *rudentis B*, x 17 *cantantis B*, xii 30 *albentis B*). But more usually all manuscripts, including *B* and *C*, have the accusative in *-es*: compare for example ii 27 *partes*, iii 53 *purgantes*, ix 35 *praesentes*, and ix 42 *fasces*. The manuscripts show a similar variation in the earlier books of the *Ex Ponto*. The ninth-century Hamburg manuscript (*A*) sometimes offers accusatives in *-is* where the other manuscripts, even *B* and *C*, have *-es* (I iv 23 *partis*, I v 11 *talis*, I vi 39 *ligantis*, I vi 51 *turris*). At I ii 4, *A* has *omnes*, where C^1 has *omnis*, and in general even in *A* the accusative in *-es* is the predominant form. For example, *A* offers *auris* at II iv 13 and II ix 25, but *aures* at I ii 127, I ix 5, II v 33, and II ix 3. In view of the instability of the manuscript evidence[10], I have normalized the ending to *-es* in all cases, considering the instances of *-is* to be scribal interpolations.

Similarly, I have used the form *penna* at iv 12 and vii 37, where *C* offers *pinna*. *Penna* is the form given in the ancient manuscripts of Virgil, and attested by Quintilian.

MFHILT

The other manuscripts I have collated belong to the vulgate class. They are not related to each other in the sense that *B* and *C* are related, nor does any of them possess independent authority as does *G*. Within the group firm lines of affiliation are hard to establish, and each of the manuscripts attests a handful of good readings that are found in few or none of the others, either by happy conjecture, or because a reading that was in circulation at the time as a variant chanced to get copied into a few surviving manuscripts. Professor R. J. Tarrant has noted that the presence of the *Ex Ponto* in north-central France 'can be traced from the eleventh century onwards, first from echoes in Hildebert of Lavardin and Baudri de Bourgeuil, later from the extracts in the *Florilegium Gallicum*, and finally from the complete texts [which include our *H* and *F*] ... that emanate from this region toward the end of the twelfth century' (*Texts and Transmission* 263); the vulgate manuscripts seem to have been propagated from the text current in the region of Orléans.

M and *F* show some originality. Their readings at xvi 33 differ somewhat from the version of that passage in *HILT*. F^1's interpolation for the missing pentameter at iii 44 differs from that of *MHILT*, while *M* has an interpolated distich following x 6 that is not otherwise attested.

Of the other manuscripts, *I* agrees with *C* in reading *horas* (=*oras*) for *undas* at vii 1, while *T* is the only manuscript collated to have the correct *laeuus* at ix 119 in the original hand (F^2 gives it as a variant reading). Similarly, *H* and *L* each have a few peculiar variants.

As a group *MFHILT* offer a good picture of the readings current in the later mediaeval period, and only rarely have I been obliged to cite a vulgate manuscript from the editions of Heinsius, Burman, or Lenz as testimony for a variant.

M

Heinsius did not have knowledge of *B* or *C*, and seems to have considered his *codex Moreti* (preserved at the Museum Plantin-Moretus in Antwerp as 'Latin, n° 68 [anc. 43] [salle des reliures, n° 32]' in Denucé's catalogue of the museum's collection) to be the best of the poor selection of manuscripts available; at xvi 33, understandably despairing of restoring the true reading, he accepted *M*'s reading pending the discovery of better manuscripts.

M was dated by Heinsius to the twelfth or thirteenth century; Denucé assigns it to the twelfth century.

At viii 85 *M* alone has the correct *ullo* for the other manuscripts' *illo*; this could naturally have been recovered by conjecture. At x 1 it has *cumerio*, the closest reading in the manuscripts collated to the correct *Cimmerio*; but Professor R. J. Tarrant informs me that *Cimmerio* is also found in *British Library Harley 2607*.

M has suffered from a certain degree of interpolation. Following x 6 there is the spurious distich *set cum nostra malis uexentur corpora multis / aspera non possum perpetiendo mori.* At ii 9 *Falerno* is a deliberate alteration of *Falerna*. At x 49 *Niphates* is an interpolation from Lucan III 245. At xiii 47 *duorum* (also given as a variant reading by F^2) looks like an attempt to correct the cryptic transmitted reading *deorum*, and at xv 15 *tellus regnata* is presumably a metrical correction following the loss of *-que* from *regnataque terra*, the reading of the other manuscripts. At xvi 25 *eticiusque* looks to be a deliberate alteration of *Trinacriusque*, but I am not sure what the interpolation means.

F

Francofurtanus Barth 110, used by Burman, shows some signs of independence. At iii 44, where a pentameter has been lost, B and C omit the line, while the other manuscripts, including M, have the interpolation *indigus effectus omnibus ipse magis*; F has the separate interpolation *Achillas Pharius abstulit ense caput*, also found in Heinsius' *fragmentum Louaniense*. F omits viii 51-54, at xi 1 reads *Pollio* for *Gallio*, and at xvi 33 has a reading somewhat different from those offered by the other manuscripts.

F alone of the manuscripts collated offers the correct *audisse* (for *audire*) at x 17. At xi 21 it and B alone have the correct *mihi* for *tibi* (omitted by C). At xiv 7 it has the probably correct *muter* for *mittar*, also found in *Bodleianus Canon. lat. 1* and *Barberinus lat. 26*, both of the thirteenth century. With the exception of *muter*, these readings could have been recovered by conjecture; given the separative interpolation at iii 44, F differs surprisingly little from the other manuscripts.

H

The thirteenth-century *Holkhamicus 322*, now *British Library add. 49368*, contains (with I) the correct *hanc* at i 16, the other manuscripts having *ha, ah* (B), or *a* (C). At xvi 30, where I have printed *leuis*, the reading of most manuscripts, H has *leui*, the conjecture of Heinsius; Professor R. J. Tarrant informs me that the same reading is found in *Othob. lat.*

36

1469. At iv 45 *H*'s *qua libet* is the manuscript reading closest to Heinsius' correct *quamlibet*; most manuscripts have *quod licet*.

Most other variants in *H* are trivial errors, although there seems to have been deliberate scribal alteration at x 18 (*sucus amarus erat* for *lotos amara fuit*), xiv 38 (*Celsius* for the usual *Septius*; Scaliger restored *Scepsius*), xvi 3 (*ueniet* for *uenit et*; presumably the intermediate step was *uenit*), and perhaps at xiv 31 (*miserabilis* for *uitabilis*).

I

The thirteenth-century *Laurentianus 36 32*, Lenz's and André's *m*, has the correct *perstas* at x 83 for *praestas*; its reading is also found in *P* and as a variant of F^2. At vii 1 it shares with *C* the reading *horas* (=*oras*), which I have printed in preference to the usual *undas*.

At viii 15 *I* has the hypercorrect *nil* for *nihil*, and at xiii 26 *ethereos ... deos* for *aetherias ... domos*, but in general has few signs of deliberate alteration.

L

Lipsiensis bibl. ciu. Rep. I 2° 7, of the thirteenth century, has *haec* at ix 103 for the other manuscripts' *et*. *Haec* restores sense to the passage, and was the preferred reading of Heinsius; I consider it a scribal conjecture, now rendered obsolete by Professor R. J. Tarrant's more elegant *quae*. *L*'s text has clearly been tampered with at xiv 41 (*populum ... uertit in iram* for *populi ... concitat iram*), but in general seems to have suffered little from interpolation. It is, however, of little independent value as a witness to the text.

T

Turonensis 879, written around the year 1200, was first fully collated by André for his edition; Lenz had earlier reported its readings for IV xvi and part of I i. At ix 119 only *T* and

F^2 of the manuscripts collated have the correct *laeuus*, although other manuscripts come close, and the reading could have been recovered by conjecture. At xv 40 *T* reads *transierit saeuos* for *transit nostra feros*; clearly *nostra* was at some point lost from the text, and metre forcibly restored.

P

I have also collated the thirteenth-century *Parisinus lat. 7993*, Heinsius' *codex Regius*. At ix 46 *P* offers the correct *cernet* for *credet*; *cernet* is also the reading of *M* after correction by a later hand and of the thirteenth-century *Gothanus membr. II 121*. At vi 7 *P* alone of collated manuscripts agrees with *C* in reading *praestat* for the correct *perstat*. *P* agrees with *L* in reading *niuibus* for the other manuscripts' *nubibus* at v 5, *adeptum* for *ademptum* at vi 49, *signare* for *signate* at xv 11, and in the orthography *puplicus* for *publicus* at ix 48, ix 102, xiii 5, and xiv 16. The manuscript has many corruptions: a few examples are i 30 *igne* for *imbre*, ii 18 *supremo* for *suppresso*, iv 6 *pace* for *parte*, vi 34 *uirtus* for *uirus*, vii 15 *piacula* for *pericula*, ix 42 *praeterea* for *praetextam*, x 63 *in harena* for *marina*, xiv 39 *conuiuia* for *conuicia*, and xvi 24 *sacri* for *scripti*. However, *P* has no unique variants with any probability of correctness. To have given a full report of *P* would have involved a considerable expansion of an already long apparatus, and I have cited the manuscript only occasionally, where a reading is only weakly attested by the other manuscripts.

Titles

MF and $B^2H^2I^2T^2$ usually supply titles for the poems. As will be seen from the apparatus, there is considerable variation among the titles, and there is no reason to suppose that they form an authentic part of the transmitted text.

The manuscript authority for the text of *Ex Ponto* IV

By and large the manuscripts of the fourth book of the *Ex Ponto* offer a remarkably uniform text of the poems, and one which, considering the late date of the manuscripts, is in surprisingly good condition. I believe that all the manuscripts, with the exception of *G*, are descended from a single archetype. *B* and *C* are the best witnesses to the text of the archetype, although the other, more heavily contaminated and interpolated manuscripts are indispensable, since they correct the peculiar errors of *B* and *C*.

The present edition

The apparatus of this edition is intended to be a full report of *BCMFHILT* and of the fragmentary *G*; some reports are also given of *P*. It includes corrections by original and by later hands.

When no manuscripts are specified for the lemma in an entry, the lemma is the reading for those manuscripts not otherwise specified. For instance, the entry

deductum carmen] carmen deductum *M*

indicates that *deductum carmen* is the reading of *BCFHILT*, while *carmen deductum* is the reading of *M*.

I have from time to time cited from earlier editions readings of manuscripts which I have not collated. To make it clear that I have not personally verified these readings, I have added in parentheses after the citation the name of the editor whose report I am using. Professor R. J. Tarrant has inspected some nine manuscripts to see what readings they offered in some particularly vexed portions of the poems; I have similarly indicated when I am obliged to him for information on a manuscript.

The *excerpta Scaligeri* mentioned at xiii 27 I know of through Heinsius' notes as printed in Burman's edition; according to M. D. Reeve (*RhM* CXVII [1974] 163), the original excerpts are still extant in Diez 8° 2560, a copy of the *editio Gryphiana* of 1546. Reeve also gives identifications of certain of Heinsius' manuscripts; when citing Heinsius' codices, I give the modern name when the manuscript has been identified and is still extant.

The greater number of the manuscripts dealt with have been corrected, some heavily. In my apparatus B^1 means "the original hand in B" and B^2 means "a correcting hand in B". B^{2ul} indicates that the reading of B^2 is clearly marked as a variant reading. B^{2gl} indicates that the entry is marked in the manuscript as a gloss; $B^{2(gl)}$ indicates a gloss not marked as such. I have reported glosses where they contribute to the understanding of a textual problem.

If different correctors have been at work in different passages, both are called B^2. If a later hand has made a correction after B^2, the later hand is called B^3. When I place B^1 in an entry but do not report B^2, it can be assumed that B^2 has the lemma as its reading.

Sometimes a corrector has altered the original text so much (without however erasing it entirely) that only the altered reading can be made out. In such cases I have used the siglum B^{2c}. Where a corrector has inserted or altered only certain letters of a word, I have indicated this in the HTML version of this edition by underlining the letters involved. In the Text version, these letters are capitalized.

Where the correction is apparently by the original scribe, B^{ac} indicates the original reading, and B^{pc} the correction.

The asterisk is used to indicate illegible letters, and the solidus (/) erasures.

When reporting variants, I have tried to indicate the spellings actually found in the manuscripts, but since mediaeval spellings do not in themselves constitute variant readings, they have not usually been reported when the text is not otherwise disturbed. I have been more generous with proper names, but have often excluded confusions of *ae, oe,* and *e,* of *i* and *y,* of *ph* and *f,* of *c* and *t,* the doubling of consonants, and the loss or addition of the aspirate.

The apparatus is intended to include a comprehensive listing of all conjectures proposed. When the author of a conjecture is not a previous editor of the poems, I have given a reference either to the publication where the emendation was first proposed, or to the earliest edition I have consulted which reports the emendation. Conjectures of Bentley are from Hedicke's *Studia Bentleiana*. Conjectures of Professor R. J. Tarrant, Professor J. N. Grant, and Professor C. P. Jones were communicated to me by their authors.

Printed editions

The first editions of the works of Ovid were printed in 1471 by Balthesar Azoguidus at Bologna and by Conradus Sweynheym and Arnoldus Pannartz at Rome. The Bologna edition was edited by Franc. Puteolanus, and the Rome edition by J. Andreas de Buxis. Lenz's edition gives numerous readings from both editions; to judge from his reports, their texts of the *Ex Ponto* were derived from late manuscripts of no great value. The Roman edition, however, contained the elegant correction of *iactate* to *laxate* at ix 73.

For my knowledge of other early editions of the *Ex Ponto* I have relied upon Burman's large variorum edition of the complete works of Ovid, published at Amsterdam in 1727. The edition contains notes of various editors of the sixteenth and early seventeenth centuries, among them Merula, Naugerius, Ciofanus, Fabricius, and Micyllus. Although I have occasionally quoted from these notes, they are in general of surprisingly little use, containing for the most part unlikely variant readings from unnamed manuscripts and explanations of passages not really in need of elucidation.

The principal event in the history of the editing of the *Ex Ponto* was the appearance at Amsterdam in 1652 of Nicolaus Heinsius' edition of Ovid. Heinsius took full advantage of the opportunity his travels as a diplomat gave him of searching out manuscripts, thereby gaining a direct knowledge of the manuscripts of the poems which has never since been equalled[11]. Heinsius also possessed an unrivalled felicity in conjectural emendation. Some of his conjectures are unnecessary alterations of a text that was in fact sound, some of his necessary conjectures are trivial, and are already found in late manuscripts of the poems or could have been made by critics of less outstanding capacities; but many are alterations which are subtle and yet necessary to restore sense or Latinity. The present edition returns to the text many conjectures and preferred readings of Heinsius that were ejected by editors of the nineteenth and twentieth centuries.

The edition of Heinsius formed the basis of all editions published during the two centuries that followed. Of these editions the most important was the 1727 variorum edition of Burman already referred to. It is from the copy of that edition at the University of Toronto Library that I have obtained my knowledge of Heinsius' notes. Burman was apparently the first editor to make use of F. On occasion he differs from Heinsius in his choice of readings. At xvi 44 he made the convincing conjecture *Maxime* (codd *maxima*), subsequently confirmed by B and C. His notes are informative; and my note on x 37-38 in particular is greatly indebted to him.

For poem x Burman reproduced some notes from an anthology of Latin verse for use at Eton, produced by an anonymous editor in 1705[12].

In 1772 Theophilus Harles published at Erlangen his edition of the *Tristia* and *Ex Ponto* 'ex recensione Petri Burmanni'. Harles was the first editor to make use of B. In the introduction to his edition Harles relates how he wrote von Oeffele, librarian to the Elector of Bavaria, asking if there was any manuscript in the Elector's library that might be helpful in preparing his edition, and thereby learned of the existence of B. It is clear from Harles' introduction that he fully appreciated the manuscript's importance; and in his notes he gives many of its readings, pointing out where it confirmed suggestions of Heinsius and Burman. However, his text is simply reprinted from Burman's variorum edition.

W. E. Weber's text of *Ex Ponto* IV in his 1833 *Corpus Poetarum Latinorum* is in effect a reprint of the Heinsius-Burman vulgate, except that at viii 59 he prints the manuscripts' incorrect accusative form *Gigantes* (Heinsius *Gigantas*). But this fidelity to the vulgate text seems not to have been the editor's intention: in his introduction he speaks of

'Heinsianae emendationes felices saepe, superuacuae saepius ... quarum emendationum partem Mitscherlichius eiecit [Göttingen, 1796; I have not seen the edition], maiorem eiicere Iahnius coepit [Leipzig, 1828: the part of the edition containing the *Ex Ponto* was never published]. dicendum tamen, etiamnunc passim haud paucas fortasse latere Heinsii et aliorum correctiones minus necessarias in uerbis Ouidianis, quas accuratior codicum inter se comparatio, opus sane immensi laboris, extrudet'. It would be understandable enough if Weber, faced with the labour of editing the entire corpus of Latin poetry, found himself unable to effect a radical revision of the text of the *Ex Ponto*.

In 1853 there appeared at Leipzig the third volume of Rudolf Merkel's first Teubner edition of the works of Ovid, containing his text of the *Ex Ponto*. The part of Merkel's introduction dealing with the *Ex Ponto* is entirely concerned with describing the appearance, orthography, and readings of the ninth-century *Hamburgensis scrin. 52 F*. The manuscript ends, however, at III ii 67, and Merkel says nothing of the basis for his text of the later poems, which in general is the Heinsius-Burman vulgate.

In 1868 B. G. Teubner published at Leipzig Otto Korn's separate edition of the *Ex Ponto*. Korn's apparatus is the first to have a modern appearance; but this appearance is deceptive, for of the twenty sigla Korn uses, ten are for individual or several manuscripts collated by Heinsius, and only five are for manuscripts collated by Korn himself. The edition is important, since Korn was the first editor to make substantial use of *B* in constituting his text. Usually he printed the text of *B* in preference to the vulgate: 'Ceterum eas partes in quibus *A* caremus, β [=*B*] libri uestigia secutus restitui, prorsus neglectis recentiorum exemplarium elegantiis, quorum ad normam N. Heinsius, cuius in tertio quartoque libro R. Merkelius assecla est, textum conformauit' (xv).

There was some reason to review critically the vulgate established by Heinsius and Burman. Even Heinsius was capable of error; examples of this in *Ex Ponto* IV include his preference for the inelegant *idem* for *ille* at iii 17, for the impossible *ullo* instead of the better attested *nullo* at v 15, and for the obvious interpolation *domitam ... ab Hercule* at xvi 19 instead of *domito ... ab Hectore*. His most pervasive fault is a partiality for elegant but unnecessary emendation: often he is guilty of rewriting passages which are in themselves perfectly sound. A typical instance is vii 30: Heinsius' *globos* is elegant enough, but there is no reason to suspect the transmitted *uiros*.

Some of the readings proposed or preferred by Heinsius had been unnecessary or wrong, but many had been necessary to make sense of the text; and Korn is often guilty of damaging the text by excluding readings not found in *B*. The supreme example of this is his restoration of the manuscripts' reading *iactate* for *laxate* at ix 73.

Korn used the collation of *B* by Harles, which had errors and omissions (in his preface Harles had warned that his report might contain errors[13]), so that at i 9 Korn prints *in istis* and at x 83 *perstas*, without noting in his apparatus that *B*'s false readings were *ab istis* and *praestas* respectively. He was aware that at xi 21 *B* read *mihi*, but printed *tibi* nonetheless, although Burman had already explained why *mihi* was the correct reading.

A curious feature of Korn's edition is its dual apparatus: below the report of manuscript variants is a listing of passages where his text differs from those of Heinsius and Merkel: 'Lectiones discrepantes editionum Heinsii et Merkelii adposui, ut et quantopere Ouidius Heinsianus a genuina forma discrepet dilucide perspiciatur, et quibus locis a Merkelio discesserim facilius adpareat' (xxxii). Korn ejects such obviously correct readings as *leuastis* at vi 44 and *laxate* at ix 73; in each instance the true reading is printed in large type at the bottom of the page. In addition, Korn rather unfairly included as different readings what were in fact only spellings which did not conform to the purified orthography then coming into use. *Cymba* does not differ from *cumba* (viii 28), nor is *Danubium* a variant for *Danuuium* (ix 80), nor again is *Vlysses* different from *Vlixes* (x 9). Finally, the second apparatus at several points misrepresents what Heinsius actually thought.

Korn's confusion on this point is understandable, since determining Heinsius' textual preferences is often more difficult than it might at first appear. Editions were published under his name which did not incorporate all his preferred readings[14]; even the lemmas to his notes are taken from the edition of Daniel Heinsius, and are not a guide to Heinsius' own view of the text, which can only be discovered by reading the actual notes[15]. A good example of this can be found at x 47. Here Heinsius' text reproduces the standard reading *Cratesque*. The lemma in his note is *Oratesque*, the reading of Daniel Heinsius' edition. In the note itself Heinsius indicates his preference for the conjecture *Calesque*, communicated to him by his friend Isaac Vossius. Here Korn, along with all modern editors, prints *Calesque* in his text; he reports *Cratesque* as Heinsius' reading.

Korn made one important conjecture in *Ex Ponto* IV, printing *decretis* at ix 44 for the manuscripts' *secretis*.

For the third volume of his complete edition of Ovid, published at Leipzig in 1874, Alexander Riese drew on Korn's edition, but was less radical in following the readings of *B*: 'nec eclecticam quam dicunt N. Heinsii nec libri optimi rigide tenacem O. Kornii rationem ingressus mediam uiam tenere studui' (vii). Riese restores Heinsius' preferred reading in only about a quarter of the places where it was deserted by Korn; even so, no editor since has shown such independence in the selection of readings.

In 1881 there appeared at London a text of *Ex Ponto* IV with accompanying commentary by W. H. Williams. The text, which Williams says is drawn from the "Oxford variorum edition of 1825", seems in general to be a reprint of the Heinsius-Burman vulgate with some readings drawn from Merkel's first edition. In spite of occasional conjectures and notes on variant readings, based on information drawn from Burman and Merkel, Williams is not generally concerned with the constitution of the text: his note on x 68 *curasque fefelli* is 'so Tennyson in the "In Memoriam"'. The commentary, which is about eighty pages long, consists largely of discussions of the cognates of various Latin words in other Indo-European languages, 'though the limits of the work preclude more than the *data* from which a competent teacher can deduce the principles of comparative philology'. A typical note is that on i 11 *scribere*: 'from [root] skrabh = to dig, whence scrob-s and scrofa = 'the grubber,' *i.e.* the pig; Grk. γράφω by loss of sibilant and softening'. The edition has been only occasionally useful in editing the poems or writing the commentary.

In 1884 Merkel published his second edition of the poems of exile. In his previous edition he had in general followed Heinsius and Burman in the fourth book; in the new edition, without specifically saying so (although in his introduction he mentions the "codex Monacensis uetustior"), he generally alters his text so as to conform with *B*'s readings. He does not always desert his former text, rightly retaining *hanc* at i 16, *quamlibet* at iv 45, and *tempus curasque* at x 67; he also keeps *lux* at vi 9 and *domitam ... ab Hercule* at xvi 19.

In his 1874 monograph *De codicibus duobus carminum Ouidianarum ex Ponto datorum Monacensibus* Korn had made known the existence of *C*. S. G. Owen's first edition of the *Ex Ponto*, printed in Postgate's *Corpus Poetarum Latinorum* in 1894, was the first edition to report this manuscript as well as *B*. His text is unduly partial to the readings of *B* and *C*, and his well-organized apparatus is so abbreviated as to be deceptive. It cannot be relied upon even for reports of *B* and *C*. At ix 73 it gives no hint that for four centuries editors had read *laxate*; many of Heinsius' preferred readings are similarly consigned to oblivion. At vi 5-6 he reports Housman's ingenious repunctuation, presumably communicated to him by its author.

In 1896 Rudolf Ehwald published his monograph *Kritische Beiträge zu Ovids Epistulae ex Ponto*. I am often indebted to Ehwald for references he has collected; my notes on i 15 *ad summam* and xiii 48 *quos laus formandos est tibi magna datos* could not have been written without the assistance of his monograph. This said, the fact remains that Ehwald's judgment and linguistic intuition were exceptionally poor. He had not relied on Korn's apparatus for his knowledge of

B, but had collated it himself; and the intent of his monograph was to establish *B*'s authority as paramount. A typical example can be seen at ix 71. Here *FILT* offer *cum ... uacabit* and *MH* have *ut ... uacabit*, while the reading of *B* and *C* is *quod uacabit*. In one of the examples Ehwald adduces, *Fast* II 18, *uacat* is found in only a few manuscripts, and it can easily be seen how it arose from *uacas*; all the other examples are instances of *quod superest* or *quod reliquum est*. The cumulative effect of these examples is to demonstrate that *quod ... uacabit* is not a possible reading. This insensitivity to the precise meaning of the passages he discusses is usual with Ehwald, and his book, although useful, is an extremely unsafe guide to the textual criticism of the poems. It has unfortunately exercised a decisive influence on all succeeding editions.

The first of these editions was Owen's 1915 Oxford Classical Text of the poems of exile. In the preface Owen acknowledges the influence of Ehwald: "adiumento primario erat R. Ehwaldi, doctrinae Ouidianae iudicis peritissimi, uere aureus libellus ... in quo excussis perpensisque codicibus poetaeque locutione ad perpendiculum exacta rectam Ponticarum edendarum normam uir doctus stabilire instituit' (viii). In most instances Owen follows Ehwald's recommendations, altering *in* to *ab* at i 9, *prospicerem* to *aspicerem* at ix 23, and at ix 44 abandoning Korn's *decretis* for the manuscripts' *secretis*.

Owen's reliance on Ehwald was noticed by Housman (903-4) in his short and accurate review of Owen's edition: 'In the *ex Ponto* Mr Owen had displayed less originality [than in his 1889 and 1894 editions of the *Tristia*] and consequently has less to repent of. Most of the changes in this edition are made in pursuance of orders issued by R. Ehwald in his *Kritische Beiträge* of 1896; but let it be counted to Mr Owen for righteousness that at III.7.37 and IV.15.42 he has refused to execute the sanguinary mandates of his superior officer'.

As in Owen's earlier edition, the apparatus is so short as to be misleading. His choice of manuscripts is too small, and exaggerates the importance of *B* and *C*; even of these two manuscripts his report is inadequate. At ix 73 he rightly prints *laxate*; the apparatus gives no indication that this is a conjecture, and that all manuscripts, including *B* and *C*, read *iactate*, which he had printed in 1894. At xi 21, where *B* gives *mihi*, indicated by Burman as the correct reading, Owen prints *tibi* and does not mention the variant in the apparatus. The situation is naturally worse with readings of manuscripts other than *B* and *C*, and with conjectures. In general, Owen's apparatus can be trusted neither as a report even of the principal readings of the few manuscripts he used, or as a register of critics' views of the constitution of the text.

In the same year as Owen's second text there appeared at Budapest Geza Némethy's commentary on the *Ex Ponto*, of which twenty-six pages are devoted to the fourth book. The notes are too sparse and elementary to form an adequate commentary, consisting largely of simple glosses. They are a useful supplement to a plain text of the poems, however, and Némethy sometimes notices points missed by others: he correctly glosses *Augusti* as "Tiberii imperatoris" at ix 70. The notes are based on Merkel's second edition; Némethy lists in a preface his few departures from Merkel's text.

In 1922 Friedrich Levy published his first edition of the *Ex Ponto* as part of a new Teubner edition of the works of Ovid. The apparatus was a reduced version of that prepared by Ehwald, 'Qui ut totus prelis subiceretur ... propter saeculi angustias fieri non potuit'. Levy's text is virtually identical to Owen's, but the apparatus is more complete. It contains a full report of *B* and *C*, and also of the thirteenth-century *Gothanus memb. II 121*. This last manuscript has the correct *cernet* at ix 46, where most manuscripts read *credet*; but otherwise its readings are of very poor quality, consisting of simple misreadings (i 24 *magnificas* for *munificas*, vii 30 *uento* for *uenit*, viii 37 *habendus* for *abunde*), simplified word order (vi 25 *tuas lacrimas pariter* for *tuas pariter lacrimas*, xvi 39 *et iuuenes essent* for *essent et iuuenes*), and intrusive glosses (viii 61 *captiuis* for *superatis*, xvi 47 *me laedere* for *proscindere*). The manuscript does not deserve the important place it has in the editions of Levy, Luck, and André[16]; Ehwald presumably included it in his apparatus because of its easy accessibility to him at Gotha, where he lived. No other manuscripts are regularly reported, so Levy's apparatus gives a false impression of the evidence for the text, although he often reports isolated readings from the manuscripts of Heinsius.

Levy omitted conjectures 'quatenus falsae uel superuacuae uidebantur'; the result is that Korn's elegant *decretis* does not appear even in the apparatus at ix 44, and the same fate befalls Scaliger's *coactus* at xiii 27.

In 1924 the Loeb Classical Library published A. L. Wheeler's text and translation of the *Tristia* and *Ex Ponto*. His text is based on Merkel's second edition, on Ehwald's *Beiträge*, and on Owen's Oxford Classical Text. In several places he rightly abandons *B*'s reading, printing *hanc* for *ah* at i 16 and *perstas* for *praestas* at x 83; at iv 45 he was clearly tempted to print Heinsius' *quamlibet*. His judgment is good, and if Ehwald and Owen had supplied him with more information on other manuscripts and on the Heinsius-Burman vulgate, his text might well have superseded all previous editions. His translation is accurate, and in corrupt passages indicates the awkwardness of the original; I have often quoted from it.

In 1938 there appeared the elaborate Paravia edition of F. W. Levy, who in the period following his earlier edition had altered his name to F. W. Lenz. The text is virtually unchanged from his edition of 1922, but has a much larger apparatus, which includes a large number of conjectures omitted from the earlier edition; I am indebted to Lenz for many of the conjectures I report, particularly at xvi 33. The large size of the apparatus is, however, deceptive; most of the manuscripts he knew of only from the reports of Heinsius, Korn and Owen, and the reports are therefore incomplete: the only manuscripts reliably reported are *B* and *C*. Since Lenz does not usually give the lemma for the variants reported, it is difficult to tell which manuscripts offer the reading in the text. Much space is wasted by reports of the readings of several heavily interpolated mediaeval florilegia; more is wasted by an undue attention to mediaeval spellings and attempts to reproduce abbreviations and to show the precise appearance of secondary corrections. These factors combine to render the apparatus virtually unreadable.

In 1963 Georg Luck published the Artemis edition of the *Tristia* and *Ex Ponto*, with a German translation by Wilhelm Willige. Luck shows some independence from Lenz, at i 16 printing *hanc* for *ah*, at iii 27 *sed et* for *subito*, at viii 71 *mauis* for *maius*, at viii 86 *distet* for *distat*, at ix 73 *laxate* for *iactate*, at xii 13 *producatur* for *ut dicatur*, and at xiv 7 *muter* for *mittar*, each time rightly. He suggests a new conjecture for the incurable xvi 33, and a new and possibly correct punctuation of xii 19. The apparatus is misleading, consisting of isolated readings from *B* and *C* and a small number of readings from other manuscripts. No indication is given that *hanc* at i 16 or *pars* at i 35 are found only in a few manuscripts, and not in *B* or *C*. Luck criticizes modern editors for ignoring the discoveries of their predecessors, and rightly prints Heinsius' *Gigantas* (codd -*es*) at viii 59. However, he shows no direct knowledge of Heinsius' notes or of the Burman vulgate, making no mention of such readings as *Gete* for *Getae* at iii 52, *leuastis* for *leuatis* at vi 44, or *fouet* for *mouet* at xi 20. The oldest edition named in his apparatus is that of Riese.

In 1977 F. Della Corte published an Italian translation of the *Ex Ponto* with an accompanying commentary, of which fifty-eight pages are devoted to the fourth book. Most of the commentary consists of extended paraphrase of the poems; I have found it of little assistance.

The most recent text of the *Ex Ponto* is the 1977 Budé edition of Jacques André. His text is essentially that of Lenz, although at ix 23 he rightly prints *prospicerem* instead of *B*'s *aspicerem*. There are a significant number of misprints in the text, apparatus, and notes, and other signs of carelessness as well.

André makes full reports of only four manuscripts in his apparatus, *B, C, T*, and *Gothanus membr. II 121*[17]. This is an inadequate sampling. *B* and *C* form a distinct group, and the Gotha manuscript is too corrupt to merit a central part in an apparatus. The result is that *T* is the sole good representative of the vulgate class of manuscripts that is regularly cited.

For knowledge of many of his secondary manuscripts, André seems to have depended on the edition of Lenz. Since much of Lenz's information was drawn from Heinsius and other earlier editors, this means that André is often giving unverified information from collations made more than three centuries previously. He did not realize that the Antwerp manuscript he collated (our *M*) was Heinsius' *codex Moreti*, whose readings Lenz sometimes reports; the result is that he reports the same manuscript twice, under the sigla *M* and *N*.

At ix 127 he cites the sixth-century Wolfenbüttel fragment in support of the unassimilated spelling *adscite* (the assimilated form *ascite* is supported by the inscriptions and by the ancient manuscripts of Virgil). In fact, the word is not found in the fragment, which preserves only the first three letters of the line.

Finally, André shows insufficient knowledge of the Heinsius-Burman vulgate; this is evident not only from the text but from the introduction, where he prefaces his list of principal editions by saying 'Nous ne mentionnerons que les editions fondées sur des principes scientifiques, dont la première est celle de R. Merkel, Berlin, 1854' (the edition was published at Leipzig in 1853).

In spite of what I have said against it, André's edition has considerable merit. His apparatus is the first to supply a lemma for each variant reading reported, and is clear and easy to read. His selection of manuscripts is inadequate, but at least he makes a full report of the four manuscripts he uses. The apparatus is in every way a great improvement on that of Lenz. At the same time, he provides a clear prose translation, an informative introduction, ample footnotes, and thirteen pages of "notes complémentaires". His notes sometimes come close to forming a true commentary, and I often quote from them.

In preparing this edition of the fourth book of the *Ex Ponto*, I have carefully read all the editions discussed above, and have attempted to include a comprehensive list of conjectures in the apparatus. I have read Burman's variorum edition with particular attention, and have often restored readings favoured by Heinsius to the text. A complete examination of the manuscripts must await a full edition of all four books of the *Ex Ponto*; but on the basis of published editions I have selected the nine manuscripts that appeared most likely to assist in establishing the text, and have included full reports of their readings in the critical apparatus. I believe that even this preliminary apparatus gives a clearer picture of the evidence for the text of *Ex Ponto* IV than any previous edition.

P. OVIDI NASONIS

EPISTVLARM EX PONTO LIBER QVARTVS

CONSPECTVS SIGLORVM

G

Herzog August Bibliothek Wolfenbüttel: Cod. Guelf. 13.11
Aug. 4°
(fragmentum Guelferbytanum)
saec v/vi

continet ix 101-8 et 127-33, xii 15-19 et 41-44. uersus saepe
non integri.

B

Monacensis lat. 384
saec xii

C

Monacensis lat. 19476
saec xii

M

Antuerpiensis Musei Plantiniani Denucé 68
saec xii/xiii
codex Moreti Heinsianus

F

Francofortanus Barth 110
saec xiii

H

Holkhamicus 322, nunc British Library add. 49368
saec xiii

I

Laurentianus 36 32
saec xiii
primus Mediceus Heinsii

L

Lipsiensis bibl. ciu. Rep. I 2° 7
saec xiii

T

Turonensis 879
saec xii/xiii

―――――――――――――

Interdum aduocatur:

P

Parisinus lat. 7993
saec xiii
Regius Heinsii

―――――――――――――

I

Accipe, Pompei, deductum carmen ab
   illo
   debitor est uitae qui tibi, Sexte, suae.
qui seu non prohibes a me tua nomina
   poni,
   accedet meritis haec quoque summa
   tuis;
siue trahis uultus, equidem peccasse
   fatebor,
5
   delicti tamen est causa probanda
   mei.
non potuit mea mens quin esset grata
   teneri;
   sit precor officio non grauis ira pio.
o quotiens ego sum libris mihi uisus in
   istis
   impius in nullo quod legerere loco!
10
o quotiens, alii uellem cum scribere,
   nomen
   rettulit in ceras inscia dextra tuum!

incipit liber quartus B^2 incipit quartus sexto pompeio M
liber ·iiii· sexto pompeio F incipit ·iiii· sexto pompeio $H^{2(?)}$ ad
pompeium lib ·iiii· I^2 hanc epistulam mittit sexto pompeio L
|| 1 deductum carmen] carmen deductum M || qui] cui
Williams || seu] si ILF^{2ul} || 4 accedet] accedat M || summa]
summe C || 5 trahis] trahes *Owen (1894)* || uultus *om* C ||
equidem] equid e B || 7 quin esset] esset quin H || 9-10 *add*
F^2 *in marg* || 9 o] di B dii I || in] ab B || istis] illis F || 10

57

quod] quid F^2 || 11 alii] aliis L aliis M^{2c} || uellem cum scribere] cum uellem scribere B uellem conscribere F^1 uellem describere P

ipse mihi placuit mendis in talibus
  error,
 et uix inuita facta litura manu est.
'uiderit! ad summam,' dixi 'licet ipse
  queratur,
15
 hanc pudet offensam non meruisse
   prius.'
da mihi, si quid ea est, hebetantem
  pectora Lethen,
 oblitus potero non tamen esse tui;
idque sinas oro, nec fastidita repellas
 uerba, nec officio crimen inesse putes,
20
et leuis haec meritis referatur gratia
  tantis;
 si minus, inuito te quoque gratus ero.
numquam pigra fuit nostris tua gratia
  rebus,
 nec mihi munificas arca negauit
  opes.
nunc quoque nil subitis clementia
  territa fatis
25
 auxilium uitae fertque feretque meae.

13 mendis] mensis C || 14 manu est] manu T || 15 summam] summum LT finem $F^{2(gl)}$ || ipse FTP ille $BCMHIL$ || 16 hanc HI ha $MFLT$ ah B a C hunc $J.$ $N.$ $Grant$ || meruisse] merunisse M^{ac} || 18 non] nec L || 19 *quid pro* nec H, *incertum* || fastidita] fastidia F^1 || 20 putes] putas L puta I puto B^{ac}, *ut uid* || 21 et] sed *fort legendum* || leuis] lenis L ||

58

haec meritis] e meritis F^1T emeritis HM^2 || 23 numquam]
non quam M || 24 mihi *om* C || negauit] negabit C || 25
nunc] hunc C || quoque] quisque C || nil] non $M^{pc}F^1$ nunc
P || 26 feretque *Heinsius* refertque $MFHILTB^2$ referta C refert
B^1

> unde rogas forsan fiducia tanta futuri
>   sit mihi? quod fecit quisque tuetur
>   opus,
> ut Venus artificis labor est et gloria Coi,
>   aequoreo madidas quae premit
>   imbre comas,
> 30
> arcis ut Actaeae uel eburna uel aerea
>   custos
>   bellica Phidiaca stat dea facta manu,
> uindicat ut Calamis laudem quos fecit
>   equorum,
>   ut similis uerae uacca Myronis opus,
> sic ego sum rerum non ultima, Sexte,
>   tuarum
> 35
>   tutelaeque feror munus opusque
>   tuae.

27 unde] un* B^1 || futuri] futura ITF^2 || 28 quisque *ex*
quique C, *ut uid* || 29 ut] et T || est] et I^{ac} || 30 aequoreo]
equoreas T^{ac} || 31 arcis] artis LP || ut Actaeae] et actee T ut
athee L uta^{a}ceae C, *ut uid* || eburna] uberna C || aerea
fragmentum Louaniense Heinsii (Korn, Lenz), codex Iunianus
Heinsii (Korn); uide Haupt Opuscula 584 aurea *Heinsius* enea
(=*aenea*) *BMFHILT, contra metrum* anea C || 32 Phidiaca]
phasadica C || facta] ficta *Heinsius* || 33 Calamis $BCI^{ac}L$
calais $MFI^{pc}TP$ cala bis H, *ut uid* || laudem] laudes B^2 ||
quos] quas B^{ac} que I^{ac}, *ut uid* || sum] pars *excerpta Politiani*

59

res $M^{2(gl?)}$ || non] pars *F om P* || ultima] ultimę (=ultimae) *C* || 36 tuae] teuę (=teuae) *C*

II

Quod legis, o uates magnorum maxime
      regum,
  uenit ab intonsis usque, Seuere, Getis;
cuius adhuc nomen nostros tacuisse
      libellos,
  si modo permittis dicere uera, pudet.
orba tamen numeris cessauit epistula
      numquam
5
  ire per alternas officiosa uices;
carmina sola tibi memorem testantia
      curam
    non data sunt—quid enim quae facis
      ipse darem?
quis mel Aristaeo, quis Baccho uina
      Falerna,
    Triptolemo fruges, poma det Alcinoo?
10
fertile pectus habes, interque Helicona
      colentes
  uberius nulli prouenit ista seges.
'mittere ad hunc carmen frondes erat
      addere siluis.'
    haec mihi cunctandi causa, Seuere,
      fuit.

seuero B^2H^2 seuero amico suo M ad mauximum F^1 [sic] ad
seuerum F^2I^2 hanc epistulam mittit seuero L || 1 regum]
rerum C uatum M^1FIL || 2 intonsis] intensis H euxinis M^1
inuisis F^{2ul} || 5 orba ... numeris] uerba ... numerus C ||

61

cessauit] cessabit B^1 || 6 uices] uias T || 8 quae] quod T || 9
Falerna] falerno M || 10 triptolemo] triptolomo CL tritolemo
F tritolomo IT || det] dat FT || 11 interque] inter I || 13 ad
hunc carmen] carmen ad hunc *fragmentum Louaniense Heinsii
(Lenz)* || 14 cunctandi] cunctanti FH cunctadi I

nec tamen ingenium nobis respondet ut
    ante,
15
    sed siccum sterili uomere litus aro;
scilicet ut limus uenas excaecat †in
    undis†,
    laesaque suppresso fonte resistit
    aqua,
pectora sic mea sunt limo uitiata
    malorum,
    et carmen uena pauperiore fluit.
20
si quis in hac ipsum terra posuisset
    Homerum,
    esset, crede mihi, factus et ipse Getes.
da ueniam fasso: studiis quoque frena
    remisi,
    ducitur et digitis littera rara meis.
impetus ille sacer qui uatum pectora
    nutrit,
25
    qui prius in nobis esse solebat, abest;
uix uenit ad partes, uix sumptae Musa
    tabellae
    imponit pigras, paene coacta, manus,

17 uenas excaecat *MFIT* cum uenas cecat *BCHL* uenas cum
caecat *Castiglioni (Lenz)* || in undis] in unda F in aruis *Dalzell*
inundans *Madvig (Lenz)* apertas *uel* aquarum *Tarrant* hiulcas
Merkel olim (1884) || 18 laesaque] lessaque M^{ac} lapsaque
Merkel (1884) || resistit] resistat L || 21 Homerum]

homorum H^1 *quid* C^{ac}, *incertum (hameo?)* || 22 ipse *MFH* ille *BCILT* || 23 studiis] studii *FIM^{pc}* || quoque frena] frena quoque I^{ac} || 26 *quid pro* qui *HP, incertum* || nobis] uobis *M* || abest] adest *T* || 27 uix sumptae ... tabellae *BCMFHL* (uix *ex* uin *C, ut uid*) uix sumpta ... tabella *T* assumpte ... tabelle *I* || 28 imponit] imposuit *I*

> paruaque, ne dicam scribendi nulla
>   uoluptas
> est mihi, nec numeris nectere uerba
>   iuuat,
> 30
> siue quod hinc fructus adeo non
>   cepimus ullos,
> principium nostri res sit ut ista mali,
> siue quod in tenebris numerosos ponere
>   gestus
> quodque legas nulli scribere carmen
>   idem est.
> excitat auditor studium, laudataque
>   uirtus
> 35
> crescit, et immensum gloria calcar
>   habet.
> hic mea cui recitem nisi flauis scripta
>   Corallis,
> quasque alias gentes barbarus Hister
>   obit?
> sed quid solus agam, quaque infelicia
>   perdam
> otia materia surripiamque diem?
> 40

29 ne] nec *L* || uoluptas] uolumptas *CM^1* uoluntas *FL* || 30 numeris] humeris C^{ac} || nectere] flectere *T* || 32 *add in marg* $I^{1,\ ut\ uid}$ || 32 sit ut] fuit *I (in ras?)* fiat ut H^1 fiat H^2 || ista]

illa *FIP* ‖ 33 gestus] gressus I^1PF^{2ul} gestus [*sic*] F^{3ul} ‖ 34 legas] legam *L* legant F^{2ul} ‖ idem est] obest F^1I^1LP ‖ 36 calcar] carcar *C* ‖ habet] habes B^{ac} ‖ *37 om P* ‖ 37 hic] haec *T* ‖ Corallis] coraillis M^{ac} ‖ 38 Hister] inster *L* ‖ obit *Damsté (Mnemosyne LXVI 32)* habet *codd* ‖ 39 quaque] quamque *BC* ‖ 40 materia] materiam B^{ac} ‖ diem] **dem M^{ac}

> nam quia nec uinum nec me tenet alea
>> fallax,
>> per quae clam tacitum tempus abire
>> solet,
> nec me, quod cuperem si per fera bella
>> liceret,
>> oblectat cultu terra nouata suo,
> quid nisi Pierides, solacia frigida,
>> restant,
>
> 45
>
>> non bene de nobis quae meruere
>> deae?
> at tu, cui bibitur felicius Aonius fons,
>> utiliter studium quod tibi cedit ama,
> sacraque Musarum merito cole,
>> quodque legamus
>> huc aliquod curae mitte recentis
>> opus!
>
> 50

41 quia nec $BCH(I^{ac})$ me nec $I^{pc}P$ neque me *MFLT* ‖ uinum] unum *C* ‖ nec me] neque me *T* ‖ 42 tacitum *add I^1 in marg tantum C* ‖ 43 nec me] nec I^{ac} hec me *C, ut uid* ‖ 45 frigida] frigora *C* ‖ restant] restat *IP* ‖ 46 meruere] metuere *L* ‖ 47 at] ac *LP* ‖ Aonius] adonius *I* ‖ 48 cedit] cedat *T* ‖ ama] amas M^{2ul} ‖ 50 aliquod] aliquid *CP*

III

Conquerar an taceam? ponam sine
       nomine crimen,
   an notum qui sis omnibus esse
       uelim?
nomine non utar, ne commendere
       querela,
   quaeraturque tibi carmine fama meo.
dum mea puppis erat ualida fundata
       carina,
5
   qui mecum uelles currere primus
       eras;
nunc, quia contraxit uultum Fortuna,
       recedis,
   auxilio postquam scis opus esse tuo.
dissimulas etiam, nec me uis nosse
       uideri,
   quisque sit audito nomine Naso
       rogas.
10
ille ego sum, quamquam non uis
       audire, uetusta
   paene puer puero iunctus amicitia;

ad ingratum MFB^2H^2 ad inuidum I^2 || 1 conquerar]
con****ar M^1 (confitear *primitus?*) || sine *add* M^2 || 2 qui sis]
quis sis $HLTM^2$ || 3 ne] nec $(B^{ac})CH$ || commendere]
commendare CL || querela] querelam C^{pc} quelelam C^{ac} || 4
carmine] carmi/ne I nomine H || 5 dum] cum M || 7 nunc
quia] dum mea F^1 || contraxit] traxit M^1 abtraxit [*sic*] M^2 ||

9 me uis] uis me $I^{pc}T$ uis I^{ac} || uideri] fateri $M^{2ul}F^{2ul}$ tueri P || 10 quisque] quique $H^{ac}P$ || sit *add* $C^{1?}$ || 11-12 *post 13-14 ponit B* || 11 quamquam] q̲u̲a̲m̲q̲u̲a̲m̲ $I^{2?c}$ qūm C (*=quoniam*) quamuis M^{2ul} || 12 iunctus] uinctus HP || amicitia] amicia M

ille ego qui primus tua seria nosse
    solebam,
  et tibi iucundis primus adesse iocis;
ille ego conuictor densoque domesticus
    usu;
15
  ille ego iudiciis unica Musa tuis.
ille ego sum quem nunc an uiuam,
    perfide, nescis,
  cura tibi de quo quaerere nulla subit.
siue fui numquam carus, simulasse
    fateris;
  seu non fingebas, inueniere leuis.
20
aut age, dic aliquam quae te mutauerit
    iram;
  nam nisi iusta tua est, iusta querela
    mea est.

13 tua] sua L || 14 iocis] locis M^{2ul} locus P || 15 ille ego] ille B^{ac} || d̲o̲m̲e̲s̲ticus F^{1c} denso (F^{ac}) || 16 unica] uinea L || 17 ille] i/l̲e̲ B^{1c} idem (B^{ac})CM^1H || ego sum] ego T^{ac} ego iudicii B^{ac} || quem nunc an uiuam *Leidensis Heinsii* qui nunc an uiuam $BCMFHILT$ quem nunc an uiuat *Heinsius* || 18 subit *Heinsius* fuit *codd* || 19 fui] fuit (B^{ac})CP || simulasse] simulare F^1 || fateris] fereris *Heinsius* || 20 leuis] lenis H || 21 aut age] eia age *'uterque Medonii* [=*Bodleianus Rawl G 105, 106*] *pro diuersa lectione', probante Heinsio* || aliquam quae te mutauerit [mutauerat C mutauit F] iram $BCMFHIL$ aliquid quod te mutauit in iram T || 22 est, iusta] est ista I^{ac}

quod te nunc crimen similem uetat esse
    priori?
an crimen coepi quod miser esse
    uocas?
si mihi rebus opem nullam factisque
    ferebas,
25
uenisset uerbis charta notata tribus.
uix equidem credo, sed et insultare
    iacenti
te mihi nec uerbis parcere fama
    refert.
quid facis, a demens? cur, si Fortuna
    recedat,
naufragio lacrimas eripis ipse tuo?
30
haec dea non stabili quam sit leuis orbe
    fatetur
quem summo dubium sub pede
    semper habet.
quolibet est folio, quauis incertior aura:
par illi leuitas, improbe, sola tua est.

---

23 quod te nunc crimen similem] quod te nunc similem
crimen *H* quae te consimilem res nunc *FIL* || uetat] ueta L^1
|| 24 an] aut *B* || 25 fac̣tisque B^{2c} || 26 charta notata
tribus] parcere fama refert *C* || 27 sed et] sed te *I* subito
$(B^1)C$ || 28 te … nec] et … non *T* || parcere fama refert]
charta notata tribus *C* || 29 a] o M^1FILT || recedat TM^2
recedit BCM^1FHIL 30 tuo] meo *HI* || 31 stabili] stabilis *L* ||
quam sit leuis orbe] quam leuis orbe *C* quantum sit in orbe
L || 32 quem *fragmentum Boxhornianum Heinsii (=Leid. Bibl.*
Publ. 180 G) quae *BCMFHILT* || summo dubium *scripsi*
summo dubio *C* summum dubio *BMFILT* mundum dubio *H*
dubio summum *fort scribendum* || 33 quauis] quamuis *MLP*
|| aura] aura est *MF* || 34 par *ex* per *M, ut uid* || sola] f̄ta

68

L(=facta) || tua est] tuē ē C

> omnia sunt hominum tenui pendentia
> filo,
35
> et subito casu quae ualuere ruunt.
> diuitis audita est cui non opulentia
> Croesi?
> nempe tamen uitam captus ab hoste
> tulit.
> ille Syracosia modo formidatus in urbe
> uix humili duram reppulit arte
> famem.
40
> quid fuerat Magno maius? tamen ille
> rogauit
> summissa fugiens uoce clientis opem.
> cuique uiro totus terrarum paruit orbis

> . . . .

35 omnia] omina *M¹FILT* euentus $F^{2(gl)}$ || pendentia]
pedentia *I* || 36 ruunt] cadunt M^{2ul} || 38 tamen] etiam *Riese*
|| 39 Syracosia *Heinsius* syracusia *CMFHILT* siracu̲na B^{2c}
syracusa *Gothanus II 121, saec xiii (André) 'etiam bene'*—
Heinsius || formidatus] fortunatus *M* || 40 famem] famen *C*
famē *L* || 41 Magno maius] maius magno *I* || ille] ipse *MI*
|| 43-44 *damnat Bentley* || 44 *om* B^1C indigus effectus
omnibus ipse magis $MHILTF^2$ [[indigus: indiguus *M*
indigens F^{2ul}) (indigus ... omnibus: omnibus ... indigus *I*)
(effectus: est factus *IL* effectis *Ellis[Owen 1894]*) (ipse: ille *T*)
(magis: fuit F^{2ul})] achillas pharius abstulit ense caput F^1
fragmentum Louaniense Heinsii (Burman)

> ille Iugurthino clarus Cimbroque
> triumpho,
45

quo uictrix totiens consule Roma fuit,
in caeno latuit Marius cannaque
      palustri,
   pertulit et tanto multa pudenda uiro.
ludit in humanis diuina potentia rebus,
   et certam praesens uix facit hora
      fidem.
50
'litus ad Euxinum' si quis mihi diceret
      'ibis,
   et metues arcu ne feriare Gete',
'i bibe' dixissem 'purgantes pectora
      sucos,
   quicquid et in tota nascitur Anticyra'.
sum tamen haec passus nec, si mortalia
      possem,
55
   et summi poteram tela cauere dei.
tu quoque fac timeas, et quae tibi laeta
   uidentur
   dum loqueris fieri tristia posse puta.

---

45 ille] ipse *I* || Iugurthino] iuigurtino *M, ut uid* ||
Cimbroque] cimboque *B* || 47 latuit Marius *M* iacuit marius
H marius latuit *L* marius iacuit *BCFIT* || 50 uix] non M^{2ul}
|| facit *R.J. Tarrant* feret *BC* habet *MFHILT* || 52 Gete
Heinsius e codicibus Getae *edd* || 53 i bibe] ebibe *B* ||
purgantes pectora sucos] purgantia pocula sompnos F^{2ul} ||
54 Anticyra] anticera *MI* || 55 nec] ne *L* || 57 laeta] lenta I^{ac}

IIII

Nulla dies adeo est australibus umida
    nimbis
    non intermissis ut fluat imber aquis,
nec sterilis locus ullus ita est ut non sit
    in illo
    mixta fere duris utilis herba rubis;
nil adeo Fortuna grauis miserabile fecit
5
    ut minuant nulla gaudia parte
        malum.
ecce domo patriaque carens oculisque
        meorum,
    naufragus in Getici litoris actus
        aquas,
qua tamen inueni uultum diffundere
        causam
    possim fortunae nec meminisse
        meae.
10
nam mihi cum fulua solus spatiarer
    harena
    uisa est a tergo penna dedisse sonum.

de consulatu sexti pompe(i)i FB^2H^2 pompeio amico suo M ad
sextum pompeium I^2 || 3 nec] non F || 4 rubis *ex* iubis F ||
6 ut] quin M^{2ul} || nulla] ulla M^{2ul} || parte *BCMFHILT, sicut
coni Bentley* pace P || 8 aquas] aquis H || 9 uultum]
uultumque L || diffundere] defendere *P, I ut uid* || causam]
causa *BCT* || 10 possim] possem L possum F || nec] non I
|| 11 cum] dum *FIT, sicut coni Bentley* || solus *BC* tristis
MFHILT || spatiarer] spatiare F^{ac} paciarer M^{pc} paciare M^{ac}

respicio, neque erat corpus quod
　　cernere possem;
　uerba tamen sunt haec aure recepta
　　mea:
'en ego laetarum uenio tibi nuntia
　　rerum,
15
　Fama, per immensas aere lapsa uias:
consule Pompeio, quo non tibi carior
　　alter,
　candidus et felix proximus annus
　　erit.'
dixit et, ut laeto Pontum rumore
　　repleuit,
　ad gentes alias hinc dea uertit iter.
20
at mihi dilapsis inter noua gaudia curis
　excidit asperitas huius iniqua loci,
ergo ubi, Iane biceps, longum
　　reseraueris annum,
　pulsus et a sacro mense December
　　erit,
purpura Pompeium summi uelabit
　　honoris,
25
　ne titulis quicquam debeat ille suis.
cernere iam uideor rumpi paene atria
　　turba
　et populum laedi deficiente loco,

penetralia *I*, *F²ul ut uid* laeta atria *Burman, qui et* plena atria
coniecit

> templaque Tarpeiae primum tibi sedis
>   adiri
> et fieri faciles in tua uota deos,
>
> 30
> colla boues niueos certae praebere
>   securi,
> quos aluit campis herba Falisca suis,
> cumque deos omnes, tum quos
>   impensius aequos
> esse tibi cupias, cum Ioue Caesar
>   erunt.
> curia te excipiet, patresque e more
>   uocati
>
> 35
>   intendent aures ad tua uerba suas.
> hos ubi facundo tua uox hilarauerit ore,
>   utque solet tulerit prospera uerba
>   dies,

29 tibi ... adiri] tibi ... adire *L* te ... adire *H²ul* || 31 certae]
cerno *Owen (1915)* certant *Damsté (Mnemosyne XLVII 33-34)*
|| 32 Falisca] falesca *B* palistra *F²ul ut uid* || *post 32 distichon
excidisse putat Ehwald (KB 63)* || 33 omnes, tum quos *HL*
omnes tunc quos *BCMFIT* tunc hos ores *P* omnes, tunc hos
Ehwald || 34 cupias] capias *B, ut uid* cupies *fort scribendum* ||
erunt *B, sicut coni Heinsius* erit *MFHILT om C* || 35 curia te]
cura te *H* curiaque *Heinsius* || excipiet] excipias *C* ||
patresque] partesque *C* || e *BCM* ex *FHILT* || uocati] uocari
C || 36 intendent] intendunt *BC* || ad *ex* at *C* || 37
hilarauerit] hilauerit *Mᵃᶜ*

> egeris et meritas superis cum Caesare
>   grates
> (qui causam facias cur ita, saepe

dabit),
40

inde domum repetes toto comitante
    senatu,
   officium populi uix capiente domo.
me miserum, turba quod non ego
    cernar in illa
   nec poterunt istis lumina nostra frui!
quamlibet absentem, qua possum,
    mente uidebo:
45

   aspiciet uultus consulis illa sui.
di faciant aliquo subeat tibi tempore
    nostrum
   nomen, et 'heu' dicas 'quid miser ille
    facit?'
haec tua pertulerit si quis mihi uerba,
    fatebor
   protinus exilium mollius esse meum.
50

---

40 qui] que B^{ac}, *ut uid* || facias cur ita, saepe dabit *Riese* facias
cur ita saepe, dabit *edd* || dabit] dabunt LF^{2ul} || 43 cernar]
cernor *MIL* cenor *H* || 45 quamlibet *Heinsius* qua libet H^1
qua licet $M^{ac}P$ quo licet *L* quod licet $BCM^{pc}FIT$ et licet H^{2ul}
scilicet *Castiglioni (Lenz)* || mente *in ras* F^2 || 46 aspiciet I^{1c}
aspicuum (I^{ac}) || 47 di *B* dii *CMFHILT* || nostrum] nomen
nostrum *C* || 48 miser ille facit] facit ille miser *T* || 49
pertulerit] protulerit *H* || 50 mollius] micius $F^{2ul}(=mitius)$

V

Ite, leues elegi, doctas ad consulis aures,
   uerbaque honorato ferte legenda
      uiro.
longa uia est, nec uos pedibus
      proceditis aequis,
   tectaque brumali sub niue terra latet.
cum gelidam Thracen et opertum
      nubibus Haemon
5
   et maris Ionii transieritis aquas,
luce minus decima dominam uenietis in
      urbem,
   ut festinatum non faciatis iter.
protinus inde domus uobis Pompeia
      petetur;
   non est Augusto iunctior ulla foro.
10
si quis ut in populo qui sitis et unde
      requiret,
   nomina decepta quaelibet aure ferat;

sexto pompeio B^2H^2 pompeo amico suo M ad sextum pompeium F ad eundem sextum pompeium I^2 || 4 latet] letet C^{ac} || 5 cum gelidam] congelidam F^1 || Thracen] tracem I tracē F || opertum] opertam L || nubibus] niuibus LP || Haemon *Laurentianus 38 39, saec xv (Lenz); Ven. Marcianus XII 106, saec xv (Lenz); editio princeps Bononiensis (Lenz)* hemum *BCMFHILT* || 6 Ionii] ycarii F^{2ul} || aquas] aquis M^{ac}? iter aquas C *quid* F^{2ul}*, incertum (extasis?)* || 7 luce F^{2c} 8 faciatis] facietis C^{pc} facetis C^{ac} || 9 Pompeia] ponpeia C || petetur FT petatur *BCMHIL* || 10 ulla] illa CI || 11 qui] que I^{ac} ||

ut sit enim tutum, sicut reor esse, fateri
    uera, minus certe ficta timoris
        habent.
copia nec uobis nullo prohibente
        uidendi
15
    consulis, ut limen contigeritis, erit:
aut reget ille suos dicendo iura Quirites,
    conspicuum signis cum premet altus
        ebur,
aut populi reditus positam componet
        ad hastam,
    et minui magnae non sinet urbis
        opes,
20
aut, ubi erunt patres in Iulia templa
        uocati,
    de tanto dignis consule rebus aget,
aut feret Augusto solitam natoque
        salutem,
    deque parum noto consulet officio.
tempus ab his uacuum Caesar
        Germanicus omne
25
    auferet; a magnis hunc colit ille deis.

---

13 fateri] fatendum *F* futuri *(B^{ac})* uerum *L$^{2(gl)}$* || 14 uera
Hilberg, Die Gesetze der Wortstellung im Pentameter des Ovid 35-
36 (fateri uera) uerba *codd (uerba ... habent)* ficta *ex* minus ficta
M || 15 uobis] nobis *L* || nullo] ullo *P, probante Heinsio* || 18
cum premet] comprimet *F^1* || altus] alter *B^1* || 19 positam]
ualidam *H* || componet] componit *L* || ad] in *F* || 20 opes]
opem *I* || 21 aut] at *H^1* || ubi erunt] ubi *C* || uocati]
uoocati *M* || 23 aut feret *BCFHILTM^{3ul}* afferet *M^{2c}* || 24

78

parum noto] parum nato *C* patrum toto *Burman* || 25 ab] et
BC || uacuum] uacuo *Heinsius*

cum tamen a turba rerum requieuerit
    harum,
ad uos mansuetas porriget ille
    manus,
quidque parens ego uester agam
    fortasse requiret.
talia uos illi reddere uerba uolo:
30
'uiuit adhuc uitamque tibi debere
    fatetur,
quam prius a miti Caesare munus
    habet.
te sibi, cum fugeret, memori solet ore
    referre
barbariae tutas exhibuisse uias,
sanguine Bistonium quod non
    tepefecerit ensem,
35
effectum cura pectoris esse tui,
addita praeterea uitae quoque multa
    tuendae
munera, ne proprias attenuaret opes.
pro quibus ut meritis referatur gratia,
    iurat
se fore mancipii tempus in omne tui.
40

27 turba] cura *Heinsius* || requieuerit] requierit C^{ac}
requieurit F^1 || 30 reddere uerba] uerba reddere *I* || 32 a
miti] * miti F^{ac} amiti BM^1H amitti *L* om I^{ac} || 33 referre] fateri
F || 35 Bistonium] bistanium *L* || tepefecerit] tepefecerat *M*
tepecerit I^{ac} || 36 cura] pura I^{ac} || 37-40 *add* B^2 *in margine* ||
37 uitae quoque] sunt uite *M* || 40 mancipii ... tui CB^2

mancipium ... tuum *MFHILTB*[3] mancipio ... tuo *Brissonius* (*'lib. VI. de Form. pag. 517'* —*Burman*) mancipio ... tuum *Merkel (1853)* || tempus] tepus *M*

> nam prius umbrosa carituros arbore
>   montes,
>   et freta ueliuolas non habitura rates,
> fluminaque in fontes cursu reditura
>   supino,
>   gratia quam meriti possit abire tui.'
> haec ubi dixeritis, seruet sua dona
>   rogate;
> 45
>   sic fuerit uestrae causa peracta uiae.

41 carituros] carituras *L* || ueliuolas] ueliferas *M*[1] || 44 possit] posset *L* 45 haec] hoc *MT* || 46 peracta] peracta *F*[2c]

VI

Quam legis ex illis tibi uenit epistula,
    Brute,
  Nasonem nolles in quibus esse locis.
sed tu quod nolles, uoluit miserabile
    fatum;
  ei mihi, plus illud quam tua uota
    ualet.
in Scythia nobis quinquennis Olympias
    acta

5

  iam tempus lustri transit in alterius.
perstat enim Fortuna tenax, uotisque
    malignum
  opponit nostris insidiosa pedem.
certus eras pro me, Fabiae laus,
    Maxime, gentis,
  numen ad Augustum supplice uoce
      loqui;

10

bruto B^2H^2 bruto amico suo M ad brutum FI^2 || 1 illis] ipsis T || 3 tu quod] tu qui L^{ac}, *ut uid* quod tu IT || 4 ei *edd* hei *Barberinus lat. 26, saec xiii (Lenz)* et BCM^1FILT si H heu M^{2ul} || illud] istud H || ualet] ualent FIT H, *ut uid* || 5 Scythia] sythia HIL scithica M || Olympias acta LT olympias acta est $BMFHI$ olimpia facta est C || 5-6 Olympias acta iam *Housman (Owen)* Olympias acta est. iam *edd* || 7 perstat] praestat CP || 8 opponit] opposuit H || nostris *in loco a prima manu relicto add* F^2 nostris B^{2c} || insidiosa] insidiosam C^{ac} inuidiosa FHM^2 || 9 eras] erat $(B^1)C$ || pro me, Fabiae] fabie pro me I || laus $BCMHILTF^3$ dux F^1 lux F^2, *probante Burman* ||

maxime] maxima *CP*

> occidis ante preces, causamque ego,
>> Maxime, mortis
> (nec fueram tanti) me reor esse tuae.
> iam timeo nostram cuiquam mandare
>> salutem;
>> ipsum morte tua concidit auxilium.
> coeperat Augustus detectae ignoscere
>> culpae;
> 15
>> spem nostram terras deseruitque
>>> simul.
> quale tamen potui de caelite, Brute,
>> recenti
>> uestra procul positus carmen in ora
>>> dedi;
> quae prosit pietas utinam mihi, sitque
>> malorum
>> iam modus et sacrae mitior ira
>>> domus.
> 20
> te quoque idem liquido possum iurare
>> precari,
>> o mihi non dubia cognite Brute nota;
> nam cum praestiteris uerum mihi
>> semper amorem,
>> hic tamen aduerso tempore creuit
>>> amor,

11 occidis] occidit *(B¹)C* || preces] pedes *M* || causamque]
causa̲q̲u̲e̲ *B²ᶜ* || ego *add F²* || 12 fueram] fuero *BC* fuerim
British Library Burney 220, saec xii-xiii (André) || 13 timeo
nostram cuiquam] timeo cuiquam nostram *F* nostram
cuiquam timeo *I* || 14 tua] tue̲ *C(=tuae)* || concidit] consul
Bᵃᶜ constitit *Némethy* || 15 Augustus] augstus *Iᵃᶜ* augustum

L^{ac} || detectae *scripsi* deceptae *codd* decepti *J. N. Grant* || 18
positus] positis *C* || 21 te quoque] teque *I* || idem] iam *F* ||
possum] possim *F* possem *T* || 22 cognite] condite M^{2ul} ||
nota] fide $LTM^{2ul}F^{2ul}$ || 24 hic] plus *T* || aduerso] auerso *H*
|| creuit *ex* creauit *H*

> quique tuas pariter lacrimas nostrasque
> uideret
> 25
> passuros poenam crederet esse duos.
> lenem te miseris genuit Natura, nec ulli
> mitius ingenium quam tibi, Brute,
> dedit,
> ut qui quid ualeas ignoret Marte forensi
> posse tuo peragi uix putet ore reos.
> 30
> scilicet eiusdem est, quamuis pugnare
> uidentur,
> supplicibus facilem, sontibus esse
> trucem.
> cum tibi suscepta est legis uindicta
> seuerae,
> uerba uelut taetrum singula uirus
> habent;
> hostibus eueniat quam sis uiolentus in
> armis
> 35
> sentire et linguae tela subire tuae,
> quae tibi tam tenui cura limantur ut
> omnes
> istius ingenui pectoris esse negent.

26 crederet] diceret F^{2ul} || 27 lenem] lene *C* || 29 ignoret]
ignorat *TP* || Marte *BCHI* in arte *MFLT* || 30 tuo] tuos *M*
|| 31 eiusdem est] eisdem est F^{ac}, *ut uid* eiusdem *Heinsius 'cum*
tribus libris' || uidentur *BMFH*, *sicut coni Bentley* uidetur *CILT*

|| 33 est] est seuere M^{ac} || 34 taetrum *R. J. Tarrant* tinctum *BCM¹FHILT* tritum M^{2ul} coctum M^{2ul} tinctu *Ehwald (KB 83)* tinguat *Merkel (1884)* || 36 linguae *ex* linge *B* || 37 limantur] limatur *C* || 38 ingenui pectoris *scripsi* ingenium corporis *codd* ingenium nominis *D. R. Shackleton Bailey*

at si quem laedi fortuna cernis iniqua,
    mollior est animo femina nulla tuo;
40
hoc ego praecipue sensi, cum magna
      meorum
    notitiam pars est infitiata mei.
immemor illorum, uestri non immemor
      umquam
    qui mala solliciti nostra leuastis, ero,
et prius hic nimium nobis conterminus
      Hister
45
    in caput Euxino de mare uertet iter,
utque Thyesteae redeant si tempora
      mensae,
    Solis ad Eoas currus agetur aquas,

40 auxilium subito tu sibi [*sic*] ferre soles M^2 *in marg* || 41 hoc] haec *FHL* || 43 uestri] uestrum *Heinsius* || 44 mala F^2 *in ras* || solliciti BCM^{2ul} sollicite M^1FHILT || leuastis *Barberinus lat. 26, saec xiii (Heinsius)* leuatis *BCMFHILT* || ero] ope *C* || 45 hic] hinc *HTP* || nimium nobis] nimium uobis *BC* nobis nimium $I^{ac}T$ || Hister] inster *L* || 46 Euxino] euxini *I* euxinum *T* eximio *F* || uertet] uertit *FP* || 47 utque] atque BHL^2 *ante codd Feschii et Hafniensis Heinsii* || si] ceu *Heinsius ('ante, Thyesteae redeant ceu tempora mensae, / solis ad Eoas currus agetur aquas')* || tempora] fercula *'malim reponi, sed obstant libri ueteres' —Heinsius*

    quam quisquam uestrum qui me
      doluistis ademptum

arguat ingratum non meminisse sui.
50

49 doluistis] lugetis *T* || ademptum] adempto *Basileensis F IV 26, saec xiii-xiv (Korn), probante Heinsio* adeptum *LP* || 50 arguat] arguar *B*

VII

Missus es Euxinas quoniam, Vestalis, ad
  oras,
ut positis reddas iura sub axe locis,
aspicis en praesens quali iaceamus in
  aruo,
nec me testis eris falsa solere queri;
accedet uoci per te non irrita nostrae,
5
  Alpinis iuuenis regibus orte, fides.
ipse uides certe glacie concrescere
  Pontum,
ipse uides rigido stantia uina gelu,
ipse uides onerata ferox ut ducat Iazyx
  per medias Histri plaustra bubulcus
  aquas,
10
aspicis et mitti sub adunco toxica ferro,
et telum causas mortis habere duas;

uestali B^2H^2 ad uestalem amicum suum M ad uestalem FI^2
hanc epistulam misit uostali L || 1 Euxinas] exunias I ||
horas [=*oras*] CI undas $BMFHLT$ || 2 locis] getis T || 3
praesens] praeses P || iaceamus] aceamus C^{ac} || 4 queri]
loqui IM^{2ul} || 5 nostrae] semper I^{ac} || 6 Alpinis] Arpinis
Verpoorten (Lenz) || 8 uina] rura F^{2ul} || 9 ut ducat Iazyx
$BCMFHIT$ [Iazyx *Merula (Burman)* iahis B ayzys C^1 iazys $C^{1?}$
^{ul} iatis M iazis F yacis H hiacis I yases T] trahat ut glatiati L
educat ut altas P || 10 bubulcus] bububcus B || 11-12 *post*
13-14 *ponit* T || 11 et mitti] et miti I^{ac} admitti F^{2ul} || adunco]
aduuco L^{ac} || 12 telum] ferum T uulnus F^{2ul}

atque utinam pars haec tantum
      spectata fuisset,
  non etiam proprio cognita Marte tibi!
tenditur ad primum per densa pericula
      pilum,
15
    contigit ex merito qui tibi nuper
        honor;
sit licet hic titulus plenis tibi fructibus
      ingens,
    ipsa tamen uirtus ordine maior erit.
non negat hoc Hister, cuius tua dextera
      quondam
puniceam Getico sanguine fecit
      aquam,
20
non negat Aegissos, quae te subeunte
      recepta
    sensit in ingenio nil opis esse loci;

---

13 spectata] speculata *L* || 14 *quid pro* etiam *H, incertum* ||
proprio] propria *B* || 15 tenditur *Owen* tenditis *BCMFHI*^{pc}*L*
tendis et *T* tendet *I*^{ac}, *ut uid* tendisti *Merkel* tendit is *Oberlin*
('*sc. Mars, cf. 45*'—*Owen 1894*) tendis at [*uel* et] ad *temptauit*
Castiglioni (Lenz) || 17 plenis] plenus (*F*^{ac})*I* || plenis tibi
fructibus ingens, *edd* plenus tibi fructibus, ingens *Ehwald* ||
ingens '*corruptum*'—*Riese; om M*^{ac} || 18 erit] erat *duo codd*
Burmanni inest *Heinsius* adest *Heinsius* || 19 hoc] hic *B*^{2c} haec
I, ut uid || 19-21 negat ... negat] neget ... negat *unus ex*
Thuaneis Heinsii (=Parisinus lat. 8256 uel 8462) neget ... neget
Burman || 21 Aegissos *uide* CIL *III pag. 1009* egisos *I*^{1}*T* ecisos
I^2, *ut uid* egiros *FLP* egyros *H* egilos *C* egylos *B* egypsos *M* ||
recepta] recepto *F*^{1}*HP* || 22 opis] opi̲s̲ *I*^{1c} opus *FH(I*^{ac})

nam, dubium positu melius defensa

　　　　　manune,
　　urbs erat in summo, nubibus aequa,
　　　　　iugo.
Sithonio regi ferus interceperat illam
25
　　hostis, et ereptas uictor habebat opes,
donec fluminea deuecta Vitellius unda
　　intulit exposito milite signa Getis.
at tibi, progenies alti fortissima Donni,
　　uenit in aduersos impetus ire uiros;
30
nec mora: conspicuus longe fulgentibus
　　　　　armis
　　fortia ne possint facta latere caues,
ingentique gradu contra ferrumque
　　　　　locumque
　　saxaque brumali grandine plura
　　　　　subis.
nec te missa super iaculorum turba
　　　　　moratur,
35
　　nec quae uipereo tela cruore madent:

23 dubium] dubium est *CL* dubum *I^{ac}* || manune *BCT* manuue *M^{pc}FHIL* manu *M^{ac}* || 24 urb<u>s</u>/ *F^{2c}* || iugo] loco *I* || 25 Sit(h)onio *BCMFIT* sidonio *H* scithonio *L* || 26 ereptas] erectas *B^{ac}* eruptas *C* || 27 deuecta] deuectus *L* || 29 Donni *CB^{1?ul}* domni *IT, M ut uid* dōni *H* dompni *L* dauni *F* domu *B^1* || 30 uiros] globos *Heinsius* || 31 conspicuus] conspicuis *IP* || 34 saxaque ... plura] pluraque ... saxa *F* || subis] su/bis *H* || 35 moratur] miratur *C* || 36 madent] rubent *Gottorphianus Heinsii* uirent *Heinsius*

　　spicula cum pictis haerent in casside
　　　　　pennis,
　　parsque fere scuti uulnere nulla

uacat.

nec corpus cunctos feliciter effugit ictus,
    sed minor est acri laudis amore dolor;
40
talis apud Troiam Danais pro nauibus
        Aiax
    dicitur Hectoreas sustinuisse faces.
ut propius uentum est admotaque
        dextera dextrae,
    resque fero potuit comminus ense
        geri,
dicere difficile est quid Mars tuus egerit
        illic,
45
    quotque neci dederis quosque
        quibusque modis:
ense tuo factos calcabas uictor aceruos,
    impositoque Getes sub pede multus
        erat.
pugnat ad exemplum primi minor
        ordine pili,
    multaque fert miles uulnera, multa
        facit,
50

---

37 haerent] horrent *L* || pennis] pinnis *C* || 38 parsque *ex*
pasque *M* || fere] fero *Heinsius* || uacat] caret $PM^{2(gl)}F^{2(gl)}$ ||
39 ////ictus *I* || 40 minor] minus $B^{ac}P$ || acri] acro *B* acer *P*
actae *Iunianus Heinsii* altae *auctor electorum Etonensium* || 41
Aiax] iaiax *C* || 42 Hectoreas] hectoas B^{ac} || 43 ut] et M^{2ul}
|| propius] proprius $F^{ac}H$ || dextera dextrae] dextre dextera
I^{ac} dextera dextre est *B (dextre ē)* dextera dextra est *C (dextraē)*
|| 44 potuit *om C* || ense] esse *C* || 46 quotque] quodque *CP*
|| dederis] dederas *L* || quosque] quotque *H* || 47 aceruos]
acerbos *C*, M^{ac} *ut uid* || 48 multus] uictus *H* || erat] eat C^{ac}

sed tantum uirtus alios tua praeterit
　　　　omnes
ante citos quantum Pegasus ibat
　　　　equos.
uincitur Aegissos, testataque tempus in
　　　　omne
sunt tua, Vestalis, carmine facta meo.

51 tantum] tamen et M || alios $M^{2?c}$ || 52 ibat] ibit BP || 53
Aegissos *uide ad 21* egisos T egiros $CFHL$ egyros B egipsos I
egypsos M || 54 sunt] sint F^1 || facta] ficta C

VIII

Littera sera quidem, studiis exculte
    Suilli,
  huc tua peruenit, sed mihi grata
    tamen,
qua, pia si possit superos lenire rogando
  gratia, laturum te mihi dicis opem.
ut iam nil praestes, animi sum factus
    amici

5

  debitor: et meritum uelle iuuare uoco.
impetus iste tuus longum modo duret
    in aeuum,
  neue malis pietas sit tua lassa meis.
ius aliquod faciunt adfinia uincula
    nobis
  (quae semper maneant inlabefacta
    precor),

10

nam tibi quae coniunx, eadem mihi
    filia paene est,
  et quae te generum, me uocat illa
    uirum.
ei mihi, si lectis uultum tu uersibus istis
  ducis, et adfinem te pudet esse
    meum!

swillio B^2 suillo amico suo M ad suillium F suillo H^2 ad
suillum I^2 hanc epistulam mittit suillo L || 1 exculte] exculta
L exulte M || Suilli] suille TP || 3 possit *Gothanus II 121, saec
xiii (Lenz), Barberinus lat. 26, saec xiii (Lenz)* posset *BCMFHILT*
|| rogando] precando T || 5 iam nil] mihi nil HT mihi non

92

ILP || 6 uoco] uolo B^1C || 7 modo] mihi *MFT* || d̲uret F^{2c}
|| 12 generum] gerum H^1, *ut uid* || 14 te] t* B^1(*tu?*)

> at nihil hic dignum poteris reperire
> > pudore
> 15
> > praeter fortunam, quae mihi caeca
> > > fuit;
> seu genus excutias, equites ab origine
> > prima
> > usque per innumeros inueniemur
> > > auos,
> siue uelis qui sint mores inquirere
> > nostri,
> > errorem misero detrahe, labe carent.
> 20
> tu modo si quid agi sperabis posse
> > precando,
> > quos colis exora supplice uoce deos.
> di tibi sunt Caesar iuuenis: tua numina
> > placa.
> > hac certe nulla est notior ara tibi.
> non sinit illa sui uanas antistitis
> > umquam
> 25
> > esse preces; nostris hinc pete rebus
> > opem.

15 at] et *T* || nihil] nil *I* || reperire] re/perire *F* || pudore]
pudoris *T* || 16 caeca] saeua *Riese* laeua *fort legendum* || 17
seu] si M^1 || excutias] inquiras F^1M^{2ul} || 18 inueniemur
$HILB^{2ul}F^{2ul}$ inuenientur MF^1T perueniemus B^1C || 19 uelis̲/
F^{2c} || qui sint mores] qui sunt mores *I, ut uid* mores qui sint
M || inquirere] inquire *M* || nostri] nostros *I, probante
Heinsio* || 20 detrahe] dete I^1 || 22 exora] excola B^{ac} || 23 di]
at *C* || sunt] sint $BCFM^{2ul}$ || 24 nulla est] nulla *FT* ||

notior] certior *I* || 25 non] nec *I* || sinit] sinet *I* || illa] ara *M¹* || 26 rebus] *ebus *B*

> quamlibet exigua si nos ea iuuerit aura,
>> obruta de mediis cumba resurget
>>> aquis;
> tunc ego tura feram rapidis sollemnia
>> flammis,
> et ualeant quantum numina testis
>> ero.

30
> nec tibi de Pario statuam, Germanice,
>> templum
> marmore; carpsit opes illa ruina
>> meas.
> templa domus facient uobis urbesque
>> beatae;
> Naso suis opibus, carmine, gratus
>> erit.
> parua quidem fateor pro magnis
>> munera reddi,

35
> cum pro concessa uerba salute
>> damus;
> sed qui quam potuit dat maxima
>> gratus abunde est,
> et finem pietas contigit illa suum,

27 quamlibet] qualibet *I* qua libet *B^{pc}C* || iuuerit] pauerit *unus Vaticanus, unde* fouerit *Heinsius* || 29 tunc] nunc *C* || 30 ualeant quantum] quantum ualeant *F* || 31 Pario] phario *LF²H²I²* || 32 carpsit] carsit *C^{ac}* carp*it *B^{2c}* capsit *F^{ac}* || meas] meos *L* || 33 facient uobis] facient nobis *C* faciant uobis *FI, probante Heinsio* uobis faciant *M^{2c, ut uid}* || urbesque] urbeque *F¹* || beatae] bate *C^{ac}* bate *F* || 37 sed] si *T* || quam] quantum *B²* || abunde *C* ab unde *B* habunde

nec quae de parua pauper dis libat
  acerra
 tura minus grandi quam data lance
   ualent,
40
agnaque tam lactens quam gramine
   pasta Falisco
 uictima Tarpeios inficit icta focos.
nec tamen officio uatum per carmina
  facto
 principibus res est aptior ulla uiris.
carmina uestrarum peragunt praeconia
   laudum,
45
  neue sit actorum fama caduca
   cauent;
carmine fit uiuax uirtus, expersque
  sepulcri
 notitiam serae posteritatis habet;
tabida consumit ferrum lapidemque
  uetustas,
 nullaque res maius tempore robur
   habet.
50

39 nec quae] neque C || pauper dis libat] pauper delibat *F*
dis pauper libat *ML* || acerra] acerba *C (=acerua)* || 40
minus] minos *C* || lance] luce *M* || 41 lactens] lactans *F^1* ||
43 officio] in uita *C* || 44 aptior] altior *P* aptior *F^{2c}* gratior
Heinsius ex tredecim codicibus || ulla] illa *B^{1}C* || 45 uestrarum]
uastarum *Burman* certarum *Heinsius* || laudum] laudem *I^{ac}*,
ut uid rerum *M^{2ul}* || 46 actorum *MFIT* auctorum *BCHL* || 47
sepulcri] sepul**ri *M^{ac}* || 49-50 *in marg add F^2; post* 51-52 *ponit*

> scripta ferunt annos: scriptis
>> Agamemnona nosti,
> et quisquis contra uel simul arma
>> tulit;
> quis Thebas septemque duces sine
>> carmine nosset
>> et quicquid post haec, quicquid et
>>> ante fuit?
> di quoque carminibus, si fas est dicere,
>> fiunt,
55
>> tantaque maiestas ore canentis eget:
> sic Chaos ex illa naturae mole prioris
>> digestum partes scimus habere suas;
> sic adfectantes caelestia regna Gigantas
>> ad Styga nimbiferi uindicis igne
>>> datos;
60
> sic uictor laudem superatis Liber ab
>> Indis,
>> Alcides capta traxit ab Oechalia;
> et modo, Caesar, auum, quem uirtus
>> addidit astris,
>> sacrarunt aliqua carmina parte
>>> tuum.

capta I^{ac} || Oechalia *edd* oethalia *BI* ethalia $C(F^{ac})L$ etholia
$MHPTF^{pc}$ || 63 addidit] addiuit B^{ac} addit F^1I^{ac} abdidit L

> si quid adhuc igitur uiui, Germanice,
>> nostro
> 65
>> restat in ingenio, seruiet omne tibi.
> non potes officium uatis contemnere
>> uates;
>> iudicio pretium res habet ista tuo.
> quod nisi te nomen tantum ad maiora
>> uocasset,
>> gloria Pieridum summa futurus eras.
> 70
> si dare materiam nobis quam carmina
>> mauis,
>> nec tamen ex toto deserere illa potes:
> nam modo bella geris, numeris modo
>> uerba coerces,
>> quodque aliis opus est, hoc tibi lusus
>>> erit,
> utque nec ad citharam nec ad arcum
>> segnis Apollo,
> 75
>> sed uenit ad sacras neruus uterque
>>> manus,
> sic tibi nec docti desunt nec principis
>> artes,
>> mixta sed est animo cum Ioue Musa
>>> tuo.

65 igitur *om* H^{ac} || uiui] riui *Hertzberg ad Prop IV i 59* || 68
iudicio B^{2c} || tuo *ex* suo *T, ut uid* || 69 quod] qui *T* ||
nomen] numen *'unus Heinsii cum prima editione, ut Augustus
intelligatur' —Burman* || tantum] tanto *C* || 71 si *R. J. Tarrant
sed codd* || mauis IF^{2ul} maius BF^1 *utrumque legere possis in*

CMHLT || 72 nec] non *I* || 74 quodque] quod B^{ac} || lusus]
ludus MLI^2 leue $L^{2(gl)}$ || 75 citharam] citharum *C* || Apollo
FILT apollo est *BCMH* || 77 docti desunt nec BF^1T docte
desunt nec LF^2 docti nec desunt *CM* desunt docti nec *HI*

quae quoniam nec nos unda summouit
　　ab illa
ungula Gorgonei quam caua fecit
　　　equi,
80
prosit opemque ferat communia sacra
　　tueri
atque isdem studiis imposuisse
　　manum,
litora pellitis nimium subiecta Corallis
ut tandem saeuos effugiamque
　　　Getas,
clausaque si misero patria est, ut ponar
　　in ullo
85
qui minus Ausonia distet ab urbe
　　　loco,
unde tuas possim laudes celebrare
　　recentes
magnaque quam minima facta
　　referre mora.
tangat ut hoc uotum caelestia, care
　　Suilli,
numina, pro socero paene precare
　　tuo.

79 nos] uos H^{ac} || summouit] dimouit *H* || 81 tueri] tuenti
$B^{pc}F^1$ || 82 atque] at sit F^{2ul} || isdem CFI^{ac} iisdem *T*
hi(i)sdem $MHI^{pc}L$ his dem B^1 his det B^2, *ut uid* || 83 pellitis]
peditis *ex* proditis *C, ut uid* || Corallis] coraulis *M* || 84

effugiamque] effugi*m F^1 || 85 misero patria est] misero est patria H || in *add* M^2 || ullo M illo $BCFHILT$ || 86 minus] minor F^{2ul} || Ausonia] ausonio C ausoni$\underline{a}$ F^{2c} || distet] distat BCT dist$\underline{et}$ $M^{2c,\ ut\ uid}$ || loco] locus F || 87 recentes] recenter *Heinsius* || 88 quam] cum H || minima $BCHILTM^2$, F^2 *in ras* nimia M^1 || 89 tangat] tangant $C^{ac}H$ || care] cara $B^{ac}C$ || Suilli] suille T || 90 socero *ex* cero M || paene] pena B^{ac}

99

IX

Vnde licet, non unde iuuat, Graecine, salutem
    mittit ab Euxinis hanc tibi Naso uadis;
missaque di faciant auroram occurrat ad illam
    bis senos fasces quae tibi prima dabit,
ut, quoniam sine me tanges Capitolia consul,

5

    et fiam turbae pars ego nulla tuae,
in domini subeat partes, et praestet amici
    officium festo littera nostra die.
atqui ego si fatis genitus melioribus essem,
    et mea sincero curreret axe rota,

10

quo nunc nostra manus per scriptum fungitur, esset
    lingua salutandi munere functa tui,

racino B^2 grecino amico suo M ad grecinum FI^2 grecino H^2 hanc epistulam mittit grecinno L || 1 unde] inde T || iuuat] uiuat F || Graecine] grecinne LT || 2 Euxinis] exinis C, *ut uid* (ecinis *Lenz, André*) || 3 di BC dii $MFHILT$ || 4 fasces] fascis C faces $F^1I^{ac}P^{ac}$ || 5 ut] et $MITF^{2ul}H^{2ul}$ || 7 domini] domino I^{ac} *om* M^1 || partes et praestet F^2 *in ras* || partes] partis C || praestet] prāt L || 8 officium] officium et M^{ac}, *ut uid* || festo *Burman* iusto T, *sicut coni Merkel* iusso $BCMFHIL$ || littera] litora C || 9 atqui *unus e duobus Hafniensibus Heinsii*

atque BCM^1FHILT ast M^{2ul} || genitus] genitis F^1 || 12
lingua] linga I^1 || salutandi] salutanti C

> gratatusque darem cum dulcibus
> > oscula uerbis,
> > nec minus ille meus quam tuus esset
> > > honor;
> illa, confiteor, sic essem luce superbus
> 15
> > ut caperet fastus uix domus ulla
> > > meos.
> dumque latus sancti cingit tibi turba
> > senatus,
> > consulis ante pedes ire iuberer eques,
> et quamquam cuperem semper tibi
> > proximus esse,
> > gauderem lateris non habuisse
> > > locum;
> 20
> nec querulus, turba quamuis eliderer,
> > essem,
> > sed foret a populo tum mihi dulce
> > > premi.
> prospicerem gaudens quantus foret
> > agminis ordo,
> > densaque quam longum turba
> > > teneret iter;
> quoque magis noris quam me uulgaria
> > tangant,
> 25
> > spectarem qualis purpura te tegeret;

14 minus ... meus quam] meus ... minus quam M minus ...
meusque C minor ... meus quam T || tuus *add I in marg* ||
16 ulla] illa $B^{ac}M^{ac}$ || 17 cingit] cinget MIF^2 tanget F^{2ul} ||
tibi *add* F^2 || 18 iuberer] uiderer *unus Vaticanus, probante*

Heinsio || 19 cuperem *add* F^2 cuper** *H* || 20 lateris] lateri *MFL* || 22 sed] sic *F* || tum] tunc *MFH* || 23 prospicerem] aspicerem *B* respicerem *Riese* || 25-26 *damnant Heinsius Bentley* || 25 quoque] quodque *L* utque $F^{2ul}M^{2gl}$ || tangant *BC* tangunt *MFHILT* || 26 tegeret] regeret *L*

> signa quoque in sella nossem formata
>   curuli
> et totum Numidae sculptile dentis
>   opus.
> at cum Tarpeias esses deductus in arces,
>   dum caderet iussu uictima sacra tuo,
> 30
> me quoque secreto grates sibi magnus
>   agentem
> audisset media qui sedet aede deus,
> turaque mente magis plena quam lance
>   dedissem,
>   ter quater imperii laetus honore tui.
> hic ego praesentes inter numerarer
>   amicos,
> 35
>   mitia ius urbis si modo fata darent,
> quaeque mihi sola capitur nunc mente
>   uoluptas,
>   tunc oculis etiam percipienda foret.

27-28 damnat Merkel (1884) || 27 curuli] curili *I* || 28 Numidae *edd* numidi *BCMHILT* nimidi *F* || sculptile] scalpule *C* scutile F^1 sculptile M^{2c} || opus] ebur *T* || 29 at] et *HL* || arces] artes B^{ac} || 30 dum] cum *CL* || iussu] iusso *B* || 31 grates *ex* magnus *T* || 33 plena quam] plenaque CF^1 quam plena *I* || 34 ter] terque B^2 || laetus] plenus *T* || 35 hic] tunc *Housman (Owen 1894)* hinc *Merkel (1884), Schenkl (Owen)* sic *Merkel (1853)* || ego] mihi *C* || 36 ius urbis si *editio Aldina 1502* ius uerbis si B^1CMF^1IT ius uerbi si *H* ius

nobis si F^2 uim uerbis si B^2, F^3 *ut uid* si uerbis uim L || 37
quaeque] quoque *C, ut uid*

> non ita caelitibus uisum est, et forsitan
>> aequis:
> nam quid me poenae causa negata
>> iuuet?
40
> mente tamen, quae sola domo non
>> exulat, usus
> praetextam fasces aspiciamque tuos.
> haec modo te populo reddentem iura
>> uidebit,
> et se decretis finget adesse tuis,
> nunc longi reditus hastae supponere
>> lustri
45
> cernet et exacta cuncta locare fide,
> nunc facere in medio facundum uerba
>> senatu
> publica quaerentem quid petat
>> utilitas,

39 aequis] aequos *C* || 40 causa] culpa *Heinsius* || negata]
nagata *C* || iuuet] foret B^{ac}, '*unde uerum eliciendum*' —*Riese* ||
41 domo *scripsi* loco *codd* foco *fort legendum* || usus *Heinsius*
utor *BCL* utar *MFHIT* utens *Williams (utens ... aspiciamque)* ||
42 aspiciamque] aspiciensque *Williams (utar ... aspiciensque)* ||
43 haec] nec B^{ac} || 44 decretis *Korn* secretis *codd* secreto
Wheeler || finget] fingit *B, C ut uid* || tuis] locis *Etonensis B. k.*
6.18, saec xiii (Lenz), probante Heinsio (secretis ... locis) || 45
longi] longe TF^2 (=*longae*) || lustri] lutri H^{ac} lustra F^{2ul} || 46
cernet *P, Gothanus membr. II 121, saec xiii (André)* credet
BCFHILT cernet M^{2c} || exacta] perfecta $M^{2(gl)}I^{2(gl)}$ || 47 *om C*
|| 48 publica] puplica *LP* || petat] petit *M*

> nunc pro Caesaribus superis decernere

grates,
　albaue opimorum colla ferire boum.
50
atque utinam, cum iam fueris potiora
　　precatus,
　ut mihi placetur principis ira roges;
surgat ad hanc uocem plena pius ignis
　　ab ara,
　detque bonum uoto lucidus omen
　　apex.
interea, qua parte licet, ne cuncta
　　queramur,
55
　hic quoque te festum consule tempus
　　agam.
altera laetitiae est nec cedens causa
　　priori:
　successor tanti frater honoris erit.
nam tibi finitum summo, Graecine,
　　Decembri
　imperium Iani suscipit ille die,
60
quaeque est in uobis pietas, alterna
　　feretis
　gaudia, tu fratris fascibus, ille tuis;

---

50 albaue *BCI* albaque *MFHLT* || opimorum] primorum *IT* || 51 iam] tu *FT* || potiora] maiora *P* || 52 principis] numinis *M* || 53 pius] prius I^{ac} || 57 laetitiae est *LT* laetitia est *BCFHI* letici* est *M* laetitiae *Heinsius e tribus codd* || cedens *BCL^{pc}T* credens L^{ac} cendens *M* cedet *FHI* || *59-60 fort spurii* || 59 Graecine] <u>de</u>grecine M^{1c} (= grecine *ex* decembri[-is?]) || Decembri] decembris *M* || 60 suscipit] suspicit (B^{ac})*C* suscipiet $M^{2(gl)}$ || 61 uobis] nobis (F^1)*H* || alterna] aterna *C, ut uid*

104

sic tu bis fueris consul, bis consul et ille,
  inque domo binus conspicietur
    honor,
qui quamquam est ingens, et nullum
    Martia summo
65
  altius imperium consule Roma uidet,
multiplicat tamen hunc grauitas
    auctoris honorem,
  et maiestatem res data dantis habet;
iudiciis igitur liceat Flaccoque tibique
  talibus Augusti tempus in omne frui!
70
cum tamen a rerum cura propiore
    uacabit,
  uota precor uotis addite uestra meis,
et si quae dabit aura sinum, laxate
    rudentes,
  exeat e Stygiis ut mea nauis aquis.

63 fueris consul] consul fueris *T* fueris *B¹* || bis consul et
ille] bis consul et ipse *H* et ille *M^{ac}* || 64 binus] bimus
Gudianus 228 (Owen 1894), probante Heinsio || honor] honos *L*
|| 65 quamquam] quamque *C* || nullum] nullium *B^{ac}P* ||
67 auctoris] actoris *MFI* || 69 Flaccoque] flacco *T* || 71 cum
FILT quod *BC* ut *MH* quum *Weise (Ehwald KB 48)* || a] ab *B*
|| propiore] propriore *CFL* || uacabit] uacabis *Riese* || 72
uotis] uestris *M^{ac}* || 73 et] *quid B, incertum* || quae *scripsi* qua
CMFHIL quem *BT* || sinum] sonum *Williams* || laxate *editio*
princeps Romana 1471 iactate *codd* || rudentes] rudentis *B* ||
74 exeat] et exeat *C* || e *BCH* a *MFILT* || Stygiis] stigis *C^{ac}*

praefuit his, Graecine, locis modo
    Flaccus, et illo
  ripa ferox Histri sub duce tuta fuit:
hic tenuit Mysas gentes in pace fideli,

hic arcu fisos terruit ense Getas,
      hic raptam Troesmin celeri uirtute
             recepit,
      infecitque fero sanguine Danuuium.
80
      quaere loci faciem Scythicique
             incommoda caeli,
      et quam uicino terrear hoste roga,
      sintne litae tenues serpentis felle
             sagittae,
      fiat an humanum uictima dira caput,
      mentiar, an coeat duratus frigore
             Pontus,
85
      et teneat glacies iugera multa freti.

75 praefuit] praefugit *C* || 77 Mysas gentes *BT* misas gentis
C missas gentes *FI* missus gentes *L* gentes missas *MH* sibi
commissas *F*$^{2(gl)}$ commissas *H*$^{2(gl)}$ || 78 fisos] fortes *M*^{2ul} ||
79 Troesmin *Heinsius; uide CIL V 6183-88, 6195* troesmen *C*
troesenen *B*^{1} troien *L* troezen *HITB*^{2} troezem *F* trozenam *M*
|| 80 infecitque] infecit *M*^{1} || Danuuium *Korn* danubium
codd || 81 quaere] queri *T* || Scythicique incommoda caeli
add F^{2} || Scythicique] siticique *I* || 82 terrear] terreat *C* ||
hoste] ense *H* || 83 serpentis] serpentes *I*^{ac} || felle] sola *C* ||
85 mentiar] effluat *FL* anfluat *P* * flu<u>at *M*^{2c}

      haec ubi narrarit, quae sit mea fama
             require,
      quoque modo peragam tempora
             dura roga.
      non sumus hic odio, nec scilicet esse
             meremur,
      nec cum fortuna mens quoque uersa
             mea est;
90

illa quies animo quam tu laudare
      solebas,
  illa uetus solito perstat in ore pudor,
[sic ego sum longe, sic hic, ubi barbarus
      hostis
  ut fera plus ualeant legibus arma
      facit,]
re queat ut nulla tot iam, Graecine, per
      annos
95
  femina de nobis uirue puerue queri.

87 ubi] ubi *uel* tibi *B* || narrarit] narraret *C* narrauit *F¹* || fama] fata *F²* || 90 nec] hec *C* || uersa mea] mea uersa *H¹* rapta mea *F* || 91 animo *'optimus Vaticanus', probante Heinsio* animi *BCMFHILT* || 92 perstat] praestat *BC* || 93-94 *damnat Merkel*; 93 *'uersus suspectus'—Heinsius; post* longe *hexametri finem, pentametrum, hexametri initium excidisse putat Ehwald* || 93 sic ego sum longe [-e C] sic hic *BCMFHILT* sic ego sum, sic hic sanctis *Korn* sic ego sum longe, Scythicis *Owen* (*ed. Tristium 1889, p. xxxviii*) || longe] lenis *Némethy* || 95 re ... nulla *MHIL* rem ... nullam *BCFT* tot iam] iam tot *L* || 96 uirue] uirque *M*

hoc facit ut misero faueant adsintque
      Tomitae
  (haec quoniam tellus testificanda
      mihi est):
illi me, quia uelle uident, discedere
      malunt;
  respectu cupiunt hic tamen esse sui.
100
nec mihi credideris: extant decreta
      quibus nos
  laudat et immunes publica cera facit;
conueniens miseris quae quamquam
      gloria non sit,

proxima dant nobis oppida munus
    idem.
nec pietas ignota mea est: uidet hospita
    terra
105
    in nostra sacrum Caesaris esse domo.

97 hoc] hec *H* quies animi *H*$^{2(gl)}$ || facit ut] facit et *BC* fac<u>it</u>ut *F*^{2c} faciunt *(F^1)* || misero faueant adsintque] faueant assint miseroque *T* || adsintque] adsinque *C*^{ac} a<u>d</u>sintque *F*^{2c} absintque *(F^1)* || 98 quoniam] *quid M*^{2c} *in ras, incertum (ipsum?)* || mihi est] michi *M* || 99 illi] ille *I*^{ac} || malunt] malint *Heinsius* || 100 respectu ... sui] respectu ... suo *ML* || cupiunt] cupiant *Heinsius* || 101 nec] neu *Heinsius* || mihi] si *B*$^{2(gl?)}$ || 102 immunes] in munem *B* || publica] puplica *LP* || cera *BCMHILF*^{2ul} cura *T* causa *F*^{1}*F*^{2ul}*(sic)* terra *F*^{2ul} || 103 quae *R. J. Tarrant* haec *L, probante Heinsio* et *BCMFHIT* ea *Heinsius* || gloria] gratia *Heinsius* || sit *G* est *CMFHILT quid B, non liquet*

stant pariter natusque pius coniunxque
    sacerdos,
    numina iam facto non leuiora deo,
neu desit pars ulla domus, stat uterque
    nepotum,
    hic auiae lateri proximus, ille patris.
110
his ego do totiens cum ture precantia
    uerba,
    Eoo quotiens surgit ab orbe dies;
tota (licet quaeras) hoc me non fingere
    dicet
    officii testis Pontica terra mei.
[Pontica me tellus, quantis hac
    possumus ora,
115

natalem ludis scit celebrare dei,]
nec minus hospitibus pietas est cognita
talis,
misit in has si quos longa Propontis
aquas;

107 pariter *GBMFHILT* pariterque *C* || coniunxque *GBCM^{pc}FHILT* natusque *M^{ac}* || 108 iam ... non *GBCMFHLT* non ... iam *I* || facto] fato *G* || 109 neu] ne *BC* || 110 auiae *BCILM^{2ul}* liuie *M^{1}FHTI^{2gl}* || proximus] protimus [*sic*] *H^{1}* || 112 surgit] fugit *M* || orbe] ore *H^{1}* || *113-14 damnat Williams* || 113 licet] uelim *fort legendum* || hoc me non *BCT,H^{ac}?* hec me non *FHIL* me numquam *M* || *115-16 damnat R. J. Tarrant* || 115 possumus] nos possumus *I* || ora] ara *B* || 116 dei] diem *HP* || 117 cognita] condita *F* || 118 longa] loga *M*

is quoque, quo laeuus fuerat sub
praeside Pontus,
audierit frater forsitan ista tuus.
120
fortuna est impar animo, talique
libenter
exiguas carpo munere pauper opes,
nec uestris damus haec oculis, procul
urbe remoti,
contenti tacita sed pietate sumus;
et tamen haec tangent aliquando
Caesaris aures:
125
nil illum toto quod fit in orbe latet.
tu certe scis haec, superis ascite,
uidesque,
Caesar, ut est oculis subdita terra tuis;

119 is] hic *M^{1}* his *P* || laeuus fuerat *TF^{2ul}* letus fuerat *BC* leuius fuerat *LP* leuuus fuerat *M* leuior fuerat *F^{1}H* fuerat

letuus ^{I} || 120 audierit] audierat F || ista] illa M || 121
fortuna est] fortuna H^1 || 122 exiguas] exiguus B^{ac} || 123
haec] hoc F || urbe] orbe I^{ac} || 124 sed pietate] haec pietate
ex haec pietate haec pietate I || /s<u>u</u>mus B^{2c} || 125 et] ut C set
L || tamen haec tangent] tanget tamen hoc F || aures] iram
I^{ac} || 126 nil] non CL || illum] illi B^1 || fit *BFI* sit *LT possis*
alterutrum legere in CMH || 127 tu certe] tu c *seruat G spatium*
quinque litterarum reliquit C en certe M^{2ul} || haec] hoc *FIT* ||
ascite] adscite B accite M ac⊙cite F || 128 ut *'legendum ex*
ueteribus' — Naugerius et *BCMFHILT*

> tu nostras audis inter conuexa locatus
> sidera sollicito quas damus ore
>> preces.
> 130
> perueniant istuc et carmina forsitan illa
> quae de te misi caelite facta nouo;
> auguror his igitur flecti tua numina,
>> nec tu
> immerito nomen mite parentis habes.

129 conuexa] onu *seruat G* connexa L || 130 sollicito
$GB^2CMFHILT$ sollito B^1 || preces *CMHIT* praeces G p̄ces *BFL*
|| 131 perueniant *GBC* peruenient *FHILT* peruenient M ||
istuc *GBCMFHI* illuc *LT* || forsitan *GBCFHILT* forsita M ||
132 misi] miss G || facta $GBC^{pc}MFHILT$ facto C^{ac} || 133-34
nec ... immerito] nec *seruat G* nam ... e merito [*unde* ex merito
C. P. *Jones] fort legendum* || 134 mite] mitte F^{ac} || habes]
habet B^1

110

X

Haec mihi Cimmerio bis tertia ducitur
    aestas
  litore pellitos inter agenda Getas.
ecquos tu silices, ecquod, carissime,
    ferrum
  duritiae confers, Albinouane, meae?
gutta cauat lapidem, consumitur
    anulus usu,

5

  atteritur pressa uomer aduncus
    humo.
tempus edax igitur praeter nos omnia
    perdit;
  cessat duritia mors quoque uicta
    mea.

albinouano B^2 albino uano H^2 albinouano amico suo M ad albino uanom F ad albinouanum I^2 hanc epistulam mittit albinouano L || 1 Haec] hic MF || Cimmerio *British Library Harley 2607 (Tarrant)* cumerio M^1 in etiam memori C in ********* B^1 in hemonio *HITP* in euxino F in exino B^{2c} bistonio LM^{2ul} || aestas] aetas C || 2 pellitos] pellitas BH pellito C || 3 ecquos ... ecquod *Laurentianus 36 2, saec xv (Lenz)* et quos ... et quod *BMFHILT* at quos ... et quod C || carissime] hine L || 4 Albinouane] albino uane H || 6 atteritur *Heinsius* et teritur *codd* deteritur *Heinsius* || *post 6 hos uersus habet M:* set cum nostra malis uexentur corpora multis / aspera non possum perpetiendo mori || 7 perdit I perdet *BCMFHLT* || 8 cessat duritia] duritia cessat C^{ac} cesset duritia *Castiglioni (Lenz)* || mea. *edd* mea? *Riese, Castiglioni*

exemplum est animi nimium patientis

                    Vlixes

            iactatus dubio per duo lustra mari;
10
            tempora solliciti sed non tamen omnia
                    fati
                pertulit, et placidae saepe fuere
                    morae.
            an graue sex annis pulchram fouisse
                    Calypso
                aequoreaeque fuit concubuisse deae?
            excipit Hippotades, qui dat pro munere
                    uentos,
15
                curuet ut impulsos utilis aura sinus,
            nec bene cantantes labor est audisse
                    puellas,
                nec degustanti lotos amara fuit:
            hos ego qui patriae faciant obliuia sucos
                parte meae uitae, si modo dentur,
                    emam.
20

---

9 exemplum est animi *BCMFLT* (anini *T*) exemplum animi
est *H* exemplum animi *I* || 10 dubio ... mari] ćbio ... mori *C*
|| 11 non] quae *'liber unus Bers[manni]. & ego inueni in editione*
Vicentina. & Ciofano pro textu est' — *Auctor Electorum Etonensium*
|| 12 pertulit] non tulit *Auctor Elect. Eton. (quae tamen ... non*
tulit) || morae] m-ore *F* || 13 pulchram *ex* pulcham *M* ||
Calypso] calipson *FH* || 14 aequoreaeque] equoreque *I^{ac}*
Aeaeaeque *Merkel* || concubuisse] incubuisse *T* || deae] deo
C || 15 Hippotades] hypodates *FHT* || 17 cantantes]
cantantis *B* || audisse *F* audire *BCMHILT* || 18 lotos *B^{1}C*
lothos *MFLTH^{2}I^2* lethes *I^{1}P* sucus *H^1 quid B^2, incertum (votos?)*
|| amara] amarus *H^1* || fuit] erat *H* || 19 faciant] faciunt *H*
|| sucos] lucos *C* || 20 meae] mee est *C*

nec tu contuleris urbem Laestrygonos

113

umquam
gentibus obliqua quas obit Hister
aqua,
nec uincet Cyclops saeuum feritate
Piacchen,
qui quota terroris pars solet esse mei!
Scylla feris trunco quod latret ab
inguine monstris,
25
Heniochae nautis plus nocuere rates.
nec potes infestis conferre Charybdin
Achaeis,
ter licet epotum ter uomat illa fretum,
qui, quamquam dextra regione
licentius errant,
securum latus hoc non tamen esse
sinunt.
30

21 urbem *BCMT* urbes *FHIL* || Laestrygonos *BC* lestrigonis *MFIT* listrigonis *HL* || 22 quas] quos *T* || Hister] inster *L* **ster *C* || 23 feritate] pietate *BC*, *I*^{ac} *ut uid* || Piacchen *B* piaechen *C* phiacem *T* piacē *MFHIL* || 24 mei] mihi *T* || 25 Scylla] silla *CP* || feris] ferox *IT* || quod] quae *M*^{2ul} quamuis *H* || latret] latrat *FM*^{2ul} || 26 Heniochae *edd* enioche *CFH* en*oche *B*^{1} emioche *M*, *ut uid* enochie *ITB*^{2} emochee *L* || nautis] multis *I* nobis *B*^{2} || 27 nec] non *L* || Charybdin] caripdin *I* charydin *C* || Achaeis] ach—eis *I* || 28 epotum *B* et potum *C* epotet *MFHILT* || ter uomat] ter uomet *H*^{1} euomat *C* || illa] ore *M*^{2ul} || 29 quamquam] quamuis *T* || errant *BCFH* errent *MILT* || 30 latus] natus *C* || hoc non] non *M*^{ac} *I*^{1}

hic agri infrondes, hic spicula tincta
uenenis;
hic freta uel pediti peruia reddit
hiemps
ut, qua remus iter pulsis modo fecerat
undis,
siccus contempta naue uiator eat.
qui ueniunt istinc uix uos ea credere
dicunt;
35
quam miser est qui fert asperiora
fide!
crede tamen; nec te causas nescire
sinemus
horrida Sarmaticum cur mare duret
hiemps.
proxima sunt nobis plaustri praebentia
formam
et quae perpetuum sidera frigus
habent;
40
hinc oritur Boreas, oraeque domesticus
huic est,
et sumit uires a propiore polo.

---

31 infrondes] frondes *C* || 32 hic] hec *L* || uel] quae *I¹* ||
reddit] fecit *M²ᵘˡ* || 34 naue] nauu *Cᵃᶜ, ut uid* || 35 istinc]
istuc *MFI* || uix uos] uix nos *BL* uos uix *T* || credere]
crederer *H* || 36 fert] foret *Cᵃᶜ* || 37 tamen] tantum *L* mihi
M²ᶜ in ras || nec te causas *BCMFHLT* (te *in ras M²ᶜ*) causas
nec te *I* || 39 praebentia] ducentia *F, probante Burman* || 40
perpetuum *M2ul* praecipuum *BCM¹FHILT* || 41 hinc] hic *FL*
|| huic] hinc *L* 42 uires ... polo *'Meynke, recte?' — Riese* uires
... loco *codd* mores ... locus *Merkel (1884)* || a propiore]
asperiore *H¹* a superiore *H²ᵘˡ*

at Notus, aduerso tepidum qui spirat
    ab axe,
  est procul, et rarus languidiorque
    uenit.
adde quod hic clauso miscentur
    flumina Ponto,
45
  uimque fretum multo perdit ab amne
    suam.
huc Lycus, huc Sagaris Peniusque
    Hypanisque Calesque
influit, et crebro uertice tortus Halys;
Partheniusque rapax et uoluens saxa
    Cinapses
  labitur, et nullo tardior amne Tyras,
50

43 at $BCMF^2HILT$ et F^1 set $F^2[sic]$ || aduerso] auerso *Bentley*
|| tepidum] tepidus MH^{2c} tepide F^{2ul} || 46 multo] misto
$M^{2ul}(=mixto)$ || 47 Lycus] lucus I || Peniusque *Heinsius ex
Plin.* NH *VI* 14 peneusque CI paneusque $BMHT$ poneusque L
panesque F || Hypanisque *Heinsius 'ex libris antiquis'*
hitanisque B hyranisque C *ut uid*, M *ut uid* hytanusque F
hytanesque T hitaneusque *ex* hitanque I hythausque H
iponesque L || Calesque I. *Vossius ex 'Eustathio Scholiis in
Periegeten' (Heinsius)* catesque $BCMFHLT$ charesque I || 48
crebro] crebo B torto I || tortus] pulsus M || Halys B halis
H alis $MFILT$ hilas C || 49 Partheniusque BHL
partheniasque C, *ut uid* parthemiusque IT parthiniusque M
partenusque F || Cinapses BC; *fluuius prorsus ignotus*
Cynapses *edd* cinapsis L tynapses H cinaspes FIT niphates M
(ex Luc. III 245) Cinolis *Auctor Electorum Etonensium 'Cinolis
emporium Arriano'* || 50 et nullo] et ullo I hanc aliquo
Leidensis Heinsii haud aliquo *Heinsius*

et tu, femineae Thermodon cognite
    turmae,

et quondam Graiis Phasi petite uiris,
cumque Borysthenio liquidissimus
     amne Dirapses
et tacite peragens lene Melanthus iter,
quique duas terras, Asiam Cadmique
     sororem,
55
separat et cursus inter utramque
     facit,
innumerique alii, quos inter maximus
     omnes
cedere Danuuius se tibi, Nile, negat;
copia tot laticum quas auget adulterat
     undas,
nec patitur uires aequor habere suas.
60
quin etiam, stagno similis pigraeque
     paludi,
caeruleus uix est diluiturque color;

51 Thermodon] themodon *C* | | turmae *BCM* turbe *FHILT* | |
52 Graiis *CM* grais *BHILT* a grais *F* | | Phasi] phasis H^1 | | 53
Borysthenio *editio princeps Romana 1471* boristenico *BCML*
boristonico *F* boistronico *I* boistonico *T* boistenio *H* | |
liquidissimus] rapidissimus *T* | | Dirapses *BCFHLT; fluuius*
ignotus diraspes *I* daraspes *M* Lycastus *Auctor Electorum*
Etonensium, probante Riese | | 54 Melanthus] melantis *T* | |
Cadmique] *add* I^2 *in loco a prima manu relicto* cathmique *B* | |
56 inter] interque *M* | | 57 alii] amnes M^1 | | omnes] omnis *B*
| | 58 Danuuius *Korn* danubius *codd* | | negat] neget F^1 | | 59
laticum] liticum *L* | | 61 quin] qui *CP, fort* F^{ac} | | pigraeque]
nigreque *T*

innatat unda freto dulcis, leuiorque
     marina est,
quae proprium mixto de sale pondus

habet.
si roget haec aliquis cur sint narrata
Pedoni,

65

quidue loqui certis iuuerit ista modis,
'detinui' dicam 'tempus, curasque
fefelli;
hunc fructum praesens attulit hora
mihi.
abfuimus solito dum scribimus ista
dolore,
in mediis nec nos sensimus esse
Getis.'

70

at tu, non dubito, cum Thesea carmine
laudes,
materiae titulos quin tueare tuae,
quemque refers imitere uirum; uetat ille
profecto
tranquilli comitem temporis esse
fidem.

63 marina est] marina *ILT* || 64 pondus] nomen *ILB²*
momen *Wakefield ad Lucr. VI 474* || 65 roget] rogat *CT* || 67
detinui ... tempus, curasque *excerpta Politiani* detinui ...
tempus curamque *LT* detinui ... curas tempusque *BCMFHI*
diminui ... curas tempusque *codex Petri Daniel^{ul}* (*Burman*),
sicut coniecerat Burman distinui ... curas, tempusque *Auctor
Electorum Etonensium* || 68 fructum praesens] praesens
fructum *F* || 69 abfuimus] afluimus *B¹* aff*uimus *C* absumus
a *M* || scribimus] scripsimus *MFL* || dolore] labore *M* || 71
dubito] dub<ins>ito</ins> *M^{2c}F^{2c, ut uid}* dubites *F^{3ul}, ut uid* || cum] tum
C || 73 quemque] queque *C* || imitere] imite** *C* (*folium
lacerum*) imitare *HLT, I^{pc} ut uid* imita *I^{ac} ut uid*

qui quamquam est factis ingens et

conditur a te
75
uir tantus quanto debuit ore cani,
est tamen ex illo nobis imitabile
quiddam,
inque fide Theseus quilibet esse
potest.
non tibi sunt hostes ferro clauaque
domandi,
per quos uix illi peruius isthmos erat,
80
sed praestandus amor, res non operosa
uolenti:
quis labor est puram non temerasse
fidem?
haec tibi, qui perstas indeclinatus
amico,
non est quod lingua dicta querente
putes.

75 quamquam est] quamquam *MP* || factis ingens] ingens
factis *F* ingens actis *T* factis uiges *P* || conditur] conditus
HT cognitus *F* || a te] arte *L* || 76 uir] uix *LT* || tantus
quanto *L* tanto quantus $B^{ac}CFHIT^{pc}$ tant<u>s</u> quantus M^{2c}
tanto quanto $B^{pc}T^{ac}$ quanto tantus *fort legendum* || 77 est] et
I || ex] in *C* || nobis] uobis *H* || imitabile] imitabibe *C* ||
quiddam] quoddam *L* quidquam M^{2ul} || 78 fide *MFH* fidem
BCILT || 80 quos *in ras* M^2 || illi *MFHIL* ulli *BCT* || 81
operosa] o<u>n</u>erosa M^{2c} laboriosa $I^{2(gl)}$ || 83 qui] quae *C* cum
L || perstas IPF^{2ul} praestas $BCMF^1HT$ prās *L* || 84 non est]
non B^1

XI

Gallio, crimen erit uix excusabile nobis
  carmine te nomen non habuisse meo.
tu quoque enim, memini, caelesti
    cuspide facta
  fouisti lacrimis uulnera nostra tuis.
atque utinam rapti iactura laesus amici
5
  sensisses ultra quod quererere nihil;
non ita dis placuit, qui te spoliare
    pudica
  coniuge crudeles non habuere nefas.
nuntia nam luctus mihi nuper epistula
    uenit,
  lectaque cum lacrimis sunt tua
      damna meis.
10
sed neque solari prudentem stultior
    ausim
  uerbaque doctorum nota referre tibi,
finitumque tuum, si non ratione,
    dolorem
  ipsa iam pridem suspicor esse mora.

---

gallioni B^2H^2 gallioni amico suo M pollioni F ad gallionem
I^2 hanc epistulam mittit gallioni L || 1 Gallio] pollio F || 3
cuspide] cupide M^{ac} || 6 quererere] querere BCP || 7 dis
placuit] displicuit (B^1) || spoliare *ex* poliare F || 8 habuere]
hūere IT *(=habuere)* hubuere C^{ac} || 9 nam] iam F || 10
damna] uerba TF^{2ul} || meis] nostris M mihi *Ehwald* || 12
uerbaque] uerba B^1 || nota] uota L uerba C || 13 dolorem]

putarem *C* || 14 iam] tam *I* || pridem] prima C^{ac}

> dum tua perueniens, dum littera nostra
> > recurrens
> 15
> > tot maria ac terras permeat, annus
> > > abit.
> temporis officium est solacia dicere
> > certi,
> > dum dolor in cursu est, et petit aeger
> > > opem.
> at cum longa dies sedauit uulnera
> > mentis,
> > intempestiue qui fouet illa, nouat.
> 20
> adde quod (atque utinam uerum mihi
> > uenerit omen!)
> > coniugio felix iam potes esse nouo.

15 perueniens *scripsi* peruenit *codd* || 16 ac *BCML* et *FHIT* ||
17 officium est ... certi] officium ... certi est *M* || 19 at] aut *C*
|| longa] longua *uel* longna *M* || dies] quies *L* || 20 fouet
Heinsius mouet *codd* || nouat] mouet $T(M^1)(F^1)$ || 21
utinam] utinam ut *F* || mihi BF^1 tibi $MHILTF^2$ *om C*

XII

Quominus in nostris ponaris, amice,
    libellis,
  nominis efficitur condicione tui.
aut ego non alium prius hoc dignarer
    honore,
  est aliquis nostrum si modo carmen
    honor.
lex pedis officio fortunaque nominis
    obstat,
5
  quaque meos adeas est uia nulla
    modos.
nam pudet in geminos ita nomen
    scindere uersus
  desinat ut prior hoc incipiatque
    minor,
et pudeat si te qua syllaba parte
    moratur
  artius appellem Tuticanumque
    uocem.
10
et potes in uersum Tuticani more
    uenire,
  fiat ut e longa syllaba prima breuis,

---

tuticano B^2H^2F tu[ti *add* M^2]cano amico suo M han [*sic*] epistulam mittit tuticano L || 3 aut BC ast $MFHILT$ || 5 fortunaque] naturaque *excerpta Scaligeri, probante Heinsio* || 6 modos] pedes I || 8 desinat] desinet I^{ac} || hoc] hic T || 9 pudeat] pudet H || te qua] te qu$\underline{a}$ B^{2c} qua te H^1P || moratur] moretur FHT || 10 Tuticanumque] Tuditanumque

Heinsius olim (Burman); uide Val Max VII viii 1 || 11 et] non *M*
nec *FI^{pc}* at *Camps (CQ n.s. IV [1954] 206-7)*

> aut producatur quae nunc correptius
> > exit,
> et sit porrecta longa secunda mora.
> his ego si uitiis ausim corrumpere
> > nomen,
>
> 15
>
> > ridear, et merito pectus habere neger.
> haec mihi causa fuit dilati muneris
> > huius,
> > quod meus adiecto faenore reddet
> > > amor,
> teque canam quacumque nota, tibi
> > carmina mittam,
> > paene mihi puero cognite paene puer,
>
> 20
>
> perque tot annorum seriem, quot
> > habemus uterque,
> > non mihi quam fratri frater amate
> > > minus,
> tu bonus hortator, tu duxque comesque
> > fuisti,
> > cum regerem tenera frena nouella
> > > manu;

13 aut] nec *R. J. Tarrant (nec potes ... nec producatur)* ||
producatur *MHI (ut M^{2[gll]})* ut ducatur *LTB^2F^{2ul}* ut dicatur
B^1CF^1 || correptius *BFLT* correptior *C, fort recte* correctius
MHI || 14 sit] si *B^{ac}P* || porrecta] producta *F^1* || 16 merito
GBCFHILT cunctis *M* || 17 dilati] lati *G* || muneris
GBCMF^1HILT nominis *F^{2ul}* || 18 reddet *GCMIT* reddit *BFHL*
|| amor *GBCFHI^1L* ager *TI^2; add M^2 (in ras?)* || 19 canam
quacumque nota, tibi *edd* canam, quacumque nota tibi *Luck*
|| quacumque nota] quacumquenaia *G* quantumque licet *I*

‖ tibi *GBCMFHIL* mea *T* ‖ 20 mihi ... puer] mihi *om I^{ac}*
puer ... mihi *CT* ‖ 22 frat<u>ri</u> *F^{2?c}* ‖ 23 tu duxque] mihi
duxque *FL*

saepe ego correxi sub te censore libellos,
25
    saepe tibi admonitu facta litura meo
        est,
dignam Maeoniis Phaeacida condere
        chartis
    cum te Pieriae perdocuere deae.
hic tenor, haec uiridi concordia coepta
        iuuenta
    uenit ad albentes inlabefacta comas.
30
quae nisi te moueant, duro tibi pectora
        ferro
    esse uel inuicto clausa adamante
        putem.
sed prius huic desint et bellum et
        frigora terrae,
    inuisus nobis quae duo Pontus habet,
et tepidus Boreas et sit praefrigidus
        Auster,
35
    et possit fatum mollius esse meum,

25 saepe] nempe *M^1* ‖ 26 tibi] tui *L* tuo *T* mihi *H^{2ul}, ut uid* ‖
litura] lit<u>u</u>/ra *F^{2c}* littera *(F^1)* ‖ meo] mea *T* tuo *H^{2ul}, ut uid* ‖
27 dignam *(B^1)CT^{pc}* dignum *MFHILT^{ac}B^{2c}* ‖ Phaeacida]
pheatica *IL* eacida *C* ‖ 28 cum] cū/ *I (=cum)* ‖ Pieriae *BCF^1T*
pieride *HF^2* pierides *IL* pyeri<u>des</u> *M^{2c}* ‖ deae] tue *M^{2ul}* ‖ 29
uiridi] in uiridi *L* ‖ 30 albentes] albentis *B* ‖ 31 nisi *ex* ubi
L ‖ 32 inuicto] inuito *uel* inuecto *'libri nonnulli ueteres', unde*
inducto Heinsius olim ‖ 33 desint] desunt *M^1* deerint *M^{2ul}, ut*
uid ‖ 35 praefrigidus] praefigidus *B^1H^{ac}* perfrigidus *ILF^2*

quam tua sint lapso praecordia dura
    sodali;
  hic cumulus nostris absit abestque
    malis.
tu modo per superos, quorum
    certissimus ille est
  quo tuus assidue principe creuit
    honor,
40
effice constanti profugum pietate
    tuendo
  ne sperata meam deserat aura ratem.
quid mandem quaeris? peream nisi
    dicere uix est,
  si modo qui periit ille perire potest.
nec quid agam inuenio, nec quid
    nolimue uelimue,
45
  nec satis utilitas est mihi nota mea.
crede mihi, miseros prudentia prima
    relinquit,
  et sensus cum re consiliumque fugit;

37 lapso] lasso *BCM* || dura] clausa M^{2ul} || sodali *ex* sobali
B || 38 nostris *add* F^2 || abestque *ex* absitque *M* || malis]
meis *C* || 40 honor] amor *C* || 42 ne *GBCMFHIT* nec *L* ||
deserat *GBCMHILT* desinat *F* || 45 nolimue] molimne *B* ||
uelimue] uelim B^1 || 46 mihi ... mea] mea ... mihi *CFT* ||
nota] mora *L* || 47 relinquit] reliquit *MF* relinquat I^{ac}, *ut uid*
refugit C^{ac} || 48 re] me M^{ac}, *ut uid* spe *Heinsius*

ipse, precor, quaeras qua sim tibi parte
    iuuandus,
  quaque uia uenias ad mea uota, uide.
50

49 quaeras] uideas M^1 || qua sim] qua sum L sim qua C ||
tibi *add* M^2 || iuuandus] iuuanda C^{ac} || 50 quaque ... uide
LF^3 quaque ... uale F^1T quoque ... uide $I^{ac}M^{2ul}$ quoque ...
uado $BCHI^{pc}$ quoque ... modo M^1 quoque ... uale F^2I^{2ul} ||
uia uenias *scripsi* uiam facias *codd*

XIII

O mihi non dubios inter memorande
    sodales,
    qui quod es, id uere, Care, uocaris,
        aue!
unde saluteris color hic tibi protinus
    index
    et structura mei carminis esse potest,
non quia mirifica est, sed quod non
        publica certe;
5
    qualis enim cumque est, non latet
        esse meam.
ipse quoque ut titulum chartae de
    fronte reuellas
    quod sit opus uideor dicere posse
        tuum;
quamlibet in multis positus noscere
    libellis,
    perque obseruatas inueniere notas;
10
prodent auctorem uires, quas Hercule
    dignas
    nouimus atque illi quem canis ipse
        pares.

ad sodalem B^2 caro amico suo M ad carum FI^2 caro H^2 || 1
memorande] numerande C || 2 qui quod es, id $BCFI$ qui
quod id es MH quique quod es LT, *fort recte* || aue] ades T ||
3 saluteris MFT salutaris $BCHIL$ || protinus] proximus CT
|| 5 mirifica] miririfica B murifica C || publica] puplica LP
|| certe] certe est BC || 6 cum<u>que</u> $B^{2c?}$ || est, non] non L ||

7 ut *add* M^2 || 8 quod ... uideor] quid ... uidear *Heinsius* || tuum] meum F^{2ul} || 11 prodent] produnt ILF^{2ul} credent C || auctorem] actorem MF || dignas] dipnas C^{ac} || nouimus] contra uiam C *(cont̄ uiā)* || illi] ille C || quem] que C || ipse] esse MT

> et mea Musa potest proprio deprensa
>> colore
>> insignis uitiis forsitan esse suis;
> tam mala Thersiten prohibebat forma
>> latere
> 15
>> quam pulchra Nireus conspiciendus
>> erat.
> nec te mirari si sint uitiosa decebit
>> carmina quae faciam paene poeta
>> Getes.
> a pudet, et Getico scripsi sermone
>> libellum,
>> structaque sunt nostris barbara uerba
>> modis,
> 20
> et placui (gratare mihi) coepique poetae
>> inter inhumanos nomen habere
>> Getas.
> materiam quaeris? laudes de Caesare
>> dixi;
>> adiuta est nouitas numine nostra dei.

13 et] at C || colore] colure C^{ac}, *ut uid* || 14 insignis] insignis $B^{2c,\ ut\ uid}$ ansignis C^{ac} || suis] meis F^1 || 15 Thersiten] therseten C || prohibebat] prohibebit H^1, *ut uid* || forma latere] latere forma I^{ac} || 16 Nireus *edd* nereus *codd* deus maris $F^{2(gl)}$ || 17 sint] sunt L || decebit] licebit L *(fort ex* decebit*)* || 18 Getes] gethas F^1 || 19 Getico scripsi] geticos

scripsi *(Bᵃᶜ)* | | libellum] libellos *I* | | 20 structaque] scriptaque *I* | | nostris] nobis *H¹* | | 22 inhumanos] inhumanas *Cᵖᶜ* humanas *Cᵃᶜ* | | 23 laudes de Caesare dixi *edd olim* laudes: de Caesare dixi *J. Gilbert, Jahrb. für kl. Ph. 1896, 62 (Owen 1915)* | | laudes] laudem *M*

> nam patris Augusti docui mortale fuisse
> 25
> > corpus, in aetherias numen abisse
> > > domos,
> > esse parem uirtute patri qui frena
> > > coactus
> > saepe recusati ceperit imperii,
> > esse pudicarum te Vestam, Liuia,
> > > matrum,
> > > ambiguum nato dignior anne uiro,
> > 30
> > esse duos iuuenes firma adiumenta
> > > parentis
> > > qui dederint animi pignora certa sui.
> > haec ubi non patria perlegi scripta
> > > Camena,
> > > uenit et ad digitos ultima charta
> > > > meos,
> > > et caput et plenas omnes mouere
> > > > pharetras,
> > > 35
> > > > et longum Getico murmur in ore fuit,

25 mortale] immortale *Tᵃᶜ* | | 26 aetherias ... domos] ethereos ... deos *I* | | numen] nomen *BC(M¹)L* | | 27 parem ... patri] parem ... patr* *B* patrem ... patri *(Hᵃᶜ)* patri ... parem *M* | | uirtute] in uirtute *L* | | coactus *excerpta Scaligeri* rogatus *codd* | | 28 recusati] recusari *C* | | ceperit] ceperat *L* cepit *F, fort ex recepit* | | inperii *F²ᶜ* | | 29 Vestam] uestem *M* deam *M²⁽ᵍˡ⁾* uastam *FᵃᶜP* testem *H* | | 30 ambiguum] ambiguum est

$MFIL^{2(gl)}$ || 31-32 esse duos iuuenes firma adiumenta parentis qui *interpunxi* esse duos iuuenes, firma adiumenta parentis, qui *edd* || 32 qui] cui *'editi plures'—Burman* || dederint] deder<u>a</u>nt M^{2c} dederit L^1 || certa] cara I || sui] fui C

atque aliquis 'scribas haec cum de
      Caesare,' dixit
  'Caesaris imperio restituendus eras.'
ille quidem dixit; sed me iam, Care,
      niuali
  sexta relegatum bruma sub axe
      uidet.

40

carmina nil prosunt; nocuerunt
      carmina quondam,
  primaque tam miserae causa fuere
      fugae.
at tu, per studii communia foedera
      sacri,
  per non uile tibi nomen amicitiae
(sic uincto Latiis Germanicus hoste
      catenis

45

materiam uestris adferat ingeniis,
sic ualeant pueri, †uotum commune
      deorum†,
  quos laus formandos est tibi magna
      datos),

37 haec] hac C || de] tu $B^{ac}C$ tu de B^{pc} || 38 imperio] imperii C || eras] eris M^1ILF^{2ul} || 39 me iam] iam me T || Care] kare M || 40 uidet] tenet F || 43 at tu] ast ego F^1 || studii] studui C || foedera] federe B^{ac} || 45 uincto *scripsi* capto *codd* || 46 uestris] nostris *MIL* || adferat] afferet F^1 praebeat I offerat *Heinsius* 47 pueri, uotum commune deorum *edd* pueri, uotum commune, deorum *Postgate (Owen 1894)* || uotum

commune deorum *corruptum* || deorum] duorum M^1F^{2ul}
augusti et liuie F^{2gl} suorum *Heinsius* || 48 quos ...
formandos] quos ... forman<u>do</u>s M^{2c} quis ... formandis LPF^{2ul}
|| laus est] est laus F tibi ... est H (laus $H^{2[gl]}$ *ad finem uersus*)
|| magna] mag** L maga F^1 || datos] dat<u>o</u>s M^{2c} deos $I^{?ul}$
data L datis $F^{2ul}P$ datur F^{2ul}

> quanta potes, praebe nostrae momenta
> saluti,
> quae nisi mutato nulla futura loco
> est.
> 50

49 potes] potest B^{ac} || praebe nostrae] nostrae praebe FI ||
momenta *Vaticanus 1595, saec xv (Mercati [Lenz]), sicut coni
Scaliger et Gronouius* monimenta $BCMFHILT$ || 50 mutato *ex
muto B*

XIV

Haec tibi mittuntur quem sum modo
    carmine questus
  non aptum numeris nomen habere
    meis,
in quibus, excepto quod adhuc
    utcumque ualemus,
  nil te praeterea quod iuuet inuenies.
ipsa quoque est inuisa salus, suntque
    ultima uota
5
  quolibet ex istis scilicet ire locis;
nulla mihi cura est terra quo muter ab
    ista,
  hac quia quam uideo gratior omnis
    erit.

epistula ad tuticanum B^2 tuticano amico suo M tuticano
F^2H^2 ad tuticanum I^2 || 1 quem *BMFLT; add I^2 in spatio a
prima manu relicto* que *CH* || sum modo] summo (B^1) || 4 te
*Berolinensis Diez. B. Sant. 1, saec. xiii (Lenz), Bodleianus
Rawlinson G 105^{ul} (Tarrant)* me *BCMFHILT* || 5 est *om I^1* ||
inuisa] non uisa *C* || 6 ex istis] ex illis *C* Euxinis *Castiglioni
(Lenz)* || scilicet] ilicet *fort legendum* || 7 terra quo muter
[mutar F^2] ab ista F^1, *Bodleianus Canon. lat. 1, saec xiii
(Tarrant), Barberinus lat. 26, saec xiii (Lenz)* terra quo mittar ab
ista *BCMFHILT* terra quam muter ut ista *Heinsius* [nulla
prior cura est] terra quam muter ut ista *Heinsius* terra nisi
muter ut ista *Heinsius* terrae quo muter ab Histro *Williams* ||
8 quia quam] quamquam *C*

  in medias Syrtes, mediam mea uela
    Charybdin

mittite, praesenti dum careamus
humo.

10

Styx quoque, si quid ea est, bene
commutabitur Histro,
si quid et inferius quam Styga
mundus habet.
gramina cultus ager, frigus minus odit
hirundo,
proxima Marticolis quam loca Naso
Getis.
talia suscensent propter mihi uerba
Tomitae,

15

iraque carminibus publica mota
meis.
ergo ego cessabo numquam per
carmina laedi,
plectar et incauto semper ab ingenio?
ergo ego, ne scribam, digitos incidere
cunctor,
telaque adhuc demens quae nocuere
sequor?

20

---

9 medias] medi*s *B* || Syrtes] syr*tis *B¹, ut uid* systes *C* ||
Charybdin *CH* caribdim *BT* caribdī *MFL* caripdī *I* || 10
mittite *BᵖᶜILF²ᵘˡ* mitte *MH* mittat *BᵃᶜC* mittant *F¹* mutē *T*
(mittē *legit André*) || 12 inf<u>erius</u> *F¹ᶜ* || 13 gramina] carmina *C*
flamina *Bentley* || 14 Marticolis] in articolis *C* || 15
suscensent *C* succensent *BMᵖᶜFHILT* successent *Mᵃᶜ* || 16
publica] puplica *LP* || mota meis] nota meis *H* meis *I¹* est
[meis] *I²⁽ᵍˡ?⁾* || 17 laedi] le̦de *Cᵃᶜ* || 18 plectar] plectat *L* ||
incauto] incapto *M* || 19 incidere] incindere *F* || 20 telaque]
tela *M* || sequor] sequar *CP*

ad ueteres scopulos iterum deuertor et
   illas
in quibus offendit naufraga puppis
   aquas?
sed nihil admisi, nulla est mea culpa,
   Tomitae,
quos ego, cum loca sim uestra
   perosus, amo.
quilibet excutiat nostri monimenta
   laboris:
25
littera de uobis est mea questa nihil.
frigus et incursus omni de parte
   timendos
et quod pulsetur murus ab hoste
   queror.
in loca, non homines, uerissima crimina
   dixi;
culpatis uestrum uos quoque saepe
   solum.
30
esset perpetuo sua quam uitabilis Ascra
   ausa est agricolae Musa docere senis;

21 deuertor] deuertar *B* || et] ad *M²*, *'quinque libri. quod
placet'* —*Heinsius* || 22 offendit] effudit *F¹* || naufraga]
naufagra *H* || 23 sed] at *fort legendum* || 24 q̣uos *B²ᶜ* || 25
excutiat] excuriat *L* || 27 frigus] frugus *C* || de *om I¹* ||
timendos] timendus *L* || 29 in] non *C* || crimina] carmina *H*
|| 30 culpatis] culpatus *BᵃᶜC* || solum] locum *MH* || 31
'uersus   suspectus' —*Heinsius* || quam   uitabilis]   quam
miserabilis *H* quam uitiabilis *A. G. Lee (PCPhS 181 [1950-51]
3), fort recte* ut illaudabilis *Bentley* || Ascra] ascre *BCH, fort
recte* || 32 agricolae] argolici *I²ᵘˡ*

et fuerat genitus terra qui scripsit in illa,

intumuit uati nec tamen Ascra suo.
quis patriam sollerte magis dilexit
     Vlixe?
35
  hoc tamen asperitas indice docta loci
     est.
non loca, sed mores scriptis uexauit
     amaris
  Scepsius Ausonios, actaque Roma rea
     est;
falsa tamen passa est aequa conuicia
     mente,
  obfuit auctori nec fera lingua suo.
40
at malus interpres populi mihi concitat
     iram,
  inque nouum crimen carmina nostra
     uocat.

33 et] **t M^1 at *Puteaneus Heinsii (=Parisinus lat. 8239, saec xiii)* *(Lenz), Laurentianus 36 2, saec xv (Lenz), edd ante Korn* non *uel* nec *fort legendum* || in] ut *L* || 34 intumuit] intimuit I^1 || Ascra] illa *I* || 36 indice] iudice *IL* || docta *B* doctus *C* dicta *MFHILT* nota *excerpta Scaligeri, sex codd Heinsii, probante Riese* || loci est] loci *FT* in est *C* (ī ē) || 37 om *C* || 37 non] nec *L* || sed mores] sermones *L* || 38 Scepsius *Scaliger, Castig. in Catull. 15, 19 (=32, ed. 2) (Lenz)* sceptius *C* septius *MFT* septius B^{2c} septius L^{2c} septi L^1, *ut uid* sepcius *I* celsius *H* || Ausonios] ausononios *uel* ausonomos *L* || actaque *MFT* actaue *BHIL* acte ue *C* || 39 falsa] fassa M^1 || est om *C* || 40 auctori] actori $C^{ac}F^1$ || fera] sua F^1 || 41 populi ... concitat iram] populum ... uertit in iram *L* || 42 inque] isque *F*

tam felix utinam quam pectore
    candidus essem!
  extat adhuc nemo saucius ore meo.

adde quod Illyrica si iam pice nigrior
    essem,
45

non mordenda mihi turba fidelis erat.
molliter a uobis mea sors excepta,
    Tomitae,
    tam mites Graios indicat esse uiros;
gens mea Paeligni regioque domestica
    Sulmo
    non potuit nostris lenior esse malis.
50

quem uix incolumi cuiquam saluoque
    daretis,
    is datus a uobis est mihi nuper honor:
solus adhuc ego sum uestris immunis in
    oris,
    exceptis si qui munera legis habent;

43 tam] iam C || pectore] pectorore H || candidus] callidus
H || 44-45 *in marg add* B^1F^2 || 44 nemo ... meo] meo ... nemo
H^1 || 45 Illyrica] ilira L || essem] eem M || 46 non] nec
$(F^{ac}?)L$ || mordenda] mordeda M || 47 uobis] nobis L || 48
Graios *edd* gratos $BCMFHIL$ raros T geticos *'unus Vaticanus ...
aeque bene [ac "Graios"!], nisi uis rectius'* —*Ciofanus* || 49 gens]
ius C || Paeligni] pēligni L || 50 lenior $M^{pc}F^{pc}HIT$ leuior
$BC(M^{ac})F^{ac}L$ || 51 uix] uos F^2] || incolumi] ịncolumi B^{2c} in
colonia C || 52 is] i/s B est M || est] is M || 53 adhuc] ad
hunc C || sum *om* F^1 || oris] aruis L || 54 si qui] siquid T
|| munera] mumera C

tempora sacrata mea sunt uelata
    corona,
55

publicus inuito quam fauor imposuit.
quam grata est igitur Latonae Delia
    tellus,

erranti tutum quae dedit una locum,
tam mihi cara Tomis, patria quae sede
fugatis
tempus ad hoc nobis hospita fida
manet.
60
di modo fecissent placidae spem posset
habere
pacis, et a gelido longius axe foret.

57 grata] gata H^{ac} || igitur latone F^{2c} || 59 cara] cala C^{ac} grata B^2 || 59 Tomis HLB^2 tomus B^1T thomus $I^{2c,\ ut\ uid}$ domus CF^1 thomos MF^{2ul} || quae $BMLT$ quae a $CFHI$ || 61 placidae] placidam B || 62 foret] forent F^2, *ut uid*

XV

Si quis adhuc usquam nostri non
    immemor extat,
  quidue relegatus Naso requirit,
    agam:
Caesaribus uitam, Sexto debere
    salutem
  me sciat; a superis hic mihi primus
    erit.
tempora nam miserae complectar ut
    omnia uitae,
5
  a meritis eius pars mihi nulla uacat,
quae numero tot sunt, quot in horto
    fertilis arui
  Punica sub lento cortice grana
    rubent,

sexto pompeio B^2MFH^2 ad sextum pompeium I^2 || 1
usquam ... extat] usquam ... extet *Guethling (Lenz)* extat ...
usquam *M* || 2 requirit *Bodleianus Auct. F 2 1 (Tarrant)*,
*Laurentianus 38 39 (Lenz), editio princeps Bononiensis (Lenz), 'ex
duobus' Heinsius* requirat *BCMFHLT* requiret *I, British Library
Burney 220 (Tarrant), Bodleianus Rawlinson G 105 (Tarrant),
Othob. lat. 1469, saec xv (Tarrant)* || agam] agat *fort legendum*
|| 5 miserae] supere *H* || 6 pars] noster pars B^{ac} || 7 horto
... arui] hasto ... arui *C* horto ... agri *TP* horti ... aruo
Williams || 8 lento] lecto *'Basil. et hoc probat Barth. Aduers.
xxxvii.10'—Burman*

  Africa quot segetes, quot Tmolia terra
    racemos,
  quot Sicyon bacas, quot parit Hybla

140

fauos.

10

confiteor; testere licet—signate,
  Quirites!
    nil opus est legum uiribus, ipse
      loquor.
inter opes et me, rem paruam, pone
  paternas,
    pars ego sum census
      quantulacumque tui;
quam tua Trinacria est regnataque terra
  Philippo,

15

    quam domus Augusto continuata
      foro,
quam tua rus oculis domini Campania
  gratum,
    quaeque relicta tibi, Sexte, uel empta
      tenes,
tam tuus en ego sum, cuius te munere
  tristi
    non potes in Ponto dicere habere
      nihil.

20

9 Tmolia terra BM^{2ul} tinolia t. C thimolia t. L thimola t. T timula t. I, *ut uid* mollia t. HP etholia t. F^1 gnosia t. F^{2ul} habet methina M^1 || racemos] ramos M^{ac} || 10 Sicyon] sicio B^1 scithion T || Hybla] hilba B^{ac} || 11 testere] testare $(M^1)LI^1P$ tristare F^1 narare I^{2ul} || signate] signare LP || 12 est *om* F^{ac} || loquor] loquar M^{pc} || 13 rem paruam $MHIT$ paruam rem $BCFL$, *fort recte* || 15 Trinacria] tinacria H || regnataque terra] regnaque terra I^1 tellus regnata M || philippo] phiūppo C || 19 tristi] cristi L || 20 potes H^{2c}

141

atque utinam possis, et detur amicius
     aruum,
   remque tuam ponas in meliore loco!
quod quoniam in dis est, tempta lenire
     precando
   numina perpetua quae pietate colis.
[erroris nam tu uix est discernere nostri
25
   sis argumentum maius an auxilium.]
nec dubitans oro; sed flumine saepe
     secundo
   augetur remis cursus euntis aquae.
et pudet et metuo semperque
     eademque precari
   ne subeant animo taedia iusta tuo;
30
uerum quid faciam? res immoderata
     cupido est;
   da ueniam uitio, mitis amice, meo.

21 amicius] micius B^{pc} (=mitius) amicitius L || aruum] auum
M^{ac} || 23 precando] rogando HF^{2ul} || 25-26 spurios puto.
'ambiguus hic locus est, eoque difficilior quoque, et obscurior' —
Micyllus; 'xv 25 libri "Erroris nam", quod nisi aegre intellegi
nequit, quamquam nec correctio satisfacit' — Merkel (1884), qui
maeroris pro erroris coniecit || 25 nam] iam FI discernere]
decernere MI^1 || 26 maius] magis I nauis F^1 || auxilium]
axilium M xilium I^1 || 27 flumine] fla̲mine M^{2c}, ut uid ||
saepe secundo] saepe F^1 secundo saepe I^{ac} || 29 semperque]
semper C || 30 iusta] iussa F^1 || 31 uerum quid] colloquio C
|| faciam] fac in I

   scribere saepe aliud cupiens delabor
     eodem;
   †ipsa locum per se littera nostra
     rogat.†

seu tamen effectus habitura est gratia,
     seu me
35
  dura iubet gelido Parca sub axe mori,
semper inoblita repetam tua munera
     mente,
  et mea me tellus audiet esse tuum;
audiet et caelo posita est quaecumque
     sub ullo
  (transit nostra feros si modo Musa
     Getas),
40

33 aliud cupiens] uolens aliud I || delabor] dilabor L || 34 *uix sanus; seclusit Merkel (1884)* || 34 ipsa locum ... rogat] inque locum ... redit *temptauit Tarrant* || per se littera ... rogat] pro se tristia ... rogant [*uel* petunt] *temptaui* || per se ... rogat] per se ... petit *unus Heinsii* per se ... facit *unus Heinsii* pro se ... facit *Heinsius* || 35 me] nos M^{2ul} || 37 munera] carmina F^1 munere F^{2ul} nomina F^{3ul}, *ut uid* || 38 mea] tua H || me] te (F^1) || audiet *FHIT* audiat *BCML* || 39 audiet] audiat L || est *om M* || ullo] illo M^{ac}, *sicut coni Bentley* || 40 transit nostra feros] transierit seuos T

teque meae causam seruatoremque
salutis
meque tuum libra norit et aere
magis.

41 seruatoremque] seru⊚atoremque *M* seruataremque *L* || 42 meque] neque *C* || tuum libra norit et aere magis *Barberinus lat. 26²ᵘˡ (Lenz), F³? (m̄ = magis)* tuum libra norit et aere minus *BCMHILT* (libra *ex* liba *I*) tuum libra norit et aere datum *F¹* || suum [libra norit et aere] minus *F²ᵘˡ* [tellus ... quaecumque ...] meque, tuum libra, nouit, et aere, minus *Gronouius*, Obs. *II i* meque tuum libra norit et aere tuum *Heinsius* tuae libra norit et aere manus *Rappold (Owen 1915)* tuae libra norit et aere domus *temptaui; cf Suet* Aug *61 1*

XVI

Inuide, quid laceras Nasonis carmina
     rapti?
  non solet ingeniis summa nocere dies,
famaque post cineres maior uenit. at
     mihi nomen
  tum quoque, cum uiuis adnumerarer,
     erat.
cum foret et Marsus magnique Rabirius
     oris
5
  Iliacusque Macer sidereusque Pedo,
et, qui Iunonem laesisset in Hercule,
     Carus,
  Iunonis si iam non gener ille foret,
quique dedit Latio carmen regale,
     Seuerus,
  et cum subtili Priscus uterque Numa,
10

ad inuidum B^2MI^2 ad inimicum H^2 || 1 carmina] carmia M
|| 3 uenit. at *scripsi* uenit et *BCMFILT* ueniet H || nomen]
uoto H (*noto?*) || 4 tum] tunc F || uiuis] uiuus H || erat]
eat C^{ac} || 5 cum foret et *FHT* cumque foret *BCMIL* ||
Rabirius *MFI* sabirius *BC* rabarius T rabirtius H rabilinus L
Sabellius *Barth,* Adu. *xxxvii 10 (Burman)* || 6 Iliacusque]
iliacus H || sidereusque] sidere/usque B Cecropiusque
Bentley; cf x 71 'cum Thesea carmine laudes' || p̱edo M^{2c} || 7
Iunonem laesisset] iunonem lesissent B^{ac}, *ut uid* lesisset
iunonem M || Carus] karus B || 8 Iunonis] iunonisque H
|| si iam] siam C^1 || gener ... foret *BCMFHT* (f̱oret M^{1c})
neger foret L foret genus I

quique uel imparibus numeris,
Montane, uel aequis
sufficis, et gemino carmine nomen
habes,
et qui Penelopae rescribere iussit
Vlixem
errantem saeuo per duo lustra mari,
quique suam †Trisomen†
imperfectumque dierum
15
deseruit celeri morte Sabinus opus,
ingeniique sui dictus cognomine
Largus,
Gallica qui Phrygium duxit in arua
senem,

11 imparibus numeris] imparibus *[spatium septem litterarum]* his *H* || 12 sufficis, et] sufficis M^{ac} || 13 Penelopae] penelopi *H* penelope *CI* || 13 solinus $H^{2(gl)}$ *in marg* || 15 Trisomen *C* *(trisom̄)* trisomem B^1 trosenē *L* trionē *F* troinē *I* trozenen *M* troezen *T* tr****m *H* troilem B^2 Troezena *quidam apud Micyllum* Tymelen *temptauit Heinsius* Thressen *[=Hero] M. Hertz (Lenz)* Chrysen *Roeper (Riese)* Troesmin *Ehwald* Troesmen *Owen* Sinatroncen *['Parthorum regis nomen'] Bergk*, Opusc. I 664 *pro* suam t. || imperfectumque] imperfectamque *H* imperfectum I^1 interruptumque *Bergk* || 16 deseruit] destituit *Bergk* || Sabinus] salinus $(M^1)T$ solius F^{2ul} || 17 dictus] dignus *I* || 18 Gallica] gallia M^1 || duxit] dixit M^1 || arua] arma $B^{1?ul}HI$

quique canit domito Camerinus ab
Hectore Troiam,
quique sua nomen Phyllide Tuscus
habet,
20
ueliuolique maris uates, cui credere

posses
carmina caeruleos composuisse deos,
quique acies Libycas Romanaque
proelia dixit,
et Marius scripti dexter in omne
genus,
Trinacriusque suae Perseidos auctor, et
auctor
25
Tantalidae reducis Tyndaridosque
Lupus,

19 domito ... ab Hectore] domitam ... ab hectore FM^{2ul}
domitam ... ab hercule *Gothanus II 121, saec xiii (André),*
probante Korn || Camerinus] camīnus *T* caminus *F* || 20 sua
nomen Phyllide Tuscus] fata nomen pillide tuscus *C* sua
tuscus phillide nomen *L* sua nomen Phyllide Fuscus *Heinsius*
('nomen magis Romanum') || 21 ueliuolique] ueiiuolique *C* ||
uates] nomen *Merkel ad Ibin p. 377 (Owen)* || posses
BCMHILT possis *F, fort recte* || 23 quique] cuique *C* ||
proelia] pretia *C* || dixit] salustius M^{2gl} || 24 Marius scripti]
marius scriptor *C* scriptor marius *B* || 24 dexter] promptus
M, fort in ras P || 25 Trinacriusque *BCFL* tinacriusque *IT*
tenar*sque *H* eticiusque *M* || Perseidos] perseidis *BCI*
Peneidos *Ehwald (=Daphnes)* || auctor ... auctor] auctor ...
actor *H* actor ... actor *F* || et] set F^2 || Tyndaridosque]
tyndaridisque *MI*

et qui Maeoniam Phaeacida uertit, et
une
Pindaricae fidicen tu quoque, Rufe,
lyrae,
Musaque Turrani tragicis innixa
coturnis,
et tua cum socco Musa, Melisse, leuis;
30
cum Varius Gracchusque darent fera

147

dicta tyrannis,
Callimachi Proculus molle teneret
iter,

27 Maeoniam] meonidē *H* || Pheacida *L* ph̲e̲acida *M²ᶜ*
pheatida *I* pheicida *H* ecaeida *B¹* aeacida *C* hetaterā *F*
hecateida *T* ecateida *B²* || et une *HLB²* et un̲e̲ *M²ᶜ* et una *IT*
et uni *B¹C* in anguem *F;* '*latet aliquid*' — *Burman* || 28 lyrae]
l*re‚*Cᵃᶜ* || 29 Musaque] uisaque *C* || 29 Turrani *BCMLT*
turani *FI* tiranni *H* Thorani *Heinsius* || tragicis] gtragicis *T*
|| innixa] innexa *T* || *30 (in ras?) add* *C²* || 30 et tua]
ipseque *C²* || socco] socio *C²*, *ut uid* || Melisse *MFB²* mel isse
B¹ molisse *IL* molasse *T* melose *H* molesse *C²* (malesse *legunt*
Lenz, Andrê) || leuis] leui *H* *Othob. lat. 1469, saec xv (Tarrant),*
sicut coni Heinsius || 31 Varius *LTB²ᵘˡ* uariis *C* uarus *B¹MFHI*
|| Gracchusque *edd olim* graccusque *T, probante Ehwald*
gra*ccusque *B* gracusque *HIL* gratusque *CMF* || 31 darent]
daret *F* parent *(B¹)C* || tyrannis *BC, sicut coni Heinsius*
tyranni *MFHILT* || 32 Proculus] proculuus *M* pro cuius *B²ᶜ*
prochius *C*

†Tityron antiquas Passerque rediret ad
herbas,†
33
aptaque uenanti Grattius arma daret,

33 locus desperatus. 'haec nec Latina sunt, nec satis intelligo quid
sibi uelint' — Heinsius

Tityron antiquas Passerque rediret ad herbas *B¹C* (Passerque
ex passerque *Riese*)
titirus antiquas et erat qui pasceret herbas *HILT* (titirus:
tiarus *Iᵃᶜ*) (pasceret: diceret *L*)
[tityron antiquas] et erat qui gigneret [herbas] *B³ᵘˡ*
titirus eternas caneret qui procreet herbas *F* (procreet:
pasceret *F²ᵘˡ*)
titirum et antiquas recu◉basse referret ad umbras *M*

148

[tityron antiquas] recubasse refertur [ad herbas] B^2
Tityron aprica recubantem pangeret umbra *Heinsius (Korn)*
Tityron aprica recubasse referret in umbra *Heinsius (Korn)*
Tityron apricus recubasse referret ad umbras [*uel* undas] *Heinsius (Korn)*
Tityrus antiquis armentaque pasceret herbis *Withof (Korn)*
Tityrus antiquas pastorque rediret ad herbas *Korn*
Tityrus antiquas rursus reuocaret ad herbas *Madvig (Adu. crit. II praef)*
Tityrus antiquas capras ubi pasceret herbas *Madvig (Adu. crit. II 105)*
Tityrus apricans, ut erat, qui pasceret, herbas *Bergk (Opusc. I 667)*
Tityron Andinasque esset qui diceret herbas *Roeper (Korn)*
Tityron antiquas pastorem exciret ad herbas *Owen (1915)*
Tityron antiquas carmenque referret ad herbas *Schneiderhan (Lenz)*
Tityron antiquas Passer reuocaret ad herbas *Luck*

33 antiquas] eternas *F* intactas *uel* ac uacuas *uel* ac uirides *Riese* ‖ 34 aptaque ... arma] altaque ... arma *M* armaque ... apta *I* ‖ uenanti] uenati *C* uenandi $F^{2\,ul}$ ‖ Grattius *Buecheler e cod illius poetae (RhM 35 [1880] 407)* gratius *CFLT* gracius *BMHI*

> Naiadas Satyris caneret Fontanus
> amatas,
35
> clauderet imparibus uerba Capella
> modis,
> cumque forent alii, quorum mihi
> cuncta referre
> nomina longa mora est, carmina
> uulgus habet,
> essent et iuuenes quorum, quod inedita
> cura est,
> appellandorum nil mihi iuris adest
40
> (te tamen in turba non ausim, Cotta,

silere,
            Pieridum lumen praesidiumque fori,

35 Naiadas *C. P. Jones* naiadas a *HLI*^{2} nayades a *MT* naidas a
BCFI^2 || Fontanus] fontusanus *M* montanus *H, ut uid* || 38
longa mora] mora longa *L* || uulgus habet] uulgus habent
HI^{ac} fama tenet *T* || *39-40 spurios putat Williams* || 39 essent
et iuuenes] *quid pro* essent *C, incertum* et iuuenes essent *H* ||
iuuenes quorum, quod *interpunxi* iuuenes, quorum quod *edd*
|| cura *unus Thuaneus Heinsii (=Parisinus lat. 8256 uel 8462)*
causa *BCMFHILT* || 41 tamen in] tanta in *M*^{1}*L* tamen e
Heinsius || 42 lumen] numen *'editi aliquot'—Burman* ||
praesidiumque fori] praesidiumque meum *H*^{1}*; uide Hor* Carm
I i 2

            maternos Cottas cui Messallasque
                    paternos,
                Maxime, nobilitas ingeminata dedit),
            dicere si fas est, claro mea nomine
                    Musa
    45
                atque inter tantos quae legeretur erat.
            ergo summotum patria proscindere,
                    Liuor,
                desine neu cineres sparge, cruente,
                        meos.
            omnia perdidimus; tantummodo uita
                    relicta est,
                praebeat ut sensum materiamque
                        mali.
    50
            [quid iuuat extinctos ferrum demittere
                    in artus?
                non habet in nobis iam noua plaga
                        locum.]

150

43 maternos] fraternos B^1CH || Cottas] coctas L || cui *om*
FIL || Messallasque BCM messalosque IL messalinosque HT
messalanosque F || 44 Maxime B^1CM^{pc}, *sicut coni Burman*
maxima $M^{ac}FHILTB^2$ || ingeminata] cui geminata F || 46
legeretur] regeretur BC^{pc} regaretur C^{ac} || 47 proscindere]
procindere F^{ac} praescindere T discindere I || 48 neu] nec IF
ne H || 49 relicta] retenta T, *ut uid (retn̄ta)* || 50 ut] ut ca T^{ac}
|| *51-52 spurios puto* || 51 demittere *Berolinensis Diez. B. Sant.*
1, saec xiii (Lenz), Laurentianus 36 2, saec xv (Lenz), editio princeps
Bononiensis (Lenz) dimittere *BCMFHILT* || artus] albis C
(astus *Lenz; André dubitanter*) || explicit liber ouidii de ponto
fe li ci ter sint bona scribenti sint uita salusque legenti B
explicit liber ouidii de ponto C explicit liber publii·o·n·de
ponto M explicit ouidius de ponto uade sed incultus qualem
decet exulis esse F explicit o de ponto H hic liber explicit
gratia christo detur L

COMMENTARY

EPISTVLARVM EX PONTO LIBER QVARTVS. The precise title of these poems is uncertain. The one mention Ovid makes of the poems' title is of little assistance: 'inuenies, quamuis non est miserabilis index, / non minus hoc illo triste quod ante dedi' (*EP* I i 15-16). The earliest manuscript of the poems, the ninth-century *Hamburgensis scrin. 52 F* (extant to III ii 67), gives no title at the start of the poems, but has 'EX PONTO LIBER ·II· EXPLICIT' at the end of the second book. Later manuscripts generally call the poems the *De Ponto* or *Epistulae de Ponto*. The original name was probably not present in the archetype; these titles were perhaps invented with the aid of the first distich of the first poem: 'Naso Tomitanae iam non nouus incola terrae / hoc tibi *de Getico litore* mittit opus'. Heinsius strongly preferred *Ex Ponto* to *De Ponto* ('nihil magis inscitum aut barbarum hac inscriptione'), citing in its support the first line of *Tr* V ii 'Ecquid, ut *e Ponto* noua uenit epistula, palles'. In reality *ex* and *de* are equally acceptable Latin (Cic *Att* XV xxvi 5; *Fam* XIV xx), but *Ex Ponto* is the title found in the oldest manuscript of the poems and has become usual since Heinsius' time; in the absence of further evidence it may be allowed to stand.

Heinsius made two other suggestions for the poems' title. The first, *Pontica*, seems best suited for a poem describing the geography of the area around Tomis or the characteristics of its inhabitants. His second suggestion, *Epistulae Ponticae*, is attractive, but without any particular probability.

I. To Sextus Pompeius

Sextus Pompeius, *consul ordinarius* in AD 14, is the most illustrious of Ovid's correspondents in the *Ex Ponto*; patron of Valerius Maximus, he was related to Pompey the Great (Sen *Ben* IV 30 2) and to Augustus (Dio LVI 29 5). For discussions of his career, see Syme *HO* 156-62, Pauly-Wissowa XXI,2 2265 61, and Dessau *PIR* P 450. He is the recipient of four poems in the fourth book, but is nowhere mentioned in the first three books of the *Ex Ponto*. Since Pompeius helped Ovid during his journey to exile (v 31-38), their relationship must have been of long standing; clearly Pompeius had indicated to Ovid his preference not to be mentioned in his verse, even after it had become clear to most of Ovid's friends that being named by him would carry no penalty. In *EP* III vi, Ovid exhorts a timid friend to allow him to name him; there is no indication, however, that the poem was addressed to Pompeius.

Ovid seems to have been best served in exile by those of his friends who were of no particular eminence. In *Tr* III iv 3-8 & 43-44 he complains not only of the treatment he has received from Augustus, but also of the lack of assistance from those of his friends most in a position to help. Once Sextus Pompeius had indicated he was willing to be named publicly, Ovid could not ignore the influence that a man of such position could bring to bear; hence the number of poems addressed to him in the fourth book.

Ovid starts the poem with an elaborate assertion of his past and present desire to mention Pompeius in his verse (1-22), and then briefly recounts the services Pompeius has rendered to him, and will continue to render (23-26). The reason he is confident that Pompeius will continue to assist him is that Pompeius' past assistance has been such that he is now, in effect, Pompeius' creation, and brings glory to him in the way that great works of art do for their creators (27-36).

1. DEDVCTVM. 'Composed'. *Deducere* is often used in reference to the drawing of fibres from the wool on the distaff and the shaping of the thread (Catullus LXIV 311-14). From this meaning derive the two senses the word can have when referring to poetry, 'composed' and 'finely spun, delicate'. The first sense is seen here and at *Tr* I i 39, *EP* I v 13, and at *Tr* V i 71 'ipse nec emendo, sed ut hic *deducta* legantur', and the second at *Ecl* VI 4-5 'pastorem, Tityre, pinguis / pascere oportet ouis, *deductum* dicere carmen', where *deductum* ... *carmen* represents the Μοῦσαν ... λεπταλέην of Callimachus *Aetia* I 24; Servius comments on the metaphor from spinning. It has been suggested that *Met* I 4 'ad mea perpetuum *deducite* tempora carmen' shows this meaning as well; see Kenney *Ouidius Prooemians* 51-52.

Hor *Ep* II i 225 'tenui deducta poemata filo' stands somewhere between the two senses.

2. DEBITOR ... VITAE. See v 33-36 (Ovid's letter speaking to Pompeius) 'te sibi, cum fugeret, memori solet ore referre / barbariae tutas exhibuisse uias, / sanguine Bistonium quod non tepefecerit ensem, / effectum cura pectoris esse tui'. The passage suggests that Pompeius supplied Ovid with a bodyguard for his journey overland from Tempyra to Tomis, either in an official capacity—Dessau suggests (*PIR* P 450) that Pompeius might have been proconsul of Macedonia—or, more probably, from his Macedonian estates, for which Dessau and Syme (*HO* 157) cite xv 15.

3. QVI. Williams' CVI is possibly correct; the line would then refer to the *titulus* of the poem in a published text.

3. SEV NON PROHIBES. 'If you do not try to prevent'. The context makes it clear that Pompeius will not in fact prevent Ovid from mentioning Pompeius in his poem. This conative sense is much more commonly found with the imperfect than with the present; the only way it can be dispensed with in this passage is if *cui* is read and, as Professor R. J. Tarrant suggests, *prohibes* taken to refer to the later inclusion of the poem in a published collection.

4. ACCEDET MERITIS. Pompeius' even allowing Ovid to name him would count as a favour. Nowhere in the poem does Ovid specify why Pompeius might prefer not to be named.

4. ACCEDET MERITIS HAEC QVOQVE SVMMA TVIS.
'This sum will be added to the favours you have done me'. Professor J. N. Grant points out to me the technical terms of finance used in the passage: *debitor ... accedet ... summa*. I once thought that *summa* was equivalent in sense to *cumulus* ('addition') at *EP* II v 35-36 'hoc tibi facturo, uel si non ipse rogarem, / *accedat cumulus* gratia nostra leuis', but have found no parallel for this sense of *summa*.

5. TRAHIS VVLTVS. 'Frown'—compare iii 7 'contraxit uultum Fortuna', viii 13-14 'ei mihi, si lectis uultum tu uersibus istis / ducis', *Am* II ii 33 'bene uir traxit uultum rugasque coegit', and *Met* II 774 'ingemuit uultumque una ac [*Housman*: ima ad *codd*] suspiria duxit'.

5-6. EQVIDEM PECCASSE FATEBOR, / DELICTI TAMEN EST CAVSA PROBANDA MEI. 'Yes, I shall certainly confess my guilt, but the reason for my offence is one that necessarily wins approval'. Ovid uses the correct legal terminology; compare Cic *Mur* 62 '*fatetur* aliquis se *peccasse* et sui [*Halm*: cui *uel* eius *codd*] *delicti* ueniam petit'. Other instances in Ovid of *peccasse fateri* at hexameter-ends are *Am* III xiv 37, *Met* III 718, VII 748 & XI 134, and *EP* II iii 33.

For Ovid's close acquaintance with the law see at xv 12 (pp 434-35).

7. NON POTVIT MEA MENS. Compare *Tr* V ix 25-26 'nunc quoque se, quamuis est iussa quiescere, quin te / nominet inuitum, uix mea Musa tenet'.

8. OFFICIO. Used again of Ovid's writing of verse-epistles at *Tr* V ix 33-34 'ne tamen *officio* memoris laedaris amici, / parebo iussis—parce timere—tuis'.

8. OFFICIO ... PIO. The words similarly combined at *Tr* III iii 84 and *Tr* V vi 4 'officiique pium ... onus'. The adjective ('loyal') is a favourite term of commendation in the poems of exile, applied to *fides* (*Tr* V xiv 20, *EP* III ii 98), coupled with *memor* (*Tr* IV v 18, V iv 43), or used to characterize the inseparable friends of myth such as Theseus and Pirithous

(*Tr* I ix 31) or Castor and Pollux (*Tr* IV v 30).

9. IN. *B*'s AB is possibly correct, *ab istis* meaning 'to judge by them, on the basis of their evidence'. Professor R. J. Tarrant cites Prop III iii 38 'ut reor *a facie*, Calliopea fuit'.

11. ALII VELLEM CVM SCRIBERE. The line confirms that Ovid was not at liberty to name Sextus Pompeius in his poems even after he had begun the composition of the first three books of the *Ex Ponto*.

Ovid similarly indicates his frustrated desire to name his correspondent at *Tr* IV v 10 'excidit heu nomen quam mihi paene tuum' and at *EP* III vi 1-2 'Naso suo (posuit nomen quam paene!) sodali / mittit ... hoc breue carmen'.

11. VELLEM CVM. *B* offers CVM VELLEM, which I take to be a simple corruption to prose word-order. It is however the reading printed by Owen; and it could be argued that *cum uellem* is the correct reading, and was altered to *uellem cum* for metrical reasons. Lucretius and Catullus were fond of placing a spondaic word in the fourth foot of the hexameter; in the Augustan age practice altered, and the pattern was generally avoided; compare *Aen* I 1 'Arma uirumque cano, *Troiae qui* primus ab oris'. It was, however, permitted occasionally, especially when the previous foot ended in a long monosyllable (Platnauer 20-22). Scribes quite often alter such lines so as to remove the spondaic word from coinciding with the fourth foot; an instance of this can be seen at line 7 'non potuit mea mens quin esset grata teneri', where *H* offers the scribal alteration *esset quin*. For a full discussion see Housman 269.

13. MENDIS. This is probably a form of *mendum* rather than of *menda*; compare Cic *II Ver* II 104 'quid fuit istic antea scriptum? quod *mendum* ista litura correxit?' and *Att* XIII xxiii 2 ' tantum librariorum *menda* tolluntur'. I have found no earlier instance in verse of *mendum* meaning 'error' in this sense; Ovid in his poems of exile uses the terms of his craft more readily than any of his predecessors.

14. VIX INVITA FACTA LITVRA MANV EST. *Vix* goes with *facta*; André seems to take it with *inuita* ('ma main l'effaçait presque à regret').

15. VIDERIT is a complete sentence meaning 'let him look to himself'. Compare the following examples: 'nona terebatur miserae uia; *"uiderit* [*sc* Demophoon]" inquit / et spectat zonam pallida facta suam' (*RA* 601-2), '"uiderit! insanos" inquit "fateamur amores"' (*Met* IX 519), 'cur tamen est mihi cura tui tot iam ante peremptis? / *uiderit*! intereat, quoniam tot caede procorum / admonitus non est' (*Met* X 623-25), '*uiderit*! audentes forsque deusque iuuat' (*Fast* II 782), '*uideris*! [*cod Ambrosianus G 37 sup (saec xiv), sicut coni Heinsius*: uiderit *codd plerique*] audebo tibi me scripsisse fateri' (*EP* I ii 9). The idiom is found with an expressed subject at *AA* II 371 '*uiderit* Atrides: Helenen ego crimine soluo' and *AA* III 671-72 '*uiderit* utilitas: ego coepta fideliter edam: / Lemniasin gladios in mea fata dabo'. It is clearly derived from the use of *uiderit* 'look after, take care of' with an expressed object, as at *Her* XII 209-11 'quo feret ira sequar! facti fortasse pigebit— / et piget infido consuluisse uiro. / *uiderit* ista deus qui nunc mea pectora uersat!'. Although *uiderit* in these passages clearly has a jussive sense, it is probably future perfect in origin, since *uidero* 'I shall look after' is quite frequent in Terence and Cicero: see Martin on Ter *Ad* 437 'de istoc ipse uiderit' and *OLD uideo* 18b.

15. AD SVMMAM means 'in short' or 'to sum up', and is used to introduce a recapitulation of what has just been expressed or concluded. The line should therefore be taken as the end of a debate which Ovid has had with himself. For the idiom, Ehwald (*KB* 45) cites Cic *Att* VII vii 7, XIV i 1, Hor *Ep* I i 106 'ad summam, sapiens uno minor est Ioue, Petronius *Sat* 37 5 'ad summam, mero meridie si dixerit illi tenebras esse, credet', 37 10, 57 3 & 9, 58 8 (in all these passages the narrator's neighbour at table is the speaker) and 71 1 (Trimalchio speaking). Professor R. J. Tarrant cites Sen *Apoc* 11 3 'ad summam, tria uerba cito dicat et seruum me ducat'.

AD SVMMVM is the reading of *L* and *T* and is printed by Burman (who punctuates *uiderit ad summum*) and Merkel (*ad summum dixi*). *OLD summus* 8b gives only one instance of *ad summum*, where it means 'at most' (Scribonius Largus 122).

The phrase does not seem appropriate to the present context.

15. IPSE (*FTP*) is so much better in sense ('although *he* may object') than the ILLE of most manuscripts that I have followed all previous editors in accepting it.

16. HANC. This, the reading of *H* and *I* (perhaps recovered by conjecture), must be preferred to HA (AH, A), the reading of the other manuscripts, since without it *licet ipse queratur* would have to be linked to *uiderit*, which seems awkward. The corruption of *hāc* to *ha* is not difficult, especially in view of the following *pudet*; compare *Met* IX 531 'pudet, a pudet edere nomen'.

17. SI QVID EA EST. 'If it really exists'. The affirmation would be 'est aliquid Lethe'; compare Prop IV vii 1 'Sunt aliquid Manes: letum non omnia finit'.

17. HEBETANTEM PECTORA. I have found no other instance in Ovid of this transferred sense of *hebetare*, but compare *Aen* II 604-6 'omnem quae nunc obducta tuenti / mortalis hebetat uisus tibi ... nubem eripiam' and *Aen* VI 731-32. The transferred sense is found at Celsus II i 11 'Auster aures hebetat ... omnis calor ... mentem hebetat'; compare as well Pliny *NH* XVIII 118 '[faba ...] hebetare sensus existimata' and Suet *Cl* 2 'animo simul et corpore hebetato'.

Oblitus in 18 indicates that *pectus* is virtually equivalent to 'mind' or even 'memory'. In Ovid it often has the sense 'poetic feeling', as at xii 16 'pectus habere neger'.

17. LETHEN. Compare *Tr* IV i 47-48 'utque soporiferae biberem si pocula Lethes, / temporis aduersi sic mihi sensus abest'.

21. ET can be construed, as connecting with the preceding *nec*; compare *Fast* VI 325 '*nec* licet *et* longum est epulas narrare deorum'. SED should however possibly be read, the word contrasting with the preceding *nec* as at ii 15-16 'nec tamen ingenium nobis respondet ut ante, / *sed* siccum sterili uomere litus aro'. The error could easily be induced by the final *s* of the preceding *putes*; compare *Med* 55-56 'par erui mensura decem madefiat ab *ouis* / (*sed* [*uar* et] cumulent libras hordea nuda duas)'.

21. LEVIS HAEC ... GRATIA. 'This unimportant expression of gratitude'. The same use of *leuis* at *EP* II v 35-36 'hoc tibi facturo, uel si non ipse rogarem, / accedat cumulus gratia nostra leuis'.

21. HAEC MERITIS REFERATVR GRATIA. Similar phrasing at *Met* V 14-15 'meritisne haec gratia tantis / redditur?', *Tr* V iv 47 'plena tot ac tantis referetur gratia factis', *EP* I vii 61 'emeritis referenda est gratia semper', and *EP* III i 79-80 'nec ... debetur meritis gratia nulla meis'.

23. NVMQVAM PIGRA FVIT NOSTRIS TVA GRATIA REBVS. Wheeler rightly points out Ovid's play in 21-23 on the varying senses of *gratia* (thanks), *gratus* (grateful), and *gratia* (favour, kindness).

26. FERETQVE is Heinsius' correction for the REFERTQVE of the manuscripts (REFERT B^1, REFERTA C); it is made necessary by the following *fiducia tanta futuri*. Owen, Lenz, and André report *feretque* as the reading of the thirteenth-century *Canonicianus lat 1*, but Professor R. J. Tarrant, who has examined the manuscript, informs me that it in fact reads *refertque*.

For the pattern compare *Tr* III viii 12 'quae non ulla tibi *fertque feretque* dies' and *Tr* II 155-56 'per superos ... qui *dant* tibi longa *dabuntque* / tempora'.

The corruption was natural enough, particularly in view of such passages as *Fast* VI 334 'errantes *fertque refertque* pedes', *Tr* I vii 5-6 (to a friend who owned a ring with Ovid's portrait) 'hoc tibi ... senti ... dici, / in digito qui me *fersque refersque* [*codd*: ferasque *Heinsius*] tuo', and *Tr* V xiii 29 'sic *ferat ac referat* tacitas nunc littera uoces'.

28. QVOD FECIT QVISQVE TVETVR OPVS. 'Everyone protects the work he has created'. This is hardly a commonplace of ancient poetry, and the catalogue which follows of famous works of art does not serve to illustrate it.

29-34. Ovid's description of the works of Apelles, Phidias,

Calamis, and Myron was influenced by Propertius' catalogue of artists at III ix 9-16; in particular, he imitates 10-12 'exactis Calamis se mihi iactat equis; / in Veneris tabula summam sibi poscit Apelles; / Parrhasius parua uindicat arte locum', and 15 'Phidiacus signo se Iuppiter ornat eburno'. Professor E. Fantham points out to me the inclusion of Apelles, Calamis, and Myron as canonical figures in a catalogue of artists at Cic *Brut* 70 and of all four in a similar catalogue at Quint XII x 6-9.

29. VENVS. Ovid is speaking of the famous Aphrodite Anadyomene painted by Apelles (fourth century BC) in Cos; hence the epithet *Coi* later in the line—Apelles was in fact from Colophon. Ovid had probably seen the picture in Rome, for Augustus brought it there from Cos (Strabo XIV 2 19; Pliny *NH* XXXV 91).

Ovid refers to the painting at *Am* I xiv 33-34 and *Tr* II 527-28. At *AA* III 223-24 (quoted in the next note) Ovid seems to be describing a cut gem copied from the painting.

30. AEQVOREO MADIDAS QVAE PREMIT IMBRE COMAS. *Imbre* depends on *madidas*. *Premit* is equivalent to *exprimit*, as is shown by *AA* III 224 'nuda Venus madidas *exprimit* imbre comas'. For *exprimere* taking as object that out of which something is pressed or squeezed see Celsus IV 24 and Pliny *NH* XXIX 31.

The Romans would not have found *aequoreo ... imbre* strange. Although the primary transferred sense of *imber* would be rain-water, it is used of sea-water as early as Ennius *Ann* 497-98 Vahlen 'ratibusque fremebat / imber Neptuni', and without defining qualifier at *Aen* I 123.

31. ACTAEAE = the metrically difficult *Atheniensis*. The word is generally confined to high poetry (*Ecl* II 24, *Met* II 554 & 720, VI 711, VII 681 & VIII 170), but its first occurrence is in prose, at Nepos *Thras* 2 1 'hoc initium fuit salutis Actaeorum'; some manuscripts read *Atticorum*, which may be right.

31. VEL EBVRNA VEL AEREA CVSTOS. There were at Athens two famous statues of Athena sculpted by Phidias:

'Phidias ... fecit ex *ebore auroque* [*Mayhoff*: aeque *codd*] Mineruam Athenis quae est in Parthenone stans, ex *aere* uero ... Mineruam tam eximiae pulchritudinis ut formae cognomen acceperit ['was named the Minerva Formosa']' (Pliny *NH* XXXIV 54); the second, less famous statue is described at Pausanias I 28 2.

Heinsius' note is something of an oddity. He begins by reading AVREA for the AENEA of most manuscripts, taking *uel eburna uel aurea custos* to refer to the chryselephantine statue in the Parthenon, 'sed altius consideranti locum apparet de duplici statua Mineruae agi, altera eburnea, altera aenea'. *Aenea* therefore continued to be the accepted reading until 1873, when Haupt (*Opuscula* 584) pointed out that it was unmetrical, and restored *aerea*, found in some manuscripts.

The inverse error occurs at *Her* VI 32, where most manuscripts have the unmetrical *aeripedes* for *aenipedes*. But Merkel, followed by Palmer, considered 31-38 an interpolation; and *aeripedes* may have been what the interpolator wrote.

32. PHIDIACA ... MANV. Ovid is recalling Prop III ix 15 'Phidiacus ... Iuppiter'. For the Latin poets' use of a personal adjective for the genitive of the noun, see Austin's interesting note on *Aen* II 543 *Hectoreum*.

33. VINDICAT VT CALAMIS LAVDEM QVOS FECIT EQVORVM. 'As Calamis lays claim to the praise given his horses'. Calamis, a sculptor of the fifth century BC, was particularly famous for his statues of horses; see Pliny *NH* XXXIV 71 'habet simulacrum et benignitas eius ['Praxiteles' generosity is seen in one of his statues']; Calamidis enim quadrigae aurigam suum imposuit, ne melior in equorum effigie defecisse in homine crederetur. ipse Calamis et alias quadrigas bigasque fecit equis sine aemulo expressis'.

33. QVOS FECIT EQVORVM. Similar instances of hyperbaton at 28 'quod fecit quisque tuetur opus', *Met* IV 803 'pectore in aduerso quos fecit sustinet angues', and *Fast* VI 20 'tum dea quos fecit sustulit ipsa metus'.

34. VT SIMILIS VERAE VACCA MYRONIS OPVS. The *Cow* of Myron (late fifth century BC) was his most famous work. Praise of the statue's lifelike appearance was a stock theme of Hellenistic writers of epigram; it appears from Pliny *NH* XXXIV 57 that the poetry written about the statue was as notable as the statue itself. Thirty-six poems of the Palatine Anthology deal with the theme (IX 713-42 & 793-98). Ausonius wrote eight epigrams on the same subject (*Ep* LXVIII-LXXV), of which I quote LXVIII as a typical example of what both the Greek and Latin epigrams are like:

> Bucula sum, caelo *['chisel']* genitoris
> facta Myronis
> aerea: nec factam me puto, sed
> genitam,
> sic me taurus init, sic proxima bucula
> mugit,
> sic uitulus sitiens ubera nostra petit.
> miraris quod fallo gregem? gregis ipse
> magister
> inter pascentes me numerare solet.

The statue was in Athens during Cicero's lifetime (*II Verr* IV 135); Ovid is likely to have seen it during his visit to the city (*Tr* I ii 77). He would certainly have seen the four statues of cattle sculpted by Myron which Augustus placed in his temple of Apollo, and which Propertius described: 'atque aram circum steterant armenta Myronis, / quattuor artificis, uiuida signa, boues' (II xxxi 7-8).

35. VLTIMA. 'Smallest, least important'. For this rare sense compare Hor *Ep* I xvii 35 'principibus placuisse uiris non ultima laus est', *Cons ad Liuiam* 44 'ultima sit laudes inter ut illa tuas', Vell Pat I 11 1, and the other instances cited by *OLD ultimus* 9.

35. SVM ('I am not the least of your possessions') seems unobjectionable enough; most editors have, however, accepted PARS from the *excerpta Politiani*.

36. MVNVS OPVSQVE is a Latin phrase with the general meaning of 'creation'. It is used in this sense at Cic *Tusc* I 70 'haec igitur et alia innumerabilia cum cernimus, possumusne dubitare quin iis praesit aliquis uel effector ... uel ... moderator tanti *operis et muneris?*', *ND* II 90, *Off* III 4 'nulla enim eius ingenii [*sc* Africani] monumenta mandata litteris, nullum *opus* otii, nullum solitudinis *munus* extat', and *Met* VII 435-36 (to Theseus) 'quodque suis securus arat Cromyona colonus, / *munus opusque* tuum est'.

II. To Cornelius Severus

Cornelius Severus (Schanz-Hosius 268-69 [§ 317]) was one
of the most famous poets contemporary with Ovid; of him
Quintilian said 'etiam si uersificator quam poeta melior
['even if his facility outruns his inspiration'], si tamen (ut est
dictum) ad exemplar primi libri bellum Siculum
perscripsisset, uindicaret sibi iure secundum locum [*sc* after
Virgil]' (X i 89). The elder Seneca quoted with approval
Severus' lines on the death of Cicero, as the finest lament
produced on the subject (*Suas* VI 26: Winterbottom *ad loc*
refers to a commentary by H. Homeyer, *Annales univ.
Saraviensis [phil. Fak.]* 10 [1961], 327-34). *EP* I viii was
addressed to a different Severus: in the third and fourth
lines of the present poem, Ovid expresses his embarrassment
at having addressed no poem to Severus previously, and in
the earlier poem no mention is made of the addressee's
poetry.

The poem is an apology to Severus for Ovid's not having
sent a poem to him before; he offers two excuses for the
omission. In the first fourteen lines, he flatters Severus by
saying that so good a poet hardly needs to receive verse
from someone else; in the twenty-four lines that follow he
describes how his poetry, because of the conditions at Tomis,
is now less abundant and of poorer quality than before. The
subject is one Ovid had employed before: *Tr* III xiv, a request
for indulgence to Ovid's verse, and *Tr* V xii, a reply to a
friend who had urged him to write more poetry, treat the
same topic in much the same way. The theme is similar to
that of Catullus LXVIII 1-40, where the poet explains that
his brother's death has caused his lack of interest in poetry.

In 39-46 Ovid moves to the somewhat discordant topic
(which serves however to re-emphasize his misery at Tomis)
of how he continues to write poetry to take his mind off
present evils, a theme he had used several times before, most
notably in *EP* I v. He ends the poem with a request that
Severus send him some of his recent work (47-50).

165

1. QVOD LEGIS. Similar beginnings to verse-epistles at *Her* III 1 '*Quam legis* a rapta Briseide littera uenit', *Tr* V vii 1, *EP* I vii 1-2 'Littera pro uerbis tibi, Messaline, salutem / *quam legis* a saeuis attulit usque Getis', and *EP* III v 1 '*Quam legis* unde tibi mittatur epistula quaeris?'.

Compare as well *Her* X 3-4 '*Quae legis* ex illo, Theseu, tibi litore mitto / unde tuam sine me uela tulere ratem'. This poem has suffered from two separate interpolations at its beginning. Certain manuscripts start the poem with the distich 'Illa relicta feris etiam nunc, improbe Theseu, / uiuit et haec aequa mente tulisse uelis', which is universally condemned; but the formulaic nature of 3-4 suggests that 1-2 'Mitius inueni quam te genus omne ferarum, / credita non ulli quam tibi peius eram', found in all manuscripts, is a second interpolation. Micyllus was the first to see this; a recent discussion at Kirfel 69-70.

1. VATES MAGNORVM MAXIME REGVM. Severus apparently wrote a poem dealing with pre-Republican Rome, to judge from xvi 9 his most famous work: 'quique dedit Latio carmen regale, Seuerus'. Heinsius took the two passages as meaning that Severus was a writer of tragedy, citing *Tr* II 553 'et dedimus tragicis scriptum regale cothurnis'; compare as well Hor *Sat* I x 42-43 'Pollio regum / facta canit pede ter percusso ['in iambic trimeter']'. Heinsius' suggestion is possible enough, but since Seneca and Quintilian speak of Severus as an epic poet and there is no mention of the stage in this poem, it should be rejected.

Similar language is used of epic poetry at *Ecl* VI 3 'cum canerem *reges* et proelia' and Prop III iii 1-4 'Visus eram ... reges, Alba, tuos et *regum facta* tuorum, / tantum operis, neruis hiscere posse meis'.

1. REGVM. VATVM (*M¹FIL*) is a conscious or unconscious attempt to extend the etymological figure seen in *magnorum maxime*.

5-6. ORBA TAMEN NVMERIS CESSAVIT EPISTVLA NVMQVAM / IRE PER ALTERNAS OFFICIOSA VICES. Other mentions of what was clearly an extensive prose correspondence between Ovid and his friends at *Tr* V xii 1-2 and *EP* I ix 1-2.

6. OFFICIOSA. 'Attentive'. The preface to Martial XII gives a good illustration of the sense: 'consequimur ut molesti potius quam ut officiosi esse uideamur'.

Officiosus occurs five times in the *Ex Ponto*, but only four times in the rest of Ovid's poetry.

9-10. Aristaeus was famous for his beekeeping (Virgil *G* IV 315-558). Bacchus was the god of wine, and Triptolemus had disseminated the knowledge of grain-farming (*Met* V 646-61). Alcinous might seem a strange companion to these three, but evidently Homer's description of Alcinous' orchard (*Od* VII 112-31) made a strong impression on the Latin poets. From Ovid compare *Am* I x 56 'praebeat Alcinoi poma benignus ager' and *Met* XIII 719-20 'proxima Phaeacum felicibus obsita pomis / rura petunt', from Propertius III ii 13 'nec mea Phaeacas aequant pomaria siluas', and from Virgil *G* II 87 'pomaque et Alcinoi siluae' 'the fruit-trees of Alcinous'.

9. BACCHO VINA FALERNA. Heinsius preferred *M*'s BACCHO VINA FALERNO. But the passage he cited in its support, Silius III 369-70 'Tarraco ... uitifera, et Latio tantum cessura Lyaeo' is not in fact parallel: *Lyaeo* there stands for *uino*, and the passage means 'Tarraco, rich in vines, conceding priority to Latin wine alone'. Ovid wished to balance the hexameter with the pentameter, and used a standard epithet to fill out the metre.

10. ALCINOO. Note the quadrisyllable ending, and compare *EP* II ix 41-42 'quis non Antiphaten Laestrygona deuouet? aut quis / munifici mores improbet *Alcinoi*?'. In his later poetry Ovid shows a steadily increasing willingness to allow his pentameters to end with words other than disyllables. Every pentameter of the amatory poems and the first fifteen *Heroides* ends in a disyllable. Two quadrisyllabic endings occur in the later books of the *Fasti*: V 582 *fluminibus* and VI 660 *funeribus*. In the first five books of the *Tristia* there are eight such endings, in the first three books of the *Ex Ponto* there are seven, while in the fourth book there are no less than fourteen instances of quadrisyllabic endings:

nearly as many as in all the rest of Ovid's corpus put together.[18] 'Sermo magis etiam quam illic [*sc* in the *Tristia*] ... neglectus est et degenerauit' Riese remarked, but it can reasonably be doubted that a poet of Ovid's facility would break the rule of the disyllabic ending except by choice. A moderation of the rule became general: the author of *Her* XVI-XXI (whom I do not believe to have been Ovid) allowed *pudicitiae* (XVI 290), *superciliis* (XVII 16), and *deseruit* (XIX 202) (Platnauer 17); a count of pentameters in Martial V shows the proportion of non-disyllabic endings at 20%—the shorter the poem, the more freely they are admitted. Quadrisyllable endings are frequent in the metrically strict Claudian.

Ovid admitted quadrisyllable endings more freely if they were proper names. Of the twenty-one quadrisyllable verse-endings in the *Ex Ponto*, six involve proper nouns: II ii 76 *Dalmatiae*, ix 42 *Alcinoi*, the present passage, IV iii 54 *Anticyra*, viii 62 *Oechalia*, and ix 80 *Danuuium*. Professor E. Fantham points out to me that Ovid follows Propertius' similar practice: 42 of the 166 quadrisyllable pentameter endings in Propertius are proper names (Platnauer 17).

The fifteen other instances in the *Ex Ponto* of quadrisyllabic pentameter-endings are II ii 6 *perlegere*, ii 70 *imperium*, iii 18 *articulis*, v 26 *ingenium*, III i 166 *aspiciant*, IV v 24 *officio*, vi 6 *alterius*, vi 14 *auxilium*, ix 48 *utilitas*, xiii 28 *imperii*, xiii 46 *ingeniis*, xiv 4 *inuenies*, xiv 18 *ingenio*, xiv 56 *imposuit*, and xv 26 *auxilium*.

For Ovid's use of trisyllabic and pentasyllabic endings, see at ix 26 *tegeret* (page 294) and iii 12 *amicitia* (p 181).

11. FERTILE PECTVS HABES. Compare *Tr* V xii 37-38 'denique non paruas animo dat gloria uires, / et *fecunda* facit *pectora* laudis amor'.

11. INTERQVE HELICONA COLENTES. Poets are also described as being on Parnassus at *Tr* IV i 50, x 23 & x 120. Helicon is the goal of poets at Hor *Ep* II i 218 (cited at 36).

12. PROVENIT continues the agricultural metaphor of *fertile pectus*. For *prouenire* = 'grow', see *AA* III 101-2 'ordior a cultu:

cultis bene Liber ab uuis / prouenit', *Fast* IV 617 'largaque prouenit cessatis messis in aruis', and *Nux* 10; for the metaphorical sense see *Am* I iii 19-20 'te mihi materiem *felicem* in carmina praebe— / *prouenient* causa carmina digna sua' and *Her* XV 13-14 'nec mihi dispositis quae iungam carmina neruis / *proueniunt*'.

For *uberius* ... *prouenit* compare Caesar *BG* V 24 'eo anno frumentum in Gallia propter siccitates *angustius prouenerat*'.

13. MITTERE AD HVNC CARMEN. Burman printed without comment MITTERE CARMEN AD HVNC, the reading of Heinsius' *fragmentum Louaniense*. It seems to be a mere normalization of the hyperbaton; the elimination of the elision (*mittere ad*) may have been a factor as well.

13. AD HVNC indicates that Ovid cannot have addressed these words in the first instance directly to Severus, but must here be recollecting his earlier thoughts. I have therefore placed the line in quotation marks.

15. NEC TAMEN. 'This was the principal reason; a second reason, however, was that ...'

15. INGENIVM = 'poetic talent', as often. Compare viii 66, xvi 2, *Tr* III vii 47, *EP* II ii 103, *EP* II v 21 (quoted at 20 *uena pauperiore*), *EP* II v 26, and *EP* III iv 11.

15. RESPONDET introduces the agricultural image of 18 'sed siccum sterili uomere litus aro', for the word here means 'yield'. *OLD respondeo* 8c cites for the literal sense Virgil *G* II 63-64 'truncis oleae melius, propagine uites / respondent', Columella II 1 3 'humus ... magno faenore ... colono respondet', Col III 3 4; for a transferred use see Sen *Ep* LXXXI 1 'non respondeant [*sc* beneficia] potius quam non dentur'.

16. SICCVM ... LITVS ARO. Proverbial for a useless activity. See Otto *harena* 4 and compare *Tr* V iv 47-48 'plena tot ac tantis referetur gratia factis, / nec sinet ille [Ovid] litus arare boues'.

Sterili is transferred by hypallage from *litus*; *siccum* serves no purpose beyond providing a balancing epithet.

169

17. VENAS EXCAECAT, the reading of most codices, is obviously correct as against the VENAS CVM CAECAT of *BCHL*. Ovid uses *excaecare* again at *Met* XV 270-72 'hic fontes natura nouos emisit, at illic / clausit ... flumina prosiliunt aut *excaecata* [*uar* exsiccata] residunt'.

17. IN VNDIS is probably corrupt; if it is retained, from the context it must mean 'in the water of springs' (Professor A. Dalzell). Williams suggests 'in the case of water', marking the analogy with *pectora sic mea sunt limo uitiata malorum* in 19.

For *undis* as a corrupt hexameter ending, compare *Met* XV 276 'redditur Argolicis ingens Erasinus in aruis [*codd*: in undis *Sen NQ III 26* 4]', *Met* VIII 162 'liquidus Phrygiis Maeandros in aruis [*uar* liquidis Phrygius ... in undis]', and *Met* XIV 155 'sedibus Euboicam Stygiis emergit in urbem [*uar* sedibus euboicis stigiis emersus ab undis]'.

The line seems to have passed without comment until Merkel's second edition: '*in undis* minus bene positum uidetur; temptabam *hiulcas*, quod expressisset Statius Theb. VIIII 450 *hiulcis flumina uenis Suggerit* ['he (the river Asopos) opens his springs wide and adds his streams']'. There seems no obvious reason, however, for Ovid to define the springs as 'gaping'.

Madvig conjectured INVNDANS, the corruption of which would be easy; but *uenas* seems more in need of a modifier than *limus*—Professor R. J. Tarrant suggests APERTAS or AQVARVM, Professor A. Dalzell IN ARVIS.

Professor Tarrant also suggests to me that *in undis* could well have originated as a gloss on *uenas*.

18. LAESAQVE. There seems no reason to replace this with Merkel's LAPSAQVE ('flowing back'?), which even seems to contradict the sense of *resistit*.

The same sense of *laesus* at *Am* III vii 32 'deficiunt laesi carmine ['spell'] fontis aquae'.

20. VENA PAVPERIORE. The same image of Ovid's poetic talent at *Tr* III xiv 33-34 'ingenium fregere meum mala, cuius et ante / fons infecundus *paruaque uena* fuit' and *EP* II v 21-22 'ingenioque meo, *uena* quod *paupere* manat, / plaudis, et e riuo flumina magna facis'.

23. DA VENIAM FASSO. As a poet himself, Severus would be particularly shocked at Ovid's admission he has virtually ceased to write poetry. Similar phrasing at III ix 45-46 'confesso ignoscite, docti: / uilior est operis fama salute mea'.

23. FRENA REMISI. 'I have let go of the reins' = 'I have stopped writing poetry'; for the sense, compare *Aen* VII 599-600 (of Latinus) 'nec plura locutus / saepsit se tectis rerumque reliquit habenas'.

The metaphor of the poet as driver is found as early as Bacchylides (V 176-78) and Pindar (*Ol* VI 22 ff). A full list of Greek and Latin passages is included in Henderson's note on *RA* 397-98; the image is particularly frequent in Roman didactic poetry, being found even at Columella X 215-16. See as well Kenney *Nequitiae Poeta* 206. In Ovid the image is found at *AA* I 39-40 & 264, II 426, III 467-68 & 809-10, *RA* 397-98, *Fast* I 25-26, II 360, IV 10, and VI 586. The only instances I have found that are not from Ovid's didactic verse are the present passage and xii 23-24 'tu bonus hortator, tu duxque comesque fuisti, / cum regerem tenera frena nouella manu'.

24. DVCITVR. 'Is formed, written'. The same sense at *Met* I 649 (of Io) '*littera* ... quam pes in puluere *duxit*' and *Met* X 215-16 'AI AI / flos habet inscriptum, funestaque *littera ducta* est'.

25. IMPETVS ILLE SACER. 'The famous divine impulse'. Similar phrasing at *Fast* VI 5-6 'est deus in nobis; agitante calescimus illo: / impetus hic sacrae semina mentis habet'.

25. VATVM PECTORA NVTRIT. *Nutrit* here seems to mean 'sustain'. Its usual transferred sense is 'cause to grow', as at III iv 26 (the only other passage I have found where the verb is used of poetry) and Hor *C* IV iv 26.

27. VIX VENIT AD PARTES ... MVSA. 'My Muse with difficulty performs her functions'. *Partes* in the sense of 'theatrical role' (Ter *Ph* 27) early acquired the extended sense of 'role', 'function', or 'duty'. Burman cites as parallels *Am* I viii 87 'seruus et *ad partes* sollers ancilla parentur' and *Nux* 68; compare as well *AA* II 546 'cum, tener, *ad partes* tu quoque, somne, uenis' and *EP* III i 41-42 'utque iuuent alii, tu debes uincere amicos, / uxor, et *ad partes* prima uenire tuas'.

27. SVMPTAE ... TABELLAE. Compare *Met* IX 523-25 'scribit damnatque *tabellas* ... inque uicem *sumptas* ponit positasque *resumit*'.

29. NE DICAM. I have found no other instance of the expression in verse, but it is common in Cicero (Kühner-Stegmann II i 825).

30. NVMERIS NECTERE VERBA. 'Bind words to metre'. I take *numeris* as a dative; no close parallel presents itself, but compare *Aen* IV 239-40 'pedibus talaria nectit / aurea'.

33. NVMEROSOS ... GESTVS. Compare *Am* II iv 29 'illa placet *gestu numerosaque bracchia* ducit', *AA* II 305 '*bracchia* saltantis, uocem mirare canentis', and Prop II xxii 5-6 'siue aliquis molli diducit candida *gestu* / bracchia, seu uarios incinit ore modos'. Heinsius thought GRESSVS (I^1PF^{3ul}) possible as well, citing Varro *LL* IX 5 '*pedes* male *ponere* atque imitari uatias ['bow-legged men'] coeperit', Martianus Capella IX 909 'licet pulchris rosea numeris ac libratis *passibus* moueretur', and Maximianus (6th century) *El* III 27 'suspensos ponere *gressus*'. But the strong manuscript authority for *gestus* and the parallels in Ovid mark it as clearly preferable to *gressus*.

33. PONERE. The verb seems strange, but Burman cited in its support Val Max VIII vii 7 'Roscius ... nullum umquam spectante populo *gestum*, nisi quem domi meditatus fuerat, *ponere* [*codd*: promere *E. Schulze*] ausus est'.

35-36. LAVDATAQVE VIRTVS / CRESCIT. For this commonplace of ancient literature see *Otto ars* 3 and compare *RA* 393 'nam iuuat et studium famae mihi creuit honore', *Tr* V xii 37-38 'denique non paruas animo dat gloria uires, / et fecunda facit pectora laudis amor', *EP* III ix 21 'scribentem iuuat ipse fauor minuitque laborem', Prop IV x 3, and Cic

172

Tusc I 4.

36. IMMENSVM GLORIA CALCAR HABET. The same metaphor at *Tr* V i 75-76 'denique nulla mihi captatur gloria, quaeque / ingeniis *stimulos subdere* fama solet', *EP* I v 57-58 'gloria uos *acuat*; uos, ut recitata probentur / carmina, Pieriis inuigilate choris', and Hor *Ep* II i 217-18 'uatibus addere *calcar* / ut studio maiore petant Helicona uirentem'.

Immensum seems rather strange; I have found no good parallel for it.

37. HIC MEA CVI RECITEM ... CARMINA. A constant complaint of Ovid in exile. Compare *Tr* III xiv 39-40 'nullus in hac terra, recitem si carmina, cuius / intellecturis auribus utar, adest', *Tr* IV i 89-90, and *Tr* V xii 53 'non liber hic ullus, non qui mihi commodet aurem'. Perhaps it is significant that Ovid does not complain in the present passage that he has no books available: certainly he must have had a substantial library at hand when he composed the *Ibis*.

38. BARBARVS HISTER. The same phrase in the same position (leaving space for the disyllable) at *EP* III iii 26 'et coit astrictis *barbarus Hister* aquis'.

Hister was the name of the lower course of the Danube (Pliny *NH* IV 79). Ovid uses the metrically convenient *Hister* fifteen times in the *Ex Ponto*, as against two instances only of *Danuuius* (IV ix 80 & x 58).

38. OBIT *Damsté* HABET *codd*. In support of *obit* Damsté cited x 22 'gentibus obliqua quas *obit* Hister aqua' (*Mnemosyne* XLVI 32). As Professor R. J. Tarrant points out, the only meaning that can be attached to *quasque alias gentes barbarus Hister habet* is 'the other people that live in the Danube'; he compares *Her* VI 135-36 'prodidit illa patrem; rapui de clade Thoanta. / deseruit Colchos; me mea Lemnos habet' and *Aen* VI 362 (Palinurus speaking) 'nunc me fluctus habet'. *EP* III ii 43-44 'nos ... quos procul a uobis Pontus et [*uar* barbarus] Hister habet', cited by Lenz in support of *habet*, is not a good parallel in view of the different subject (*Pontus et Hister* instead of *Hister* alone).

Lenz cited *Tr* II 230 'bellaque pro magno Caesare Caesar obit' for a variant *habet*; Professor Tarrant cites another instance of the corruption at *Met* I 551-52 'pes modo tam uelox pigris radicibus haeret, / ora cacumen obit'.

39. MATERIA = 'means' (*OLD materia* 8).

41. NEC VINVM NEC ME TENET ALEA FALLAX. The same statement at *EP* I v 45-46 'nec iuuat in lucem nimio marcescere uino, / nec tenet incertas alea blanda manus'. For Ovid's temperance, compare *EP* I x 30 'scis mihi quam solae paene bibantur aquae'.

Me tenet in the present passage should perhaps be translated 'holds my attention' (*OLD teneo* 22) rather than 'attracts' (Wheeler).

41. VINVM. For wine as a diversion from sorrow, compare Tib I ii 1 'Adde merum uinoque nouos compesce dolores' (with Smith's note) and Tib I v 37 'saepe ego temptaui curas depellere uino'.

42. TACITVM TEMPVS. Similar phrases at *AA* II 670 'iam ueniet *tacito* curua senecta pede', *Fast* VI 771 '*tacitis* ... senescimus annis', *Tr* III vii 35-36 'senectus / quae *strepitus passu non faciente* uenit', *Tr* IV vi 17 '*tacito* pede lapsa uetustas' and *Tr* IV x 27 '*tacito* passu labentibus annis'.

43. QVOD CVPEREM. At *EP* I viii 39-62 Ovid, having detailed the urban pleasures he has lost, speaks of his agricultural pursuits in Italy, and laments that this diversion is not available to him at Tomis. The two passages add personal meaning to his description at *Met* XIV 623-34 of Pomona's gardening and his prescription at *RA* 169-98 of agriculture as a diversion from an unhappy love-affair.

43. SI PER FERA BELLA LICERET. Compare *EP* II vii 69-70 'tempus in agrorum cultu consumere dulce est: / non patitur uerti barbarus hostis humum' and *EP* III viii 6 'hostis ab agricola uix sinit illa [*sc* loca] fodi'. At *Tr* III x 57-66 Ovid gives a vivid description of what could happen to the farmers of Tomis in a raid.

44. NOVATA = 'restored to fertility through ploughing'. Ovid more commonly uses *renouare*, as at *Tr* V xii 23-24 'fertilis, assiduo si non renouetur aratro, / nil nisi cum spinis gramen habebit ager', *Am* I iii 9, *Met* I 110 & XV 125, *Fast* I 159, and *Tr* IV vi 13.

45. RESTANT is not strictly logical, but a similar attraction of number is confirmed by metre at *Tr* I ii 1 'Di maris et caeli —quid enim nisi uota *supersunt*?'; RESTAT (*IP*) must therefore be rejected.

Similar confusions occur in the manuscripts at *Met* XIV 396 'nec quicquam antiqui [*Berolinensis Heinsii*: antiquum *codd plerique*] Pico nisi nomina *restant*' and *Tr* IV x 85 'si tamen extinctis aliquid nisi nomina *restant*'.

47. TV, CVI BIBITVR FELICIVS AONIVS FONS. For the image of the poet drinking from Hippocrene see Prop III iii 5-6 'paruaque tam magnis admoram fontibus ora, / unde pater sitiens Ennius ante bibit'. Both here and at II x 25 Propertius speaks of Hippocrene as the spring of epic poetry specifically.

47. FELICIVS. 'With happier result'; compare *Ibis* 559 'nec tibi, si quid amas, felicius Haemone [=*quam Haemoni*] cedat'.

47. AONIVS FONS. Platnauer (13) cites only four instances from the elegiac poets of hexameters ending in monosyllables: Prop II xxv 17 'amor, qui', *Am* II ix 47 'Cupido, est', the present passage, and *EP* IV ix 101 'quibus nos'. Ehwald and Levy compare *Met* V 573 'quae tibi causa fugae, cur sis, Arethusa, sacer *fons*'. The coincidence suggests that in both passages Ovid was recalling a line-ending from an earlier poet. Alternatively, Professor E. Fantham suggests to me that Ovid may here have deliberately created an awkward line-ending so as to mock himself and bear out his claim of waning inspiration.

47-50. Ovid returns to the subject of his poem's opening, Severus' poetry.

48. VTILITER ... CEDIT. Similar phrasing at *EP* II vii 19 '[iam liquet ...] obseruare deos ne quid mihi *cedat amice*'.

49. MERITO. 'With justification'; Severus' previous service to the Muses has brought him fame and not, as in Ovid's case, disaster.

50. HVC ALIQVOD CVRAE MITTE RECENTIS OPVS. A similar request at *EP* III v 29-30 (to Cotta Maximus) 'quod licet, ut uidear tecum magis esse, legenda [*Burman*: legendo *uel* loquendo *codd*] / saepe precor studii pignora mitte tui'.

50. CVRAE = 'poetic toil', as at *Tr* II 11-12 'hoc pretium *curae* [*fragmentum Treuirense (saec x)*: uitae *codd plerique*] uigilatorumque laborum / cepimus', *EP* I v 61 'cur ego sollicita poliam mea carmina *cura*?', and *EP* III ix 29. At xvi 39 and *Tr* II 1 the word means 'product of poetic toil'.

176

III. To An Unfaithful Friend

By the time Ovid wrote this poem, the letter of reproach was a genre familiar to him: each book of the *Tristia* (with the obvious exception of II) contains such a poem (I viii; III xi; IV ix; V viii), and in the *Ibis* Ovid had, by the extended treatment of a number of standard topics within the subject, created a poem of over six hundred lines.

Ovid begins the poem by stating that he has heard about his friend's faithlessness; he asks what possible excuse there might be for this behaviour (1-28). He then warns his friend that Fortune is changeable, and gives four examples of famous men who fell from prosperity (29-48). He ends the poem by stating once again that Fortune is undependable, and gives his own catastrophe as an instance; his friend should remember this, and moderate his behaviour accordingly (49-58).

The poem has points of contact with the earlier poems of reproach. *Tr* I viii is addressed to a friend who failed to visit Ovid after his disaster: he can scarcely believe his friend is human. In *Tr* III xi, Ovid asks his enemy why through his actions he makes his punishment even worse. *Tr* IV ix is a warning that if Ovid's enemy does not cease attacking him, he will through his poetry make his enemy's name infamous throughout the world. *Tr* V viii, the poem closest in theme to the present one, is a warning to his enemy that Fortune is changeable and Augustus merciful, so he and Ovid might one day change situations.

The *Ibis*, being primarily a catalogue of literary curses, stands somewhat apart from the other poems of reproach in structure as in size; yet the opening of the poem, in which Ovid describes his enemy's conduct and the ways he might respond, offers a number of parallels to the present poem.

1. CONQVERAR AN TACEAM. Kenney (*Nequitiae Poeta* 204-5), commenting on *AA* I 739 'conquerar an moneam', cites other instances of the same rhetorical device at *Aen* III 39 ' eloquar an sileam?' and *Met* IX 147 'conquerar an sileam?', as well as the present passage.

1. CONQVERAR. The choice of verb is significant: this poem is a rhetorical *conquestio* transferred to verse. Kenney cites Cicero's definition of *conquestio* at *Inu* I 106: 'conquestio est oratio auditorum misericordiam captans ... id locis communibus efficere oportebit, per quos Fortunae uis in omnes et hominum infirmitas ostenditur; qua oratione ... animus hominum ... ad misericordiam comparatur, cum in alieno malo suam infirmitatem considerabit'.

1. PONAM SINE NOMINE CRIMEN. 'Shall I put my accusation in my poem without naming you?'. The same sense of *ponere* at *Tr* I v 7 '*positis* pro nomine signis', *Tr* IV iv 7, and *EP* III vi 1-2 'Naso suo (*posuit* nomen quam paene!) sodali / mittit ab Euxinis hoc breue carmen aquis'.

2. QVI SIS. The boundary between adjectival *qui* and pronominal *quis* in Latin was not absolute; and just as one finds such forms as *quis clamor* (*Met* III 632), so it seems to have been Latin practice to use *qui* before forms of *esse* in indirect discourse, perhaps in order to avoid a double *s*-sound. Some instances of this from verse are *Ecl* I 18 'iste deus *qui sit* da, Tityre, nobis', *Ecl* II 19 'nec *qui sim* quaeris, Alexi', *Aen* III 608-9 '*qui sit* fari ... hortamur', *Met* XIV 841 'mihi nec *quae sis* dicere promptum est', *Met* XV 595 'is *qui sit* signo, non nomine dicam', *Fast* V 191 'ipse doce *quae sis*', *Ibis* 52 'teque breui *qui sis* dissimulare sinam', *Ibis* 61 '*qui sis* nondum quaerentibus edo', and *EP* III vi 57 'teque tegam, *qui sis*'. In some of these passages *quis* is found as a variant reading; given the ease of corruption, the rule should perhaps be made canonical, and such passages as *Met* I 248-49 '*quis sit* laturus in aras / tura' supplied with forms of *qui* even when, as in this instance, there is only weak manuscript support. (Professor R. J. Tarrant prefers, however, to retain *quis* at *Met* I 248, seeing a difference between expressions of identity [*qui sis ... dicam*] and of description [*sit* and *laturus* go closely together]).

The use of *qui* seems to have extended to past subjunctives of *esse* as well as present: compare *Met* XI 719 'qui [*uar* quis] foret ignorans'. For discussions see Löfstedt II 79-96 and Shackleton Bailey on *Att* III x 2 'possum obliuisci *qui fuerim, non sentire qui sim?*'.

In preclassical Latin *qui* is found for *quis* even in direct questions: *OLD qui* A4a cites Pl *Capt* 833 'qui uocat', Ter *Ph* 990 'qui nominat me', and Scipio minor V 19 Malcovati[3] 'qui spondet mille nummum'. The usage must have continued in spoken Latin, for it is found at Vitruvius VII 5 6 and Petronius 62 8.

3. NOMINE NON VTAR, NE COMMENDERE QVERELA. An interesting indication of the confidence Ovid felt in his poetry. In his earlier poems of reproach, Ovid had represented his not naming the person as an act of forbearance (*Tr* IV ix 1-4; *Ibis* 51-54).

3. COMMENDERE QVERELA. Oxymoron.

5. DVM MEA PVPPIS ERAT VALIDA FVNDATA CARINA. The common ancient metaphor of shipwreck also used of Ovid's exile at *Tr* I i 85-86, *Tr* II 99-102, *Tr* III iv 15-16 'dum tecum uixi, dum me leuis aura ferebat, / haec mea per placidas cumba cucurrit aquas', *Tr* V xii 50, and *EP* II iii 25-28.

7. CONTRAXIT VVLTVM. See at i 5 *trahis uultus* (p 149).

9-10 form a tricolon, where each phrase represents the same action in progressively more specific terms: (1) 'dissimulas etiam' (2) 'nec me uis nosse uideri' (3) 'quisque sit audito nomine Naso rogas'.

9. DISSIMVLAS. The same word in similar contexts at *Tr* I i 62 'dissimulare uelis, te liquet esse meum', *Tr* III vi 2, *Tr* IV iii 54, *Tr* IV iv 28, and *EP* I ii 146.

9. NEC ME VIS NOSSE VIDERI. 'You don't want others to think you know me'. Similar thought and language at *Tr* IV iii 51 'me miserum si turpe putas mihi nupta uideri!' and *EP* II iii 29-30 'cumque alii *nolint* etiam *me nosse uideri,* / uix duo proiecto tresue tulistis opem'.

10. QVISQVE SIT. QVIQVE SIT (*H^{ac}P*) could be defended, *sit* determining the form *qui*, even with the intervening enclitic, but given the prevalence of relative *quique* at line-beginnings in Ovid (compare xvi 9, 11, 15, 19 & 23) it seems better to take it as a trivial error.

11, 13, 15, 17. ILLE EGO. The same idiom to stir someone's memory at *Fast* III 505-6 '*illa ego sum* cui tu solitus promittere caelum: / ei mihi, pro caelo qualia dona fero' and *EP* I ii 129-32 '*ille ego sum* qui te colui, quem festa solebat / inter conuiuas mensa uidere tuos: / *ille ego qui* duxi uestros Hymenaeon ad ignes, / et cecini fausto carmina digna toro'. R. G. Austin, discussing the spurious proem to the *Aeneid* (*CQ* LX, n.s. XVIII [1968] 110-11), cites *Tr* V vii 55-56 '*ille ego* Romanus uates—ignoscite, Musae!— / Sarmatico cogor plurima more loqui', *Met* I 757-58 '*ille ego* liber, / ille ferox tacui', Statius *Sil* V v 38 & *Theb* IX 434, and Silius XI 177-82: 'It will be noticed ... that all these examples represent the new situation as a fall from grace'.

12. AMICITIA. Ovid allows pentasyllabic words to end the pentameter only in the poetry of exile (Platnauer 17). There are eight such words in the *Tristia*, and four in the *Ex Ponto*: I ii 68 *patrocinium*, II ix 20 *Ericthonius*, this passage, and xiii 44 *amicitiae* (Platnauer 17; Riese vii). This distribution contrasts with Ovid's increasing fondness in the *Ex Ponto* for trisyllabic and quadrisyllabic endings, for which see at ix 26 *tegeret* and ii 10 *Alcinoo*.

The later *Heroides* have two pentasyllabic pentameter-endings, XVI 290 *pudicitiae* and XVII 16 *superciliis*.

13-14. ILLE EGO QVI PRIMVS TVA SERIA NOSSE SOLEBAM, / ET TIBI IVCVNDIS PRIMVS ADESSE IOCIS. The same joining of *seria* and *ioci* (or *lusus*) at *Tr* I viii 31-32, *EP* I ix 9-10, *EP* II iv 9-10 '*seria* multa mihi tecum conlata recordor, / nec data *iucundis* tempora pauca *iocis*', and *EP* II x 41-42. It is found in prose and early Latin: Luck at *Tr* I viii 31-32 cites Cic *Fin* II 85 'at quicum *ioca, seria, ut dicitur,* quicum arcana, quicum occulta omnia? tecum, optime', Pliny *Ep* II xiii 5 'cum hoc *seria,* cum hoc *iocos* miscui', Pliny *Ep* IV xvii 5 'nihil a me ille secretum, non *ioculare,* non *serium,* non triste, non laetum', and Ennius *Ann* 239-40 Vahlen[3] 'cui res audacter magnas paruasque iocumque / eloqueretur'.

15. CONVICTOR. The word belongs properly to prose, the only other occurrences in verse being two passages in Horace's *Satires*: I iv 96 'me ... *conuictore* usus amicoque' & I vi 47 'quia sim tibi, Maecenas, *conuictor'*. *Conuictus* is similarly found in verse twice only, in Ovid's poetry of exile (*Tr* I viii 29-30 '*conuictu* causisque ualentibus ... temporis et longi iunctus amore tibi' & *EP* II x 9-10 'quam [*sc* curam] tu uel longi debes *conuictibus* aeui, / uel mea quod coniunx non aliena tibi est').

15. DENSOQVE. 'Frequent, often recurring'. This sense of *densus* is not found elsewhere in Ovid, but compare Virgil *G* IV 347 '*densos* diuum numerabat amores', Statius *Theb* VI 421, and Juvenal IX 35-37 'quamuis ... blandae assidue *densaeque* tabellae / sollicitent'. The closest parallel for the poetic singular cited by *OLD densus* 3a is Martial IX lxxxvii 1-2 'Septem post calices Opimiani / *denso* cum iaceam triente[19] blaesus'.

15. DOMESTICVS. Apparently the only instance of the substantive in verse. The word is common enough in prose, and formed part of the spoken language, for it is found in reported speech at Petronius 45 6.

17. QVEM *Leidensis Heinsii* QVI *codd plerique*. *Qui* cannot be connected with *nescis*, and so is without antecedent. The scribe was probably influenced by 11, 13, and 15, in which *ille ego* is completed by a nominative clause.

For *quem ... an uiuam* compare *EP* III vi 57 '*teque* tegam, *qui sis'*.

17. VIVAM. Heinsius' VIVAT is unnecessary: the assimilation of person seems reasonable enough in view of such passages as *EP* I ii 129-31 'ille ego sum qui te *colui* ... ille ego qui *duxi* uestros Hymenaeon ad ignes'.

18. SVBIT *Heinsius* FVIT *codd*. The preceding *nescis* requires a verb with present meaning; and *fuit* seems impossible to construe as a true perfect (with present result). Heinsius' *subit* seems an elegant solution: certain manuscripts offer the same corruption of *subit* to *fuit* at *Met* IX 93-94 'lux *subit*, et

181

primo feriente cacumina sole / discedunt iuuenes' and *Met* XIV 827-28 'pulchra *subit* facies et puluinaribus altis / dignior'.

19-20. SIVE FVI NVMQVAM CARVS, SIMVLASSE FATERIS; / SEV NON FINGEBAS, INVENIERE LEVIS. For a similar opposition (either alternative being discreditable), see *Met* IX 23-24 'nam, quo te iactas, Alcmena nate, creatum, / Iuppiter aut falsus pater est aut crimine uerus'.

21. AVT. 'Otherwise'. For the use of *aut* as a disjunctive adverb rather than a conjunction compare xii 3 'aut ego non alium prius hoc dignarer honore' and the passages there cited. Here, as at xii 3, the idiom has been misunderstood by scribes, with such resulting variants in late manuscripts as EIA ('uterque Medonii pro diuersa lectione'; accepted by Heinsius) and DIC (*Gothanus II 121*; printed by Burman).

21. IRAM. 'Cause for anger'. This seems to be the only instance of the meaning, *ira* not being found even as a predicative dative; but compare the use of *laudes* to mean 'acts deserving praise', as at viii 87 'tuas ... laudes ... recentes'.

23. QVOD TE NVNC CRIMEN SIMILEM seems to be the correct reading; the line connects with the *an crimen ...* of 24. QVAE TE CONSIMILEM RES NVNC (*FIL*) looks like a rewriting of the line, perhaps following the loss of *crimen* by haplography (*crim͞similē*). There seems no good reason why Ovid would have used the emphatic *consimilem* instead of the more usual *similem*.

25. SI ... OPEM NVLLAM ... FEREBAS. 'If you had no intention of assisting me'—the inceptive or conative imperfect (Woodcock 200). Similar phrasing at *Tr* I viii 9-10 'haec ego uaticinor, quia sum deceptus ab illo / *laturum* misero quem mihi rebar *opem*' and *EP* II vii 46 'et nihil inueni quod mihi *ferret opem*'.

25. REBVS ... FACTISQVE. 'Through financial help or action on my behalf'. Ovid does not use this sense of *res* elsewhere in his poetry.

26. VERBIS ... TRIBVS. 'A few words'. For the idiom

Williams cites Plautus *Mil* 1020 '"breuin an longinquo sermoni?" "tribu' uerbis"' and *Trin* 963 'adgrediundust hic homo mi astu.—heus, Pax, te tribu' uerbis uolo'; from comedy, *OLD tres* b cites Ter *Ph* 638. From the classical period compare Sen *Apocol* 11 3 'ad summam, tria uerba cito dicat, et seruum me ducat', Sen *Ep* 40 9, and Quint IX iv 84 'haec omnia in tribus uerbis'; Camps sees *tres* as having the same indefinite meaning at Prop II xiii 25-26 'sat mea sit magno [*Phillimore*: sit magna *uel* sat magna est *codd*] si tres sint pompa libelli / quos ego Persephonae maxima dona feram'.

27. SED ET was the standard reading until Ehwald's defence (*KB* 63) of SVBITO, the reading of (*B¹*) and C.

Ehwald's reasoning was that *sed et* would indicate that the news of his friend's slandering him was additional information, and that Ovid already knew something of his friend's behaviour. But this is precisely the case: Ovid has just finished saying that his friend has done nothing to help him (9-10), and now he gives the additional information that his friend is even working against him. Ehwald supported the asyndeton that *subito* creates by quoting *Met* XV 359-60 'haud equidem credo: sparsae quoque membra uenenis / exercere artes Scythides memorantur easdem', where in fact *quoque* seems a convincing parallel to *sed et*.

27. INSVLTARE IACENTI. 'Torment in my misery'. Ovid plays on the literal meanings of *iacere* and *in-saltare*; for the latter, see *Aen* XII 338-39 'caesis / hostibus insultans'. Ovid uses *insultare* in only three other passages. All are from the poems of exile, and all are about the ill-treatment accorded Ovid: *Tr* II 571 'nec mihi credibile est quemquam *insultasse iacenti*', *Tr* III xi 1, and *Tr* V viii 3-4 'curue / casibus insultas quos potes ipse pati?'.

29. A DEMENS. *A* indicates a certain amount of sympathy with the person addressed, as can be seen from *Tr* V x 51-52 'quid loquor, *a demens*? ipsam quoque perdere uitam, / Caesaris offenso numine, dignus eram' and *Ecl* II 60-61 'quem fugis, *a demens*? habitarunt di quoque siluas / Dardaniusque Paris'. *O* (*M¹FILT*) would indicate rather less sympathy: compare *Met* III 640-41 'dextera Naxos erat:

183

dextra mihi lintea danti / "quid facis, *o demens*? quis te furor"
inquit "Acoete?"'.

29. RECEDAT (*TM²*) is no doubt a scribal conjecture, but a
correct one: 'Why, in case disaster should strike ...'. Most
manuscripts have RECEDIT.

31. ORBE probably means 'wheel'; compare Tib I v 70
'uersatur celeri Fors leuis orbe *rotae*' and *Cons ad Liuiam* 51-52
(quoted in the next note). However, Professor E. Fantham
points out to me that it could also mean 'sphere': she cites
Pacuvius 366-67 Ribbeck² (*Rhet Her* II 36) 'Fortunam
insanam esse et caecam et brutam perhibent philosophi, /
saxoque instare in *globoso* praedicant *uolubilei*'. Smith at Tib I
v 70 gives numerous instances of both images.

32. QVEM, found in Heinsius' *fragmentum Boxhornianum*
(=Leid. Bibl. Publ. 180 G), must be right as against the
QVAE of the other manuscripts; if a definition is to be given
after the preceding 'haec dea non stabili quam sit leuis orbe
fatetur', it should be a definition of the wheel, not the
goddess. But the resulting *quem summum dubio* seems very
awkwardly phrased, and further emendation is probably
needed.

The obvious solution would be to read 'quem summo [*C* in
fact reads *summo*] *dubium* sub pede semper habet'. This
would give *orbis* a standard epithet, as at *Tr* V viii 7-8 'nec
metuis *dubio* Fortunae stantis in *orbe* / numen' and *Cons ad
Liuiam* 51-52 'nempe per hos etiam Fortunae iniuria mores /
regnat et *incerta* est hic quoque nixa *rota*'. In support of the
rather more difficult *summo ... pede* (='toes') Professor R. J.
Tarrant cites Sen *Suas* II 17 'insistens *summis digitis* ['toes']—
sic enim solebat quo grandior fieret', Sen *Tro* 1090-91 'in
cacumine / erecta *summos* [*uar* summo] turba librauit *pedes*',
and *Met* IV 562 'aequora destringunt *summis* Ismenides *alis*';
compare as well *Met* IX 342-43 'in adludentibus undis /
summa pedum taloque tenus uestigia tingit'.

A second solution might be to read 'quem *dubio summum* sub
pede semper habet'; the transfer of *dubius* from *orbis* to *pes*
seems acceptable enough, and *Met* IV 134-36 'oraque buxo /
pallidiora gerens exhorruit aequoris instar, / quod tremit

exigua cum summum stringitur aura' offers a good parallel to *summum*.

The image of Fortune standing on her wheel occurs elsewhere in Ovid's poems of exile at *Tr* V viii 7-8 (quoted above) and *EP* II iii 55-56 'scilicet indignum, iuuenis carissime, ducis / te fieri comitem stantis in orbe deae'.

33. QVOLIBET EST FOLIO ... INCERTIOR. For the proverb, see Otto *folium* 1; and from Ovid compare *Am* II xvi 45-46 'uerba puellarum, foliis leuiora caducis, / inrita qua uisum est uentus et unda ferunt', *Her* V 109-10 'tu leuior foliis tum cum sine pondere suci / mobilibus uentis arida facta uolant', and *Fast* III 481-82 (Ariadne speaking) 'Bacche leuis leuiorque tuis quae tempora cingunt / frondibus'.

33. QVAVIS INCERTIOR AVRA. Compare *Her* VI 109-10 'mobilis Aesonide uernaque incertior aura, / cur tua polliciti pondere uerba carent?'. Otto (*uentus* 1) cites as well Prop II v 11-13 'non ita Carpathiae uariant Aquilonibus undae, / nec dubio nubes uertitur atra Noto, / quam facile irati uerbo mutantur amantes', *Her* XVIII 185-86 (Leander to Hero) 'cumque minus firmum nil sit quam uentus et unda, / in uentis et aqua spes mea semper erit?', and Calpurnius *Ecl* III 10 'mobilior uentis o femina!'.

The *folium* and *uentus* images of the present line are found together at Prop II ix 33-35 'non sic incerto mutantur flamine Syrtes, / nec folia hiberno tam tremefacta Noto, / quam cito feminea non constat foedus in ira'.

34. PAR ILLI = *par illius leuitati*. Similar compressions at vi 40 'mollior est animo femina nulla tuo' and commonly.

37-38. Ovid gives four instances of unexpected catastrophe, two from Greek history, two from Roman; the greater importance of the Roman examples is emphasized by their position and by the doubling of the space allotted to each example from two lines to four. There is a similar transition at Prop II vi 19-20 'cur exempla petam Graium? tu criminis auctor / nutritus duro, Romule, lacte lupae'.

The Greek examples may have been a traditional pairing: Croesus and Dionysius are mentioned together at Lucian

Gall 23 as notable instances of personal catastrophe.

37. OPVLENTIA CROESI. Croesus as the archetype of wealth also at *Tr* III vii 41-42 'nempe dat ... Fortuna rapitque, / Irus et est subito qui modo Croesus erat'.

The story of Croesus' downfall and the subsequent sparing of his life by Cyrus is taken from Herodotus I 86-88.

It is clear from his poetry that Ovid had a good knowledge of at least the first book of Herodotus:

(1) *Met* III 135-37 'sed scilicet ultima semper / expectanda dies homini est, dicique beatus / ante obitum nemo supremaque funera debet' may have been drawn from Solon's advice to Croesus at Herodotus I 32 7: 'εἰ δὲ πρὸς τούτοισι [if in addition to having prosperity while alive] ἔτι τελευτήσει τὸν βίον εὖ, οὗτος ἐκεῖνος τὸν σὺ ζητέεις, [ὁ *add Stein*] ὄλβιος κεκλῆσθαι ἄξιός ἐστι· πρὶν δ' ἂν τελευτήσῃ, ἐπισχεῖν μηδὲ καλέειν κω ὄλβιον, ἀλλ' εὐτυχέα'.

(2) At *Fast* II 79-118 Ovid tells the story of Arion found at Herodotus I 23-24.

(3) At *Fast* II 663-66 there occurs the clearest instance of borrowing: Ovid uses the story of the border dispute between Sparta and Argos (Herodotus I 82) in the course of his discussion of the god Terminus: 'si tu signasses olim Thyreatida terram, / corpora non leto missa trecenta forent, / nec foret Othryades congestis lectus [*Barth*: tectus *codd*] in armis. / o quantum patriae sanguinis ille dedit!'.

37. AVDITA EST CVI NON. Compare *Met* XV 319-20 'cui non *audita est* obscenae Salmacis undae / Aethiopesque lacus?'.

38. NEMPE TAMEN VITAM CAPTVS AB HOSTE TVLIT. 'Even so, it is undeniable that he became a prisoner, and received his life as a gift from his enemy'. *Vitam ferre* also at *EP* II i 45 (from a description of Germanicus' triumph of AD 12) 'maxima pars horum *uitam* ueniamque *tulerunt*'.

39. ILLE ... FORMIDATVS. Equivalent to *ille* with a defining *qui*-clause: 'The famous man who had once been feared ...'. Ovid is referring to Dionysius II, the student of Plato, who was expelled from Syracuse in 344 and became a schoolmaster in Corinth. Valerius Maximus (VI ix ext 6) also gives Dionysius as an example of unexpected disaster, and Plutarch (*Timoleon* 14) cites him as an example of the operations of Fortune. For an account of Dionysius' life at Corinth, see Justinus XXI v. There was a Greek proverb 'Διονύσιος ἐν Κορίνθῳ' (Cic *Att* IX ix 1; Quintilian VIII vi 52), apparently referring to his continued lust for power: 'Dionysius ... Syracusis expulsus Corinthi pueros docebat: usque eo imperio carere non poterat' (Cic *Tusc* III 27). Discussions of the proverb at Otto *Dionysius* and Shackleton Bailey on *Att* IX ix 1.

39. SYRACOSIA ... IN VRBE. Restored by Heinsius from the manuscripts' unmetrical SYRACVSIA, as at *Fast* VI 277. The same confusion between Συρακόσιος and Συρακούσιος is found in the manuscripts of Pindar (*Ol* I 23), the Attic form supplanting the original Doric. The same corruption is found in some ninth-century manuscripts of Virgil at *Ecl* VI 1 'Prima Syracosio dignata est ludere uersu' and in the Veronese scholia, and in the manuscripts of Claudian *carm min* LI 6 (Housman 1273).

40. HVMILI ... ARTE. For the low social position of the schoolmaster in antiquity, see Bonner 146-62, and compare especially Juvenal VII 197-98 'si Fortuna uolet, fies de rhetore consul; / si uolet haec eadem, fiet de consule rhetor' and Pliny *Ep* IV xi 1 'nunc eo decidit ut exul de senatore, rhetor de oratore fieret'.

41. MAGNO MAIVS. 'Greater than (Pompey) the Great'. Even in the letters of Cicero, Pompey is occasionally called *Magnus* without further identification (*Att* I xvi 12). Other plays on the name at *Fast* I 603-4 'Magne, tuum nomen rerum est mensura tuarum; / sed qui te uicit nomine maior erat' and Lucan I 135 'stat magni nominis umbra', where Getty cites Velleius II 1 4 'Pompeium magni nominis uirum'.

42. CLIENTIS OPEM. After the final defeat at Pharsalus, Pompey fled to Egypt and sought the protection of Ptolemy XIII (Caesar *BC* III 103, Plutarch *Pomp* 77).

Pompey similarly treated as the victim of Fortune at Cic *Tusc*

I 86 and through much of Lucan VII-VIII; compare as well *Anth Lat* Riese 401 'Quam late uestros duxit Fortuna triumphos, / tam late sparsit funera, Magne, tua'.

Compare as well *Anth Lat* 415 39-40 'spes Magnum profugum toto discurrere in orbe / iusserat et pueri regis adire pedes'; the distich follows a description of the hardships undergone by Marius.

44. The line is omitted by B^1 and C; other manuscripts offer (with minor variations) INDIGVS EFFECTVS OMNIBVS IPSE MAGIS or ACHILLAS PHARIVS ABSTVLIT ENSE CAPVT, a line apparently devised with the aid of Juvenal X 285-86 'Fortuna ... uicto *caput abstulit*' and Lucan VIII 545-46 'ullusne in cladibus istis / est locus Aegypto *Phariusque* admittitur *ensis*?', both passages concerned with Pompey's murder by Achillas. Clearly a line of the poem was lost in transmission.

Heinsius and Bentley felt that the entire distich should be deleted; but 43 seems acceptable enough, and it is appropriate that the description of Pompey's downfall be balanced with the four-line mention of Marius that follows. It would be strange if Pompey's sensational murder were overlooked, as this was regarded by the poets as the ultimate reversal of his fortunes: compare Manilius IV 50-55, Juvenal X 283-86 (which is joined to a mention of Marius' reversal) and *Anth Lat* 401-3 Riese.

45. ILLE goes with Marius two lines on—'the famous Marius'.

45. IVGVRTHINO ... CIMBROQVE TRIVMPHO. Marius rose to prominence in the Jugurthine war, celebrating his triumph in 104; in 101 his defeat in the Po valley of the Cimbri, a Germanic tribe originally from Jutland, ended a twelve-year military threat to Rome.

47. IN CAENO LATVIT MARIVS. In 88 Sulla, whose command against Mithridates had been transferred to Marius by a special law, marched on Rome and induced the Senate to name Marius an outlaw; Marius was forced to escape to Africa, at one point on the route hiding in the marshes of Minturnae. This ordeal is mentioned by the poets who deal with Marius, but they consider that he reached the low point of his fortunes when he arrived at Carthage. Compare Manilius IV 47-49, Juvenal X 276-77 'exilium et carcer Minturnarumque paludes / et mendicatus uicta Carthagine panis' and *Anth Lat* 415 33-38 Riese.

47. LATVIT MARIVS *M* IACVIT MARIVS *H* MARIVS LATVIT *L* MARIVS IACVIT *BCFIT*. *Iacere* and *latere* could each be corrupted to the other with ease: such corruptions occur in certain manuscripts at *Met* I 338 and *Fast* II 244 (*iacere* corrupted to *latere*) and *Fast* II 467, II 587 & III 265 (*latere* corrupted to *iacere*). Although it is weakly attested, *latuit* should be read here in view of the use of *abdere* at Velleius II xix 2 'paludem Maricae, in quam se fugiens consectantis Sullae equites *abdiderat*' and Lucan II 70 'exul limosa Marius caput *abdidit* ulua', and of κρύπτειν at Plutarch *Marius* 37 5: *latere* is often virtually a passive form of *abdere*.

Marius latuit looks like a normalization of word order from the emphatic *latuit Marius*.

47. CANNAQVE PALVSTRI. *Canna palustris* is a standard feature of Ovid's marshes; see *AA* I 554, *RA* 142, and *Met* IV 298 & VIII 337. At *RA* 142 Henderson comments 'Ovid probably means the plant called in this country [Scotland] Reed (*Phragmites communis*, a grass), which the Italians call *canna di palude*; smaller than *harundo* (*Arundo donax*, the Greek κάννα and Italian canna), it nevertheless often reaches a height of 6 or 7 feet'.

48. MVLTA PVDENDA. The entire sequence of events during Marius' flight to Africa.

50. FACIT *R. J. Tarrant*. For *fidem facere* ('induce belief') compare *Met* VI 565-66 'dat gemitus fictos commentaque funera narrat, / et lacrimae *fecere fidem*' and Caesar *BC* II 37 1 'nuntiabantur haec eadem Curioni, sed aliquamdiu *fides fieri* non poterat: tantam habebat suarum rerum fiduciam'. Ehwald (*KB* 63) defends FERET (*BC*), quoting *Aen* X 792 'si qua *fidem* tanto est operi *latura* uetustas', but the true meaning of this line is 'if antiquity can ever win belief for a deed so grand' (Jackson Knight); the idiom cannot be fitted into the present passage with acceptable meaning. HABET, the reading of most manuscripts, does not account for FERET, but is in itself acceptable enough; compare *Her* XVI 59-60 'ecce pedum pulsu uisa est mihi terra moueri— / uera loquar ueri [*Heinsius*: uero *codd*] uix *habitura fidem*' and Cic *Flac* 21 'sed fuerint incorruptae litterae domi; nunc uero quam *habere* auctoritatem aut quam *fidem* possunt?'.

51. SI QVIS MIHI DICERET. Compare *Tr* IV viii 43-44 'hoc mihi si Delphi Dodonaque diceret ipsa, / esse uideretur uanus uterque locus'.

52. GETE is read from the manuscripts by Heinsius; the form is the same as at *Met* X 608 'Hippomene uicto', *Fast* IV 593 'uictore Gyge', *EP* II iv 22 'in Aeacide Nestorideque', and *EP* I viii 6 'dura pharetrato bella mouente Gete [*uar* Geta]'. All editors but Heinsius print GETAE, but this is contrary to Ovid's usage: compare (to take only a few instances) *Ibis* 637 '*Sarmaticas* inter *Geticasque sagittas*', *EP* I i 79 'inque locum *Scythico* uacuum mutabor ab *arcu*', and *EP* III v 45 'ipse quidem *Getico* peream uiolatus ab *arcu*'. The only apparent exceptions to the rule I have found are *Tr* IV i 21 'Sinti [*Ehwald*: inter *codd* Sintae *Iac. Gronouius*] nec militis ensem', where the compound expression alters matters somewhat, and *Fast* V 580 '*Parthi* [*uar* Parthis] signa retenta *manu*', where *Partha* should probably be read; compare *Fast* VI 244 '*Mauras* pertimuere *manus* [*codd*: minas *Alton*]' and *EP* I iii 59-60 'altera Bistonias pars est sensura sarisas, / altera *Sarmatica* spicula missa *manu*'.

Getes is also used as an adjective at xiii 18 'paene poeta Getes'.

53. I BIBE ... ANTICYRA. A hendiadys for 'Go drink all the mind-purging hellebore that grows in Anticyra'.

53. PVRGANTES ... SVCOS. For discussions of *elleborus* see Theophrastus *HP* IX 10, Pliny *NH* XXV 47-61, and Aulus Gellius XVII xv. There were two varieties of the plant, black and white (from the colour of their roots): the former was a laxative, the latter induced vomiting and was thought to sharpen the intellect; compare Val Max VIII vii ext 5, Pliny

190

NH XXV 52, Martianus Capella IV 327, and the other passages cited by Brink at Hor *AP* 300.

54. ANTICYRA. Three places of this name are known from ancient sources; it is not known which of them Ovid had in mind. One was a city in Locris on the north side of the entrance to the Corinthian Gulf; the second was a city near Mount Oeta (Strabo IX v 10), and the third an island of uncertain location (Pliny *NH* XXV 52). It is possible that Hor *AP* 300 'tribus Anticyris caput insanabile' should be taken to mean that all three places were famous for hellebore, but ps-Acron glosses *tribus Anticyris* as 'tribus ... potionibus [*Keller*: potus *codd*] ... aut multo elleboro', which Brink accepts, citing Hor *Sat* II iii 82-83 'danda est ellebori multo pars maxima auaris; / nescio an Anticyram ratio illis destinet omnem' and Persius IV 16 'Anticyras ... sorbere meracas' for the metonymy, and Petronius 88 4 'Chrysippus, ut ad inuentionem sufficeret, ter elleboro animum detersit' for the number. The last two places at least seem to have been known for their hellebore; compare Pliny *NH* XXV 49 'plurimum autem nascitur in Oete monte et optimum uno eius loco circa Pyram' and XXV 52 'Drusum quoque apud nos ... constat hoc medicamento liberatum comitiali morbo ['epilepsy'] in Anticyra insula'.

57. TV QVOQVE FAC TIMEAS. That is, his friend should start to behave better towards him. For a similar exhortation at the end of a poem of reproach, see *Tr* I viii 49-50 'effice peccati ne sim memor huius, et illo / officium laudem quo queror ore tuum'; even in the *Ibis* there is a veiled offer of reconciliation: 'et neque nomen in hoc nec dicam facta libello, / teque breui qui sis dissimulare sinam. / postmodo, *si perges*, in te mihi liber iambus / tincta Lycambeo sanguine tela dabit' (51-54).

58. DVM LOQVERIS. Compare *Am* I xi 15 'dum loquor, hora fugit' and Hor *Carm* I xi 7-8 'dum loquimur, fugerit inuida / aetas'; Nisbet and Hubbard cite *ad loc* Persius V 153 and Petronius 99 3, noting that the *sententia* is not found before Horace.

191

IV. To Sextus Pompeius

In this second poem addressed to Sextus Pompeius, Ovid
celebrates the news that Pompeius is to be *consul ordinarius* in
the following year. As Pompeius was consul in 14, Ovid
probably wrote the poem shortly after the election of
magistrates in 13.

Poems iv and v form a pair, the first being an account of
Ovid's reaction on learning of Pompeius' election, the second
being a letter to the new consul. Both poems have points of
contact with poem ix, a letter of congratulation sent to
Graecinus on his becoming suffect consul.

The poem begins with general reflections that no sadness is
absolute, which prepare for the description of how the news
came to Ovid of Pompeius' election (1-20). He pictures to
himself the ceremonies that will take place (21-42), and ends
with the hope that in the midst of the festivities Pompeius
will still be able to remember him (43-50).

1-6. In these lines Ovid reverses the usual ancient sentiment
that no pleasure is unalloyed. Compare Hor *Carm* II x 17-18
'non, si male nunc, et olim / sic erit'. For the more usual
thought, see *Met* VII 453-54 'nulla est sincera uoluptas, /
sollicitique aliquid laetis interuenit' and *Fast* VI 463
'interdum miscentur tristia laetis'.

1. AVSTRALIBVS VMIDA NIMBIS. An image used
elsewhere by Ovid as a metaphor of his unhappiness: see *Tr* I
iii 13 'hanc animo nubem dolor ipse remouit', *Tr* V v 22 'pars
uitae tristi cetera nube uacet', and *EP* II i 5-6 'tandem aliquid
pulsa curarum nube serenum ['cloudless'] uidi'.

1. VMIDA. For the dampness of the south wind, compare
Met I 65-66 'contraria tellus / nubibus assiduis pluuiaque
madescit ab Austro'.

2. NON INTERMISSIS ... AQVIS. *Non intermissis* in the
same metrical position at *EP* I iv 16 'non intermissis

cursibus ibit equus'; *intermissus* used of bad weather at *Tr* II 149-51 'uentis agitantibus aera [*uar* aequora] non est / aequalis rabies continuusque furor, / sed modo subsidunt *intermissique* silescunt'.

7. DOMO PATRIAQVE CARENS OCVLISQVE MEORVM. Similar phrasing at *Tr* III vii 45 'cum caream patria uobisque domoque', *Tr* III xi 15-16 'quod coniuge cara, / quod patria careo pignoribusque meis', *Tr* V v 19 (of his wife) 'illa domo nataque sua patriaque fruatur', *Tr* I v 83, *Tr* IV vi 19, *Tr* IV ix 12, *Tr* V x 47, *EP* I iii 47, and *EP* II ix 79.

7. OCVLISQVE MEORVM. Compare *Tr* V iv 27-30 'nec patriam magis ille suam desiderat ... quam uultus *oculosque* tuos, o dulcior illo / melle quod in ceris Attica ponit apis'. *Oculisque meorum* seems to mean 'regards des miens' (André) rather than 'the sight of my own' (Wheeler); compare *Aen* XI 800-1 'oculosque tulere / cuncti ad reginam', *Met* VII 256 'et monet arcanis oculos remouere profanos', Persius V 33 'permisit sparsisse oculos ['to look where I chose']', and from prose Cic *Fam* IX ii 2 'ut uitemus oculos hominum'.

9. VVLTVM DIFFVNDERE. The action opposite to *trahis uultus* (i 5); compare *Met* XIV 272 'diffudit uultus' and from prose Sen *Ep* 106 5 'nisi dubitas an uultum nobis mutent, an frontem astringant, an *faciem diffundant*'. It is probably from this expression that *diffundere* acquired the extended sense of 'mentally relax' (*OLD diffundo* 5), for which compare *Met* IV 766 'diffudere animos', *Met* III 318 'Iouem ... diffusum nectare', and *AA* I 218 'diffundetque animos omnibus ista dies'.

9. CAVSAM. CAVSA (*BCT*) is grammatical enough, but corruption from *qua ... causam* to *qua ... causa* is more likely than the inverse.

The construction of the sentence is rather complex: Ovid's normal practice would be to employ an objective genitive with *causa*.

10. POSSIM *BCMHIT* POSSEM *L* POSSVM *F*. The clause is in primary tense sequence following the true perfect *inueni*, which represents the present result of a past action.

Compare *fecit ... minuant* in 5-6.

10. NEC MEMINISSE = *et obliuisci. Nec (non) meminisse* is metrically useful for filling the second hemistich of the pentameter up to the disyllable; so used at vi 50 'arguat ingratum non meminisse sui', *Tr* IV iv 40 & V xiii 18, and *EP* II iv 6.

11. SOLVS *BC.* TRISTIS, the reading of the other six manuscripts, is tempting, as being the less neutral of the two adjectives, and was accepted without question by Heinsius and Burman. If it is accepted, one could argue that Ovid refers back to the word at 21 'dilapsis ... curis'. But *solus* is shown to be correct by the passage Ovid is here imitating, Virgil *G* I 388-89 'tum cornix plena pluuiam uocat improba uoce / et *sola* in sicca secum *spatiatur harena*'. *Solus* was lost through haplography ('fulua solus': the elongated 's' form common in manuscripts would have facilitated the error) and *tristis* interpolated to restore the metre. Ehwald believed (*KB* 63) that the error arose from *tristis* having been written above *solus* in the archetype, but there is no reason to accept this, since the one could not stand as a gloss for the other.

11. SPATIARER HARENA. The phrase is taken from Virgil *G* I 388-89 (quoted in the previous note); Ovid imitates the passage again at *Met* II 572-73 'lentis / passibus, ut soleo, summa *spatiarer harena*'.

12. VISA EST A TERGO PENNA DEDISSE SONVM. 'I thought I heard a wing rustle behind me'. A similar advent of an unseen deity at *Met* III 96-98 'uox subito audita est; neque erat cognoscere promptum / unde, sed audita est: "quid, Agenore nate, peremptum / serpentem spectas? et tu spectabere serpens"'. Compare as well *Met* V 294-98 'Musa loquebatur: pennae sonuere per auras, / uoxque salutantum ramis ueniebat ab altis. / suspicit et linguae quaerit tam certa loquentes / unde sonent hominemque putat Ioue nata locutum; / ales erat'.

12. PENNA *BMFHILT* PINNA *C. Pinna* and *penna*, perhaps from different roots, were confused even in antiquity. The ancient manuscripts of Virgil offer *pinna* as the spelling even for the meaning 'wing', but Quintilian clearly took *penna* as the correct spelling for this sense: 'quare ['therefore'] discat puer ... quae cum quibus cognatio; nec miretur cur ... a pinno quod est acutum [*sc* fiat] securis utrimque habens aciem *bipennis*, ne illorum sequatur errorem qui, quia a pennis duabus hoc esse nomen existimant, pennas auium dici uolunt'. (I iv 12).

13. NEQVE ERAT *CMHL* NEC ERAT *BFIT*. Virgil had a very strong preference for *neque* before words starting with a vowel, but Ovid did not follow this rule: compare *Met* I 101 'nec ullis', 132 'nec adhuc', 223 'nec erit', 306 'nec ablato', and 322 'nec amantior'. However, it seems better to accept *neque* as the true reading in view of the good manuscript support and the parallel at *Met* III 96-97 'uox subita audita est (neque [*uar* nec] erat cognoscere promptum / unde, sed audita est)'.

13. NEQVE ERAT CORPVS. 'But there was no body'. *Neque* (*nec*) represents *sed ... non* as well as *et ... non*.

It is one of Ovid's favourite devices to describe the aspect of gods when they appear to him, as at *Am* III i 7-14 (Elegy and Tragedy), *Fast* I 95-100 (Janus), *Fast* III 171-72 (Mars), *Fast* V 194 (Flora), *Fast* V 637-38 (Tiber), and *EP* III iii 13-20 (Amor). The only other passage where Ovid says he did not see the god is *Fast* VI 251-54, but Vesta had no traditional appearance that Ovid could make use of: compare *Fast* VI 298 'effigiem nullam Vesta ... habet'.

The reason that Ovid did not describe Fama was that the picture of Fama as a winged monster which Virgil had made standard (*Aen* IV 174-88) could not easily be integrated into the poem. The only description of Fama in Ovid is at *Met* IX 137-39 'Fama loquax praecessit ad aures, / Deianira, tuas, quae ueris addere falsa / gaudet, et e minima sua per mendacia crescit'. At *Met* XII 39-63 there is a memorable description of Fama's dwelling-place. Fama is also personified (but with no descriptions) at *EP* II i 19-20 & II ix 3.

16. PER IMMENSAS AERE LAPSA VIAS. Similar phrasing at *EP* III iii 77-78 (Amor speaking) 'ut tamen aspicerem consolarerque iacentem, / *lapsa per immensas est mea penna* *uias'*.

17. QVO NON TIBI CARIOR ALTER. Compare *Tr* III vi 3 'nec te mihi carior alter', *Tr* IV vi 46 'qua nulla mihi carior, uxor', and *EP* II viii 27 'per patriae nomen, quae te tibi carior ipso est'.

18. CANDIDVS ET FELIX PROXIMVS ANNVS ERIT. Compare *Fast* I 63-64 'ecce tibi *faustum*, Germanice, nuntiat *annum* / inque meo primus carmine Ianus adest'. No doubt both passages echo the phrasing of a New Year wish or prayer.

18. CANDIDVS. 'Favourable'. Compare *Tr* V v 13-14 (on his wife's birthday) 'optime natalis! quamuis procul absumus, opto / *candidus* huc uenias', Prop IV i 67-68 'Roma, faue, tibi surgit opus, date *candida* ciues / omina, et inceptis dextera cantet auis!', and *Fast* I 79-80 'uestibus intactis Tarpeias itur in arces, / et populus *festo concolor* ipse suo est'.

19. DIXIT ET has a definite epic flavour, being found in Virgil at *Aen* I 402 & 736, II 376, III 258, IV 659, V 477, VI 677, VIII 366 & 615, IX 14, X 867, XI 561 & 858, XII 266 & 681, and *G* IV 499; from Ovid compare *Met* I 466-67 'dixit et eliso percussis aere pennis / impiger umbrosa Parnasi constitit arce', I 762 'dixit et implicuit materno bracchia collo', III 474, IV 162 & 576, V 230 & 419, VIII 101, and VIII 757. A close parallel at *EP* III iii 93-94 (Amor has been speaking with Ovid) 'dixit et aut ille est tenues dilapsus in auras, / coeperunt sensus aut uigilare mei'.

22. EXCIDIT. 'I forgot'; the opposite of *subit* 'I remember'. The idiom is standard Latin (*OLD excido*[1] 9b); Ovidian instances at *Her* XII 71, *Am* II i 18, *Met* VIII 449-50 'excidit omnis / luctus et a lacrimis in poenae uersus amorem est', *Met* XIV 139, *Fast* V 315, *Tr* I v 14, *EP* II iv 24, and *EP* II x 8 'exciderit tantum ne tibi cura mei'.

23. VBI ... RESERAVERIS ANNVM. 'When you have unlocked the year'. Compare Ovid's descriptions of Janus at *Fast* I 99 'tenens baculum dextra *clauemque* sinistra' and *Fast* I 253-54 '"nil mihi cum bello: pacem postesque tuebar / et" *clauem* ostendens "haec" ait "arma gero"'.

23. LONGVM ANNVM. André translates, 'l'année longue à venir', citing Cic *Phil* V 1 'Nihil umquam longius his Kalendiis Ianuariis mihi uisum est', to which *OLD longus* 14a adds (among other passages) Caesar *BG* I 40 13 'in longiorem diem collaturus' and Sen *Ep* 63 3 'non differo in *longius* tempus'; but the meaning 'far off' seems unsuited to the present context. *Longum* should be taken in its usual sense; it perhaps emphasizes that the whole year is still ahead.

24. SACRO MENSE. *Sacer* because of the religious ceremonies marking the New Year.

25-28. The first action of the new consul was to take auspices at his home and to assume the consular toga: compare Livy XXI 63 10 (217 BC; Flaminius has entered his consulship while absent from Rome) 'magis pro maiestate uidelicet imperii Arimini quam Romae magistratum initurum et in deuersorio hospitali quam apud penates suos praetextam sumpturum' (Mommsen *Staatsrecht* I^3 615-17).

26. NE TITVLIS QVICQVAM DEBEAT ILLE SVIS. There are two possible ways of understanding this line.

One way is to take *titulis* as referring to Pompeius' earlier magistracies, 'as if the series of offices were a score which Pompey would pay in full when he became consul' (Wheeler). A similar use at *Her* IX 1 'Gratulor Oechaliam titulis accedere nostris'.

Titulis does not have to be taken as a strict reference to the offices Pompeius had already held, but can have the wider sense of 'reputation, honour'. Compare the opening line of *Her* IX quoted above; Professor R. J. Tarrant cites *Met* XV 855 'sic magnus cedit *titulis* Agamemnonis Atreus' and Juvenal VIII 241.

The second way to take the passage is, with Némethy, to understand *titulis ... suis* as being equivalent to *maioribus suis, qui magnos titulos habent*, the *tituli* being the inscriptions below the *imagines* of Pompeius' ancestors. A parallel for the sense at *EP* III i 75-76 'hoc domui *debes* de qua censeris, ut illam / non magis officiis quam probitate colas'. Professor E.

Fantham suggests a refinement: *titulis ... suis* should be taken in the sense 'achievements of his ancestors'. Compare Prop IV xi 32 'et domus est titulis utraque fulta suis'.

27. PAENE ATRIA. Heinsius preferred PENETRALIA, the reading of *I* and *F²* ('sed ne sic quidem locus mihi uidetur plane in integrum restitutus'), apparently objecting to *paene*. The word seems weak enough, especially in view of Virgil *G* I 49 'illius immensae *ruperunt* horrea messes', but Professor R. J. Tarrant points out to me a similarly weak *paene* at *Tr* III xi 13-14 'sic ego belligeris a gentibus undique saeptus / terreor, hoste meum paene premente latus'. Burman conjectured LAETA and PLENA; neither seems very convincing.

For *atria* compare *Her* XVI 185-86 'occurrent denso tibi Troades agmine matres, / nec capient Phrygias *atria* nostra nurus'. *Penetralia*, although poorly attested, is in itself appropriate enough, since the new consul began his magistracy in front of his *penates*: Festus (Mueller 208; Lindsay 231) defined the *penetralia* as the 'penatium deorum sacraria'.

28. ET POPVLVM LAEDI DEFICIENTE LOCO. The jostling of a crowd similarly described at *Am* III ii 21-22 'tu tamen a dextra, quicumque es, parce puellae; / contactu lateris laeditur ista tui'.

29-34. The new consul, accompanied by lictors, left his house and went in solemn procession to the Capitoline, where he took his place on the curule chair, and then sacrificed to Iuppiter Optimus Maximus. A meeting of the Senate followed, held in the temple of Jupiter.

At ix 17-32 Ovid gives a similar description of the consul's entering on his office.

29. TARPEIAE ... SEDIS. *Capitolinus* is metrically awkward; hence the synecdoche from the *Tarpeia rupes*, the part of the Capitoline from which criminals were hurled. Similar tropes at viii 42 'uictima Tarpeios inficit icta focos', ix 29 'at cum Tarpeias esses deductus in arces', and commonly in the poets.

199

30. FACILES IN TVA VOTA. 'Receptive to your prayers'; for this frequent sense of *facilis* compare *Her* XII 84 'sed mihi tam *faciles* unde meosque deos?', *Met* V 559 'optastis *facilesque* deos habuistis', *Tr* IV i 53 'sint precor hae [the Muses] saltem *faciles* mihi', *EP* II ii 19-20 'esse ... fateor ... *difficilem* precibus te quoque iure meis', *Her* XVI 282 'sic habeas *faciles in tua uota deos*', and Grattius 426.

31-32. The asyndeton in this distich is odd, given the preceding series of connectives. If the text is unsound, however, alteration of *certae* to *certant* (Damsté) or *cerno* (Owen) is not the cure. By using *certae* Ovid is indicating that there will be a clean blow with the axe, a good omen for the coming year. For the opposite omen, see *Aen* II 222-24 (describing Laocoon) 'clamores simul horrendos ad sidera tollit: / qualis mugitus, fugit cum saucius aram / taurus et *incertam* excussit ceruice securim'.

31-32. BOVES NIVEOS ... QVOS ALVIT CAMPIS HERBA FALISCA SVIS. Compare *Am* III xiii 13-14 'ducuntur *niueae* populo plaudente *iuuencae*, / quas aluit campis herba Falisca suis' and *Fast* I 83-84 (a description of the sacrifices on January 1st) '*colla* rudes operum *praebent* ferienda iuuenci, / quos aluit campis herba Falisca suis'.

33-34. CVMQVE DEOS OMNES, TVM QVOS IMPENSIVS AEQVOS / ESSE TIBI CVPIAS, CVM IOVE CAESAR ERVNT. *Cupias* must be supplied with *deos omnes* —'You will wish the favour of all the gods; those gods whose favour you will particularly wish will be Caesar and Jupiter'. The omission of the verb from the *cum*-clause seems very strange, however, and Ehwald (*KB* 63-64) is possibly correct in supposing a distich to have fallen from the text after 32; in this case, *cumque deos omnes* is probably far removed from its original form.

33. OMNES, TVM QVOS. Ehwald wished to read OMNES, TVNC HOS (*P* reads TVNC HOS ORES), *hos* referring to the gods of the Capitol who had been named in the distich missing after 32; but this would leave *cum Ioue Caesar erunt* without a predicate.

33. AEQVOS. 'Favourable'; compare *Her* I 23 'sed bene

consuluit casto deus *aequus* amori'; *Tr* I ii 6 '*aequa* Venus Teucris, Pallas *iniqua* fuit', *Tr* III xiv 29 '*aequus* erit scriptis', and *Tr* IV i 25.

35. E MORE VOCATI. 'Convened, as is traditional'. After the sacrifice on the Capitoline, the new consul addressed the assembled Senate; compare Livy XXVI 26 5 'M. Marcellus cum idibus Martiis consulatum inisset, senatum eo die *moris modo causa* habuit ['held a session of the Senate simply because it was traditional to do so']' and Livy XXI 63 8 'ne die initi magistratus Iouis optimi maximi templum adiret, ne senatum inuisus ipse et sibi uni inuisum uideret consuleretque'.

36. INTENDENT AVRES. The expression is not found elsewhere in Ovid, or in Virgil; but compare Manilius II 511 'at nudus Geminis *intendit* Aquarius *aurem*'. The expression is presumably an extension of *oculos (aciem) intendere*, for which see Cic *Tusc* IV 38, *Ac* II 80, and Tac *Ann* IV 70.

37. FACVNDO TVA VOX ... ORE. For Pompeius' eloquence, Némethy cites Val Max II vi 8 '*facundissimo* ... sermone, qui ore eius quasi e beato quodam eloquentiae fonte manabat' and IV vii ext 2 'clarissimi ac *disertissimi* uiri'.

37. HILARAVERIT. The verb is rare and elevated in tone. Compare Cic *Brut* 44 (of Pericles' oratory) 'huius suauitate maxime hilaratae Athenae sunt', Catullus LXIII 18, and *Ecl* V 69.

38. VTQVE SOLET, TVLERIT PROSPERA VERBA DIES. Compare *Fast* I 175-76 (Ovid to Janus) '"at cur *laeta* tuis dicuntur *uerba* Kalendis, / et damus alternas accipimusque preces?"'.

40. Riese's punctuation 'facias cur ita, saepe dabit' seems preferable to the alternate 'facias cur ita saepe, dabit', as placing more emphasis on Augustus and being perhaps an echo of *Tr* IV ii 12 'munera det meritis, *saepe datura*, deis'.

42. OFFICIVM POPVLI = *populum officium facientem*; the same metonymy at *Met* XV 691-93 (of Aesculapius) 'restitit hic agmenque suum *turbaeque sequentis / officium* placido uisus dimittere uultu / corpus in Ausonia posuit rate'.

44. NEC POTERVNT ISTIS LVMINA NOSTRA FRVI.
Other non-personal subjects at Cic *Am* 45 (*animus*) and ps-
Quint *Decl* VII 10 'uulneribus illis non fruentur *oculi*'. In all
of these passages the transition from an expressed personal
subject to a faculty or part of the personality seems fairly
natural.

45. QVAMLIBET is a correction by Heinsius: 'far away as
you might be ...'. The QVOD (QVA) LICET of most
manuscripts anticipates the following *qua possum*, contrary
to Ovid's practice.

45. QVA POSSVM, MENTE. A commonplace of the poems
of exile: compare ix 41-42 'mente tamen, quae sola domo non
exulat, usus / praetextam fasces aspiciamque tuos', *Tr* III iv
56, *Tr* IV ii 57 'haec ego summotus *qua possum mente uidebo*',
EP I viii 34 'cunctaque mens oculis peruidet usa suis', *EP* II
iv 8, *EP* II x 47, and *EP* III v 47-48.

47. SVBEAT TIBI. See at xv 30 *subeant animo* (p 440).

V. To Sextus Pompeius

The poem was written shortly after Pompeius' accession to the consulship (compare 4 'tectaque brumali sub niue terra latet' and 24 'deque *parum noto* consulet officio'). It takes the form of a set of instructions to the poem on what it should do when it reaches Rome. Ovid tells the poem it should look for Pompeius, and includes a short description of some of the consular functions Pompeius might be carrying out (1-26). He then instructs the poem in what it is to say to Pompeius: it should describe to him Ovid's gratitude for past and present services, and promise (using several *adynata* as illustrations) that this gratitude will be eternal (27-46).

A close parallel to this poem is furnished by *Tr* III vii, in which Ovid tells the poem where it is to seek his stepdaughter Perilla and what it is to say to her. Similar personifications are found in *Tr* I i, in which Ovid gives instructions to his book on what it should do when it reaches Rome and the prudence it should show, in *Tr* III i, where the book describes its arrival in Rome, in *Tr* V iv, where the letter tells of Ovid's misery and his loyalty to his friend, and in Ovid's exhortation to his *elegi* at *Fast* II 3-6. The device is not unique to Ovid, being found at Catullus XXXV, Hor *Ep* I xx, and Statius *Sil* IV iv.

1. LEVES ELEGI. The same phrase at Am II i 21 'blanditias *elegosque leues*, mea tela, resumpsi'.

1. DOCTAS AD CONSVLIS AVRES. 'To the ears of a consul who appreciates poetry'. Compare Hor *Ep* I xiii 17-18 'carmina quae possint oculos *aurisque* morari / Caesaris' and Prop II xiii 11-12.

2. HONORATO ... VIRO. Dative of agent with *legenda*.

2. HONORATO refers specifically to Pompeius' consulship. *Honor* is often used with the restricted sense of 'magistracy'.

3. LONGA VIA EST. Compare *Tr* I i 127-28 (the end of

Ovid's instructions to his book) 'longa uia est, propera! nobis habitabitur orbis / ultimus, a terra terra remota mea'.

3. LONGA VIA EST, NEC VOS PEDIBVS PROCEDITIS AEQVIS. The *uia longa* is seen as a possible cause of the metre's lameness at *Tr* III i 11-12.

3. NEC ... PEDIBVS ... AEQVIS. Ovid often mentions the alternating pattern of elegiac verse: compare xvi 11 *numeris ... imparibus ... uel aequis* and the passages there cited, *Am* III i 8 (of Elegy) 'et, puto, pes illi *longior alter* erat', and *EP* III iv 85-86 'ferre etiam molles elegi tam uasta triumphi / pondera *disparibus* non potuere *rotis*'.

5. HAEMON *Laurentianus 38 39 (saec xv), Ven. Marcianus XII 106 (saec xv), editio princeps Bononiensis* HAEMVM *BCMFHILT*. I follow Heinsius and Burman in printing *Haemon*, in consideration of the preceding *Thracen*: it seems neater to have both place-names in their Greek forms. *Haemum* is similarly the transmitted reading at *Met* VI 87 (of the tapestry created by Minerva) 'Threiciam Rhodopen habet angulus unus et *Haemon*' and *Met* X 76-77 (of Orpheus) 'in altam / se recipit Rhodopen pulsumque Aquilonibus *Haemon*', the preferable *Haemon* being found only in certain late manuscripts.

6. TRANSIERĪTIS. In early Latin this would necessarily have been a perfect subjunctive, the future perfect indicative being *transierĭtis* with the second 'i' short; but after Ennius and Plautus the forms (like *-erīs* and *-erĭs*)) are used indifferently, according to metrical necessity. See Platnauer 56 and Kühner-Stegmann I 115-16.

7. LVCE MINVS DECIMA DOMINAM VENIETIS IN VRBEM. '[Starting from Brundisium] you will arrive in Rome before the tenth day'. The same idiom at *Fast* V 379 'nocte minus quarta promet sua sidera Chiron'.

8. VT FESTINATVM NON FACIATIS ITER. The trip would probably be not much shorter than ten days. André cites Livy XXXVI 21 and Plutarch *Cato maior* 14 3 for Cato's five-day journey from Hydruntum (Livy; Hydruntum is about seventy-five kilometres southeast of Brundisium) or

Brundisium (Plutarch) in 191 to announce the victory over Antiochus III at Thermopylae; both authors mention the journey for its speed. The more leisurely journey from Rome to Brundisium described in Hor *Sat* I v seems to have taken about fifteen days; see Palmer on I v 103.

9. Either **PETETVR** (*FT*) or PETATVR (*BCMHIL*) is possible enough. *Petetur* seems the better reading in view of *uenietis* (7) and *erit* (16), the corruption perhaps having been induced by *faciatis* in the preceding line. But the jussive *petatur* could be continuing from *ite* in the first line; compare Statius *Sil* IV iv 4-5 'atque ubi Romuleas uelox penetraueris arces, / continuo dextras flaui *pete* Thybridis oras'.

10. NON EST AVGVSTO IVNCTIOR VLLA FORO. Compare xv 16 'quam domus [*sc* tua] Augusto continuata foro'.

11. SI QVIS VT IN POPULO. 'If someone in the crowd'. This seems to be the sense of *ut in populo*; Wheeler's translation 'as may happen in the crowd' will work here and at *Tr* I i 17-18 'si quis *ut in populo* nostri non immemor illi [=*illic*], / si quis qui quid agam forte requirat, erit', but not at *Tr* II 157-58 'per patriam, quae te tuta et secura parente est, / cuius *ut in populo* pars ego nuper eram' or at Hor *Sat* I vi 78-80 (Horace describes his schooldays) 'uestem seruosque sequentis / *in magno ut populo* si qui uidisset, auita / ex re praeberi sumptus mihi crederet illos'.

A similar idiom appears at *Tr* II 231-32 'denique *ut in tanto* quantum non extitit umquam / *corpore* pars nulla est quae labet imperii'

11. QVI SITIS ET VNDE. Similar phrasing at *Ilias Lat* 554-55 'nomen genusque roganti, / *qui sit et unde'*.

12. NOMINA ... QVAELIBET ... FERAT. *Ferat* = 'receive as answer'. Compare Livy V 32 8 '[M. Furius Camillus] cum accitis domum tribulibus clientibusque ... percontatus animos eorum *responsum tulisset* se conlaturos quanti damnatus esset, absoluere eum non posse, in exilium abiit' and XXI 19 11.

12. DECEPTA ... AVRE. Compare *Met* VII 821-23 'uocibus

205

ambiguis *deceptam* praebuit *aurem* / nescio quis nomenque aurae tam saepe uocatum / esse putat nymphae'.

14. VERA, MINVS *Hilberg* VERBA MINVS *codd.* For the phrase *uera fateri* Hilberg (35-36) cited as parallels *Met* VII 728 & IX 53, *Tr* I ix 16, *EP* III i 79 'si uis *uera fateri*', *EP* III ix 19 'quid enim dubitem tibi *uera fateri*?', to which add *EP* II iii 7. For the contrast of *uera* and *ficta* Hilberg cited *EP* III iv 105-6 'oppida turritis cingantur eburnea muris, / *fictaque* res *uero* [*codd*: uerae *Riese*] more putetur agi'; see as well *Tr* I ix 15-16 'haec precor ut semper possint tibi *falsa* uideri; / sunt tamen euentu *uera fatenda* meo'. For the corruption of *uera* to *uerba* he cited *Fast* I 332, *Tr* III vi 36, III xi 33 & IV iii 58, and Prop III xxiv 12 'naufragus Aegaea uera [*Passerat*: uerba *codd*] fatebar [*uar* fatebor] aqua'; for the position of *uera* he cited *EP* III i 46 & IV xiii 26. The corruption was no doubt assisted by the isolated position of *uera* at the start of the pentameter.

15-16. COPIA NEC VOBIS NVLLO PROHIBENTE VIDENDI / CONSULIS ... ERIT. 'Even if no one stops you, you will not be able to see the consul [because he will be busy]'. Heinsius preferred to read VLLO (*P*), but this does not yield sense: it would have to mean 'you will be able to see the consul if no one prevents you' or 'you will be unable to see the consul if anyone prevents you'; neither of these meanings would cohere with what follows.

15. COPIA. 'Opportunity'; compare *Met* XI 278 '*copia* ... facta est adeundi tecta tyranni', *EP* III i 135-37 'cum domus Augusti ... laeta ... plenaque pacis erit, / tum tibi di faciant adeundi *copia* fiat', and *Aen* I 520 'coram data *copia* fandi', XI 248 (=I 520) & XI 378.

16. CONTIGERĪTIS. See on 6 *transierītis*.

17. DICENDO IVRA. The plural is poetic, the standard phrase being *ius dicere*: *OLD ius*[2] 4b cites Livy III 52 6 alone for the plural.

17-26. Ovid lists in order of ascending importance some of the activities Pompeius as consul might be engaged in, starting with the hearing of lawsuits and ending with visits to the imperial family. For a shorter instance of the device of listing the recipient's possible activities, see *Tr* III vii 3-4 (Ovid tells his letter to seek Perilla) 'aut illam inuenies dulci cum matre sedentem, / aut inter libros Pieridasque suas'.

18. CONSPICVVM ... SIGNIS EBVR. *Signis* = 'bas-relief'; the sense is confined to verse (*OLD signum* 12b). Compare ix 27 'signa ... in sella ... formata curuli', *Met* V 80-82 'altis / extantem signis ... cratera', *Met* XII 235-36 'signis extantibus asper / antiquus crater', *Met* XIII 700, Lucr V 1427-28 'ueste ... purpurea atque auro signisque ingentibus apta', *Aen* V 267, V 536 & IX 263, Prop IV v 24, Statius *Theb* I 540, and Silius II 432.

18. CVM PREMET ALTVS EBUR. 'When he sits tall on the curule chair'. The same situation similarly described at *Fast* I 81-82 'iamque noui praeeunt fasces, noua purpura fulget, / et noua conspicuum pondera sentit ebur'; compare as well *Med Fac* 13 'matrona *premens altum* rubicunda sedile' and *Met* V 317 'factaque de uiuo *pressere* sedilia saxo'.

19. REDITVS ... COMPONET. 'Will be arranging the [state's] income'. For *reditus* compare *Am* I x 41 'turpe tori *reditu* census augere paternos' and *EP* II iii 17-18 'at *reditus* iam quisque suos amat, et sibi quid sit / utile sollicitis supputat ['calculates'] articulis'. For *componet* compare Cic *II Verr* IV 36 '*compone* hoc quod postulo de argento' and Tac *Ann* VI 16 5.

19. POSITAM ... AD HASTAM. A spear placed in the ground was a symbol of magisterial authority, and as such was always present at the letting of tax contracts. For the language compare Cic *Leg Agr* II 53 'ponite ante oculos uobis Rullum ... *hasta posita* ... auctionantem'. For *hasta* with the specific meaning of 'contract-letting', see Livy XXIV 18 11 'conuenere ad eos frequentes qui *hastae huius generis* adsueuerant'. The practice is recalled in the modern Italian term for 'auction', *uendita all'asta*.

20. MINVI MAGNAE. A word play on *minus* and *magis* at least; but Professor E. Fantham points out to me that Ovid probably had in mind the phrase *maiestatem populi Romani minuere* (Cic *Inu* II 53 & *Phil* I 21); Pompeius will not allow the interests of the state to be damaged.

21. IN IVLIA TEMPLA = *in curiam Iuliam*. Caesar had started the construction of a new senate-house in 44; it was opened by Augustus in 29. The building, as restored by Diocletian, survives substantially intact: see Nash I 301.

22. TANTO DIGNIS CONSVLE REBVS. Note the separation of the epithets from the nouns, and the high level of diction produced by the hyperbaton.

23. AVT FERET ... SOLITAM ... SALVTEM = *aut, ut solet, salutabit.*

23. NATOQVE. Tiberius, son of Ti. Claudius Nero, had been adopted by Augustus in AD 4.

24. DEQVE PARVM NOTO CONSVLET OFFICIO. 'Will be asking advice about his unfamiliar office'. It still being winter, Pompeius would not have been very long in office, and so would not yet have been very familiar with his duties. Burman objected to this notion ('nec Ovidium tam adulandi imperitum fuisse puto, ut ignorantiam aut seruitutem tam imprudenter obiiceret Pompeio') and conjectured DEQVE PATRVM TOTO CONSVLET OFFICIO, that is, 'consulet Caesares, *quale uelint esse officium* totius senatus'. But the conjecture is unattractive, and the problem not as great as Burman thought: both Ovid and Pompeius would wish to emphasize the importance of the Caesars.

25. AB HIS VACVVM. A prose usage, paralleled in Ovid by *EP* I i 79 alone 'inque locum Scythico *uacuum* mutabor *ab arcu*'. Elsewhere Ovid has nine instances of *uacuus* with the simple ablative and two instances of *uacuus* with the genitive, while Virgil never has *uacuus* with a complement. ET HIS VACVVM, given by *B* and *C*, is perhaps an attempt to restore normal poetic idiom.

26. A MAGNIS ... DEIS. 'After the great gods'—Augustus and Tiberius. Dio says that it was remarked after Augustus' death that both of the consuls for the year were related to the emperor (LVI 29 5); it is strange that Ovid nowhere mentions Pompeius' link with the imperial family.

For the sense of *ab*, compare for example *Ecl* V 48-49 'nec calamis solum aequiperas, sed uoce magistrum: / fortunate puer, tu nunc eris alter *ab illo*' and Statius *Theb* IV 842.

27. CVM TAMEN ... REQVIEVERIT. After it has arrived in Rome, the poem should not vex Pompeius by approaching him when he is busy. At *Tr* I i 93-96 Ovid in the same way advises his book when it should approach Augustus, and at *EP* III i 135-40 gives similar directions to his wife. Compare as well *Met* IX 572-73 (a messenger carries Byblis' declaration of love to her brother) 'apta minister / tempora nactus adit traditque fatentia [*H. A. Koch*: latentia *codd*] uerba' and *Met* IX 610-12 (Byblis' explanation of the failure of her suit) 'forsitan et missi sit quaedam culpa ministri: / non adiit apte, nec legit idonea, credo, / tempora, nec petiit *horam animumque uacantem*'.

27. A TVRBA RERVM. 'De ces multiples affaires' (André). Heinsius conjectured CVRA, citing ix 71 (addressed to Graecinus as consul) 'cum tamen *a rerum cura* propiore uacabit'. The conjecture is elegant enough, but the manuscript reading seems sufficiently supported by *Her* II 75-76 (Phyllis to Demophoon) 'de tanta *rerum turba* factisque parentis / sedit in ingenio Cressa relicta tuo' and *EP* III i 144 'per *rerum turbam* tu quoque oportet eas'; compare as well Columella XI 2 25.

28. MANSVETAS ... MANVS. The same phrase in the same position at Prop III xvi 9-10 'peccaram semel, et totum sum pulsus in annum: / in me *mansuetas* non habet illa *manus*'. *Mansuetus* is foreign to poetic vocabulary, not being found in Virgil or Horace, and only three times in Propertius (I ix 12, I xvii 28, III xvi 10): in Ovid it occurs elsewhere only at *Tr* III vi 23 'numinis ut laesi fiat mansuetior ira' and *Ibis* 26.

28. PORRIGET ILLE MANVS. *Manus* = *manum*; for the latter, compare *Her* XVIII 15-16 'protinus haec scribens "felix i littera" dixi, / "iam tibi formosam *porriget illa manum*"'. Alternatively, the phrase could be taken to indicate Pompeius' gesture of welcoming to a suppliant: at *Met* III 458 Narcissus, saying how he wished to embrace his reflection, says 'cumque ego *porrexi tibi bracchia*, porrigis ultro'.

31-32. VIVIT ADHVC VITAMQVE TIBI DEBERE FATETVR, / QVAM PRIVS A MITI CAESARE MVNVS HABET. See on i 2 *debitor ... uitae*, and compare *Tr* V ix 11-14 'Caesaris est primum munus, quod ducimus auras; / gratia post magnos est tibi habenda deos. / ille dedit uitam; tu quam dedit ille tueris, / et facis accepto munere posse frui': the similarity of phrasing makes it all but certain that the poem was addressed to Pompeius.

33. MEMORI ... ORE. The phrase belongs to high poetic diction: compare *Met* VI 508 'absentes pro se *memori* rogat *ore* salutent', *Met* X 204 (Apollo to the dead Hyacinthus) 'semper eris mecum *memorique* haerebis in *ore*', and *AA* III 700 'auditos *memori* detulit *ore* sonos'.

35. SANGVINE BISTONIVM QVOD NON TEPEFECERIT

ENSEM. Another instance of high poetic diction: compare *Her* I 19 'sanguine Tlepolemus Lyciam *tepefecerat* hastam', *Aen* IX 333-34 'atro *tepefacta* cruore / terra', *Aen* IX 418-19 'hasta ... traiecto ... haesit *tepefacta* cerebro', and Hor *Sat* II iii 136.

37-38. ADDITA PRAETEREA VITAE QVOQVE MVLTA TVENDAE / MVNERA. The dative expresses purpose. For the sense of *tueri* 'sustain', compare *Tr* V ix 13 'uitam ... quam dedit ille *tueris*', Cic *Deiot* 22 'atque antea quidem maiores copias alere poterat; nunc exiguas uix *tueri* potest', Livy V 4 5, XXIII 38 12 & XXXIX 9 5, and Pliny *NH* XXXIII 134 'M. Crassus negabat locupletem esse nisi qui reditu annuo legionem *tueri* posset'.

38. NE PROPRIAS ATTENVARET OPES. This may be a reference to the financial burden of living in exile, but more probably refers to the actual financial loss Ovid suffered in exile: 'ditata est spoliis perfida turba meis' (*EP* II vii 62). It is clear from *Tr* I vi 7-8 that Ovid had feared such losses from the beginning of his exile.

Attenuare is a very strong verb: compare *Met* VIII 843-45 (of Erysichthon) 'iamque fame patrias altique uoragine uentris / *attenuarat* ['had exhausted'—Miller] opes, sed inattenuata manebat / tum quoque dira fames'.

39. PRO QVIBVS VT MERITIS REFERATVR GRATIA. Similar language to Pompeius at i 21 'et leuis haec *meritis referatur gratia* tantis'.

40. MANCIPII ... TVI (*CB*^{2}) 'belonging to your property' seems a much more elegant construction than the other manuscripts' MANCIPIVM ... TVVM 'your slave', and was conjectured by Heinsius; in support of *mancipium ... tuum* Burman cited viii 65-66 'si quid adhuc igitur uiui, Germanice, nostro / restat in ingenio, *seruiet* omne tibi'.

41-44. Ovid uses the common device of listing *adynata*; the second version of the device at *Tr* I viii 1-10, where Ovid says that now his friend has betrayed him he expects to see the *adynata* occur. Comprehensive listings of *adynata* in ancient literature given by Smith on Tib I iv 65-66, Shackleton Bailey on Prop I xv 29, Nisbet and Hubbard on Hor *Carm* I ii 9, xxix 10 & xxxiii 7, and by Gow on Theocritus I 132-36.

42. VELIVOLAS occurs once more at xvi 21 'ueliuolique maris uates', and nowhere else in Ovid's poetry. It is found at Lucretius V 1442 and *Aen* I 224 'mare ueliuolum', and was from old Latin poetry: Macrobius (*Sat* VI v 10) cites instances from Livius Andronicus (Morel 58) and Ennius (*Ann* 380 Vahlen[3]; *Andromache* 74 Ribbeck[3]).

43. SVPINO. 'Backwards'; almost the reverse of *praeceps*. The same sense at *Med Fac* 40 'nec redit in fontes unda *supina* suos'.

45. DIXERITIS. See on 6 *transieritis*.

45. SVA DONA. Compare *Her* XII 203 (Medea to Jason) 'dos mea tu sospes' and Sen *Med* 142 'muneri parcat meo [=*uitae suae*]' & 228-30.

46. SIC FVERIT VESTRAE CAVSA PERACTA VIAE. 'So you will have carried out the reason for your journey'. The same sense of *causa* at *Met* VI 449-50 'coeperat aduentus causam, mandata referre / coniugis' and of *peragere* (always with *mandata* as object) at *Met* VII 502, XI 629 & XIV 460, *Fast* III 687, and *Tr* I i 35-36 'ut *peragas mandata*, liber, culpabere forsan / ingeniique minor laude ferere mei'.

Professor E. Fantham points out to me that Ovid may here be playing on a second sense of *causam peragere*, 'end a speech [in court]', for which see *Met* XV 36-37 'spretarumque agitur legum reus ... *peracta* est / causa prior ['the case for the prosecution'—Miller], crimenque patet' and *Her* XXI 152.

VI. To Brutus

Of the Brutus to whom this poem is addressed nothing is known beyond what Ovid here tells us. He was an advocate, by Ovid's testimony an eminent one (29-38), and had been among the few who stood by Ovid at the time of his exile (23-26). The collection of *Ex Ponto* I-III was apparently dedicated to him, since the first poem of the first book and the last poem of the third book are addressed to him, but the two poems fail to give any further information on him or on his relationship to Ovid.

Ovid starts the poem with the reflection that he has now spent five years at Tomis (1-6). Fortune has tricked him: Fabius Maximus died before he could appeal to Augustus, Augustus before he could pardon Ovid (7-16). He hopes that the poem he has written on the apotheosis of Augustus will win him pardon; Brutus' fine qualities guarantee that he shares Ovid's wishes (17-22). The poem ends with a eulogy of Brutus' character and an assurance of Ovid's eternal gratitude to those friends who stood by him (23-50).

1. QVAM LEGIS. See at ii 1 *quod legis* (p 162).

3-4. SED TV QVOD NOLLES, VOLVIT MISERABILE FATVM; / EI MIHI, PLVS ILLVD QVAM TVA VOTA VALET. For the play on *nolle/uelle* and the thought of 4, compare *Met* IX 757-58 'quodque ego, *uult* genitor, *uult* ipsa socerque futurus, / at *non uult* natura, potentior omnibus istis'.

5. QVINQVENNIS. Ovid often mentions the time he has spent in exile: see *Tr* IV vi 19-20 (AD 10) 'ut patria careo, *bis* frugibus area trita est, / dissiluit nudo pressa *bis* uua pede', *Tr* IV vii 1-2 '*Bis* me sol adiit gelidae post frigora brumae, / *bisque* suum tacto Pisce peregit iter', *Tr* V x 1-2 (AD 11-12) 'Vt sumus in Ponto, *ter* frigore constitit Hister, / facta est Euxini dura *ter* unda maris', *EP* I ii 25-26 (AD 12-13) 'hic me pugnantem cum frigore cumque sagittis / cumque meo fato

213

quarta fatigat hiemps', *EP* I viii 27-28 'ut careo uobis, Stygias detrusus in oras, / *quattuor* autumnos Pleias orta facit', *EP* IV x 1 (AD 14) 'Haec mihi Cimmerio *bis tertia* ducitur aestas', and *EP* IV xiii 39-40 'sed me iam, Care, niuali / *sexta* relegatum bruma sub axe uidet'.

Ovid's first full year of exile was AD 9; since Augustus died on 19 August 14, this poem can be securely dated to the final few months of that year.

5. OLYMPIAS in Latin can mean a period of four or of five years; Ovid may have used *quinquennis* to remove the ambiguity. *Olympias* elsewhere in classical poetry apparently only at Manilius III 596, where it also denotes a five-year period.

5-6. OLYMPIAS ACTA / IAM *Housman* OLYMPIAS ACTA EST. / IAM *edd.* The subject of *transit* must be *Olympias*, since otherwise the pentameter is without a subject. Wheeler offers 'the time is now passing to a second lustrum', which does not account for the genitive *lustri ... alterius* (a second *tempus*, in the accusative, would have to be understood), while André gives 'et déjà j'entre dans un second lustre', which does not explain the person of *transit*. The editors' reading could be retained, and *Olympias* understood as the subject of the pentameter; but it seems simpler to follow Housman in omitting *est* (with *L* and *T*) and joining the two lines in a single sentence.

Transit is in strict terms illogical, since an Olympiad once completed (*acta*) cannot pass into a second period of time, but the idiom seems natural enough in view of Ovid's use of *transire* with seasons at *Met* XV 206 '*transit in aestatem* post uer robustior annus'; compare as well *Fast* V 185 (to Flora) 'incipis Aprili, *transis in tempora Maii*'.

7. PERSTAT ENIM FORTVNA TENAX. In Ovid's case, Fortune does not show her typical inconstancy.

8. OPPONIT NOSTRIS INSIDIOSA PEDEM. Otto *pes* 7 cites this passage and Petronius 57 10 'et habebam in domo qui mihi *pedem opponerent* hac illac'.

9-10. CERTVS ERAS ... LOQVI. 'You had made up your

mind to speak'. The same idiom at *Her* IV 151-52, *Her* VII 9 'certus es, Aenea, cum foedere soluere naues ...?', *Met* IX 43, X 394 & XI 440; the impersonal construction at *Met* V 533, IX 53 'certum est mihi uera fateri' & X 38-39.

9. FABIAE LAVS, MAXIME, GENTIS. Similar phrasing at *EP* III iii 2 'o sidus Fabiae, Maxime, gentis, ades'. This passage seems to be the earliest instance of *laus* 'object of praise; reason for praise' used of a person: *TLL* VII.2 1064 73 ff. cites from classical Latin only *Eleg Maec* 17-18 'Pallade cum docta Phoebus donauerat artes; / tu decus et *laudes* huius et huius eras', Valerius Flaccus II 243-44 'decus et patriae *laus* una ruentis, / Hypsipyle', Silius XIII 824, and Martial I xlix 2-3 'nostraeque *laus* Hispaniae ... Liciniane'. LVX (F^2), printed by Burman, is acceptable enough (compare Cic *Cat* IV 11 'hanc urbem, *lucem* orbis terrarum'), but is clearly a guess based on F^1's DVX.

For a full discussion of the career of Paullus Fabius Maximus, *consul ordinarius* in 11 BC, see Syme *HO* 135-55. He is the recipient of *EP* I ii, a request to plead for Ovid with Augustus, and *EP* III iii, an account of Ovid's vision of Amor which ends with a plea for Fabius' assistance. He is prominently mentioned at Hor *Carm* IV i 9-12 as a suitable prey for Venus, and it appears from Juvenal VII 94-95 that he was a famous patron of literature: Ovid mentions his *scripta* at *EP* I ii 135. We learn from the same poem that Ovid's wife was a member of Fabius' family: 'ille ego de uestra cui data nupta domo est' (136).

10. SVPPLICE VOCE LOQVI. Similar phrasing at *Met* VI 33 '*supplice uoce* roga: ueniam dabit illa roganti'. The adjectival use of *supplex* is not confined to verse; *OLD supplex* 2 cites instances from Caesar and Suetonius.

11. OCCIDIS ANTE PRECES. 'You died before making your request'. Since Fabius is named in an inscription (*CIL* VI 2023a, line 17; cited by Froesch 209) as having participated in the election of Drusus to the Arval Brotherhood on 15 May AD 14, he must have died very shortly before Augustus.

11-12. CAVSAMQVE EGO, MAXIME, MORTIS ... ME

REOR ESSE TVAE. The death of Fabius, so soon before that of Augustus, seems to have raised popular suspicions. Tacitus (*Ann* I 5 1-2) mentions a rumour that Fabius had secretly accompanied Augustus to Planasia to visit Agrippa Postumus and that his wife had warned Livia of this; Augustus heard of this, and at Fabius' funeral she was heard blaming herself for his death. If Fabius' death occurred under strange circumstances, Ovid's accusation against himself of having been its cause may have special point.

For a full discussion of the circumstances of Fabius' death, see Syme *HO* 149-51.

12. NEC FVERAM TANTI. 'But I was not worth this much'. *Fueram* has the sense of the imperfect, as at *AA* I 103-4 'tunc neque marmoreo *pendebant* uela theatro, / nec *fuerant* liquido pulpita rubra croco'; other instances at *Her* V 69, *AA* II 137, *AA* III 429 & 618, and *Tr* III xi 25. A full discussion at Platnauer 112-14: he cites thirteen instances from Propertius, who seems to have been fondest of the idiom, and only one certain instance from Tibullus, II v 79 'haec fuerant olim'.

FVERO (*BC*) gives the sense 'but I will be discovered not to have been worth this much'; the tense seems difficult to fit to the context.

FVERIM (*British Library Burney 220, saec xii-xiii*) 'but I hope I was not worth so much' is quite possibly correct, and would account for the corruption to *fuero*.

12. NEC ... TANTI. Similar phrasing at *Met* X 613 (Atalanta ponders Hippomenes' willingness to risk death to gain her hand) '*non* sum me iudice *tanti*'.

13. MANDARE. 'Consign'; a legal term for charging others with carrying out business on one's behalf, which carried certain obligations with it. See Gaius III 155-62, Just *Inst* III 26, and the discussion at Buckland 514-21.

15. DETECTAE ... CVLPAE *scripsi* DECEPTAE ... CVLPAE *codd. Me decipit error* is a phrase used by Ovid to mean 'I am making a mistake'; see *EP* III ix 9-12 'auctor opus laudat ...

iudicium tamen hic non *decipit error* ['I do not make this error of judgment'], / nec quicquid genui protinus illud amo'. Ovid uses the expression very often for the "mistake" which led to his exile: see *Tr* I iii 37-38 (Ovid to his friends on the night of his exile) 'caelestique uiro quis me *deceperit error* / dicite pro culpa ne scelus esse putet', *Tr* IV i 23 'scit quoque [*sc* Musa] cum perii quis me *deceperit error*', and *EP* II ii 61 'quasi me nullus *deceperit error*'. He uses *decipere* once when speaking of the other cause of his exile: 'o puer [*sc* Amor], exilii *decepto* causa magistro' (*EP* III iii 23). Wheeler took *deceptae* to refer to Ovid: 'Augustus had begun to pardon the fault I committed in error'. This kind of extreme hypallage, with the true modified noun not expressed, does not however seem to be Ovid's practice, although found in the Silver poets: Statius *Theb* IX 425 'deceptaque fulmina' means 'the thunderbolts thrown by Jupiter at the request of Semele, who had been *deceived* by Juno'. Professor J. N. Grant suggests DECEPTI to me; but the genitive of the first person is rare in Ovid, and the perfect participle without expressed noun seems difficult. Owen saw the difficulty with *deceptae*, and in his second edition referred to Livy XXII 4 4 'id tantum hostium quod ex aduerso erat conspexit; ab tergo ac super caput *deceptae* insidiae'. But *deceptae* (which has been variously emended) there means *occultae*, as explained by Housman (521-22), who cited Prop II xxiv 35-36 'Phrygio fallax Maeandria campo / errat et ipsa suas *decipit* unda uias' and Sen *HF* 155 for the same sense; and *occultae* is clearly not the meaning here required, since Ovid's misdemeanour was all too visible.

Being unable to explain *deceptae*, I have conjectured *detectae*. Ovid seems to have committed his *error* in two stages. First he committed the original misdemeanour; then he kept silent about it when it might have been better for him to speak. Compare *Tr* III vi 11-13 'cuique ego narrabam secreti quicquid habebam, / excepto quod me perdidit, unus eras. / id quoque si scisses, saluo fruerere sodali'. Later this misdemeanour was discovered: for the arrival of the news of this discovery when Ovid was visiting Elba with Cotta Maximus, see *EP* II iii 83-90. It is to this discovery that *detectae* refers: 'Augustus had begun to forgive the misdemeanour that had been revealed'. For this use of *detegere* compare *Met* II 544-47 'ales / sensit adulterium Phoebeius [*coruus*, the raven], utque latentem / *detegeret culpam*, non exorabilis index, / ad dominum tendebat iter' and Livy XXII 28 8 'necubi ... motus alicuius ... aut fulgor armorum fraudem ... detegeret'.

Professor R. J. Tarrant points out to me the parallel problem at *Met* IX 711 'indecepta pia mendacia fraude latebant', where context requires *indecepta* to have the meaning 'undetected'. *Indecepta* might be taken to support *deceptae* in the present passage, but I am more inclined to read *indetecta* for *indecepta*: of the various conjectures made, Zingerle's *inde incepta* is most commonly accepted.

At *Her* IX 101-2 'tolle procul, *decepte*, faces, Hymenaee, maritas / et fuge turbato tecta nefanda pede!', *detecte* should similarly be read. *Detecte* better explains why Hymenaeus should flee; also, Hymenaeus has not been deceived, for it appears from 61-62 'spes bona det uires; fratris [*Palmer*: fratri *codd*] nam nupta futura es; / illius de quo mater, et uxor eris' that Macareus had fully intended to marry Canace.

16. SPEM NOSTRAM TERRAS DESERVITQVE SIMVL. The *-que* should of course be taken with *terras*.

This is a typical instance of Ovid's love of *syllepsis*, of giving a single verb two objects (or more), each of which uses a different meaning of the verb. Compare, from many instances, ix 90 'nec cum fortuna mens quoque uersa mea est', *Her* VII 9 'certus es, Aenea, cum foedere soluere naues', *Met* II 601-2 'et pariter uultusque deo plectrumque colorque / excidit', *Met* VIII 177, *Fast* III 225, *Fast* III 857 'hic [the messenger of Ino] ... corruptus cum semine', *Fast* V 652 'montibus his ponunt spemque laremque suum', and *EP* II vii 84 'meque simul serua iudiciumque tuum'.

16. DESERVITQVE. Ovid does not use *deserere* with things as object until his poetry of exile: compare *Tr* I ix 65 'nec amici *desere* causam'. Instances in the later *Heroides* at XV 155 'Sappho *desertos* cantat amores' and XVI 260 'orantis medias *deseruere* preces'; in both cases the objects are virtually equivalent to persons.

218

17. TAMEN. 'In spite of my dejection'.

17-18. DE CAELITE ... RECENTI ... CARMEN. The poem does not survive. At xiii 25-32 Ovid describes a similar poem on the apotheosis of Augustus, written in Getic.

17. RECENTI. 'New, freshly created'. Used in similar contexts at *Met* IV 434-35 'umbraeque *recentes* ... simulacraque functa sepulcris', VIII 488 'fraterni manes animaeque *recentes*', X 48-49 'Eurydicenque uocant: umbras erat illa *recentes* / inter', and especially XV 844-46 'Venus ... Caesaris eripuit membris nec in aera solui / passa *recentem* animam caelestibus intulit astris'.

18. VESTRA = 'of you [plural] at Rome'.

18. CARMEN IN ORA DEDI. 'I sent a poem for you to recite from and speak of'. *Dare* meaning 'send' is usually restricted to use with *litteras* (*OLD do* 10; compare Cic *Att* II i 12 & IX viiB 1, Livy XXVII 16 13).

For *in ora*, compare Catullus XL 5 'an ut peruenias *in ora* uulgi [*sc* hoc facis]?', Hor *Ep* I iii 9 '... Titius, Romana breui uenturus *in ora*', Prop III ix 32 (to Maecenas) 'et uenies tu quoque *in ora* uirum', *Tr* V vii 29-30 'non tamen ingratum est quodcumque obliuia nostri / impedit et profugi nomen *in ora* refert', and Livy II 36 3. The only instance I have found of the expression being used of a thing rather than a person other than this passage is also from Ovid: 'illud opus ... nunc incorrectum populi peruenit *in ora*, / in populi quicquam si tamen ore mei est' (*Tr* III xiv 21-24). Neither passage would have seemed strange to the Romans, given the close identification between poet and work: compare Ennius' famous 'uolito uiuo' per ora uirum' and *Met* XV 878 'ore legar populi'.

19. QVAE PIETAS. 'This demonstration of loyalty'.

20. SACRAE ... DOMVS. Augustus' house called 'magni ... Iouis ... domum' at *Tr* III i 38; compare as well *EP* III i 135 'domus Augusti, Capitoli more colenda'.

20. MITIOR IRA. Compare *EP* III iii 83 'pone metus igitur: *mitescet* Caesaris *ira*'.

21. LIQVIDO POSSVM IVRARE. 'I can swear unambiguously'. The only other instance of this sense in verse apparently III iii 49-50 'scis tamen et *liquido* iuratus dicere possis / non me legitimos sollicitasse toros'. From prose compare Cic *II Verr* IV 124 'confirmare hoc *liquido*, iudices, possum, ualuas magnificentiores ... nullas umquam ullo in templo fuisse', *II Verr* III 136, *Fam* XI 27 7 'alia sunt quae *liquido* negare soleam', and Sen *Ben* VII 9 5.

22. NON DVBIA ... NOTA. The phrase logically belongs with the preceding line: on the firm evidence of Brutus' past behaviour (described in 23-42), Ovid can confidently state that Brutus prays for his restoration. *Non dubia* by litotes for *certa* (for which see *Her* XX 207 'te ... nimium miror, *nota certa* furoris'); *nota* 'tangible sign, evidence' similarly used at *Met* I 761 (*generis*). FIDE (*LTM²ᵘˡF²ᵘˡ*) is an obvious gloss for *nota*.

23. VERVM ... AMOREM. 'Sincere love' (Wheeler); compare *Met* V 61 '*ueri* non dissimulator *amoris*' and *Tr* IV iv 71 'et comes exemplum *ueri* Phoceus *amoris*'.

25. TVAS ... LACRIMAS NOSTRASQVE. The tears of Ovid's friends at his departure described at *Tr* III iv 39-40, *EP* I ix 17-18, and *EP* II xi 9-10 (to Rufus) 'grande uoco lacrimas meritum quibus ora rigabas, / cum mea concreto sicca dolore forent'.

26. PASSVROS POENAM CREDERET ESSE DVOS. Compare *Tr* V iv 37-38 (Ovid's letter speaking) 'quamuis attonitus, sensit tamen omnia, *nec te / se minus aduersis indoluisse suis*'.

27. LENEM TE MISERIS GENVIT NATURA. Compare Cic *Tusc* II 11 'te *natura* excelsum quendam uidelicet et altum et humana despicientem *genuit*' and Ennius *Ann* 112 Vahlen³ (of Romulus) 'qualem te patriae custodem di *genuerunt*'.

29. MARTE FORENSI. Similar metaphor for the lawcourts at *Fast* IV 188 'et fora *Marte suo* litigiosa uacent', *Tr* III xii 17-18 'ludis / cedunt uerbosi garrula *bella* fori' and *Tr* IV x 17-18 'frater ... fortia uerbosi natus ad *arma* fori'. According to Ovid real wounds were suffered in the forum at Tomis: 'adde quod iniustum rigido ius dicitur ense, / dantur et in medio uulnera saepe foro' (*Tr* V x 43-44).

30. POSSE TVO PERAGI VIX PVTET ORE REOS. Similar language at *Tr* I i 23-24 'protinus admonitus repetet mea crimina lector, / *et peragar populi publicus ore reus*'. *Peragere* refers to the prosecution of a defendant carried to its end, but does not imply success for the prosecutor: see Pliny *Ep* III ix 30 and Ulpian *Dig* XLVIII v 2 1 'non alias ad mulierem possit peruenire, nisi reum peregerit [*sc* adulterii]; peregisse autem non alias quis uidetur, *nisi et condemnauerit*'.

31. QVAMVIS PVGNARE VIDENTVR *BMFH*. Given the dependent *pugnare*, it seems hardly possible to read the VIDETVR given by the other manuscripts. The same problem arises at *Met* VIII 463-64 '*pugnant* materque sororque, / et diuersa trahunt unum duo nomina pectus', where the manuscripts divide between *pugnant* and *pugnat*; for an unambiguous parallel, see *Her* XIX 173 'nunc, male res iunctae, calor et reuerentia *pugnant*'.

Heinsius further suggested deleting *est* from the preceding *scilicet eiusdem est* 'cum tribus libris', but the change in number does not seem unduly harsh.

32. SVPPLICIBVS FACILEM. See on iv 30 *faciles in tua uota*, and compare *Am* II iii 5-6 (to his girl's eunuch) 'mollis in obsequium *facilisque rogantibus* esses, / si tuus in quauis praetepuisset amor' and *Her* XVI 197-98 'da modo te *facilem*, nec dedignare maritum ... Phrygem'.

Ovid is here indirectly referring to his own situation: compare *EP* III iii 107-8 'at tua *supplicibus* domus est adsueta *iuuandis*, / *in quorum numero me precor esse uelis*'.

33. LEGIS VINDICTA. 'The exacting of punishment on behalf of the law'. The law has been broken, and therefore demands retribution; Brutus acts on its behalf. For the sense of the genitive compare Val Max I 1 ext 3: (Dionysius of Syracuse committed many acts of sacrilege, but punishment was visited on him after his death in the form of his son's ignominious career) 'lento enim gradu ad *uindictam sui* diuina procedit ira tarditatemque supplicii grauitate pensat'.

33. LEGIS ... SEVERAE. *Seuerae* here serves as a standard epithet and has no such special force as at *EP* III iii 57-58 'uetiti ... *lege seuera* / credor adulterii composuisse notas'.

34. VERBA VELVT TAETRVM SINGVLA VIRVS HABENT. The same image at *EP* III iii 105-6 'ergo alii noceant miseris optentque timeri, / *tinctaque mordaci spicula felle gerant*'.

34. TAETRVM *R. J. Tarrant* TINCTV *Ehwald* TINCTVM *codd.* *Tinctum* is impossible: if the word were used, it would have to go with *uerba*. Compare *Ibis* 53-54 'liber iambus / *tincta* Lycambeo sanguine *tela* dabit', *Ibis* 491 '[tamque cadas domitus ...] quam qui *dona* tulit Nesseo *tincta* ueneno', *EP* III i 26 '*tinctaque* mortifera tabe *sagitta* madet', and *EP* III iii 106 '*tinctaque* mordaci *spicula* felle gerant'. Ehwald's *tinctu* is linguistically and palaeographically somewhat better than Merkel's *tinguat*: for similar corruptions compare *Fast* III 612 'flet tamen *admonitu* motus, Elissa, tui', where many manuscripts read *admonitus*, and *Tr* I iv 9 'pinea texta sonant pulsu [*Rothmaler*: pulsi *codd*], stridore rudentes'. Even so, 'Each of your words carries poison, as though it had been dipped in it' seems awkward. For Professor Tarrant's *taetrum* compare Lucretius I 936 'absinthia taetra', *Dirae* 23 'taetra uenena', and *Hal* 131 'nigrum ... uirus'.

34. VIRVS HABENT. Compare *Tr* IV i 84 'aut telo *uirus habente* perit' & III x 64 'nam uolucri ferro tinctile *uirus inest*'.

35-36. HOSTIBVS EVENIAT QUAM SIS VIOLENTVS IN ARMIS / SENTIRE. *Hostibus eueniat* is a common phrase in Ovid: compare *Am* II x 16-17 '*hostibus eueniat* uita seuera meis! / hostibus eueniat uiduo dormire cubili', *Am* III xi 16, *AA* III 247, *Fast* III 493-94 'at, puto, praeposita est fuscae mihi Candida paelex! / *eueniat nostris hostibus* ille dolor [*recc quidam*: color *codd plerique*]!', and *Her* XVI 219-20 (Paris to Helen) '*hostibus eueniant* conuiuia talia nostris, / experior posito qualia saepe mero!'.

37. QVAE TIBI TAM TENVI CVRA LIMANTVR. 'Which are sharpened by you with such painstaking care'. For this meaning of *limare* compare Pliny *NH* VIII 71 'cornu ad saxa *limato*' and Cic *Brut* 236 '[M. Piso ...] habuit a natura genus quoddam *acuminis*, quod etiam arte *limauerat*'.

37-38. VT OMNES / ISTIVS INGENVI PECTORIS ESSE NEGENT. 'So that all would deny that they are the product of your kindly spirit'; for this sense of *ingenuus* compare Catullus LXVIII 37-38 'quod cum ita sit, nolim statuas nos mente maligna / id facere aut *animo* non satis *ingenuo*'. *Ingenui pectoris* is my correction for the manuscripts' INGENIVM CORPORIS, which could only mean 'so that all would deny that the talent of your body exists'; Ovid can hardly be identifying the *tela* of 36 with Brutus' *ingenium*. Wheeler translates 'On these [the missiles of your tongue] you use the file with such extreme care that none would recognize in them your real nature', and André 'que personne ne croirait qu'un tel esprit habite ton corps'; neither translation fits the Latin. Shackleton Bailey's INGENIVM NOMINIS still leaves unsolved the problem of *ingenium*.

The corruption of *ingenui* to *ingenium* (or rather, *ingeniū*) is simple enough; and the interchange of *pectus* and *corpus* is a common error.

42. NOTITIAM ... INFITIATA. *Infitiari* used similarly at *EP* I vii 27 'nec tuus est genitor nos *infitiatus* amicos'.

43. IMMEMOR ... IMMEMOR. Professor R. J. Tarrant points out the similar epanalepsis at Hor *Ep* I xi 9 '*oblitusque* meorum, *obliuiscendus* et illis'.

44. SOLLICITI *BCM*^{2ul} SOLLICITE *M*^{1}*FHILT*. The adjective with adverbial meaning would be especially liable to corruption. The same construction at *Am* II iv 25 'dulce canit flectitque *facillima* uocem'.

44. LEVASTIS *Barberinus lat. 26, saec xiii* LEVATIS *BCMFHILT*. If 44 were taken in isolation, *leuatis*, which most editors print, would be acceptable enough; compare *Tr* IV i 49 ' iure deas igitur ueneror mala nostra *leuantes*' and *EP* III vi 13-14 'nec scelus admittas si consoleris amicum, / mollibus et uerbis aspera fata *leues*'. But it is clear from 42 'est infitiata' and 49 'doluistis' that Ovid is speaking of the time of his banishment, and so *leuastis* must be read. Compare *Tr* I v 75 'me deus oppressit, nullo *mala nostra leuante*', *EP* II vii 61-62 'recta fides comitum poterat *mala nostra leuare*: / ditata est spoliis perfida turba meis', and *EP* III ii 25-26 'pars estis pauci melior, qui rebus in artis / ferre mihi nullam turpe putastis [*uar* putatis] opem'.

45-50. Compare the listing of *adynata* at the end of v (41-44), which again illustrates Ovid's eternal gratitude (to Sextus Pompeius). Here the personal detail (*hic nimium nobis conterminus Hister*) makes the *adynaton* reflect Ovid's own circumstances.

46. DE MARE. The same form of the ablative at *Tr* V ii 20 'pleno de mare'. Compare Ovid's frequent use of the metrically convenient ablative in *-e* of third-declension adjectives.

47-48. Thyestes' feast cited as a proverbial example at *Met* XV 62 (Pythagoras is urging a vegetarian diet) 'neue Thyesteis cumulemus uiscera mensis', *Tr* II 391-92 'si non Aeropen [*Politianus*: Meropen *uel* Europen *codd*] frater sceleratus amasset, / auersos Solis non legeremus equos', Lucan I 534-44, and Martial III xlv 1-2 'Fugerit an Phoebus mensas cenamque Thyestae / ignoro: fugimus nos, Ligurine, tuam'.

47. VTQVE ... SI = *et, quasi.* All of the instances of the idiom cited by Lewis & Short *ut* II A 2e and *OLD ut* 8d are from prose, except for Ter *Eun* 117 and Lucilius 330 Marx. In none of these passages is *ut* separated from *si*: the hyperbaton elevates the phrase and makes more natural its use in verse.

49. QVI ME DOLVISTIS ADEMPTVM. 'Who mourned my exile' is the meaning imposed by context, but the phrase would usually mean 'who mourned my death': compare *EP* I ix 41 'iure igitur lacrimas Celso libamus *adempto*', and the similar use of *raptus* for the exiled Ovid at xi 5 and xvi 1. For Ovid's considering his exile as his death, see xvi 1-4, *Tr* III iii 53 'cum patriam amisi, tunc me periisse putato', and *EP* I ix 56 'et nos extinctis adnumerare potest'.

VII. To Vestalis

Vestalis, a younger son of Cottius, monarch of a small kingdom in the Alps (see at 29 [p 253]), was *primipilaris* of the legion of the area (perhaps the *V Macedonica*). He had just been named administrator of the region around Tomis (see at 1); as an important local official, he was a natural choice as recipient of one of Ovid's letters.

The poem starts with a description of the harsh climate of Tomis, to which Vestalis along with Ovid can now testify, and of the savagery of the inhabitants (1-12). This serves as a bridge to a compliment to Vestalis on being named *primipilaris* (13-18), and to the main body of the poem, a long and rather conventional description of how Vestalis led the final attack in the recovery of Aegissos (19-52). In the concluding distich Ovid declares that he has rendered immortal the deeds of Vestalis.

1. ORAS (*CI*) seems more suited to the nature of Vestalis' command than VNDAS, the reading of the other manuscripts. After *Euxinas*, corruption from *oras* to *undas* would be very easy, the inverse less so. Ovid does not elsewhere use *Euxinae orae*, the usual substantives with *Euxinus* being *aquae, mare, fretum*, and, closest in meaning, *litus*, for which see iii 51 'litus ad Euxinum ... ibis', *Tr* V ii 63-64 'iussus ad Euxini deformia litora ueni / aequoris', and *Tr* V iv 1.

2. POSITIS ... SVB AXE in effect acts as a single adjective meaning 'northern'; *axe* plays a subordinate role and so does not require an epithet. The phrasing may be based on Accius 566-67 Ribbeck[2] '[ora ...] *sub axe posita* ad Stellas septem, unde horrifer / Aquilonis stridor gelidas molitur niues'. *Lycaonio ... sub axe* at *Tr* III ii 2.

3. ASPICIS EN PRAESENS. Compare ix 81-86, where Ovid invites Graecinus to ask his brother Flaccus, recently stationed in the Pontus, about conditions of life in the area.

3. IACEAMVS. 'Lie suffering': similarly used at *EP* I iii 49 'orbis in extremi *iaceo* desertus harenis', I vii 5, II ix 4 & III i 85 'ut minus infesta *iaceam* regione labora'.

4. FALSA ... QVERI. Perhaps a common phrase: Professor R. J. Tarrant cites Sallust *Iug* 1 '*Falso queritur* de natura sua genus humanum'.

5-6. ACCEDET ... FIDES. 'People will believe'. Compare Cic *Diu* I 5 'Cratippusque ... isdem rebus *fidem tribuit*, reliqua diuinationis genera reiecit' and Tac *Germ* 3 4 'ex ingenio quisque *demat uel addat fidem*' 'each can believe or disbelieve this according to his disposition'.

5-6. NON IRRITA ... FIDES = *rata fides*, a phrase meaning 'trustworthiness', *rata* having no special force. Compare *Met* III 341 'prima *fide* [genitive] ... *ratae* temptamina', *Tr* I v 49-50 'multa credibili tulimus *ratamque*, / quamuis acciderint, non habitura *fidem*', and *Tr* III x 35-36 'cum sint praemia falsi / nulla, *ratam* debet testis habere *fidem*'. Note the hyperbaton in all these passages.

6. ALPINIS IVVENIS REGIBVS ORTE. See at 29 *progenies alti fortissima Donni* (p 253). For the language, compare Hor *Carm* I i 1 'Maecenas atauis edite regibus'.

7. IPSE VIDES CERTE GLACIE CONCRESCERE PONTVM. At ix 85-86 Ovid tells Graecinus to ask his brother Flaccus 'mentiar, an coeat duratus frigore Pontus, / et teneat glacies iugera multa freti'.

Similar language at *Tr* III x 37-38 'uidimus ingentem glacie consistere pontum, / lubricaque [*codd*: lubrica cum *fort scribendum*] immotas testa premebat aquas'.

8. IPSE VIDES RIGIDO STANTIA VINA GELV. The same picture more explicitly given at *Tr* III x 23-24 'nudaque consistunt, formam seruantia testae, / uina, nec hausta meri, sed data frusta bibunt'.

9-10. IPSE VIDES ONERATA FEROX VT DVCAT IAZYX / PER MEDIAS HISTRI PLAVSTRA BVBVLCVS AQVAS. Similar descriptions at *Tr* III x 33-34 'perque nouos pontes, subterlabentibus undis, / *ducunt Sarmatici barbara plaustra* *boues*' and *Tr* III xii 29-30 'nec mare concrescit glacie, nec ut ante per Histrum / stridula Sauromates *plaustra bubulcus* agit'.

9. IAZYX. The *Iazyges Sarmatae* are mentioned by Pliny (*NH* IV 80) and by Strabo (VII 3 17), who describes them as one of several tribes living between the Borysthenes (Dnepr) and the Danube. They are also listed by Pompey, under the name of 'Iazyges Metanastae', the Wandering Iazyges (*Geog* III 7); the 'Iazyges' he describes as living along the shore of the Maeotis (III 5 19). Tacitus mentions the nation at *Ann* XII 29 4 (Vannius, king of the Suebi, is under attack) 'ipsi manus propria pedites, eques e Sarmaticis Iazygibus erat' and at *Hist* III 5 (the *principes Sarmatarum Iazygum* are enlisted to ensure the defence of Moesia in the absence of the regular troops; their offer to raise infantry as well as supplying their usual force of cavalry is rejected because of the fear of future treachery).

The name of the tribe was difficult metrically, so here Ovid calls them *Iazyges*, while at *Tr* III xii 30 (cited in the previous note) he calls them *Sauromatae*. At *EP* I ii 77 he solves the difficulty through hendiadys: 'quid *Sauromatae* faciant, quid *Iazyges* acres'.

11. ASPICIS. Ovid here uses verbs of seeing in an interesting way. At 7 and 9 he has *uides*; then *aspicis* suggests continuity but at the same time movement toward a new subject, and with a military detail introduced so as to introduce Vestalis' experience of war; then in 13-14 the emphasis is changed by the contrary-to-fact past optative *utinam ... spectata fuisset*.

11. ASPICIS ET MITTI SVB ADVNCO TOXICA FERRO. 'You behold how poison is hurled on the barbed steel' (Wheeler). The *telum* of 12 should be taken to be a spear, since *mittere* never seems to be used of arrows. At *Ibis* 135 the *hasta* is mentioned as the special weapon of the Iazyges.

11. ADVNCO. The spear had hooks. Compare *Met* VI 252-53 'quod [*sc* ferrum] simul eductum est, pars et pulmonis *in hamis* / eruta cumque anima cruor est effusus in auras', where Bömer cites among other passages Curtius IX 5 23 'corpore ... nudato animaduertunt *hamos inesse telo* nec aliter id sine pernicie corporis extrahi posse quam ut secando uulnus augerent' and Prop II xii 9 'et merito *hamatis* manus est armata sagittis'.

13-14. ATQVE VTINAM PARS HAEC TANTUM SPECTATA FVISSET, / NON ETIAM PROPRIO COGNITA MARTE TIBI. A similar opposition at *Met* III 247-48 (of Actaeon) *'uelletque uidere, / non etiam sentire* canum fera facta suorum'.

15. TENDITVR *Owen* TENDITIS *codd*. The number of *tenditis* is inappropriate to the context. Owen's *tenditur*, independently conjectured two years later by Ehwald (*KB* 84), seems a somewhat more elegant solution to the problem than Merkel's TENDISTI. It puts the weight of the line on *ad primum ... pilum* rather than on Vestalis himself; the pentameter, with its emphasis on the *honor*, suggests that this is right.

15. PRIMVM PILVM. Compare *Am* III viii 27-28 'proque bono uersu *primum* deducite *pilum*! / nox [*A. Y. Campbell*: hoc *uel* hic *codd*] tibi, si belles [*Madvig*: uelles *codd*], possit, Homere, dari'. The *primipilaris* was the commander of the first century of the first cohort of the Roman legion, and hence first in rank among the legion's centurions.

17. PLENIS is the reading of all but two of the manuscripts collated. For this sense of *plenus* ('abundant'), compare *Am* I viii 56 '*plena* uenit canis de grege praeda lupis', *Nux* 91-92 'illa [the tree that is not near a road] suo quaecumque tulit dare dona colono / et *plenos* fructus adnumerare potest', Hor *Sat* I i 57, and Cic *Sex Rosc* 6 'alienam pecuniam tam *plenam* atque praeclaram'. Ehwald read PLENVS (*F^{ac}I*), joining *ingens* with *uirtus* in the following line, arguing that the honour would not seem a great one to a member of a royal family. But Ovid devoted four lines to describing Vestalis' new rank: he must have believed that Vestalis would consider it a very great honour indeed. As well, if *ingens* is connected with *titulus, uirtus ... maior* gains point.

17. PLENIS ... FRVCTIBVS. For the wealth of the *primipilaris*, see *Am* III viii 9-10 'ecce recens diues parto per uulnera censu / praefertur nobis sanguine pastus eques'. In that poem the newly-rich *primipilaris*, Ovid's rival in love, is given a character very different from that of Vestalis.

17. INGENS is used at ix 65 of another office, the consulship.

18. IPSA TAMEN VIRTVS ORDINE MAIOR ERIT. A similar sentiment at *EP* II ix 11-14 (to king Cotys) 'regia, crede mihi, res est succurrere lapsis ... fortunam decet hoc istam ['this befits your position'], *quae maxima cum sit, / esse potest animo uix tamen aequa tuo*'.

19. NON NEGAT HOC HISTER. For the device of calling to witness the scenes of military exploits compare Catullus LXIV 357 'testis erit magnis uirtutibus unda Scamandri' and the passages there cited by Fordyce. For *non negat* Professor A. Dalzell cites Catullus IV 6-7 'negat ... negare'.

20. PVNICEAM GETICO SANGVINE FECIT AQVAM. Similar language at ix 79-80 (of Flaccus) 'hic raptam Troesmin celeri uirtute recepit, / *infecitque fero sanguine Danuuium*'.

21. AEGISSOS. The city, the modern Tulcea, is situated about 110 kilometres directly north of Tomis (Constanţa) on the southernmost branch of the Danube, 60 kilometres from the mouth of the river. At *EP* I viii 11-20 Ovid describes the recapture of the city from the Getes; evidently the city had been lost once again.

Aegissos is the spelling certified by three of the five sources cited by Mommsen (*CIL* III page 1009), namely Hierocles *Synecdemus* 637 14, *Notitia dignitatum* 99, and Procopius *Aed* IV 7 20. The *Itinerarium Antoninianum* (226 2) offers *Aegiso* (ablative); Ehwald (*KB* 41), citing Mommsen, took this as sufficient justification for retaining the single *s* of the *Ex Ponto* manuscripts, although the now lost Strasbourg manuscript had *egissus* at I viii 13 (and an indication of an alternative ending in -*os*). The *Ravenna Cosmography* (4 5), Mommsen's final source, reads *Aegypsum*.

27. TE SVBEVNTE RECEPTA. 'Recaptured on your attack'. Intransitive *subire* in this sense belongs to military vocabulary: compare Caesar *BG* VII 85 'alii tela coniciunt, alii testudine facta *subeunt*' and Curtius IV 2 23. For instances from military prose of *subire* with a direct object see Caesar *BG* II 27 '*subire* iniquissimum locum', Hirtius *BG* VIII 15, *Bell Alex* 76 2 '*subierant* iniquum locum', and *Bell Hisp* 24 2.

22. INGENIO ... LOCI. 'The nature (i.e. difficulty) of its terrain'. The same standard phrase at Tac *Ann* VI 41 'locorumque ingenio', *Hist* I 51 'diu infructuosam et asperam militiam tolerauerant *ingenio loci* caelique ['climate']', and from Ovid *Tr* V x 17-18 'tumulus defenditur ipse / moenibus exiguis ingenioque loci' and *EP* II i 52 '[oppida ...] nec satis *ingenio* tuta fuisse *loci*'.

22. NIL OPIS. The expression is rather prosaic: compare Cic *Fam* IV i 1 '*aliquid opis* rei publicae tulissemus'.

23. DVBIVM *BMFHIT* DVBIVM EST *CL*. The same variant in many manuscripts at *EP* III i 17-18 (Ovid is addressing Tomis) 'nec tibi sunt fontes laticis nisi paene marini, / qui potus *dubium* sistat alatne sitim'.

24. NVBIBVS AEQVA. 'As high as the clouds'. For this use of *aequus* compare *Aen* IX 674 'abietibus iuuenes patriis in [*Heyne*: et *codd*; *cf Il* XII 132 'ἔστασαν ὡς ὅτε τε δρύες οὔρεσιν ὑψικάρηνοι'] montibus aequos', Statius *Ach* I 173 'aequus uertice matri', Sen *Ep* 94 61 'aequum arcibus aggerem ... et muros in miram altitudinem eductos', and *Aen* IV 89 '*aequataque* machina caelo'.

25. SITHONIO = *Thracio*.

25. INTERCEPERAT. *Intercipere* 'capture' common in Livy (IX 43 3, XXI 1 5, XXVI 51 12, XXXVI 31 10); compare Ammianus XX 7 17 & XX 10 3 'locis ... recuperatis quae olim barbari intercepta retinebant ut propria'.

26. EREPTAS VICTOR HABEBAT OPES. Similar phrasing at *Fast* III 49-51 'hoc ubi cognouit contemptor Amulius aequi / (nam *raptas* fratri *uictor habebat opes*), / amne iubet mergi geminos'.

27. FLVMINEA ... VNDA. *Flumineus* does not occur elsewhere in the *Tristia* or *Ex Ponto*; *fluminea ... aqua* at *Fast* II

46 & 596.

27. VITELLIVS. This Vitellius is presumably one of the four sons of Publius Vitellius, grandfather of the emperor. Suetonius wrote of the sons, Aulus, Quintus, Publius, and Lucius, that they were 'quattuor filios amplissimae dignitatis cognomines ac tantum praenominibus distinctos' (*Vit* 2 2). Heinsius suggested Aulus (*cos* AD 32) was the one here meant, 'nisi ad L. Vitellium patrem [*sc* principis] referre mauis'. 'On the general and reasonable assumption', wrote Syme (*HO* 90), 'this is P. Vitellius'. But Suetonius calls P. Vitellius 'Germanici comes', and he is heard of in 15 assisting Germanicus in a campaign (Tac *Ann* I 70 1): it is perhaps more likely that Publius would have been with Germanicus at the time of the capture of Aegissos, and that another of the brothers is meant. Certainty is in any case not attainable.

29. PROGENIES ALTI FORTISSIMA DONNI. For the phrasing, compare *EP* II ix 1-2 'Regia *progenies*, cui nobilitatis origo / nomen in Eumolpi peruenit usque ['goes back to'], Coty'.

The Donnus here referred to is Vestalis' grandfather (*CIL* V 7817), or possibly a more distant ancestor. Vestalis' father, Cottius, became a client of Augustus; at XV 10 7 Ammianus mentions the worship still accorded Cottius 'quod iusto moderamine rexerat suos, et ascitus in societatem rei Romanae quietem genti praestitit sempiternam'. At *Nero* 18 Suetonius mentions as one of the few additions to the empire under Nero the 'regnum ... Alpium defuncto Cottio'. This Cottius would probably have been Vestalis' older brother; André is therefore right to infer that Vestalis 'n'était pas l'héritier du trône, ce qu'Ovide n'aurait pas manqué de signaler'.

30. IMPETVS. *Impetus* + infinitive usually indicates a mad impulse: the only other exception in Ovid is *Met* V 287-88 (one of the Muses speaking) '*impetus ire fuit*; claudit sua tecta Pyreneus / uimque parat, quam nos sumptis effugimus alis'.

31. CONSPICVVS LONGE FVLGENTIBVS ARMIS. Modelled on *Aen* XI 769 '*insignis longe* Phrygiis *fulgebat* in *armis'*.

32. FORTIA NE POSSINT FACTA LATERE CAVES. Vestalis would in any case have fought bravely; so that his deeds would not pass unnoticed, he led the attack.

33. INGENTIQVE GRADV. When Ovid elsewhere use *ingens gradus* (*passus*) he gives the phrase a humorous tone: see *Am* III i 11 'uenit et *ingenti* uiolenta Tragoedia *passu'*, *AA* III 303-4 'illa uelut coniunx Vmbri rubicunda mariti / ambulat *ingentes* uarica fertque *gradus'*, and *Met* XIII 776-77 (of Polyphemus) 'gradiens *ingenti* litora *passu* / degrauat'. The straightforwardness of this passage is of a piece with the rest of the poem.

For an example of the normal epic use of this detail, see *Aen* X 572 'longe gradientem'.

33. FERRVM LOCVMQVE reflects 23 'dubium *positu* melius defensa *manune'*.

34. SAXAQVE ... GRANDINE PLVRA. The same phrase in the same metrical position at *Ibis* 467-68 'aut te deuoueat certis Abdera diebus, / *saxaque* deuotum *grandine plura* petant'.

35. MISSA SVPER IACVLORVM TVRBA. 'The crowding missiles hurled from above' (Wheeler).

38. FERE. Heinsius' FERO would involve the repetition of *fero* in 44; and *fero uulnere* would be rather feeble when applied to a shield.

Professor R. J. Tarrant points out to me that Ovid's description of Vestalis' exploit may have served as a distant model for Lucan's account of how a centurion named Scaeua rallied Caesar's forces and led an attack against Pompey's encampment (VI 140-262). Scaeua was made *primipilaris* in reward for his bravery (Caesar *BC* III 53 5).

40. SED MINOR EST ACRI LAVDIS AMORE DOLOR. Similar language of a similar exploit at *Met* XI 525-28 'ut miles, numero praestantior omni, / cum saepe adsiluit defensae moenibus urbis, / spe potitur tandem *laudisque* *accensus amore* / inter mille uiros murum tamen occupat unus'. Ovid's description of Vestalis' exploit is little more than a string of conventional phrases.

40. ACRI. 'Sharp'. Compare ii 36 'immensum gloria *calcar* habet'.

41-42. TALIS APVD TROIAM DANAIS PRO NAVIBVS AIAX / DICITVR HECTOREAS SVSTINVISSE FACES. Compare *Met* XIII 7-8 (Ajax speaking of Ulysses) 'at non Hectoreis dubitauit cedere flammis, / quas ego sustinui, quas hac a classe fugaui' and *Met* XIII 384-85 (the death of Ajax) 'Hectora qui solus, qui ferrum ignesque Iouemque / sustinuit totiens, unam non sustinet iram'. All three passages are drawn from *Il* XV 674-746, the description of how Ajax repulsed Hector's attempt to set the Greek ships afire, and in particular from 730-31 'ἔνθ' ἄρ' ὅ γ' ἑστήκει δεδοκημένος, ἔγχεϊ δ' αἰεὶ / Τρῶας ἄμυνε νεῶν, ὅς τις φέροι ἀκάματον πῦρ'.

41. PRO NAVIBVS. 'In front of the ships'; a reminiscence of *Il* XV 746 (the final line of the book) 'δώδεκα δὲ προπάροιθε νεῶν αὐτοσχεδὸν οὖτα'.

43. DEXTERA DEXTRAE. Ovid used syncope in *dextera* where metrically convenient. Elsewhere when he employs the two forms he is usually describing the joining of hands in pledge or friendship. See *Her* II 31 'commissaque *dextera dextrae*', *Her* XII 90 '*dextrae dextera* iuncta meae', and *Met* VI 447-48 '*dextera dextrae* / iungitur'. For a different use, see *Met* III 640-41 '*dextera* [*uar* dextra] Naxos erat: *dextra* mihi lintea danti / "quid facis, o demens? quis te furor," inquit "Acoete?"'.

45-46. DICERE DIFFICILE EST QVID MARS TVVS EGERIT ILLIC, / QVOTQVE NECI DEDERIS QVOSQVE QVIBVSQVE MODIS. As Professor E. Fantham points out to me, this *praeteritio* takes the place of a full *aristeia* detailing Vestalis' exploits.

46. QVOSQVE QVIBVSQVE MODIS. Compare *quotque quibusque modis* in an erotic context at *Am* II viii 28, and *Tr* III xii 33-34 'sedulus occurram nautae, dictaque salute, / quid ueniat quaeram *quisue quibusue locis'*.

47. ENSE TVO FACTOS CALCABAS VICTOR ACERVOS.
Compare *Met* V 88 (of Perseus) 'extructos morientum *calcat a ceruos'*.

50. MVLTAQVE FERT MILES VVLNERA, MVLTA FACIT. A
similar conjunction of verbs at *Fast* II 233-34 'non
moriuntur inulti, / *uulneraque* alterna *dantque feruntque* manu'.

52. IBAT. IBIT (*BP*) is printed by all modern editors except
André, and is possibly correct: compare *Am* II iv 31-32 'ut
taceam de me, qui causa tangor ab omni, / illic Hippolytum
pone, Priapus *erit*' for the future tense used of a mythological
character, and *EP* II xi 21-22 'acer et ad palmae per se
cursurus honores, / si tamen horteris, fortius *ibit* [*uar* ibat]
equus' for the corruption of future to imperfect.

53. TEMPVS IN OMNE. Similar promises of immortality at
Tr I vi 36 (to his wife) 'carminibus uiues *tempus in omne* meis',
EP II vi 33-34 (to Graecinus) 'crede mihi, nostrum si non
mortale futurum est / carmen, in ore frequens posteritatis
eris', and *EP* III i 93 (to his wife) 'nota tua est probitas
testataque *tempus in omne*'.

Vestalis is known to us only through this poem.

VIII. To Suillius

This poem, nominally addressed to Suillius, husband of Ovid's stepdaughter, is in fact directed to Germanicus, of whose staff Suillius was a member (see at 23 [pp 264-65]).

Ovid begins the poem by expressing his pleasure at receiving, at last, a letter from Suillius, saying he hopes that Suillius does not feel ashamed of being related to him by marriage (1-20). He then asks him to address Germanicus on his behalf (21-26). In 27-30 he says how grateful he will be if Germanicus assists him; at 31 he begins to address Germanicus directly in a tripartite defence of poetry. The first part (31-42) builds on 34 'Naso suis opibus, *carmine*, gratus erit': Ovid is now poor, but can still offer Germanicus his poetry. The second section (43-66) builds on 43-44 'nec tamen officio uatum per *carmina* facto / principibus res est aptior ulla uiris', and explains how verse brings immortality to great men and their deeds. The third section (67-78) offers culminating evidence for the value of poetry: Germanicus is himself a poet. Ovid moves from this to a final plea that Germanicus help his fellow-poet: once removed from Tomis, he will praise him in verse (79-88). In the final distich of the poem, he asks Suillius to assist his prayer.

The structure of the poem is similar to that of *Tr* V ii. In that poem Ovid addresses his wife for the first thirty-eight lines, telling her of his misery and asking her to approach Augustus on his behalf. In the six lines that follow, he asks himself what he will do if she fails him; he answers that he will make his own direct approach to Augustus. The final thirty-four lines are his prayer to Augustus, in which he describes the hardships he endures at Tomis and begs for a mitigation of his punishment. It is remarkable that in both poems direct addresses to members of the imperial family should be disguised in this way: it seems probable that *Tr* II, Ovid's long defence of his conduct, had been received by Augustus with hostility, and that he was thenceforth more circumspect.

1-2. SERA QVIDEM ... GRATA TAMEN. *Tamen* goes with *grata*, balancing *quidem*. For instances of the separate *serus tamen* idiom ('it is late in happening, but it does in fact happen') see Nisbet and Hubbard at Hor *Carm* I xv 19.

1. SERA QVIDEM. It seems that in spite of his being a close relative of Ovid, Suillius, like Sextus Pompeius (see the introduction to i), had been reluctant to be openly associated with him.

1. STVDIIS EXCVLTE. 'Refined'. *Studiis* adds little to the force of *exculte*: the same idiom at Quintilian XII ii 1 'mores ante omnia oratori *studiis* erunt *excolendi*' and Cic *Tusc* I 4 'ergo in Graecia musici floruerunt, discebantque id omnes, nec qui nesciebat satis *excultus doctrina* putabatur'.

1. SVILLI. P. Suillius Rufus (*PW* IV A,1 719-22; *PIR¹* S 700) is otherwise chiefly known to us from three passages of Tacitus: Suillius is presented as 'strong, savage, and unbridled' (Syme *Tacitus* 332). At *Ann* IV 31, Tacitus describes how, in 24, Tiberius insisted that Suillius, convicted of accepting a bribe, be relegated to an island rather than merely be exiled from Italy; what seemed cruelty at the time later seemed wisdom in view of his later behaviour as a favourite of Claudius. At *Ann* XI 1-7 Tacitus describes how Suillius' excesses resulted in a proposal in the Senate to revive the *lex Cincia* of 204 BC, by which advocates had been forbidden remuneration: the proposal was modified by Claudius at the instance of Suillius and others affected so as to establish a maximum fee of ten thousand sesterces. At *Ann* XIII 42-43 (AD 58) Tacitus tells how Suillius, 'imperitante Claudio terribilis ac uenalis', was charged with extortion as proconsul of Asia and with laying malicious charges under Claudius. Banished to the Balearic islands, he led a luxurious existence, remaining unrepentant.

3-4. PIA SI POSSIT SVPEROS LENIRE ROGANDO / GRATIA. Compare 21 'si quid agi sperabis posse *precando*'.

5-6. ANIMI SVM FACTVS AMICI / DEBITOR. 'Your friendly purpose has placed me in your debt' (Wheeler). The genitive similarly used for the cause of indebtedness at i 2 '*debitor* est *uitae* qui tibi, Sexte, suae' and *Tr* I v 10

237

'perpetuusque *animae debitor huius* ero'.

6. MERITVM VELLE IVVARE VOCO. 'I call the desire to help a favour already given'. Otto *uelle* 2 cites *EP* III iv 79 'ut desint uires, *tamen est laudanda uoluntas*', Prop II x 5-6 'quod si deficient uires, audacia certe / laus erit: in magnis *et uoluisse sat est*', *Pan Mess* 3-7, *Laus Pisonis* 214; the same proverb at Sen *Ben* V 2 2 'uoluntas ipsa rectum petens laudanda est'.

7. IMPETVS ISTE TVVS LONGVM MODO DVRET IN AEVVM. Similar phrasing at *EP* II vi 35-36 (Graecinus has been rendering Ovid assistance) 'fac modo permaneas lasso, Graecine, fidelis, / *duret et in longas impetus iste moras*'.

9. IVS ALIQVOD. 'A certain claim on each other'. The same phrase for a similar situation at *EP* I vii 60 (to Messalinus, elder brother of Cotta Maximus) '*ius aliquod* tecum fratris amicus habet'.

9. ADFINIA. The *adfinis* was a relative by marriage, commonly, as here, a son-in-law; a relative by common descent was a *cognatus*.

9. ADFINIA VINCVLA. *Vinculum* used of family relationships at *Met* IX 550 (Byblis wishes to marry her brother) 'expetit ... *uinclo* tecum propiore ligari' and Cic *Planc* 27 'cum illo maximis *uinclis* et propinquitatis et *adfinitatis* coniunctus'.

10. INLABEFACTA. The word elsewhere in Latin only at xii 29-30 'haec ... concordia ... uenit ad albentes *inlabefacta* comas'. Ovid is fond of using negative participles of this type.

11-12. NAM TIBI QVAE CONIVNX, EADEM MIHI FILIA PAENE EST, / ET QVAE TE GENERVM, ME VOCAT ILLA VIRVM. The same type of circumlocution at *Her* III 45-48 (Briseis to Achilles) "diruta Marte tuo Lyrnesia moenia uidi; ... uidi ... tres cecidisse *quibus* [*Bentley*: tribus *codd*] quae mihi, mater erat'.

11. EADEM MIHI FILIA PAENE EST. This is presumably Perilla, the recipient of *Tr* III vii, whom Ovid there speaks of in terms appropriate to a stepfather.

13-14. EI MIHI, SI LECTIS VVLTVM TV VERSIBVS ISTIS / DVCIS, ET ADFINEM TE PVDET ESSE MEVM. A similar lament at *EP* II ii 5-6 '*ei mihi, si lecto uultus* tibi nomine non est / qui fuit, et dubitas cetera perlegere!'; both passages are followed by defences of Ovid's character.

For *uultum ... ducis* see at i 5 *trahis uultus* (p 149).

15. NIHIL *BCMFHLT* NIL *I.* Copyists were more prone to alter *nil* to *nihil* than the inverse; but in 1919 Housman demonstrated that *nihil* was Ovid's invariable form for the latter half of the first foot by pointing out that in all of the twenty-odd passages where the manuscripts offer *nihil* or *nil* at that position the following word invariably begins with a vowel (*Collected Papers* 1000-1003). There would be no reason for such an avoidance of consonants if Ovid had allowed *nil* in this position; he must therefore have used *nihil* alone.

16. FORTVNAM, QVAE MIHI CAECA FVIT. The image of Fortune being blind to a single individual seems very strange. Professor R. J. Tarrant suggests that *caeca* could mean 'unforeseeing', and by *fortunam* Ovid could be referring to his own previous circumstances; alternatively, *caeca* might be a corruption induced by the familiar image of the blind goddess, replacing an original SAEVA (Riese) or LAEVA, for which compare Silius III 93-94 'si promissum uertat *Fortuna* fauorem, / *laeuaque sit coeptis*'.

17-18. SEV GENVS EXCVTIAS, EQVITES AB ORIGINE PRIMA / VSQVE PER INNVMEROS INVENIEMVR AVOS. A similar claim at *Tr* IV x 7-8 'usque a proauis uetus ordinis heres, / non modo fortunae munere factus eques'. The status of *eques* was not hereditary except in the case of a senator's son. The Paeligni did not receive the citizenship until after the Social War; to be born to equestrian status, and to assume that he could have had a senatorial career (*Tr* IV x 35), Ovid must have belonged to one of the dominant families of the region.

17. EXCVTIAS. 'Examine'. Ovid plays on the primary meaning of the word, 'shake out', at *Am* I viii 45-46 'has quoque quae frontis rugas in uertice portant [*Burman*: quas ... portas *codd*] / *excute*; de rugis crimina multa cadent'. The transferred meaning had lost any sense of metaphor by Ovid's time, however; see especially *Tr* II 224 '*excutiasque* oculis otia nostra* ['the product of my leisure hours'— Wheeler] tuis'.

19-20. SIVE VELIS QVI SINT MORES INQVIRERE NOSTRI, / ERROREM MISERO DETRAHE, LABE CARENT. A similar claim of no fault beyond his *error* at *EP* II ii 15-16 'est mea culpa grauis, sed quae me perdere solum / ausa sit, et *nullum maius adorta nefas*'.

20. ERROREM ... DETRAHE. At *Met* II 38-39 the same phrase with a different meaning: (Phaethon to his father) 'pignora da, genitor, per quae tu uera propago / credar, et hunc animis *errorem* ['doubt'] *detrahe* nostris*.

20. LABE CARENT. The same sense of *labes* at *Tr* I ix 43 'uitae *labe carentis*' and Prop IV xi 41-42 'neque ulla *labe* mea nostros erubuisse focos'; compare as well the phrase *sine labe* at *Tr* II 110 (*domus*), *Tr* IV viii 33 (*decem lustris ... peractis*), *EP* I ii 143 (*praeteriti anni*), *EP* II vii 49 (*uita prior*), *Her* XVII 14 (*tenor uitae*), and *Her* XVII 69 (*fama*).

22. QVOS COLIS ... DEOS. A similar definition of the imperial family at *EP* II ii 123 '*quos colis ad superos* haec fer mandata sacerdos'.

23. DI TIBI SVNT CAESAR IVVENIS. *BCFM*^{2ul} read SINT; but the indicative seems to be required by the preceding 'quos *colis* ... deos' and the following '*tua numina* placa' and 'hac certe nulla est notior *ara* tibi'.

23. CAESAR IVVENIS. Germanicus; he would have acquired the cognomen *Caesar* on his adoption by Tiberius in AD 4. *Iuuenis* probably refers to Germanicus' title of *princeps iuuentutis*, which *EP* II v 41-42 indicates he must have held: 'te *iuuenum princeps*, cui dat Germania nomen, / participem studii Caesar habere solet'. Germanicus' holding of the title is not elsewhere attested.

At *Ann* IV 31 5, Tacitus identifies Suillius as 'quaestorem quondam Germanici'; at *Ann* XIII 42 4, he represents Suillius as saying of himself and Seneca 'se quaestorem Germanici, illum domus eius adulterum fuisse'. His service under Germanicus was clearly a principal fact of his life.

25-26. ANTISTITIS ... PRECES. Here *antistes* is virtually equivalent to *cultor*, as at *Tr* III xiv 1 '*Cultor et antistes* doctorum sancte uirorum'; compare as well *Met* XIII 632-33 'Anius, quo ... *antistite* Phoebus / rite *colebatur*'.

27-28. QVAMLIBET EXIGVA SI NOS EA IVVERIT AVRA, / OBRVTA DE MEDIIS CVMBA RESVRGET AQVIS. Ovid here mixes two nautical metaphors: if a ship is overwhelmed by high seas, a favouring breeze will not be of great assistance.

28. OBRVTA DE MEDIIS CVMBA RESVRGET AQVIS. Similar wording at [Sen] *Oct* 345-48 '[cumba ...] *obruta* ... ruit in pelagus rursumque salo / pressa *resurgit*'.

29. TVNC EGO TVRA FERAM RAPIDIS SOLLEMNIA FLAMMIS. Perhaps a verbal reminiscence of *Aen* IX 625-26 'Iuppiter omnipotens, audacibus adnue coeptis. / ipse tibi ad tua templa *feram sollemnia* dona'.

29. TVRA ... SOLLEMNIA. The phrase does not occur elsewhere in Ovid; but compare the passage from *Aen* IX quoted above, as well as the conjunction of words at *Tr* III xiii 16 'micaque *sollemni turis* in igne sonet'.

29. RAPIDIS is here used as a standard epithet; its full force ('destructive') at *Met* II 122-23 'tum pater ora sui sacro medicamine nati / contigit et *rapidae* fecit patientia *flammae*', *Met* XII 274-75 'correpti *rapida*, ueluti seges arida, *flamma* / arserunt crines', and *EP* III iii 60 (to Amor) 'sic numquam *rapido* lampades *igne* uacent'.

31-32. NEC TIBI DE PARIO STATVAM, GERMANICE, TEMPLVM / MARMORE. Professor R. J. Tarrant points out to me the reference to Virgil *G* III 13-16 'et uiridi in campo *templum de marmore* ponam ... in medio mihi Caesar erit templumque tenebit'; *Parii lapides* are mentioned at III 34. Here Ovid makes the temple literal, and conducts his *recusatio* in the terms used by love-poets.

32. CARPSIT OPES ... MEAS. 'Has destroyed my wealth'. This is not strictly true, since Ovid at v 38 says that Pompeius give him gifts (Ovid's letter speaking) 'ne proprias attenuaret opes'.

The same use of *carpere* at ix 121-22 'fortuna est impar animo, talique libenter / exiguas *carpo* munere pauper opes' and *Am* I viii 91 'et soror et mater, nutrix quoque *carpat* amantem'.

34. NASO SVIS OPIBVS, CARMINE, GRATVS ERIT. Compare *Am* II xvii 27 'sunt mihi pro magno felicia carmina censu' and *Am* I iii entire.

37. QVAM POTVIT ... MAXIMA. For the idiom compare Cic *Fam* XIII vi 5 '*quam maximas* ... gratias agat' and *ND* II 129 'gallinae ['hens'] ... cubilia sibi nidosque construunt eosque *quam possunt mollissime* substernunt'.

37. GRATVS ABVNDE EST. Apparently the only instance in classical poetry of *abunde* modifying an adjective. The prose authors cited by the lexica are Sallust, Livy, Valerius Maximus, Curtius, the elder Pliny, and Quintilian. *Abunde* elsewhere in Ovid only at *Met* XV 759 'humano generi, superi, fauistis abunde!' and *Tr* I vii 31 'laudatus abunde'.

38. FINEM PIETAS CONTIGIT ILLA SVVM. 'That act of piety has reached its objective', that is, has made the giver *gratus*.

39-42. For the sentiment compare *EP* III iv 81-82 'haec [*sc* laudanda uoluntas] facit ut ueniat pauper quoque gratus ad aras, / et placeat caeso non minus agna boue'.

41-42. GRAMINE PASTA FALISCO / VICTIMA TARPEIOS INFICIT ICTA FOCOS. Compare iv 29-32 'templaque Tarpeiae primum tibi sedis adiri ... colla boues niueos certae praebere securi, / quos aluit campis *herba Falisca* suis'.

42. INFICIT. 'Stain'. *Inficere* in the context of a sacrifice also at *Met* XV 134-35 '[uictima ...] percussa ... sanguine cultros / inficit' and Hor *Carm* III xiii 6.

44. PRINCIPIBVS ... VIRIS. A fixed colloquial idiom: *OLD princeps*[1] 5 cites Plautus *Amphitruo* 204 'delegit *uiros* primorum *principes*' and Hor *Ep* I xvii 35 '*principibus* placuisse *uiris* non ultima laus est'. There was a parallel expression *principes feminae*: see Pliny *NH* VIII 119 and Tac *Ann* XIII 42 (Suillius compares himself to Seneca) 'an grauius aestimandum sponte litigatoris praemium honestae operae adsequi quam corrumpere cubicula principum feminarum?'.

45. CARMINA VESTRARVM PERAGVNT PRAECONIA LAVDVM. *Praeconia* in a similar context at *Tr* II 65 'inuenies uestri *praeconia* nominis illic [in the *Metamorphoses*]'; used with *peragere* at *Tr* V i 9 'ut cecidi, subiti *perago praeconia* casus'.

45. LAVDVM. 'Deeds meriting praise'; compare 87 'tuas ... laudes ... recentes'. The meaning is found even in prose: see Caesar *BC* II 39 4 'haec tamen ab ipsis inflatius commemorabantur, ut de suis homines *laudibus* libenter praedicant' and the other passages cited at *OLD laus*[1] 3b.

46. ACTORVM. AVCTORVM (*BCHL*) is possible enough; but *actorum* accords better with the preceding *laudum*.

46. CADVCA. 'Impermanent'. The sense is frequent in Cicero: see *Rep* VI 17 'nihil est nisi mortale et *caducum* praeter animos' and *Phil* IV 13. Elsewhere in Ovid the usual sense of the word is 'ineffectual': see *Fast* I 181-82 'nec lingua *caducas* / concipit ulla preces, dictaque pondus habent' and *Ibis* 88 'et sit pars uoti nulla caduca mei'. Similar uses at *Her* XV 208 & XVI 169.

47. CARMINE FIT VIVAX VIRTVS, EXPERSQVE SEPVLCRI / NOTITIAM SERAE POSTERITATIS HABET. For the immortality given by verse, compare from Ovid *Tr* V xiv 5 (to his wife) 'dumque legar, mecum pariter tua fama legetur' and *EP* III ii 35-36 (to those friends who assisted him) 'uos etiam seri laudabunt saepe nepotes, / claraque erit scriptis gloria uestra meis'. The topic is closely related to that of the poet's own immortality, for which, in Ovid, see xvi 2-3 'non solet ingeniis summa nocere dies, / famaque post cineres maior uenit' and *Met* XV 871-79.

For other poets' treatment of the immortality given by verse, see Prop III ii 17-26, Hor *Carm* IV ix, Pindar *Nem* VII 11-16, Gow on Theocritus XVI 30, and Murgatroyd on Tib I iv 63-66.

47. VIVAX VIRTVS. Compare Hor *AP* 68-69 'mortalia facta peribunt, / nedum sermonum stet honos et gratia *uiuax*'.

47. EXPERSQVE SEPVLCRI. The diction of this line is very elevated: Professor R. J. Tarrant compares *Met* IX 252-53 (Jupiter speaking of Hercules) 'aeternum est a me quod traxit, et *expers* / atque immune *necis*' and *Cons Liu* 59-60 'Caesaris adde domum, quae certe *funeris expers* / debuit humanis altior esse malis'. The following line's *notitiam ... habet* is in comparison an anticlimax.

49. TABIDA CONSVMIT FERRVM LAPIDEMQVE VETVSTAS. Iron and flint were proverbial for hardness: compare x 3-4 'ecquos tu silices, ecquod, carissime, ferrum / duritiae confers, Albinouane, meae?', *Her* X 109-10, *AA* I 473-76, *Met* XIV 712-13, *Fast* V 131-32, *Tr* IV vi 13-14, and *EP* II vii 39-40; other passages are cited by Smith at Tib I iv 18 'longa dies molli saxa peredit aqua'. At I 313-16, Lucretius, discussing the invisible wearing away of substances, says 'stilicidi casus *lapidem* cauat, uncus aratri / *ferreus* occulte decrescit uomer in aruis, / strataque iam uolgi pedibus detrita uiarum / saxea conspicimus'.

51. SCRIPTA FERVNT ANNOS. The phrase completes the sentence begun in the previous distich, as is shown by the parallel passages *Am* I x 61-62 'scindentur uestes, gemmae frangentur et aurum; / *carmina quam tribuent, fama perennis erit*' and *Am* I xv 31-32 'ergo cum silices, cum dens patientis aratri / depereant aeuo, *carmina morte carent*'.

51. FERVNT. 'Withstand'; the same sense at *Tr* V ix 8 'scripta *uetustatem* si modo nostra *ferunt*', Cic *Am* 67 'ea uina quae *uetustatem ferunt*', Silius IV 399-400 'si modo *ferre diem* ... carmina nostra ualent', and Quintilian II 4 9 'sic et *annos ferent* et uetustate proficient'.

51-53. AGAMEMNONA ... THEBAS. The two great cycles of Greek heroic mythology. The same conjunction at *Am* III xii 15-16 'cum *Thebae*, cum *Troia* foret, cum Caesaris acta, / ingenium mouit sola Corinna meum' and *Tr* II 317-20 'cur non Argolicis potius quae concidit armis / uexata est iterum carmine *Troia* meo? / cur tacui *Thebas* et uulnera mutua fratrum / et septem portas sub duce quamque suo'; compare as well Prop II i 21 '[canerem ...] nec ueteres *Thebas* nec *Pergama*, nomen Homeri'. Lucretius, arguing that the world was created at a definite moment, wrote 'cur supera ['before'] bellum *Thebanum* et funera *Troiae* / non alias alii quoque res cecinere poetae?' (V 326-27).

52. QVISQVIS CONTRA VEL SIMVL ARMA TVLIT. The leaders of the Greeks and Trojans.

The line's structure parallels 54 'quicquid post haec, quicquid et ante fuit'. Both are conspicuous by their lack of adornment.

55. DI QVOQVE CARMINIBVS, SI FAS EST DICERE, FIVNT. This is possibly a reference to Herodotus II 53, where Herodotus says that Homer and Hesiod established the Greek pantheon; for Ovid's borrowings from Herodotus, see at iii 37 *opulentia Croesi* (p 189). The same idea previously in Xenophanes (fr. 11 Diels).

The line looks ahead to 63-64 'et modo, Caesar, auum, quem uirtus addidit astris, / sacrarunt aliqua carmina parte tuum'.

55. SI FAS EST DICERE. Ovid here apologizes for the shocking statement he is making. Up to this point poetry has helped give lasting fame to what was already a fact, but here poetry is actually making something happen (or appear to happen). At *Am* III xii 21-40 Ovid similarly describes how poets created the myths.

57-64. Ovid follows the same sequence in the *Metamorphoses*, describing the separation of Chaos at I 5-31, the attack of the Giants at I 151-55, Bacchus' conquest of India at IV 20-21 & 605-6, and Hercules' capture of Oechalia at IX 136; he foretells Augustus' apotheosis at XV 868-70. Professor R. J. Tarrant points out that these lines may well be referring specifically to the earlier poem.

57-58. SIC CHAOS EX ILLA NATVRAE MOLE PRIORIS / DIGESTVM PARTES SCIMVS HABERE SVAS. 'Thus we know Chaos now has its divisions after having been arranged in order from the famous mass that was its previous nature'. Ovid describes the separation of the elements at *Met* I 25-31 and *Fast* I 103-10; see also *Ecl* VI 31-36.

I take *illa* ('famous') to refer to the familiarity through the poets and philosophers of the notion of the separation of Chaos into the four elements. Alternatively, Professor A. Dalzell points out to me that *illa* could have a pejorative sense.

58. DIGESTVM. 'Separated'. At *Met* I 7 Ovid calls Chaos 'rudis *indigestaque* moles'.

59. ADFECTANTES CAELESTIA REGNA GIGANTAS. At *Am* III xii 27 Ovid, speaking of false legends created by the poets, says 'fecimus Enceladon iaculantem mille lacertis'.

In his youth, Ovid had attempted but later abandoned a poem on the battle of the Giants against Jupiter 'designed to glorify Augustus under the guise of Jupiter' (Owen *Tristia II* p. 77): the language he uses at *Tr* II 333-40 seems too explicit to be a mere instance of the love-poet's defence of his subject-matter: 'at si me iubeas domitos Iouis igne Gigantas [*Heinsius*: Gigantes *codd*] / dicere, conantem debilitabit onus. /

diuitis ingenii est immania Caesaris acta / condere, materia ne superetur opus. / *et tamen ausus eram*; sed detrectare uidebar, / quodque nefas, damno uiribus esse tuis.[20] / ad leue rursus opus, iuuenalia carmina, ueni, / et falso moui pectus amore meum'. He refers to the same poem again at *Am* II i 11-18 'ausus eram, memini, *caelestia* dicere bella / centimanumque Gyen—et satis oris erat— / cum male se Tellus ulta est, ingestaque Olympo / ardua deuexum Pelion Ossa tulit. / in manibus nimbos et cum Ioue fulmen habebam, / quod bene pro caelo mitteret ille suo— / clausit amica fores! ego cum Ioue fulmen omisi; / excidit ingenio Iuppiter ipse meo'.

The actual descriptions of the Giants' rebellion in Ovid's surviving poems are brief (*Met* I 151-62 & 182-86, *Fast* V 35-42), but references to the rebellion are frequent (*Met* X 150-51, *Fast* I 307-8, *Fast* IV 593-94, *Fast* V 555, *Tr* II 71, *Tr* IV vii 17, *EP* II ii 9-12). The accounts at *Met* V 319-31 of the flight of some of the gods to Egypt and at *Fast* II 459-74 of Venus' flight to the Euphrates are no doubt derived from Ovid's earlier researches.

59. ADFECTANTES. 'Unlawfully seeking to obtain'; compare *Met* I 151-52 'neue foret terris securior arduus aether, / *adfectasse* ferunt *regnum caeleste Gigantas*' and *Fast* III 439 'ausos *caelum adfectare Gigantas*'. This sense is found in prose: compare Livy I 50 4 'cui enim non apparere *adfectare* eum imperium in Latinos?'. At Livy I 46 2 the word is used without the conative sense: 'neque ea res Tarquinio spem *adfectandi* regni minuit'.

59. GIGANTAS *Heinsius*. The manuscripts have GIGANTES, which Lenz, Wheeler, and André print. In classical Latin poetry, Greek nouns of the third declension with plural nominatives in -ες and plural accusatives in -ας retained these endings. Housman 836-39 gives many instances where metre demonstrates an accusative in -ας. In Ovid when such an ending occurs, some manuscripts commonly offer the normalized -es; at *Tr* II 333, as here, all manuscripts offer *Gigantes*, again corrected by Heinsius.

Such apparent violations of the rule as *Fast* I 717 'horreat Aeneadās et primus et ultimus orbis', *Fast* III 105-6 'quis tunc aut Hyadās aut Pliadas Atlanteas / senserat' and Virgil *G* I 137-38 'nauita tum stellis numeros et nomina fecit, / Pleiadās, Hyadās, claramque Lycaonis Arcton' are of course no real exceptions, the lengthening of short closed vowels at the ictus being permitted (Platnauer 59-62).

60. AD STYGA NIMBIFERI VINDICIS IGNE DATOS.
'Hurled to the underworld by the lightning-bolt of cloud-gathering Jupiter'. This was Jupiter's first use of the weapon: see *Fast* III 439-40 'fulmina post ausos caelum adfectare Gigantas / sumpta Ioui: *primo tempore inermis erat*'.

60. NIMBIFERI VINDICIS IGNE is my correction of the
manuscripts' NIMBIFERO and NVBIFERO. The unmodified *uindicis* and modified *igne* of the manuscript readings might be defended by *EP* II ix 77 'quicquid id est [whatever Ovid has committed], habuit moderatam uindicis iram', but *uindicis* is there defined by the following 'qui nisi natalem nil mihi dempsit humum', and *moderatam* is a more suitable epithet for *iram* than is *nimbifero* for *igne* in the present passage., At *Tr* II 143-44 'uidi ego pampineis oneratam uitibus ulmum, / quae fuerat *saeuo fulmine* tacta Iouis', the manuscripts divide between *saeuo* and *saeui*, which has a good claim to be considered the true reading; in any case, *Iouis* is less in need of a defining adjective than *uindicis* in the present passage. Finally, the genitive here is strongly supported by *Ibis* 475-76 'ut Macedo rapidis icta est cum coniuge flammis, / sic precor *aetherii uindicis* igne cadas'.

The corruption may have been induced by a wish to introduce interlocking word order: for a similar instance see at ii 9 *Baccho uina Falerna* (p 164). But in fact substantive and epithet are constantly found linked at the caesura of the pentameter: the strong break in the metre at that point no doubt made the construction more readily acceptable there than in other positions.

I have printed *nimbiferi* in preference to *nubiferi* because Jupiter is linked with *nimbi* at two other passages. The first of these is *Am* II i 15-16 'in manibus *nimbos et cum Ioue fulmen* habebam, / quod bene pro caelo mitteret ille suo', and the second *Met* III 299-301, where Ovid describes Jupiter's preparations to descend on Semele: 'aethera conscendit uultuque sequentia traxit / nubila, quis *nimbos* immixtaque fulgura uentis / addidit et tonitrus et ineuitabile fulmen'.

61-62. SIC VICTOR LAVDEM SVPERATIS LIBER AB INDIS ... TRAXIT. Bacchus' conquest of India is also mentioned by Ovid at *Fast* III 465-66 'interea Liber depexos crinibus Indos / uicit et Eoo diues ab orbe redit', *Fast* III 719-20, and *Tr* V iii 23-24.

61-62. VICTOR should be taken both with *Liber* and *Alcides*.

61-62. LIBER ... ALCIDES. The same pairing (both times in the context of Augustan panegyric) at *Aen* VI 801-5 'nec uero *Alcides* tantum telluris obiuit, / fixerit aeripedem ceruam licet, aut Erymanthi / pacarit nemora et Lernam tremefecerit arcu; / nec qui pampineis uictor iuga flectit habenis / *Liber*, agens celso Nysae de uertice tigris' and Hor *Carm* III iii 9-15. Ovid may have made similar mention of Bacchus and Hercules in his panegyric of Augustus.

61-62. SIC ... LAVDEM ... ALCIDES CAPTA TRAXIT AB OECHALIA. Hercules attacked and captured Oechalia in order to carry off Iole, the king's daughter. This was his last exploit, for it led to Deianira's sending him the poisoned robe which caused his death. The capture of Oechalia is also mentioned at *Her* IX *passim* (the poem perhaps not by Ovid) and *Met* IX 136-40.

62. OECHALIA. For the quadrisyllable ending to the pentameter, see at ii 10 *Alcinoo* (p 164).

63. AVVM. Augustus. In AD 4 Augustus adopted Tiberius (son of Livia's first husband, Ti. Claudius Nero), and Tiberius adopted Germanicus, son of his brother Drusus.

63. QVEM VIRTVS ADDIDIT ASTRIS. Compare *Aen* VIII 301 (of Hercules) 'salue, uera Iouis proles, decus *addite diuis*'.

Augustus died on 19 August AD 14; on 17 September the Senate decreed *caelestes religiones* for him (Tac *Ann* I 10 8; *Fasti Amiternini, Antiates, & Oppiani*, at Ehrenberg-Jones 52). Augustus' apotheosis is also mentioned at ix 127-32 and xiii 23-26.

64. ALIQVA ... PARTE. The same phrase in the same metrical position at *Fast* I 133-34 (Janus speaking) 'uis mea narrata est. causam nunc disce figurae: / iam tamen hanc *aliqua* tu quoque *parte* uides'.

64. CARMINA. Ovid is referring to his own poems (in Latin and Getic) on Augustus' apotheosis, also mentioned at vi 17-18 'de caelite ... recenti ... carmen', ix 131-32 'carmina ... de te ... caelite ... nouo', and xiii 25-26.

65-66. SI QVID ADHVC IGITVR VIVI, GERMANICE, NOSTRO / RESTAT IN INGENIO, SERVIET OMNE TIBI. Compare Prop IV i 59-60 'sed tamen exiguo *quodcumque* e pectore *riui* / fluxerit, hoc patriae *seruiet omne meae*', which Ovid is clearly imitating. Hertzberg *ad loc* conjectured RIVI for our passage, which may well be right; but *uiui* seems to agree better with *restat*.

67. VATIS ... VATES. For an extreme instance of Ovid's favourite figure of *polyptoton* (Quintilian IX 3 36-37), see the account at *Met* IX 43-45 of Achelous' wrestling-match with Hercules: 'inque gradu stetimus, certi non cedere, eratque / cum *pede pes* iunctus, totoque ego pectore pronus / et *digitos digitis* et *frontem fronte* premebam'. Other instances of polyptoton with *uates* at *Fast* I 25 (to Germanicus) 'si licet et fas est, *uates* rege *uatis* habenas' and *EP* II ix 65 (to Cotys, king of Thrace, apparently a writer of poetry) 'ad *uatem uates* orantia bracchia tendo',

67. VATES. Approximately nine hundred lines survive of a version of Aratus generally attributed to Germanicus, who might have been composing the poem at the time Ovid was writing: Augustus' apotheosis is mentioned at 558-60. It is possible however that Tiberius was the poem's author: he is known to have written a *Conquestio de morte L. Caesaris* and to have composed Greek verse (Suet *Tib* 70). For a full discussion see the introduction to Gain's edition of the *Aratus*.

69-70. QVOD NISI TE NOMEN TANTVM AD MAIORA VOCASSET, / GLORIA PIERIDVM SVMMA FVTVRVS ERAS. Compare *Met* V 269-70 (the Muses to Minerva) 'o nisi te uirtus opera ad maiora tulisset, / in partem uentura chori

Tritonia nostri'.

There is a striking parallel to this passage in Quintilian's address to Domitian in his catalogue of poets: 'hos nominamus quia Germanicum Augustum ab institutis studiis deflexit cura terrarum, parumque dis uisum est esse eum maximum poetarum' (X i 91-92).

70. GLORIA PIERIDVM SVMMA. *Gloria* similarly used at *EP* II xi 28 'maxima Fundani *gloria*, Rufe, soli', *Aen* VI 767 'proximus ille Procas, Troianae *gloria* gentis', and Val Max IV iii 3 'Drusum ... Germanicum, eximiam Claudiae familiae *gloriam*'. The term was used in particular of fine cattle: see *AA* I 290 'candidus, armenti gloria, taurus', *Pan Mess* (*Corp Tib* III vii) 208 'tardi pecoris ... *gloria* taurus' and *Aetna* 597 '*gloria* uiua Myronis' (on Mvron's *Cow* see at i 34 *ut similis uerae uacca Myronis opus* [p 158]).

71. SI DARE *R. J. Tarrant.* The manuscripts' SED DARE is a possible reading; but Professor Tarrant's slight change removes the awkwardness of *nec tamen* following immediately upon *sed*.

71. MAVIS *IF²ᵘˡ* MAIVS *BF¹*. Either of the two variants could be read from *CMHLT*. The preferable reading is *mauis*, since it links more closely to *potes* in the pentameter, and would be especially liable to corruption after *maiora* two lines previous. I have found no good parallel for singular *maius* 'a more important thing': for the plural *OLD maior* 5 cites from verse *Fast* IV 3 'certe maiora canebas' and its model, *Ecl* IV 1 'paulo maiora canamus'.

72. NEC TAMEN EX TOTO DESERERE ILLA POTES. Graecinus was another of Ovid's addressees who, while a soldier, kept up his other pursuits: 'artibus ingenuis [=*lībĕrālibus*], quarum tibi maxima cura est, / pectora mollescunt asperitasque fugit. / nec quisquam meliore fide complectitur illas, / qua sinit officium militiaeque labor' (*EP* I vi 7-10).

72. EX TOTO. 'Altogether'. Compare *EP* I vi 27-28 'spes igitur menti poenae, Graecine, leuandae / non est *ex toto* nulla relicta meae'. The idiom was probably subliterary: the only instances from the time of Ovid cited by *OLD totum* 2 are Celsus III 3 71b 'neque *ex toto* in remissionem desistit' and Columella V 6 17 'antequam *ex toto* arbor praeualescat'.

73. NVMERIS ... VERBA COERCES. 'You arrange words in metrical patterns'. Similar wording at Cic *Or* 64 'mollis est enim oratio philosophorum ... nec *uincta numeris* ['not in rhythmic prose'], sed soluta liberius'.

Professor E. Fantham points out to me that Ovid may also be playing on *numerus* 'military contingent' (*OLD numerus* 9): 'you draft words in squads'.

75-76. NEC AD CITHARAM NEC AD ARCVM SEGNIS APOLLO, / SED VENIT AD SACRAS NERVVS VTERQVE MANVS. Apollo is similarly described at *Met* X 107-8 (of Cyparissus) 'nunc arbor, puer ante deo dilectus ab illo / *qui citharam neruis et neruis temperat arcum*'.

76. VENIT = *conuenit*. In Latin verse a simple verb can carry the sense of any of its compounds, even when this sense is quite different from the usual meaning of the simple verb. Compare Catullus LXIV 21 'tum Thetidi pater ipse *iugandum* Pelea *sensit*', "where it is plain that iugandum is for coniugandum, and this leads the reader to the conclusion that sensit is for consensit, where the omission decidedly affects the sense" (Bell 330).

The line should not be taken as an instance of the expression *uenire ad manum* (*OLD uenio* 7c), since the idiom's sense 'be convenient' does not fit the context here: for the sense compare Livy XXXVIII 21 6 'quod [*sc* saxum] cuique temere trepidanti *ad manum uenisset*' and Quintilian II xi 6 'abrupta quaedam, ut forte *ad manum uenere*, iaculantur'. *Venire in manus* offers a somewhat more satisfactory meaning, almost equivalent to 'have, hold' (compare Cic *Q Fr* II xv [xiv] i 'quicumque calamus *in manus meas uenerit*' and Persius III 11 '*inque manus* chartae nodosaque *uenit* harundo'), but seems to be a separate idiom.

79. QVAE QVONIAM NEC NOS. 'Since she continues to give poetic inspiration to myself as well as to you'. *Quae quoniam* seems very prosaic, but Ovid uses the phrase again at *Tr* I ix 53-54 '*quae* [*sc* coniectura] *quoniam* uera est ... gratulor ingenium non latuisse tuum'.

79-80. VNDA ... VNGVLA GORGONEI QUAM CAVA FECIT EQVI. Hippocrene, the spring of the Muses, said to have been created by the hoof-beat of Pegasus. Similarly described at *Met* V 264 'factas pedis ictibus undas', *Fast* V 7-8 'fontes Aganippidos Hippocrenes, / grata Medusaei signa ... equi' and Persius prol 1 'fonte ... caballino'.

80. VNGVLA ... CAVA. Professor J. N. Grant points out to me the possible borrowing from Ennius *Ann* 439 Vahlen[3] 'it eques et plausu *caua* concutit *ungula* terram'.

80. GORGONEI ... EQVI. The same phrase in the same metrical position at *Fast* III 450 'suspice [*sc* caelum]: *Gorgonei* colla uidebis *equi*'. For the birth of Pegasus from the blood of the Gorgon Medusa, see *Met* IV 784-86,

81. COMMVNIA SACRA TVERI. *Sacra* similarly used of poetry at *Tr* IV i 87, *Tr* IV x 19 'at mihi iam puero caelestia *sacra* placebant', *EP* II x 17 'sunt tamen inter se *communia sacra* poetis', and *EP* III iv 67 'sunt mihi uobiscum *communia sacra*, poetae'. For *tueri* 'observe, maintain' compare Cic *Tusc* I 2 'mores et instituta uitae resque domesticas ac familiaris nos profecto et melius *tuemur* et lautius'.

82. ISDEM STVDIIS IMPOSVISSE MANVM. Similar phrasing at *Tr* IV i 27-28 'non equidem uellem ... *Pieridum sacris imposuisse manum*'.

82. IMPOSVISSE has the sense of the present infinitive, as is shown by *tueri* in the previous line; compare as well ii 27-28 'uix sumptae Musa tabellae / *imponit* pigras, paene coacta, *manus*'. For the idiom, see Platnauer 109-12. It is particularly frequent in the latter half of the pentameter, immediately before the disyllable: compare, from many instances, *AA* III 431-32 '*ire* solutis / crinibus et fletus non *tenuisse* decet' and *Tr* IV viii 5-12 'nunc erat ut posito deberem fine laborum / *uiuere*, me nullo sollicitante metu, / quaeque meae semper placuerunt otia menti / *carpere* et in studiis molliter *esse* meis, / et paruam *celebrare* domum ueteresque Penates ... inque sinu dominae carisque sodalibus inque / securus patria *consenuisse* mea'. The idiom, although more common in elegiac verse, is also found in epic: compare *Aen* X 14 'tum *certare* odiis, tum res *rapuisse* licebit'.

83. LITORA PELLITIS NIMIVM SVBIECTA CORALLIS. Compare ii 37 'hic mea cui recitem nisi flauis scripta Corallis'. Strabo mentions the Coralli as inhabiting the region near Haemus (VII 5 12); they are rather obscurely described at Val Fl VI 89-94 'densique leuant uexilla Coralli, / barbaricae quis signa rotae, ferrataque dorso / forma suum ['of pigs'], truncaeque Iouis simulacra columnae; / proelia nec rauco curant incendere cornu, / indigenas sed rite duces et prisca suorum / facta canunt ueterumque, uiris hortamina, laudes'.

Nothing else is known of the tribe.

83. PELLITIS. Elsewhere in Ovid only at x 2 'pellitos ... Getas'.

83. NIMIVM SVBIECTA. Compare vi 45 'nimium nobis conterminus Hister'.

85. VLLO *M* ILLO *BCFHILT*. *Illo* is not a possible reading, since of course most parts of the empire would have been less isolated than Tomis. Ovid does not specify a preferred place of exile at either *Tr* IV iv 49 'nunc precor hinc alio iubeat discedere' or *EP* III i 29-30 'non igitur mirum ... altera si nobis usque rogatur humus', nor in any of the passages listed in the next two notes.

86. QVI MINVS ... DISTET. For this constant prayer of the exiled Ovid, see *Tr* II 575-78 (the concluding lines) 'non ut in Ausoniam redeam, nisi forsitan olim, / cum longo poenae tempore uictus eris; / tutius exilium pauloque quietius oro, / ut par delicto sit mea poena suo', *Ibis* 28, *EP* III i 4 & 85, *EP* III iii 64, *EP* III vii 30, *EP* III ix 38, and *EP* III ix 1-4 'Quod sit in his eadem sententia, Brute, libellis, / carmina nescio quem carpere nostra refers, / *nil nisi me terra fruar ut propiore rogare*, / et quam sim denso cinctus ab hoste loqui'.

86. DISTET *FHILM*^{2c}. Lenz and André print DISTAT (*BCT*); however, the defining subjunctive seems to be required, and is supported by *EP* II viii 36 'daque procul Scythico *qui sit* ab hoste locum'.

87. LAVDES. See at 45 *laudum* (p 268).

88. MAGNAQVE QVAM MINIMA FACTA REFERRE MORA. At *EP* III iv 53-60 Ovid speaks of how a poem of his on a recent triumph has been late in being written, and will be late in reaching Rome: 'cetera certatim de magno scripta triumpho / iam pridem populi suspicor ore legi. / illa bibit sitiens lector, mea pocula plenus; / illa recens pota est, nostra tepebit aqua. / non ego cessaui, nec fecit inertia serum: / ultima me uasti distinet [*scripsi*: sustinet *codd*] ora freti. / dum uenit huc rumor properataque carmina fiunt / factaque eunt ad uos, annus abisse potest'.

90. SOCERO PAENE ... TVO. See at 11 *eadem mihi filia paene est* (p 262).

IX. To Graecinus

C. Pomponius Graecinus (*PIR*[1] P 540), suffect consul in 16, was the recipient of *EP* I vi, an appeal for his assistance, and of *EP* II vi, a request that he be more lenient towards Ovid's faults and continue to assist him. He must have been an old friend of Ovid, for *Am* II x is addressed to him ('Tu mihi, tu certe, memini, Graecine, negabas / uno posse aliquem tempore amare duas'), and he was clearly a literary patron (*EP* I vi 7-8 'artibus ingenuis, *quarum tibi maxima cura est*, / pectora mollescunt asperitasque fugit').

The poem begins with Ovid's wish that his letter might arrive on the day Graecinus becomes consul (1-4). He imagines himself present when Graecinus enters his magistracy; since he will not be there, he will at least in his mind imagine Graecinus carrying out his consular functions (5-56). He then speaks of Graecinus' brother Flaccus, who will succeed him as *consul ordinarius* for 17: the two brothers will take pleasure in each other's office (57-65). He describes the brothers' devotion to Tiberius, and asks for their assistance in obtaining his removal from Tomis (65-74). The mention of his exile serves as a bridge to the topic of his life in Tomis. Flaccus can attest to the hardships Ovid endures, since he was recently stationed in the area (75-86). Once Graecinus has learned of these hardships from Flaccus, he should ask what Ovid's reputation in Tomis is. He will learn that Ovid is well liked, and has even received public honours (87-104). His loyalty to the imperial family is well known: Flaccus may have heard of this, Tiberius will eventually learn of it, but Augustus has certainly observed it from heaven; Ovid's poems are perhaps inducing Augustus to yield to his prayers (105-34).

The poem is the longest in the book, and combines several almost unrelated sections dealing with a number of subjects. The first section of the poem, the celebration of Graecinus' nomination to the consulship, is very heavily indebted to IV iv, Ovid's first poem on Sextus Pompeius' election to the consulship. The section detailing Flaccus' presence near Tomis owes something to IV vii, the letter to Vestalis. The description of Ovid's reputation in Tomis is new, and shows a softening of his attitude towards his fellow-townsmen, but the description of his piety to the imperial family owes much to III ii, a letter of thanks to Cotta for the gift of images of the members of the family. The poem's discursiveness and large number of derived elements suggest a hasty composition.

1. GRAECINE. Graecinus became a *frater Arualis* in 21 (*CIL* VI 2023); the C. Pomponius Graecinus of *CIL* XI 5809 (Iguvium) seems not to have survived to enter the Senate (Syme *HO* 74-75). Graecinus is not mentioned in literary sources apart from Ovid, but his brother Flaccus was rather more famous: see at 75 (p 308).

3. DI FACIANT looks like a colloquial expression. Other instances at iv 47-48 '*di faciant* aliquo subeat tibi tempore nostrum / nomen', *Tr* V xiii 17, and Prop II ix 24.

3. AVRORAM here is virtually equivalent to *diem*; it is not found elsewhere in the poetry of exile, but compare *Fast* I 461 & II 267-68 'tertia post idus nudos aurora Lupercos / aspicit'.

3. OCCVRRAT. 'Arrive', as commonly: compare Cic *Phil* I 9, Livy XXXVII 50 7 '*ad comitiorum tempus occurrere* non posse', and Pliny *Ep* VI xxxiv 3 'uellem Africanae [*sc* pantherae] quas coemeras plurimas *ad praefinitum diem occurrissent*'.

4. BIS SENOS = *dŭŏdĕcim*, metrically difficult because of its initial three consecutive short vowels. Roman poets avoid using the usual names for numbers above *nouem*, with the obvious exceptions of *centum* and *mille*; sometimes, as here, metrical exigencies left them with no alternative. For *bis seni* (*sex*) Tarrant at Sen *Ag* 812 *bis seno ... labore* cites Ennius *Ann* 323 Vahlen[2], *Ecl* I 43, *Aen* I 393, Prop II xx 7, *Met* VIII 243, *Fast* I 28, Sen *Tro* 386 & *Oed* 251, and from Greek Callimachus *Aetia* I fr. 23 19 Pfeiffer.

6. TVRBAE. Compare iv 27 'cernere iam uideor rumpi paene atria *turba'*.

7. IN DOMINI SVBEAT PARTES. *Partes* = 'function'; see at ii 27 *uix uenit ad partes ... Musa* (p 170). For *subeat* 'undertake' compare Quintilian X i 71 'declamatoribus ... necesse est secundum condicionem controuersiarum plures *subire personas'* and the passages cited at *OLD subeo* 7b.

8. FESTO *Burman* IVSSO *BCMFHIL* IVSTO *T, sicut coni Merkel. Iusso* has been explained since Merula as meaning that Ovid hopes the letter will arrive on the day it is told to; but the word seems rather strange, and lacks the point it has in the passages cited by Ehwald (*KB* 64), *AA* II 223-24 'iussus adesse foro, *iussa* maturius *hora* / fac semper uenias, nec nisi serus abi' and Prop IV vi 63-64 (of Cleopatra) 'illa petit Nilum cumba male nixa fugaci, / hoc unum, *iusso* non moritura *die'* (she would commit suicide at a time of her own choosing), or at *Aen* X 444 (cited by Owen in 1894) 'socii cesserunt *aequore iusso'*, where *iusso* stands by hypallage for *iussi*. The meaning of *iusto* is inappropriate for the present passage, as will be seen from Suet *Tib* 4 2 'retentis ultra *iustum tempus* ['the time allowed'] insignibus'. Burman's conjecture *festo* was not placed in the text even by its author, but it seems a reasonable solution to the difficulty. For it Burman cited 56 'hic quoque te *festum* consule *tempus* agam'; see as well *Fast* I 79-80 'uestibus intactis Tarpeias itur in arces, / et populus *festo* concolor ipse suo est'. The corruption of so straightforward an epithet may seem unlikely, but compare Prop IV xi 65-66 'uidimus et fratrem sellam geminasse curulem; / consule quo, *festo* [*Koppiers*: facto *codd*] *tempore*, rapta soror'.

9. ATQVI *unus e duobus Hafniensibus Heinsii*. The ATQVE of *BCMFHILT* is possibly right. For the adversative sense here required, *OLD atque* 9 cites Plautus *Aul* 287-88 'atque ego istuc, Anthrax, aliouorsum dixeram, / non istuc quod tu insimulas', *Mer* 742, and Ter *Heaut* 189 (apparently a misprint for 187 'atque etiam nunc tempus est') from comedy, but from the classical period only Cic *Att* VI i 2 'ac putaram paulo secus' and *Fam* XIV iv 5 'atque ego, qui te confirmo, ipse me non possum', and instances of *ac tamen* at *Fam* VII xxiii 1, Caesar *BC* III 87 4, and Tac *Ann* III 72. In view of the doubtful status of adversative *atque* at the time of Ovid and the ease of corruption of *atqui* to *atque* I have followed Heinsius in reading *atqui*. Heinsius similarly restored *atqui* from his *codex Richelianus* for the other manuscripts' *atque* at *Tr* II 121-24 'corruit haec ... sub uno ... crimine lapsa domus. / atqui ea sic lapsa est ut surgere, si modo laesi / ematuruerit Caesaris ira, queat'; and *atque* is found for the correct *atqui* in some manuscripts at Hor *Sat* I ix 52-53 '"magnum narras, uix credibile!" "atqui / sic habet"' and *EP* I ii 33-34 '*atqui* / si noles sanus, curres hydropicus', and in most manuscripts at *Ep* I vii 1-5 'Quinque dies tibi pollicitus me rure futurum / Sextilem totum mendax desideror. *atqui*, / si me uiuere uis sanum recteque ualentem, / quam mihi das aegro, dabis aegrotare timenti, / Maecenas, ueniam'.

10. SINCERO. 'Unbroken'.

12. SALVTANDI MVNERE ... TVI. Professor R. J. Tarrant points out to me the notably prosaic use of the defining gerundive.

13. GRATATVS has the force of a present participle, as is shown by *cum dulcibus ... uerbis*; André mistranslates 'après t'avoir félicité, je t'embrasserai avec des mots tendres'. The perfect participle of deponent verbs takes past or present meaning indifferently, according to context.

16. VT CAPERET FASTVS VIX DOMVS VLLA MEOS seems strange, as does Némethy's explanation 'poeta elatus superbia tectum uertice tangere sibi uidetur'. Perhaps the distich means something like 'on that day I would be filled with a pride which no ancestry, no matter how illustrious, could justify'.

16. FASTVS. 'Haughtiness'—Wheeler. The same sense at *AA* II 241-42 'exue *fastus*, / curam mansuri quisquis amoris habes' and *Aen* III 326-27 (Andromache speaking) 'stirpis Achilleae *fastus* iuuenemque superbum ... tulimus'. Ovid generally uses *fastus* of the arrogance of women to their suitors (*Am* II xvii 9, *Met* XIV 762, *Fast* I 419); the word is not found elsewhere in the poetry of exile.

259

17. DVMQVE LATVS SANCTI CINGIT TIBI TVRBA SENATVS. Compare iv 41 'inde domum repetes toto comitante senatu'; Ovid is here obviously referring to the earlier procession *from* the new consul's house.

20. LATERIS ... LOCVM is a strange phrase, but is made easier by *latus ... cingit* in 17. Compare also such passages as *Met* II 448-49 'nec ... iuncta deae lateri nec toto est agmine prima' and *Aen* X 160-61 'Pallas ... sinistro / adfixus lateri'. It is possible that *latus* here means 'companion', as at Martial VI lxviii 4 'Eutychos ille, tuum, Castrice, dulce latus'.

20. HABVISSE is equivalent to *habere*, as is shown by *esse* in the preceding line. For the idiom, see at viii 82 *imposuisse* (p 282) and xi 2 *habuisse* (p 361).

21. TVRBA QVAMVIS ELIDERER. *Elidere* similarly used of a crowd's jostling at Sen *Clem* I 6 1; an extended description at Juvenal III 243-48.

23. PROSPICEREM. Owen in his second edition, Wheeler, and Lenz follow Ehwald (*KB* 64) in printing *B*'s ASPICEREM. Ehwald argued that *prospicerem*, 'survey from a distance', was inappropriate in view of the preceding *turba quamuis eliderer*. But the verb should be taken not with the pentameter that precedes, but with the one that follows, 'densaque quam longum turba teneret iter': *prospicerem* seems very appropriate. Riese conjectured RESPICEREM 'look back at', but emendation seems unnecessary.

Compounds of *specere* (the simple verb is used by Plautus and Ennius) are peculiarly liable to confusion: *prospicere* is similarly corrupted to *aspicere* in some manuscripts at *Met* III 603-4 'ipse quid aura mihi tumulo promittat ab alto / prospicio' and *Met* XI 715-16 'notata locis reminiscitur acta fretumque / prospicit', and other instances of variation of prefix will be found at *Met* II 405, VI 343, XI 150, XIV 179, XV 577, 660 & 842, *Fast* I 139 & 461, V 393 & 561, and *Her* XIX 21.

25-26. Heinsius and Bentley questioned the authenticity of these lines, but the distich does not seem lame enough to warrant excision, and *tegeret* (see below) is paralleled elsewhere.

25. QVOQVE MAGIS NORIS. 'Listen: this will make you understand better'. Ovid is very fond of *quoque magis* and the corresponding *quoque minus*, particularly at line-beginnings. He generally uses the formula to denote the emotion which information he then gives should induce. Compare *Met* I 757-58 '"quo"que "magis doleas, genetrix" ait, "ille ego liber, / ille ferox tacui"', *Met* III 448-50 (Narcissus to his reflection) 'quoque magis doleam, nec nos mare separat ingens ... exigua prohibemur aqua', *Met* XIV 695-97 'quoque magis timeas ... referam tota notissima Cypro / facta', *Tr* I vii 37-38, and *EP* I viii 9-10 'quoque magis nostros uenia dignere libellos, / haec in procinctu carmina facta leges'; similar instances of *quoque minus* at *Met* II 44, VIII 579, 620 & 866, and *EP* III ii 52. The present passage shows the same idiom, but with the difference that a subordinate clause (*quam me uulgaria tangant*) depends on the verb (*noris*) introduced by the *quoque magis* clause.

The same formula is used with a different sense, the *quoque* being an ablative of degree of difference, at *Am* III ii 28 and *Met* IV 64 'quoque magis tegitur, tectus magis aestuat ignis'.

EP II v 15-16 'quoque magis moueare malis, doctissime, nostris, / credibile est fieri condicione loci' reads oddly; something has probably been lost from the text after the hexameter.

25. VVLGARIA. 'Commonplace, ordinary'. Compare Hor *Sat* II ii 38 and Cic *De or* II 347 'neque enim paruae [*sc* res] neque usitatae neque uulgares admiratione aut omnino laude dignae uideri solent'.

25. TANGANT. 'Impress'; compare *Her* V 81 'non ego miror opes, nec me tua regia tangit', *Her* VI 113, *Her* VII 11, *Met* IV 639, *Met* X 614-15 'nec forma *tangor* (poteram tamen hac quoque tangi), / sed quod adhuc puer est: non me mouet ipse, sed aetas', and *Fast* V 489, as well as *Her* XVI 83. For *tangere* with a neuter plural subject see *Aen* I 462 'mentem mortalia *tangunt*'.

26. TEGERET. There are twenty trisyllabic pentameter

endings in Tibullus, thirty in Propertius, but only five in Ovid, all in the *Ex Ponto*: I i 66 *faciet*, I vi 26 *scelus est*, I viii 40 *liceat*, III vi 46 *uideor*, and this passage (Platnauer 15-16). Quadrisyllabic endings are similarly frequent in the poetry of exile: see at ii 10 *Alcinoo* (p 164).

27. SIGNA ... IN SELLA ... FORMATA CVRVLI. For *signum* 'bas-relief' see at v 18 *conspicuum signis ... ebur* (the phrase also of the curule chair).

28. NVMIDAE SCVLPTILE DENTIS OPVS. Professor R. J. Tarrant points out to me the clear imitation of Prop II xxxi 12 'ualuae, LIbyci nobile dentis opus'.

28. NVMIDAE ... DENTIS *edd* NVMIDI ... DENTIS *codd*. The masculine first declension substantive *Numida* is occasionally used as an adjective: compare *AA* II 183 'Numidasque leones' (some manuscripts read *Numidosque*) and Juvenal IV 99-100 'ursos ... Numidas'. André prints *Numidi*, citing a nominative *Numidus* at *CIL* VIII 17328, the variant at *AA* II 183, and Apicius VI 8 4 'pullum Numidum' (where there is a variant *Numidicum*, which André printed in his 1974 edition of Apicius). But given the support for the first-declension form offered by the Juvenal passage and the better manuscripts of the *Ars Amatoria*, the danger in adducing a doubtful passage of Apicius and a single inscription to determine poetic usage, and the ease of corruption to the second declension, it seems better to assume that Ovid here used the first declension form.

Numidae ... dentis is high poetic diction: compare *Met* XI 167-68 'instructam ... fidem gemmis et *dentibus Indis*', Catullus LXIV 47-48 'puluinar ... *Indo* ... *dente* politum', Prop II xxxi 12 (quoted above), and Statius *Sil* III iii 94-95 'Indi / dentis honos'.

28. SCVLPTILE. The word does not seem to occur again in Latin until Prudentius *Steph* X 266.

29. TARPEIAS ... IN ARCES. See at iv 29 *Tarpeiae ... sedis* (p 208).

30. DVM expresses purpose; if it were temporal, the verb would be *cadit* instead of *caderet*: compare 17-18 '*dumque* latus

262

sancti *cingit* tibi turba senatus, / consulis ante pedes ire iuberer eques'.

31. SECRETO represents Ovid's response to the bidding *fauete linguis*. The word is frequent in comedy, but is very rare in verse, being virtually confined to satire (Hor *Sat* I ix 67, Juvenal I 95).

31-32. MAGNVS ... DEVS = Iuppiter Optimus *Maximus*. Compare *AA* II 540 'eris *magni* uictor in arce *Iouis*'.

33. TVRAQVE MENTE MAGIS PLENA QVAM LANCE DEDISSEM. The same notion of sincerity of feeling being more important than size of gifts at viii 35-40.

34. TER QVATER ... LAETVS. 'Infinitely happy'; compare Prop III xii 15 '*ter quater* in casta felix, o Postume, Galla!', *Aen* I 94 'o *terque quaterque* beati', *AA* II 447-48, and *Tr* III xii 25-26 'o *quater* et *quotiens non est numerare beatum* / non interdicta cui licet urbe frui!'. The phrase is common in Ovid, but he generally uses it to mean 'several times': compare *Am* III i 31-32 'mouit ... *terque quaterque* caput', *Met* II 49, *Met* IV 734 '*ter quater* exegit repetita per ilia ferrum', *Met* VI 133, *Met* IX 217, *Met* XII 288, *Fast* I 576, and *Fast* I 657 '*ter quater* euolui signantes tempora fastos'.

35. HIC. 'Hier auf dem Kapitol'—Ehwald (*KB* 65). The idiom is somewhat strange, but seems well enough supported by *Met* XIV 372-73 '"per o, tua lumina" dixit / "quae mea ceperunt, perque *hanc*, pulcherrime, formam"' and *Her* XVI 137, passages cited by R, J. Tarrant at Sen *Ag* 971 'dummodo *hac* ['your'] moriar manu'. Compare as well Prop I xi 17-18 'non quia perspecta non es mihi cognita fama, / sed quod in *hac* omnis *parte* ['at Baiae'] timetur [*codd*: ueretur *Lachmann*] amor' and Fedeli *ad loc.*

36. MITIA ... SI ... FATA DARENT. 'If the Fates had been kind, and given'.

36. VRBIS *editio Aldina 1502* VERBIS *codd. Ius urbis = ius urbis habitandae*; compare *Met* XIII 471-72 'genetrici corpus inemptum / reddite, neue auro redimat ius triste sepulcri [=*sepeliendi*]'.

37-38. MENTE ... OCVLIS. Similarly contrasted at *Met* XV 62-64 'isque, licet caeli regione remotos, / *mente* deos adiit et, quae natura negarat [*'Medic. rectius' (Heinsius)*: negabat *codd*] / uisibus humanis, *oculis* ea *pectoris* hausit'.

38. NON ITA CAELITIBVS VISVM EST. 'The gods decided otherwise'. Compare xi 7 'non ita dis placuit', *Met* VII 699, *Tr* IV viii 15-16 (Ovid had hoped for a peaceful and happy old age) 'non ita dis uisum est, qui me terraque marique / actum Sarmaticis exposuere locis'. These passages are probably all echoes of *Aen* II 426 'dis aliter uisum'.

40. IVVET *B^{pc}CMFHILT* FORET *B^{ac}* *'unde uerum eliciendum'* — *Riese*. But the correction is by the original hand (Owen suggested that the error was induced by *foret* at the end of the preceding distich), and *iuuet* is unobjectionable: Ovid is explaining his admission in the previous line that the gods were perhaps just in his case—claiming he was innocent, that is, that the gods had been unjust, would be of no assistance to him.

41. MENTE TAMEN, QVAE SOLA DOMO NON EXVLAT, VSVS. See at iv 45 *qua possum, mente* (p 211).

41. QVAE SOLA DOMO NON EXVLAT. Similar wording at *Tr* III iv 45-46 'Nasonisque tui *quod adhuc non exulat unum* / nomen ama'.

41. DOMO NON EXVLAT. *Domo* is my conjecture for the transmitted LOCO, which is strange and difficult to construe. FOCO is also possible; but the singular would be unusual. For *domo* compare Ter *Eun* 610 'domo exulo nunc'.

42. PRAETEXTAM FASCES ASPICIAMQVE. The *-que* logically belongs with *fasces*, joining it with *praetextam*: such dislocations are common in the pentameter because of its strict metrical requirements.

According to the manuscripts the preceding line ends with VTAR; I have printed Heinsius' VSVS, since there would otherwise be an asyndeton between *utar* and *aspiciam*. There are similar errors at 57 and xi 15 (*cedet* for *cedens*; *peruenit* for *perueniens*): here we may have a deliberate alteration by a scribe who did not understand the force of the delayed enclitic and sought a verb to couple *aspiciam* with.

44. DECRETIS *Korn* SECRETIS *codd* SECRETO *Wheeler*. Korn's conjecture makes the pentameter an amplification of the hexameter, a common pattern in Ovid; its corruption to *secretis* would be easy. Ehwald (*KB* 39-40) retained *secretis*, citing Tac *Ann* III 37 'secreta ['solitary designs'—Grant] patris mitigari' and Pliny *Pan* 53 6 (we should rejoice in our present good fortune under Trajan, and weep at the tribulations endured under previous emperors) 'hoc *secreta* nostra ['our private thoughts'], hoc sermones, hoc ipsae gratiarum actiones agant'. But in a list of the consul's public functions such a deviation of subject seems inappropriate. Wheeler's *secreto* is a little forced: 'my mind ... shall fancy itself present unseen at your actions'. Ehwald objected that Korn did not explain what his conjecture meant; but *decernere* was used of the consuls' judicial decisions (Cic *Att* XVI xvi a 4(6) 'consulum decretum').

45. LONGI ... LVSTRI. The epithet seems to have no special force: compare iv 23 'longum ... annum'.

45. REDITVS HASTAE SVPPONERE. See at v 19 *reditus ... componet* (p 219).

46. CERNET PM^{2c}*, Gothanus membr. II 121 (saec xiii)* CREDET *BCFHILT*. *Cernet* seems preferable to *credet* as continuing the image of *uidebit* in 43.

46. EXACTA CVNCTA LOCARE FIDE. Graecinus will be careful and incorruptible in assigning taxation contracts. For *fide* compare v 20 'et minui magnae non sinet urbis opes'; for *exacta* compare Suet *Tib* 18 'cum animaduerteret Varianam cladem temeritate et neglegentia ducis accidisse ... curam ... solita [*scripsi; confer Liu XXVII 47 1 'multitudo ... maior solita' solito codd*] *exactiorem* praestitit'.

48. PVBLICA QVAERENTEM QVID PETAT VTILITAS. The consul acted as chairman of the Senate, proposing the order of the day, and asking the senators in order of seniority for their *sententiae* on the appropriate action for the question under discussion.

48. PVBLICA ... VTILITAS. 'The people's interest'. For *utilitas* compare *Met* XIII 191 'utilitas populi', Cic *Part Or* 89 'persaepe euenit ut *utilitas* cum honestate certet', Cic *Sul* 25 '*populi utilitati* magis consulere quam uoluntati', and Livy VI 40 5 & VIII 34 2 'posthabita filii caritas *publicae utilitati*'.

49. PRO CAESARIBVS = *pro Caesarum factis*. Compare *Res Gestae* 4 'ob res a me aut per legatos meos auspicis [=*auspiciis*] meis terra marique prospere gestas quinquagiens et quinquiens *decreuit senatus* supplicandum esse dis immortalibus. dies autem per quos *ex senatus consulto* supplicatum est fuere DCCCLXXXX'.

49. CAESARIBVS. Tiberius, Germanicus, and Drusus. Similarly used at *EP* II vi 18 (to Graecinus) 'omnia *Caesaribus* [Augustus and Tiberius] sic tua facta probes'.

49. DECERNERE GRATES. 'Propose (in the Senate) the decreeing of thanks'. The sense of *decernere* is common in prose: see Cic *Prou Cons* 1, *Att* VII i 7, and the other passages at *OLD decerno* 6.

49. GRATES appears occasionally in prose (Tarrant at Sen *Ag* 380 *reddunt grates* cites Livy XXIII 11 12, Curtius IX 6 17, and Vell Pat II 25 4), but in hexameter and elegiac verse is the necessary representative for *grātiās*.

51. CVM IAM FVERIS POTIORA PRECATVS. For *potior* 'more important' compare Caesar *BC* I 8 (a reported remark of Pompey) 'semper se rei publicae commoda priuatis necessitudinibus habuisse *potiora*', Livy VIII 29 2, and the many passages at *OLD potior*[2] 4. The usage belongs to prose: Ovid elsewhere and Virgil always use *potior* to mean either 'more powerful' or 'preferable'.

53-54. SVRGAT ... DETQVE. The apodosis of an implied condition: 'If you prayed for me, the fire would rise'.

53. SVRGAT AD HANC VOCEM PLENA PIVS IGNIS AB ARA. The same favourable omen at *Met* X 278-79 (Pygmalion has finished his prayer to Venus) 'amici numinis omen, / flamma ter accensa est apicemque per aera duxit'.

53. PLENA ... AB ARA. Another indication of Graecinus'

devotion to the Caesars.

53. PIVS. 'Holy'; compare *pia tura* at *Am* III iii 33, *Met* XI 577, and *Tr* II 59, *pia sacra* at *Tr* V v 2, and *pio ... igne* at *Tr* V v 12.

54. LVCIDVS. Proleptic: 'The flame-tips would become bright and furnish a good omen for your prayer'.

55. NE CVNCTA QVERAMVR. 'So that not everything I say will be a complaint'.

57. LAETITIAE EST *LT*. Most manuscripts have LAETITIA EST. Similarly at *Met* VIII 430 'illi *laetitiae est* cum munere muneris auctor' most codices read *laetitia est*. Heinsius thought LAETITIAE possibly correct here, as might be the case also in the *Metamorphoses*: *laetitiae* could easily have been misread as *laetitia ē* [=*est*], with *laetitiae est* as a later correction.

58. FRATER. L. Pomponius Flaccus (*PIR¹* P 538), *consul ordinarius* for 17. As the greater honour would indicate (Graecinus was *consul suffectus*), Flaccus was more prominent than his brother and, unlike Graecinus, is several times mentioned in literary sources outside Ovid. At II 129 Velleius Paterculus speaks of Flaccus' ability and modesty, and Suetonius (*Tib* 42 1) names him as a drinking-companion of the emperor, made propraetor of Syria by Tiberius. Tacitus says that Flaccus proposed the *supplicationum dies* following the discovery in 16 of Libo's plot against Tiberius (*Ann* II 32 3); at *Ann* II 41 2 he names Flaccus as consul at the time of Germanicus' great triumph in 17, and at VI 27 3 mentions Flaccus' death in 34 while propraetor of Syria. For Flaccus' special mission to Thrace shortly after the time this poem was written, see at 75 (p 308).

EP I x is addressed to Flaccus, but gives little information except that Flaccus had, like Graecinus, given help to Ovid (37-40). Ovid's relations with Flaccus were clearly not as intimate as those with his brother.

59-60. The distich may be an interpolation, or at least deeply corrupted in its present form. Professor E. Fantham points out to me that the construction of *die* with both *summo ...*

Decembri and *Iani* is awkward, and that *dies Iani* does not seem to be used elsewhere in Latin literature. The tense of *suspicit* is strange as well: a future would normally be expected here.

61. QVAEQVE EST IN VOBIS PIETAS. 'Your family-feeling is so great that ...' The same idiom at *Met* V 373 'quae iam patientia nostra est', *EP* I vii 59, *EP* II ii 21-22 'quaeque tua est pietas in totum nomen Iuli, / te laedi cum quis laeditur inde [=*ex illis*] putas', and Hor *Sat* I ix 54-55 'quae tua uirtus, / expugnabis'. The sense is frequent in prose (*OLD qui*[1] A 12).

The expression is used as a simple relative with the implication of size only from context at *Tr* III v 29 'quaeque tibi linguae est facundia, confer in illud' and *Tr* III vi 7-8 'quique est in caris animi [*codd*: animo *fort legendum; uide ad 91*] tibi candor amicis— / cognitus est illi quem colis ipse uiro'.

61-62. ALTERNA ... GAVDIA. Flaccus will first rejoice to see Graecinus become consul; then Graecinus will have the pleasure of seeing Flaccus consul.

64. BINVS seems sufficiently confirmed, as Ehwald points out (*KB* 51-52) by *bis ... bis* in the preceding line; BIMVS, conjectured by Heinsius and found in certain late manuscripts, seems ingenious but unnecessary. Ehwald compares *Ecl* III 30 '*bis* uenit ad mulctram, *binos* alit ubere fetus'.

64-65. HONOR ... INGENS. At vii 17 Ovid calls the rank of *primipilaris* 'titulus ... ingens'.

65-66. MARTIA ... ROMA. The same phrase at *Tr* III vii 52 and *EP* I viii 24; compare as well *Aen* I 276-77 'Romulus ... Mauortia condet / moenia'. Mars, father of Romulus and Remus, was peculiarly the god of Rome: compare *Fast* I 39-40 & III 85-86 'Mars Latio uenerandus erat, quia praesidet armis: / arma ferae genti remque decusque dabant'.

The reference to Mars is very apt in view of the primarily military nature of the republican consul's office.

67. MVLTIPLICAT TAMEN HVNC GRAVITAS AVCTORIS HONOREM. Flaccus had been nominated for the consulship by Tiberius.

For language and sentiment compare *Met* VIII 430 'illi laetitiae est cum munere muneris *auctor*'.

67. GRAVITAS is linked with Hercules at *Met* IX 270, with Jupiter at *Met* I 207 (considered suspect by Merkel) and II 847, with all the Olympian gods at *Met* VI 73, and with Augustus at *Tr* II 512. Underneath the ostensible connection to Jupiter at *Met* II 846-47 'non bene conueniunt nec in una sede morantur / maiestas et amor' Professor R. J. Tarrant sees an allusion to Augustus.

69-70. IVDICIIS IGITVR LICEAT FLACCOQVE TIBIQVE / TALIBVS AVGVSTI TEMPVS IN OMNE FRVI. Compare *EP* II vi 17-18 (to Graecinus) 'quodque soles animo *semper*, quod uoce precari, / omnia Caesaribus sic *tua facta probes*'.

70. AVGVSTI = *Tiberii;* his name in inscriptions is TI·CAESAR·AVG (Sandys 235).

71. CVM *FILT* QVOD *BC* VT *MH* QVVM *Weise.* The archetype was illegible at this point, and the manuscripts offer various supplements. Of these *cum* seems the most appropriate. Ehwald favoured *quod* (*KB* 48), but all except one of the passages he cited are instances of *quod superest* or *quod reliquum est.* The one relevant passage he cited was *Fast* II 17-18 (to Augustus) 'ergo ades et placido paulum mea munera uultu / respice, pacando *si quid* ab hoste *uacat*'. Many manuscripts however offer *uacas* (for which compare Prop II xxxii 7 'quodcumque uacabis'), and the corruption to the third person seems an easy one. *Vacare* in general does not seem to occur with an expressed impersonal subject.

71. CVRA PROPIORE. The same phrase at *Met* XIII 578-79 '*cura* deam *propior* luctusque domesticus angit / Memnonis amissi'.

73. SI QVAE DABIT AVRA SINVM. 'If some wind should give the opportunity of filling my sails'. *Quae* is my correction for QVA (*CMFHIL*), which would make the sentence mean 'If the wind should in some way ...'. The difficulty here is with the apparently already existing *aura*: what breeze is Ovid referring to? QVEM (*BT*) presents the same difficulty ('If the breeze should offer any opportunity ...') and in any case looks like a scribal correction. I take *qua* to be an unmetrical form corrupted from the rare form *quae* of the indefinite adjective. For the form, compare Ter *Heaut* 44 'si *quae* [*Bembinus (saec iv-v)*: qua *recc*] [*sc* fabula] laboriosast, ad me curritur', Hor *Sat* I iv 93-95 'mentio si *quae* [*uar* qua] ... te coram fuerit, defendas, ut tuus est mos', Hor *Sat* II vi 10 'o si urnam argenti fors *quae* mihi monstret', and *CIL* I 583 37 'SEIQVAE CAVSA ERIT'. *Quae* in the present passage offers the same notion of a fresh breeze rising as is found at viii 27-28 'quamlibet exigua si nos ea [*sc* ara] iuuerit *aura*, / obruta de mediis cumba resurget aquis' and *Tr* IV v 19-20 'remis ad opem luctare ferendam / *dum ueniat* placido mollior *aura* deo'.

Quae should possibly be written at *Met* VI 231-33 'praescius imbris ... rector / carbasa deducit ne *qua* leuis effluat aura', but Professor R. J. Tarrant points out that *qua* can be defended by taking *leuis* to mean 'nimble', a sense supported here by *effluat*. A strong case could be made for reading *quae* at Hor *Carm* III xiv 19-20 'Spartacum si *qua* potuit uagantem / fallere testa'.

73. SINVM. *Sinus* in the sense of 'sail' is common enough (*Am* II xi 38, *AA* III 500, *Fast* V 609, and *Aen* III 455 & V 16; the origin of the metonymy seen at Prop III ix 30 'uelorum plenos ... sinus'); but the brachylogy here 'opportunity of filling my sails' is remarkable.

73. LAXATE *editio princeps Romana* IACTATE *codd*. Korn, Lenz, and André print the manuscript reading, and Korn offers three parallel passages in its defence, none of which stands up to examination. The first is *EP* III ii 5-6 'cumque labent alii *iactataque* uela relinquant, / tu lacerae remanes ancora sola rati', where *iactata* means 'storm-whipped'; compare Statius *Theb* VII 139-41 'uento / incipiente ... laxi *iactantur* ubique rudentes'. At Cic *Tusc* V 40 (a Spartan to a wealthy sea-merchant) 'non sane optabilis quidem ista ... rudentibus apta fortuna', 'Well, your fortune depends on your cables, and I don't think it something to be sought

270

for', *iactare* does not appear. The third passage, Virgil *G* II 354-55 'seminibus positis superest diducere terram / saepius ad capita ['roots'] et duros *iactare* bidentis', hardly seems relevant.

For *laxate rudentes* 'let out the sails' Heinsius cited *Aen* III 266-67 'tum litore funem / deripere excussosque iubet *laxare* rudentis' 'Next he commanded us to fling hawsers from moorings and uncoil and ease the sheets' (Jackson Knight), *Aen* VIII 707-8 'uentis ... uela dare et *laxos* iamiamque immittere funis', Cic *Diu* I 127, Lucan V 426-27 'pariter soluere rates, totosque rudentes / *laxauere* sinus', and Lucan IX 1004.

74. E STYGIIS ... AQVIS. Similar phrasing at *Met* X 697 'Stygia ... unda, *Met* XI 500 'Stygia ... unda', *Aen* VI 374 'Stygias ... aquas', *Aen* XII 91 'Stygia ... unda', and *Cons Liu* 410 'Stygia ... aqua'.

Ovid often uses the phrasing of his exile: see *Tr* I ii 65-66 'mittere me *Stygias* si iam uoluisset in *undas* / Caesar, in hoc uestro non eguisset ope', *Tr* IV v 22, *EP* I viii 27 'careo uobis, *Stygias* detrusus in *oras*', and *EP* II iii 44 'a *Stygia* quantum mors [*codd*: sors *Heinsius*] mea distat aqua?'. For Ovid's exile as the equivalent of death, see at vi 49 *qui me doluistis ademptum* (p 243).

75. PRAEFVIT HIS ... LOCIS MODO FLACCVS. At *Ann* II 64-67 Tacitus reports how, following the death of Augustus, Rhescuporis attacked and imprisoned his brother Cotys (addressee of *EP* II ix), alleging a plot against himself; on their father's death, the kingdom of Thrace had been divided between them, Cotys receiving the better regions. Tiberius insisted that Rhescuporis release his brother and come to Rome to explain the situation; Rhescuporis then killed his brother, claiming it was a suicide. 'nec tamen Caesar placitas semel artes mutauit, sed defuncto Pandusa, quem sibi infensum Rhescuporis arguerat [*scripsi*: arguebat *M*], Pomponium Flaccum, *ueterem stipendiis* et arta cum rege amicitia eoque accommodatiorem ad fallendum ob id maxime Moesiae praefecit'; the previous service mentioned by Tacitus is no doubt the command Ovid is here referring to.

Flaccus succeeded in trapping Rhescuporis and bringing him to Rome; he was found guilty and sent in exile to Alexandria, where he died. Velleius Paterculus placed the episode first in his list of memorable events of Tiberius' reign (II 129); it is briefly mentioned at Suet *Tib* 37 4.

75. FLACCVS. 'Ab hoc Flacco uolunt quidam Valachiam ['Wallachia'] fuisse dictam olim *Flacciam*, quod nomen sensim corruptela sermonis transiit in Valachiam. Vide Georgii a ['von'] Reychersdorff Chorographiam Transyluaniae. pag. 33 [first published in 1595; see *British Museum Gen Cat* 200 383] qui addit hinc [*sic*] adhuc Romanum ibi sermonem durare, licet admodum corruptum. sed hae fabulae'—Burman. Clearly the existence of Rumanian was not widely known in Western Europe at the time Burman wrote.

77. MYSAS GENTES = *Moesos*. Strabo (VII 3 10; cited by André) claims a common origin for the Μοισοί of Europe and the Μυσοί of Asia. For the Greek form, compare Ovid's use of *Getes* for *Geta* and *Sauromates* for *Sarmata*.

78. ARCV FISOS ... GETAS. For the bow as the typical Getic weapon, see iii 52 'arcu ... Gete'', *EP* III v 45 'Getico ... arcu' and *Ibis* 635 'Geticasque sagittas'.

78. ENSE. The *gladius*, typical weapon of the Roman legionary. For the precise equivalence of the two terms, see Quintilian X i 11. In Ovid's poetry, the proportion of instances of *ensis* to instances of *gladius* is about 90:30; in the poetry of exile, it is 21:3. For a discussion of *ensis/gladius*, with statistics, see Axelson 51; the only poets to admit *gladius* more freely than Ovid are Lucan and Juvenal.

79. TROESMIN *Heinsius* TROESMEN *C* TROESENEN *B[1]* TROEZEN *uel similia codd plerique*. Troesmis, the modern Galaţi, is located on the north bank of the Danube, about 160 kilometres inland from Aegissos (Tulcea). Heinsius did not have the assistance of *CIL* V 6183-88 & 6195, but seems nonetheless to have conjectured that *Troesmin* was a possible reading ('sed legendum, Τρωισμὶς uel Τρωσμίς'). Korn was the first to place *Troesmin* in the text.

79. CELERI VIRTVTE. 'With a bold surprise attack'.

80. INFECITQVE FERO SANGVINE DANVVIVM.
Compare the similar description of Vestalis' recapture of
Aegissos: 'non negat hoc *Hister*, cuius tua dextera quondam
/ *puniceam Getico sanguine fecit aquam*' (vii 19-20).

80. DANVVIVM. According to Owen at *Tr* II 192 this, and
not DANVBIVM (the reading of the manuscripts), is the
spelling certified by the inscriptions. Manuscripts divide
between the two spellings at Hor *Carm* IV xv 21 and Tac
Germ I 1.

81-86. Ovid similarly calls Vestalis as his witness at vii 3-4
'aspicis en praesens quali iaceamus in aruo, / nec me testis
eris falsa solere queri'.

81. INCOMMODA. The word is not found elsewhere in
Ovid, and is not used in verse, except for satire (Hor *AP* 169;
Juvenal XIII 21). It is particularly common in Caesar.

81. CAELI = 'climate', as commonly (*Tr* III iii 7, Prop II xxviii
5, Cic *Att* XI xxii 2).

82. QVAM VICINO TERREAR HOSTE ROGA. An
imitation of Tib I i 3 'quem labor assiduus *uicino terreat hoste*'.

**83. SINTNE LITAE TENVES SERPENTIS FELLE
SAGITTAE.** Similar descriptions of poisoned arrows at *Tr* IV
i 77 'imbuta ... tela uenenis', *Tr* IV i 84, *Tr* III x 64, *Tr* V vii 16
'tela ... uipereo lurida felle', *EP* I ii 16 'omnia uipereo spicula
felle linunt', *EP* III i 26, and *EP* III iii 106.

84. FIAT AN HVMANVM VICTIMA DIRA CAPVT.
Human sacrifice similarly mentioned at *Tr* IV iv 61-62 'illi
quos audis hominum gaudere cruore, / paene sub eiusdem
sideris axe iacent'.

85. MENTIAR. Professor J. N. Grant points out to me the asyndeton following *quaere ... sintne*. Compare the similar problem at iv 31-32.

85. AN COEAT DVRATVS FRIGORE PONTVS. Similar wording at vii 7 'ipse uides certe glacie concrescere Pontum', *Tr* II 196 'maris astricto quae coit unda gelu', and *Tr* III x 37.

86. IVGERA MVLTA FRETI. According to *TLL* VII.2 629 7-8 this is the unique instance of *iugerum* being applied to water. The transferred sense is natural enough in view of the poets' application to the sea of such words as *campus* and *arua*.

89. NON SVMVS ... ODIO. Basically a prose use; but compare *Met* II 438 'huic odio nemus est', *Fast* VI 558, *EP* II i 4 'iam minus hic odio est quam fuit ante locus', and *Ecl* VIII 33 'tibi est odio mea fistula'.

Owen's second edition has the misprint '*nec* sumus hic odio', reproduced by Wheeler. The error was induced by *nec* at the start of the pentameter.

90. NEC CVM FORTVNA MENS QVOQVE VERSA MEA EST. For Ovid's use of syllepsis, see at vi 16 *spem nostram terras deseruitque simul* (p 234). For the sentiment of this line, compare Sen *Med* 176 'Fortuna opes auferre, non animum potest', where Costa cites Accius 619-20 Ribbeck[2] 'nam si a me regnum Fortuna atque opes / eripere quiuit, at uirtutem non quiit', Sen *Ben* IV 10 5, Sen *Ep* XXXVI 6, and Euripides fr. 1066 Nauck.

91. ILLA QVIES ANIMO. *Animo* is locative; or perhaps *in* should be supplied from the following line: for the joining of a noun with a following preposition already with a complement, see Clausen on Persius I 131 'abaco numeros et secto in puluere metas'. I read *animo* (found in one of Heinsius' Vatican manuscripts) because of the parallel structure it gives with the following *in ore*, but ANIMI (*BCMFHILT*) is possible enough: *OLD quies* 7 cites *quies animi* at Celsus III 18 5.

91. QVAM TV LAVDARE SOLEBAS. The same phrase at *Her* XV 193 'haec sunt illa [*sc* pectora], Phaon, *quae tu laudare* *solebas*'. For the persistence of Ovid's old habits, compare *EP* I x 29-30 (he remains a moderate drinker, as formerly).

93-94. SIC EGO SVM LONGE, SIC HIC, VBI BARBARVS HOSTIS / VT FERA PLVS VALEANT LEGIBVS ARMA, FACIT is clearly corrupt, as will be seen from Wheeler's 'Such is my bearing in this far land, where the barbarian foe causes cruel arms to have more power than law' and André's 'Je vis au loin, ici, où un ennemi barbare donne aux armes cruelles plus de force qu'aux lois'. Merkel ejected the distich, which seems the best solution; it is not necessary to the poem's structure, and the iterated *facit ut* in unrelated clauses at 94 and 97 is suspicious. Also, as Professor R. J. Tarrant notes, the *ut* in 94 makes one expect that *ut* in 95 will be correlative, when it in fact continues the thought of 93 (or rather of 91-92, after 93-94 are excised).

Heinsius thought 93 alone to be suspect; if so, the meaning lying behind the text is probably something like 'What I once was at Rome, I still am here'.

93-94. HIC, VBI BARBARVS HOSTIS, / VT FERA PLVS VALEANT LEGIBVS ARMA FACIT. Similar statements at *Tr* V vii 47-48 'non metuunt leges, sed cedit uiribus aequum, / uictaque pugnaci iura sub ense iacent' and *Tr* V x 43-44; see also Otto *lex* 3.

93. BARBARVS HOSTIS. The same phrase at *Tr* III x 54, *Tr* IV i 82, and *EP* II vii 70.

95. RE ... NVLLA *MHIL* REM NVLLAM *BCFT*. The verb *queri* can take a direct object, or be constructed with *de* + ablative, but not both; this would in effect give the verb two objects. *Re ... nulla* removes this difficulty and is obviously prone to corruption, the true object *de nobis* being postponed to the following line.

96. FEMINA ... VIRVE PVERVE = 'anyone'; compare *Tr* III vii 29-30 'pone, Perilla, metum: tantummodo *femina nulla / neue uir* a scriptis discat amare tuis', and Ovid's use of *femina uirque* 'everyone' at *Met* VI 314-15 '*femina uirque* timent cultuque impensius *omnes* ... uenerantur numina', *RA* 814, *Tr* I iii 23, and *Tr* II 6. The repeated *u* in *uirue* would not have offended the Romans: compare for instance *Tr* III vii 30 'neue uir', *Am* I viii 97 'uiri uideat toto uestigia lecto', and *Met* XII 204 'poteratque uiri uox illa uideri'; conscious alliteration at *Am* III vii 59 'uiuosque uirosque' and *Met* XIII 386 'inuictumque uirum uicit'.

98. HAEC QVONIAM TELLVS TESTIFICANDA MIHI EST. Similar phrasing at *Ibis* 27-28 (of Augustus) 'faciet quoque forsitan idem / *terra* sit ut propior *testificanda mihi*'.

100. RESPECTV ... SVI. 'Out of consideration for themselves'. *Respectus* elsewhere in Ovid only at *Tr* I iii 99-100 (of his wife after his departure) '[narratur ...] uoluisse mali [*Madvig*: mori *codd*] moriendo ponere sensus, / *respectu* tamen non periisse *mei*'. *Respectus* is found in Phaedrus, Martial, and Juvenal, but not in Virgil, Horace, or Propertius.

101. NEC MIHI CREDIDERIS in its absolute use here seems colloquial: elsewhere Ovid uses *nec ... credideris* to introduce a dependent clause (*Tr* V xiv 43; *EP* I viii 29).

101. EXTANT DECRETA QVIBVS NOS / LAVDAT ET IMMVNES PVBLICA CERA FACIT. The same honour described in greater detail at xiv 51-56.

101. EXTANT ('there exist') is somewhat more forceful than the nearly equivalent *sunt*: compare xiv 44 '*extat* adhuc nemo saucius ore meo', Cic *Planc* 2 'uideo ... hoc in numero neminem ... cuius non *extet* in me summum meritum', and Cic *Diu* I 71.

102. PVBLICA CERA = *tabulae publicae*, 'public records', for which compare Cic *Arch* 8 & *Fl* 40, and Livy XXVI 36 11. The same metonymy at Val Max II x 1, where *tabulae* and *cera* are used as synonyms, and at Hor *Ep* I vi 62 'Caerite cera', where commentators cite Aulus Gellius' mention of *tabulae Caerites* (XVI 13).

103. QVAE R. J. *Tarrant* HAEC L, *probante Heinsio* ET BCMFHIT. *Quae* connects with *idem* in the following line and provides a more satisfactory sense than *et*, which would make the sentence mean that Ovid did not consider the decrees something to boast of. *Quae quamquam* is preferable to *haec quamquam* since it connects better with the preceding

276

line and is obviously more prone to corruption; but for a similar corruption of *haec* compare Prop II xxiii 1 'fuit indocti haec [*uar* et] semita uulgi'. For *quae* Professor Tarrant cites *EP* III v 9-10 '*quae quamquam* lingua mihi sunt properante per horas / lecta satis multas, pauca fuisse queror' and *EP* III viii 23-24 '*quae quamquam* misisse pudet ... tu tamen haec quaeso consule missa boni'.

103. QVAMQVAM ... SIT *G* QVAMQVAM ... EST *BCMFHILT*. For the subjunctive Luck compares *Met* XIV 465 'admonitu quamquam luctus renouentur amari' and *Met* XV 244-45 '*quae* [*sc* elementa] *quamquam* spatio distent, tamen omnia fiunt / ex ipsis'; in the first passage a few manuscripts and in the second the majority offer the indicative. Ovid usually has the indicative following *quamquam*; but *sit* should be taken as the correct reading here in view of *G*'s early date.

105. NEC PIETAS IGNOTA MEA EST. At xiii 19-38 Ovid describes an instance of his *pietas*, the reciting to the Getes of a poem in Getic on Tiberius.

105-10. The figures of the imperial family had been a gift of Cotta Maximus, for which *EP* II viii was a letter of thanks. For a discussion of Ovid's treatment of the imperial family, particularly in the poems of exile, see K. Scott "Emperor Worship in Ovid", *TAPA* LXI [1930] 43-69.

106. CAESARIS. Augustus, as is made clear by the next line.

107. NATVSQVE PIVS. Tiberius; see at viii 63 *auum* (p 277). For Tiberius' piety to Augustus' memory compare Tac *Ann* IV 37 4 (AD 25; Tiberius speaking) 'cum diuus Augustus sibi atque urbi Romae templum apud Pergamum sisti non prohibuisset, *qui omnia facta dictaque eius uice legis obseruem*, placitum iam exemplum ... secutus sum'.

107. CONIVNXQVE SACERDOS. Livia, priestess of the deified Augustus; Germanicus was his *flamen*. For the language compare Vell Pat II 75 3 'Liuia ... genere, probitate, forma Romanarum eminentissima, quam postea *coniugem* Augusti uidimus, quam transgressi ad deos *sacerdotem* ac filiam'.

108. FACTO ... DEO. See at viii 63 *quem uirtus addidit astris* (p 277).

109. VTERQVE NEPOTVM. Germanicus and Drusus.

111. PRECANTIA VERBA = *preces*. The same phrase at *Met* VI 164, IX 159, and XIV 365.

112. EOO ... AB ORBE. The same phrase at *Fast* III 466 & V 557.

113-14. Williams suggested deleting this distich: 'The distance between *Tota* and *Pontica terra*, the use of *licet*=if, and *Pontica terra* immediately followed by *Pontica tellus*, point to an interpolation'.

The hyperbaton of *tota ... Pontica terra* seems standard enough. Wheeler translates *licet quaeras* as 'you are free to inquire', which may be right; however, the phrase does indeed seem awkward, and *licet* may be an intrusive gloss that has displaced *uelim*: compare *Her* IV 18 'fama—*uelim quaeras*—crimine nostra uacat'. The repetition of *Pontica terra* and *Pontica ... tellus* is a very strong argument for deleting one of the two distichs. However, 115-16 seems more likely to be the interpolation in view of the difficulties discussed in the next note.

115. ORA. Ehwald (*KB* 65) read ARA (*B*), citing Dessau *ILS* 154 14-15 'ara(m) numini Augusto pecunia nostra faciendam curauimus; *ludos* / ex idibus Augustis diebus sex p(ecunia) n(ostra) faciendos curauimus'; but the *ara* and *ludi* are clearly separate items in the inscription, which does not support the phrasing *ara natalem ludis celebrare*.

Even with *ora*, 115-16 read rather oddly: the notion of an individual conducting *ludi* is strange, and the singular *dei* seems rather vague after the collective *his* of 111. If the distich is excised (as Professor R. J. Tarrant suggests) 113-14 round out the paragraph that began with 105 (note the correspondence of *uidet hospita terra* in 105 with *testis Pontica terra* in 114), and 117 introduces *hospites* as a second class of witnesses.

118. LONGA. Not 'distant' (Wheeler) but 'long'; compare *Met* XIII 407 'longus in angustum qua clauditur Hellespontus'. *Longus* meaning 'distant' is extremely rare: *OLD longus* 6 cites only Silius VI 628 'remeans longis ... oris' and ps-Quintilian *Decl* 320 6 'longas terras ... peragraui' (Lewis and Short add Justinus 18 1 'longa a domo militia'). The normal Latin words for 'distant' were *longinquus* and *longe* (ancestor of French *loin*).

119. IS in its various forms occurs only seven times in *EP* IV: the other occurrences are of feminine singular *ea* at i 17, viii 27 & xiv 11, of *eius* at xv 6 (its only occurrence in the *Ex Ponto*), of accusative *id* at i 19, and of accusative neuter plural *ea* at x 35.

The elegiac poets avoided the use of *is*, preferring *hic, ille,* and *iste*. The singular nominative forms were the only ones used relatively freely by Ovid (about forty instances of each); Tibullus and Propertius avoided even these (Platnauer 116; Axelson 70-71).

119. QVO LAEVVS FVERAT SVB PRAESIDE PONTVS. See at 75 *praefuit his ... locis modo Flaccus* (p 308).

119. LAEVVS ... PONTVS = *Euxini litora laeua* (*Tr* IV i 60). A similar brachylogy at *EP* I iv 31 'iunctior Haemonia est *Ponto* quam Roma *sinistro* [*Burman*: sit Histro *codd*]'.

119. PRAESIDE. This seems to be the first instance of *praeses* 'governor' in Latin. It is found in prose from Tacitus and Suetonius on: Trajan even uses it in his official correspondence (Pliny *Ep* X xliv).

119. FVERAT. See at vi 12 *nec fueram tanti* (p 230).

121. AVDIERIT. Probably a perfect subjunctive 'may have heard', although possibly an epistolary future perfect indicative ('when you receive this, your brother will perhaps [*forsitan*] have heard'). For the perfect subjunctive compare *Met* X 560-62 *'forsitan audieris* aliquam certamine cursus / ueloces superasse uiros'.

121. FORTVNA EST IMPAR ANIMO. Similar phrasing at *Tr* V v 46-47 (on his wife's birthday) 'at non sunt ista gaudia nata die, / sed labor et curae *fortunaque moribus impar*'; but note the different sense of *fortuna*.

121. FORTVNA. 'My means' (Wheeler). The sense is rare but classical; *OLD fortuna* 12 cites among other passages Cic *Fam* XIV 4 2 'periculum fortunarum ['possessions'] et capitis sui' and Caes *BG* V 43 4.

122. CARPO ... OPES. For the sense of *carpo* see at viii 32 *carpsit opes ... meas* (p 266).

126. ILLVM *CMFHILTB*² ILLI *B*¹. Either accusative or dative would be acceptable enough with *latere*. The earliest instances from verse given by *TLL* VII.2 997 49 are Lucretius III 280 for the dative and *Aen* I 130 for the accusative. I retain the accusative because it is the reading of most manuscripts, including *B*'s close relative *C*. There are similar variants involving the object of *latere* at *Fast* V 361: the accusative given by most manuscripts is generally read in preference to the dative.

127-29. TV ... TV. For the anaphora of *tu* in hymns or solemn prayer, see the passages collected by Nisbet and Hubbard at Hor *Carm* I x 9 and by Tarrant at Sen *Ag* 311.

127. SVPERIS ASCITE. *Asciscere* is generally used of admission to the citizenship or to the Senate: for parallels to the metaphorical use here, see Tarrant at Sen *Ag* 812-13 'tuus ille bis seno meruit labore / *adlegi caelo* magnus Alcides'.

128. Causal **VT** ['*ex ueteribus*' *Naugerius*] seems an appropriate correction for the manuscripts' lame ET.

129-30. NOSTRAS ... PRECES. The hyperbaton adds elevation and dignity to the prayer.

129-30. INTER CONVEXA ... SIDERA = *inter sidera conuexi caeli*; the hypallage adds further to the elevation of the passage. For *conuexa* compare Festus (58 Muller; 51 Lindsay) 'conuexum est ex omni parte declinatum, *qualis est natura caeli*, quod ex omni parte ad terram uersum declinatum est', *Met* I 26 'ignes *conuexi* uis et sine pondere *caeli*', *Ecl* IV 50, and Cic *Arat* 560 (314). In particular compare *Aen* I 607-8, which Ovid is clearly imitating: 'dum montibus umbrae /

lustrabunt, *conuexa* polus dum *sidera* pascet'. There is some question as to whether *conuexa* should there be taken with *sidera*, or as the object of *lustrabunt*: Ovid clearly took it with *sidera*.

130. SOLLICITO QVAS DAMVS ORE PRECES. For the general wording compare *Tr* III viii 20 'tum quoque *sollicita mente rogandus* erit' and *EP* III i 148 'nil nisi *sollicitae* sint tua uerba *preces*': for *sollicito ... ore* compare *sollicita uoce* at *Met* X 639 & XIV 706.

131. PERVENIANT ISTVC. Compare *EP* II ii 95 'si tamen haec audis et uox mea *peruenit istuc* [=*Romam*]'.

131-32. CARMINA ... QVAE DE TE MISI CAELITE FACTA NOVO. Ovid also mentions his poems on Augustus' apotheosis at vi 17-18, viii 63-64 & xiii 25-26.

133-34. NEC TV / IMMERITO NOMEN MITE PARENTIS HABES. 'Et ce n'est pas sans raison que tu portes le doux nom de Père' (André) must be correct as against Wheeler's 'for not undeservedly hast thou the gracious name of "Father"', since *nec*, although it can mean *et ... non* or *sed ... non*, cannot mean *nam ... non*; the proof of this is the frequent occurrence of *neque enim*.

The litotes *non (haud, nec) immerito* is common enough in Latin: see the many examples at *TLL* VII.1 457 26 ff. But in the four instances given of *nec immerito*, it never serves to introduce a new phrase as here. At Plautus *St* 28 'decet *neque id immerito* eueniet' it introduces a second verb which amplifies the preceding one, while it modifies preceding verbs at Ter *Ad* 615 'tanta nunc suspicio de me incidit *neque ea immerito*', Val Max IV vii 1 'inimicus patriae fuisse Ti. Gracchus existimatus est, *nec immerito*, quia potentiam suam saluti eius praetulerat', and Quintilian X i 104 'habet amatores—*nec immerito*—Cremuti libertas'. One would expect a clause of causation to follow *auguror his igitur flecti tua numina*, and I think it possible that Ovid wrote NAM TV / E MERITO (Professor C. P. Jones suggests EX MERITO). Both the corruption from *e merito* and the subsequent interpolation of *nec* would be easy enough. For *e(x) merito*, compare vii 16 'contigit *ex merito* qui tibi nuper honor'.

281

133. NEC TV. The elegiac poets admitted a monosyllabic ending to the hexameter if it was preceded by another monosyllable closely linked to it in sense: see Platnauer 13. For true monosyllabic endings, see at ii 47 *Aonius fons*.

134. NOMEN MITE PARENTIS = *nomen parentis, quod significat te mitem esse*. At *Tr* I i 73 and *EP* II viii 51 members of the imperial family are called *mitissima numina*. There is another instance of hypallage with *nomen mite* (a different sense of *mitis* being used) at *Fast* V 64 *'nomen* et aetatis *mite* [*codd*: rite *Riese*] senatus erat', 'the very name of senate signified a ripe old age' (Frazer).

134. PARENTIS = *patris patriae*. For the title compare *Res Gestae* 35 (the final achievement listed by Augustus) 'tertium decimum consulatum cum gerebam, senatus et equester ordo populusque Romanus uniuersus appellauit me *patrem patriae*, idque in uestibulo aedium mearum inscribendum esse et in curia et in foro Aug. sub quadrigis quae mihi ex s.c. positae sunt decreuit'. Suetonius describes the conferring of the title at *Aug* 58.

X. To Albinovanus Pedo

The poem is the only one in the *Ex Ponto* addressed to Albinovanus. Considering the elder Seneca's express testimony that Albinovanus was a close friend of Ovid (see at 4 [pp 327-28]), this is rather surprising; perhaps Albinovanus, an associate of Germanicus (Tac *Ann* I 60 2), had, like some of Ovid's other friends, asked not to be mentioned in his verse.

The poem begins with the statement that Ovid is now in his sixth year of exile; unlike flint and iron, he is not touched by the passing of time (1-8). He says that his tribulations are like those of Ulysses, but more severe; there follows a comparison of his experiences with those of Ulysses (9-30). He then describes the bleakness of the climate, and how the sea freezes over in winter (31-34). He has heard that his accounts are not believed at Rome, and will therefore explain the reasons for the sea's freezing over (35-38). At Tomis the north wind prevails, and the salinity of the sea is reduced by the influx of many large rivers (which are listed in a catalogue); the sea's freezing is caused by these two factors (39-64). He is telling all this to Albinovanus to pass the time; Albinovanus is writing poetry as well, about Theseus, who is an example for him to follow (65-82). Ovid does not wish to imply that Albinovanus is not already doing everything possible to assist him (83-84).

The poem combines with remarkable ease a number of quite disparate subjects, and is in this sense reminiscent of Tibullus. Most of the subjects had been used previously in the poetry of exile; in particular, see *Tr* I v 57-84 for an extended comparison of the trials of Ulysses and those of Ovid. The disquisition on the reasons for the Euxine's freezing over is, however, new. It seems to have been drawn from a geographical or physical treatise which has left its mark elsewhere in Latin literature: see at 37-38 (p 340-42).

1. CIMMERIO *British Library Harley 2607 (Tarrant)* CVMERIO

283

M^1 IN ETIAM MEMORI C IN ********* B^1 IN HEMONIO *HITP* IN EVXINO F IN <u>EXINO</u> B^{2c} BISTONIO LM^{2ul} Many centuries had passed since the Cimmerians had inhabited Scythia; even Herodotus, who tells the story of their departure, seems to regard the event as belonging to the distant past (IV 11-12). Homer was vaguely aware of the nation: at *Od* XI 13-19 (imitated at *Pan Mess* 64-66), he speaks of the 'Κιμμερίων ἀνδρῶν ... πόλις' by the stream of Ocean, which never receives sunlight.

For *Cimmerio* Burman compared Claudian *Cons Stil* I 129 'nunc prope Cimmerii tendebat litora *Ponti*'; see as well *In Eutr* I 249 'extra *Cimmerias*, Taurorum claustra, paludes'.

1. BIS TERTIA ... AESTAS. The poem is therefore dated to the summer of 14. For Ovid's mentions of the length of his exile, see at vi 5 *quinquennis* (p 227).

3. ECQVOS ... ECQVOD *Laurentianus 36 2, saec xv* ET QVOS ... ET QVOD *BCMFHILT*. The same corruption is found in certain manuscripts at *Met* III 442-45 (Narcissus speaking) "'*ecquis*, io siluae, crudelius" inquit "amauit? ... *ecquem* ... qui sic tabuerit longo meministis in aeuo?"' and commonly. Other instances of *ecquis* in emotionally heightened questions at *Fast* IV 488, *Tr* I vi 11, *EP* III i 3, and *Her* XXI 106.

3. SILICES ... FERRVM. See at viii 49 *tabida consumit ferrum lapidemque uetustas* (p 270).

4. ALBINOVANE. Albinovanus Pedo[21] and Ovid seem to have been close friends. Ovid mentions him again at xvi 6 'sidereusque Pedo', and he was the source of the famous anecdote in the elder Seneca (*Cont* II 2 12) of how Ovid chose as the three lines in his poems he most wished to retain the same three verses a group of his friends most wished to remove.

He was a famous raconteur: the younger Seneca calls Pedo *fabulator elegantissimus* at *Ep* CXXII 15-16 when repeating one of his anecdotes.

At the time this poem was written, Albinovanus was

engaged on a *Theseid* (71). Quintilian perhaps had this poem in mind when he included a rather slighting mention of Albinovanus in his catalogue of epic poets at X i 90: 'Rabirius ac Pedo non indigni cognitione, si uacet'. He may, however, have been thinking of Albinovanus' poem on Germanicus' campaigns, of which the elder Seneca preserves some twenty-three hexameters (*Suas* I 15; commentary by V. Bongi, *Istituto Lombardo di scienze e lett. Rendiconti [Classe di Lettere]* ser. 3 13 [1949], 28-48. Norden and others have attributed Morel *Incert* 46 'ingenia immansueta suoque simillima caelo' to the same poem). Martial several times mentions Albinovanus as a writer of epigrams (II lxxvii 5, V v 5 & X xx (xix) 10); this fits well with the younger Seneca's description of Albinovanus as *fabulator elegantissimus*.

At *Ann* I 60 2, Tacitus mentions Pedo as 'praefectus finibus Frisiorum' in Germanicus' campaign of 15.

5-6. LAPIDEM ... ANVLVS ... VOMER. See at viii 49 *tabida consumit ferrum lapidemque uetustas* (p 270), and compare *AA* I 473-76 'ferreus assiduo consumitur *anulus* usu, / interit assidua *uomer* aduncus humo. / quid magis est saxo durum, quid mollius unda? / dura tamen molli saxa cauantur aqua'.

6. ATTERITVR *Heinsius.* Korn and Riese printed the manuscripts' ET TERITVR, for which Riese cited *Tr* I iv 9-10 'pinea texta sonant pulsu [*Rothmaler:* pulsi *codd*], stridore rudentes, / ingemit *et* nostris ipsa carina malis' and *Tr* III iv 57-58 'ante oculos errant domus, urbsque et forma locorum, / accedunt*que* suis singula facta locis', but these are extended descriptions of single events, not lists of separate examples.

Elsewhere in Ovid, the only form found of *atterere* is *attritus*: this circumstance perhaps contributed to the corruption of the present passage.

6. ATTERITVR PRESSA VOMER ADVNCVS HVMO. Professor R. J. Tarrant points out to me the hypallage in this passage. *Pressus* is to be taken twice, with *uomer* and with *humo*: the earth is *pressed down* as the plough is *pressed* into it.

7. TEMPVS EDAX. The same phrase at *Met* XV 234; compare as well *edax ... uetustas* at *Met* XV 872.

7. PRAETER NOS. At *EP* II vii 39-45, Ovid (with a series of images parallel to that of the present passage) says that he is in fact being worn away by the hardships he is enduring: 'ut ... caducis / percussu crebro *saxa* cauantur aquis, / sic ego continuo Fortunae uulneror ictu ... nec magis assiduo *uomer* tenuatur ab usu, / nec magis est curuis Appia trita rotis, / pectora quam mea sunt serie calcata malorum'.

8. PERDIT *I* PERDET *BCMFHLT.* The tense is made probable by the preceding *cauat ... consumitur ... atteritur* and the following *cessat*; compare as well *Tr* IV vi 17-18 'cuncta pot*est* ... uetustas / praeter quam curas attenuare meas'. Third conjugation verbs in the third person are for obvious reasons peculiarly apt to corruption of tense and mood. The alteration from present to future is rather less common than the inverse corruption, for an instance of which see at xii 18 *reddet* (p 378).

8. CESSAT DVRITIA MORS QVOQVE VICTA MEA. Death does not conquer Ovid, but is conquered by him. Professor E. Fantham points out to me the baroque inversion in the phrase, citing as a parallel Sen *Tr* 1171-75, where Hecuba says that death fears her and flees her.

Riese placed a question mark at the end of the line, but since in 7 Ovid asserts unambiguously that time does not affect him, there seems no reason to make the following line a question. In his poems from exile Ovid often expresses his wish to die; see *Tr* III viii 39-40 'tantus amor necis est querar ut cum Caesaris ira / quod non offensas uindicet ense suas', *Tr* III xiii 5-6, IV vi 49-50, and V ix 37-38.

9. EXEMPLVM EST ANIMI NIMIVM PATIENTIS VLIXES. Ovid frequently compares his trials in exile to those undergone by Ulysses. The longest instance of this is *Tr* I v 57-84; compare as well *Tr* III xi 61-62 'crede mihi, si sit nobis collatus Vlixes, / Neptuni minor est quam Iouis ira fuit', *Tr* V v 1-4, and *EP* I iii 33-34, II vii 59-60 & III vi 19-20.

Ulysses' voyage was a favourite subject of the Latin poets. For a surviving example, see Prop III xii 23-36. An indication of the subject's popularity is the fact that *Pan Mess* 45-49 'nam seu diuersi fremat inconstantia uulgi, / non alius sedare queat; seu iudicis ira / sit placanda, tuis poterit mitescere uerbis. / non Pylos aut Ithace tantos genuisse feruntur / Nestora uel paruae magnum decus urbis Vlixem' is followed not by a description of Ulysses' eloquence, as would have been appropriate, but by a narrative of his travels (52-81): this illogical sequence was no doubt induced by the poet's familiarity with similar descriptions of Ulysses' voyage in the poetry of his time.

Professor E. Fantham cites Seneca's use of Ulysses as an *exemplum patientiae* at Sen *Dial* II 2 1, where Hercules is compared to Ulysses.

9. EXEMPLVM EST. Professor R. J. Tarrant points out to me the unusual baldness of the phrase. In Ovid's earlier verse *exemplum* has an instructional or minatory overtone (*AA* III 686, *Met* IX 454). The flatter use of *exemplum* seems to be typical of the poetry of exile: compare *EP* III i 44 'coniugis exemplum diceris esse bonae', and *Tr* I v 21, IV iii 72 & IV iv 71.

9. NIMIVM PATIENTIS = πολύτλας (*Il* VIII 97, *Od* V 171, et saep.). The sense of *nimium* seen here is not generally found in poetry, or even in literary prose; the instances cited by *OLD nimium*² 2 are all from comedy, Cato, and the letters of Cicero.

10. DVO LVSTRA. Compare xvi 13-14 'Vlixem / errantem saeuo per *duo lustra* mari' and *AA* III 15-16 'est pia Penelope *lustris* errante *duobus* / et totidem lustris bella gerente uiro'.

11. SOLLICITI ... FATI is based on such phrases as *sollicita uita* (Prop II vii 1) and *sollicitissima aetas* (Sen *Breu Vit* 16 1). Similar phrasing at *Tr* IV x 116 'nec me *sollicitae* taedia *lucis* habent'.

11. PLACIDAE SAEPE FVERE MORAE. Compare Prop III xii 23-24 'Postumus alter erit miranda coniuge Vlixes: / non illi *longae* tot nocuere *morae*'.

13. SEX ANNIS. According to Homer (*Od* VII 261), Ulysses

287

left Calypso in the eighth year of his stay on her island. André points out that Hyginus *Fab* CXXV 16 has Ulysses on the island for one year only; for other estimates of the length of Ulysses' stay, see Roscher III 627. Ovid was probably influenced by the *bis ... tertia* of the poem's opening. *Cimmerio* in 1 furnishes another connection with Ulysses (*Od* XI 14; quoted at 1).

13. FOVISSE. Compare *Od* V 118-120 (Calypso speaking) 'Σχέτλιοί ἐστε, θεοί, ζηλήμονες ἔξοχον ἄλλων, / οἵ τε θεαῖς ἀγάασθε παρ' ἀνδράσιν εὐνάζεσθαι / ἀμφαδίην, ἤν τίς τε φίλον ποισετ' ἀκοίτην'.

13. CALYPSO *BCMILT*. Lenz and André print CALYPSON (*FH*). Roman poets followed the Greek declension of feminine proper nouns ending in -ω; compare *Pan Mess* 77 'fecunda Atlantidos arua *Calypsus* [*uar* calipsos]'. The accusatives of such nouns are of the same form as the nominative. See for example *Aen* IV 383-84 'et nomine *Dido* / saepe uocaturum' and *Aen* VII 324-25 'luctificam *Allecto* dirarum ab sede dearum / infernisque ciet tenebris', cited by Charisius 63 (Keil); neither he nor Servius shows knowledge of an accusative in *-on*. Scribes, however, found the declension puzzling; and it is common to find the pseudo-accusative in *-on* offered by some manuscripts whenever the true form in *-o* occurs; this has happened at *Her* VI 65 'ultimus e sociis sacram conscendis in *Argo*', *Her* VII 7 'certus es ire tamen miseramque relinquere *Dido* [*edd*: Didon *codd*]', *Her* XII 9 'cur umquam Colchi Magnetida uidimus *Argo*', *Am* II ii 45 'dum nimium seruat custos Iunonius *Io*', *Am* II xix 29 'dum seruat Iuno mutatam cornibus *Io*', and Prop I xx 17-18 'namque ferunt olim Pagasae naualibus *Argo* [*edd*: Argon *codd*] / egressam longe Phasidos isse uiam'. Modern editors often print the spurious form, even at *AA* I 323 'et modo se Europen fieri, modo postulat *Io*', where all manuscripts offer the correct reading.

For a full discussion of this and the inverse corruption (for instance of *Iason* to *Iaso*), see Goold 12-14.

14. AEQVOREAEQVE. Compare *Am* II xvii 17-18 'creditur *aequoream* Pthio Nereida regi, / Egeriam iusto concubuisse Numae' and *AA* II 123-24 'non formosus erat, sed erat facundus Vlixes, / et tamen *aequoreas* torsit amore deas'. Merkel's AEAEAEQVE is ingenious but unnecessary.

15. HIPPOTADES = *Aeolus*. The same patronymic at *Met* IV 663, XI 431, XIV 86, XIV 224 & XV 707.

15. QVI DAT PRO MVNERE VENTOS. Compare *Met* XIV 223-26 'Aeolon ille refert Tusco regnare profundo, / Aeolon Hippotaden, cohibentem carcere *uentos*; / quos bouis inclusos tergo, *memorabile munus*, / Dulichium sumpsisse ducem' and *Od* X 19-26.

17. NEC BENE CANTANTES LABOR EST AVDISSE PVELLAS. The description is intentionally prosaic. For the Homeric account of the Sirens see *Od* XII 37-54 & 153-200.

17. AVDISSE *F* AVDIRE *BCMHILT*. *Audire* cannot stand, as the present tense conflicts with *fuit* in the following line. For *est audisse* representing *fuit audire*, compare *Met* IX 5-6 (Achelous hesitates before recounting his wrestling-match with Hercules) 'referam tamen ordine: nec tam / turpe *fuit uinci* quam *contendisse decorum est'*.

18. NEC DEGVSTANTI LOTOS AMARA FVIT. See *Od* IX 82-104 for Homer's account of the Lotus-eaters.

18. NEC ... AMARA = *et dulcis*. Compare *Od* IX 94 'λωτοῖο ... μελιηδέα καρπόν'.

18. DEGVSTANTI. The verb is extremely rare in the sense 'taste, sample'; this is the only instance of the meaning found in poetry, although a transferred use is found at Lucretius II 191-92 'ignes ... celeri flamma *degustant* tigna trabesque' and *Aen* XII 375-76 'lancea ... summum *degustat* uulnere corpus'.

Ovid uses the somewhat more common *gustare* in a similar context at *Tr* IV i 31-32 'sic noua Dulichio lotos *gustata* palato / illo quo nocuit grata sapore fuit'.

21. VRBEM LAESTRYGONOS = 'Λάμου αἰπὺ πτολίεθρον, / Τηλέπυλον Λαιστρυγονίην' (*Od* X 81-82) or 'Lami ueterem Laestrygonos ... urbem' (*Met* XIV 233), where the crews of all the ships but Ulysses' own were killed and eaten; accounts

289

of this at *Od* X 76-132 and *Met* XIV 233-42. Ovid refers again to the episode at *EP* II ix 41 'quis non Antiphaten Laestrygona deuouet?'.

21. LAESTRYGONOS *BC* LE(-I-)STRYGONIS *MFHILT*. *Laestrygonos* = Λαιστρυγόνος (*Od* X 106). At *Met* XIV 233 (cited above) all manuscripts offer *Laestrygonis*; the Greek genitive should probably be read as here.

22. GENTIBVS OBLIQVA QVAS OBIT HISTER AQVA. Similar wording at ii 37-38 'hic mea cui recitem nisi flauis scripta Corallis, / quasque alias gentes barbarus Hister obit?'.

22. OBLIQVA apparently refers to the swirling of a river's eddies. The sense 'winding' generally given the word would fit at *Met* IX 17-18 (Achelous to the father of Deianira) 'dominum me cernis aquarum / cursibus *obliquis* inter tua regna fluentum', but not at *Met* VIII 550-53 (Achelous to Theseus) '"succede meis" ait "Inclite, tectis, / Cecropide, nec te committe rapacibus undis: / ferre trabes solidas *obliquaque* uoluere magno / murmure saxa solent"' or *Her* VI 87 'illa refrenat aquas *obliquaque* flumina sistit'. At *Met* I 39 'fluminaque *obliquis* cinxit decliuia ripis', *obliquis* should be taken with *flumina*, and *decliuia* with *ripis*; or possibly both adjectives should be taken with both nouns.

23. VINCET. Like *superare*, *uincere* has the twin meanings of 'surpass' and 'defeat'.

23. CYCLOPS. The same pairing of the Laestrygonians and Polyphemus at *EP* II ii 113-114 (to Messalinus; he should address Augustus on Ovid's behalf) 'nec tamen Aetnaeus uasto Polyphemus in antro / accipiet uoces Antiphatesue tuas'.

23. FERITATE goes with *uincet*: 'will surpass in savagery'. I once thought PIETATE (*BCI^{ac}*) was the correct reading, connecting the word with *saeuum* and taking it as a reference to human sacrifice; but this seems strained and obscure. *Pietate* may be an intrusion from ecclesiastical Latin; Professor R. J. Tarrant suggests that it is possibly an anticipation of the following *Piacchen*.

23. PIACCHEN *B* PIAECHEN *C*. See the critical apparatus for the other forms offered by the manuscripts. As the king's name is not elsewhere recorded, its true form must remain in doubt.

24. QVI QVOTA TERRORIS PARS SOLET ESSE MEI. With Burman, Weber, and Wheeler I take the line as a statement: compare *EP* II x 31 'et *quota pars* haec sunt rerum quas uidimus ambo' (cited by Williams), where *quota*, as here, takes the meaning 'how small' from context. Most editors take it as a question, for which compare *Am* II xii 9-10 'Pergama cum caderent bello superata bilustri, / ex tot in Atridis *pars quota* laudis erat?'.

25-27. SCYLLA ... CHARYBDIN. Ovid gives similar descriptions of Scylla at *Am* III xii 21-22 and *EP* III i 122, of Charybdis at *Am* II xvi 25-26, and of Scylla and Charybdis at *Her* XII 123-26 and *Met* XIII 730-33. All such descriptions in Latin poetry of course derive ultimately from *Od* XII 73-110.

25. QVOD LATRET AB INGVINE MONSTRIS. Professor R. J. Tarrant points out to me Ovid's imitation here of *Ecl* VI 74-75 'Scyllam ... candida succinctam latrantibus inguina monstris'; the *rates* and *nautae* of Ovid's line 26 are in lines 76 and 77 of the Virgilian passage.

25. QVOD. 'Granted that'. Bömer at *Met* VII 705 claims that the only passage where this is the necessary meaning of *quod* is *Priapea* VI 1 'quod sum ligneus ... Priapus ... prendam te tamen', but it seems to be the meaning required at Lucretius II 532-35 'nam *quod* rara uides magis esse animalia quaedam / fecundamque minus naturam cernis in illis, / at regione locoque alio terrisque remotis / multa licet genere esse in eo numerumque repleri'.

All six instances of the idiom cited by the *OLD* (*quod* 6c) are from poetry. In the two instances already cited, *quod* is followed by the indicative, as is the case at Prop III ii 11-16. *Quod* in this sense followed by the subjunctive seems to be an Ovidian idiom; it is used by him at *Her* IV 157-61 'quod mihi *sit* genitor, qui possidet aequora, Minos, / quod *ueniant* proaui fulmina torta manu, / quod *sit* auus radiis frontem uallatus acutis, / purpureo tepidum qui mouet axe diem— / nobilitas sub amore iacet!' and *Met* VII 704-7 'liceat mihi uera referre / pace deae: quod *sit* roseo spectabilis ore, / quod *teneat* lucis, *teneat* confinia noctis, / nectareis quod *alatur* aquis, ego Procrin amabam', and by an imitator of Ovid at *Her* XVIII 41.

26. HENIOCHAE NAVTIS PLVS NOCVERE RATES. The Heniochi lived on the eastern shore of the Euxine and were, as Ovid indicates, known as pirates (Strabo XI 2 12-13).

27. INFESTIS ... ACHAEIS. Mela includes the Achaei and the Heniochi in his list of 'ferae incultaeque gentes uasto mari adsidentes' (I 110). The two nations are grouped together by Strabo (XII 2 12) and Pliny (*NH* VI 30).

28. EPOTVM ... VOMAT. Professor R. J. Tarrant cites the verbal similarity at (pseudo-Ovidian) *Am* III v 18 'iterum *pasto pascitur* ante cibo'.

28. EPOTVM *B* ET POTVM *C* EPOTET *MFHILT.* *Epotet* is supported by *Her* XII 125 'quaeque uomit totidem fluctus totidemque resorbet' and Od XII 105-6 'τρὶς μὲν γάρ τ' ἀνίησιν ἐπ' ἤματι, τρὶς δ' ἀναροιβδεῖ / δεινόν'. Professor A. Dalzell points out in particular 'τρὶς ... τρὶς' paralleling *ter ... ter* in the present passage. But at *RA* 740 Ovid wrote 'hic uomit epotas [*uarr* et potat; hic potat; optatas; acceptas; aequoreas] dira Charybdis aquas'; and the corruption to *epotet* seems much more probable than the inverse. Ovid elsewhere uses only the perfect participle of *epotare*.

29. LICENTIVS ERRANT. Ovid is clearly imitating *Aen* VII 557-58 (Juno to Allecto) 'te super aetherias *errare licentius* auras / haud pater ille uelit, summi regnator Olympi', apparently the only other instance of *licentius* in classical verse.

31-32 act as a bridge to the next major section of the poem, and do not in themselves contribute to what has been said.

31. INFRONDES is a *hapax legomenon*.

32. HIC FRETA VEL PEDITI PERVIA REDDIT HIEMPS. Other mentions of the sea's freezing at vii 7, *Tr* II 196, III x

35-50 & V x 2, and *EP* III i 15-16 (to the Pontus) 'tu glacie freta uincta tenes, et in aequore piscis / inclusus tecta saepe natauit aqua'.

Parts of the Black Sea do in fact freeze: 'In winter, spurs of the Siberian anticyclone (clear, dry, high-pressure air mass) create a strong current of cold air, and the northwestern Black Sea cools down considerably, with regular ice formation' (article on "Black Sea", *Encyclopaedia Britannica*, Macropaedia vol. 2, pp. 1096-98 [Chicago: 1974]).

32. HIEMPS. For the last one hundred years, the spelling given in editions of Latin texts has generally been *hiems* (some exceptions are Palmer's *Heroides*, the Paravia Virgil, and Reynolds' editions of Seneca), but the spelling in the ancient manuscripts of Virgil is invariably *hiemps*. Munro's argument for this spelling seems unanswerable: 'obeying the almost unanimous testimony of our own [i.e. *O* and *Q* of Lucretius] and other good mss. we cannot but give *umerus umor* and the like: also *hiemps*. I have heard it asked what then is the genitive of *hiemps*; to which the best reply perhaps would be what is the perfect of *sumo* or the supine of *emo*. The Latins wrote *hiemps*, as they wrote *emptum sumpsi sumptum* and a hundred such forms, because they disliked *m* and *s* or *t* to come together without the intervention of a *p* sound; and our mss. all attest this: *tempto* likewise is the only true form, which the Italians in the 15th century rejected for *tento*' (Lucretius ed. 4 vol. 1 p. 33).

33-34. VT, QVA REMVS ITER PVLSIS MODO FECERAT VNDIS, / SICCVS CONTEMPTA NAVE VIATOR EAT. Ovid has in mind Virgil's description of the freezing of a Scythian river (*G* III 360-62) 'concrescunt subitae currenti in flumine crustae, / undaque iam tergo ferratos sustinet orbis, / puppibus illa prius, patulis nunc hospita plaustris'.

35. QVI VENIVNT ISTINC VIX VOS EA CREDERE DICVNT; / QVAM MISER EST QVI FERT ASPERIORA FIDE. For Ovid's fear that his accounts of what he has undergone will not be believed, see vii 3-4 and *Tr* I v 49-50, III x 35-36 & IV i 65-66. In particular, see ix 85-86 'mentiar, an coeat duratus frigore Pontus, / et teneat glacies iugera multa freti'.

37-38. NEC TE CAVSAS NESCIRE SINEMVS / HORRIDA SARMATICVM CVR MARE DVRET HIEMPS. Ovid's principal explanation of the freezing of the Euxine, the low salinity of the water, is found in four other Latin authors. At IV 718-28, Valerius Flaccus offers a catalogue of rivers similar to that of Ovid, and, like Ovid, gives the cold winter winds as a subsidiary reason for the freezing. It is quite possible that Ovid is Valerius' source; but this is very unlikely to be the case for Macrobius *Sat* VII xii 28-38 (cited by Burman). The passage is a discussion of why, although oil congeals, wine and vinegar do not. Wine does not freeze because it contains elements of fire; this is why Homer called it αἴθοπα οἶνον. Vinegar does not freeze because it is so bitter; it is like seawater, which because of its bitterness does not congeal. 'nam quod Herodotus historiarum scriptor contra omnium ferme qui haec quaesiuerunt opinionem scripsit [IV 28], mare Bosporicum, quod et Cimmerium appellat, earumque partium mare omne, quod Scythicum dicitur, id gelu constringi et consistere, aliter est quam putatur'. It is not the seawater that freezes, but the layer of fresh water above it, which comes from the rivers that flow into the Euxine. Macrobius goes on to explain that there is an outflow of fresh water to the Mediterranean and an influx of seawater, with perfect correctness: the *Encyclopaedia Britannica* article cited at 32 notes that 'Flows in the Bosporus are complex, with surface Black Sea water going out and deep, saltier water coming in from the Sea of Marmara*.

There can be very little doubt, given the identity of the explanations and the similarity of language, that Ovid and Macrobius were drawing on a common source. The same source is reflected at Gellius XVII viii 8-16. Here Taurus the philosopher asks Gellius why oil often congeals, but wine does not. Gellius answers that wine is fiery by nature, which is why Homer called it αἴθοπα οἶνον. Taurus responds that wine is indeed known to have fire in it, for it warms the body when drunk; yet vinegar, in spite of its cooling effects, never freezes; perhaps things which are light and smooth are more prone to freezing. It is also worth asking why fresh water freezes, but seawater does not. 'tametsi Herodotus ... historiae scriptor contra omnium ferme qui haec quaesiuerunt opinionem scribit mare

Bosporicum, quod Cimmerium appellatur, earumque partium mare omne quod Scythicum dicitur, gelu stringi et consistere'. No explanation for the freezing-over is given.[22]

Ammianus Marcellinus XXII 8 48 gives the same two explanations for the Euxine's freezing as Ovid: 'quicquid autem eiusdem Pontici sinus Aquilone caeditur et pruinis, ita perstringitur gelu ut nec amnium cursus subteruolui credantur, nec per infidum et labile solum gressus hominis possit uel iumenti firmari, quod uitium numquam mare sincerum, sed permixtum aquis amnicis temptat'. At XXII 8 46 he once again mentions the sweetness of the Euxine's waters.

Lucan describes the freezing of the Euxine (V 436-41), but gives no explanation of the cause.

39. PLAVSTRI PRAEBENTIA FORMAM ... SIDERA. The Great Bear. Other mentions of the constellation at *Met* X 446-47 'inter ... triones / flexerat obliquo plaustrum temone Bootes', *Tr* III iv b 1-2 (47-48), III x 3-4 & V iii 7-8, and *EP* I v 73-74. Compare as well Germanicus *Aratea* 24-26 'axem Cretaeae dextra laeuaque tuentur / siue Arctoe seu Romani cognominis Vrsae / Plaustraue [*Grotius*:-que *codd*], quae facie [*scripsi (datiuum)*[23]: facies *codd*] stellarum proxima uerae [*Barth*: uera *uel* uero *codd*]', *Her* XVIII 152, Sen *Ag* 66-68, and Lucan V 23 'Hyperboreae plaustrum glaciale sub Vrsae'.

Praebentia formam is elevated diction: Professor R. J. Tarrant cites Lucretius V 581-83 'luna ... claram speciem certamque figuram / praebet'.

40. PERPETVVM M^{2ul} PRAECIPVVM BCM^1FHILT. *Praecipuum* could be defended by *EP* III i 13-14 (to the Pontus) 'nec tibi pampineas autumnus porrigit uuas, / cuncta sed immodicum tempora frigus habet', but *praecipuus* in fact always seems to have the notion of 'outstanding' or 'superior', which does not seem appropriate to the present passage. For *perpetuum* compare *Tr* III ii 7-8 'plurima sed pelago terraque pericula passum / ustus ab *assiduo* frigore Pontus habet', *Tr* III x 14 '[niuem ...] indurat Boreas *perpetuamque* facit', *Tr* V ii 65-66 'me ... cruciat *numquam sine* *frigore* caelum, / glaebaque canenti *semper* obusta gelu', *EP* I iii 49-50 'orbis in extremi iaceo desertus harenis, / fert ubi *perpetuas* obruta terra niues', and *EP* II vii 72 'frigore *perpetuo* Sarmatis ora riget'.

41. HINC ORITVR BOREAS. Compare *Tr* III xi 7-8 'barbara me tellus et inhospita litora Ponti / cumque suo *Borea* Maenalis ursa uidet' and *Ibis* 11-12 'ille relegatum gelidos *Aquilonis ad ortus* / non sinit exilio delituisse meo'.

41. DOMESTICVS. The word is rare in verse; Ovid uses it as a substantive at iii 15 'ille ego conuictor densoque *domesticus* usu'. Here Ovid may be recalling the language of *Met* VI 685-86 (of Boreas) 'ira, / quae solita est illi nimiumque *domestica* uento'.

42. VIRES. Merkel proposed MORES, citing Virgil *G* I 50-52 'at prius ignotum ferro quam scindimus aequor, / uentos et uarium caeli praediscere *morem* / cura sit' and Statius *Sil* III ii 87 'quos tibi currenti praeceps gerat Hadria *mores*'. The second passage is not to the point, since it means 'what sort of obedience to your wishes do you expect from the Adriatic as you make your voyage'. In any case, Professor R. J. Tarrant points out to me the poor logic of Merkel's proposed text: Ovid is deriving the *natura loci* from its surroundings; he should not now be saying that Boreas gets his *mores* from the area. The reading of the manuscripts seems acceptable enough if one accepts Meynke's *polo* for *loco* ('he gathers strength from the nearby North Pole'). For *sumit uires* compare *Met* VIII 882 (Achelous speaking) 'armenti modo dux *uires* in cornua *sumo*', *Met* XI 510-11 'ut ... solent *sumptis* incursu *uiribus* ire ... feri ... leones' and Hor *Ep* I xviii 85 'neglecta solent incendia *sumere uires*'. Professor R. J. Tarrant compares such phrases as *sumere iras* (*Met* II 175), *animos* (*Met* III 544-45), and *cornua* (*AA* I 239, *Tr* IV ix 27).

42. POLO *Meynke* LOCO *codd.* The pointlessness of *loco* is made clear enough by Wheeler's 'and he takes on strength from a place nearer to him'. Meynke's *polo* removes the difficulty, answers well to the following 'at Notus, *aduerso* tepidum qui spirat ab *axe*', and is supported by the language of *Met* II 173 'quaeque *polo* posita est glaciali *proxima* Serpens', and *Fast* IV 575-76 (of Ceres) 'errat et in caelo liquidique immunia ponti / adloquitur gelido *proxima* signa *polo*'. For the corruption, compare the common misreading of *locum* for *solum*.

43. ADVERSO ... AB AXE. Ovid here seeks a contrast with *polo* in the previous line; but clearly he means only that the south wind comes from the opposite direction, not that it originates at the South Pole.

Bentley conjectured AVERSO for *aduerso*, and the two words are obviously prone to interchange: compare *Tr* I iii 45 (of Ovid's wife, after his departure) 'multaque in auersos [*Heinsius*: aduersos *codd*] effudit uerba Penates' and the variations among the manuscripts at Virgil *G* I 218 'auerso ... astro', *Aen* XII 647 'auersa uoluntas', and Sen *Tr* 1123 'auersa cingit campus' (on which see Housman 1076). But *aduerso* 'opposite' seems to have the sense required here.

43. TEPIDVM QVI SPIRAT. For the construction compare *Met* IX 661 'sub aduentu *spirantis lene* Fauoni' and Avienus *Descr Orb* 847 'uel qua *lene* Notus *spirat*'. The trivialized TEPIDVS QVI SPIRAT is found in *MH*^{2c}. *Tepidus Notus* occurs four times in Ovid (*Am* I iv 12, I vii 56 & II viii 20, and *Tr* III xii [xiii] 42).

44. LANGVIDIORQVE VENIT. Compare *EP* II i 1-2 'Huc quoque Caesarei peruenit fama triumphi, / *languida* quo fessi uix uenit *aura Noti*'.

46. AB AMNE. Similar instrumental uses of *ab* at *Her* X 138 'tunicas lacrimis sicut *ab imbre* graues', *AA* III 545 'ingenium placida mollitur *ab arte*', *Met* I 65-66 'contraria tellus / nubibus assiduis pluuiaque madescit ab Austro', *Met* IV 162-63 'pectus ... adhuc *a caede* tepebat', and *Fast* V 323 'caelum nigrescit *ab Austris*'.

47-58. For the lengthy catalogue, typical of Ovid, compare the listing of Actaeon's dogs at *Met* III 206-25 (in particular at 217 'et Dromas et Canache Sticteque et Tigris et Alce') and the catalogue of trees that came to listen to Orpheus sing (*Met* X 90-107).

47. LYCVS. A number of rivers had this name in the ancient world. Ovid presumably means the Paphlagonian Lycus referred to by Virgil at *G* IV 366-67 'omnia sub magna labentia flumina terra / spectabat diuersa locis, Phasimque Lycumque ...'.

47. SAGARIS. The modern Sakarya; it flows into the Black Sea about 125 kilometres east of Istanbul. It is mentioned at Pliny *NH* VI 1 4 'Sangaris fluuius ex inclutis. oritur in Phrygia, accipit uastos amnes ... idem Sagiarius plerisque dictus'.

47. PENIVSQVE. The 'flumen et oppidum Penius' are mentioned at Pliny *NH* VI 14 as being in the region of the Caucasus on the Euxine coast; nearby were 'multis nominibus Heniochorum gentes'. The river seems not to be mentioned elsewhere in ancient literature.

47. HYPANISQVE. The modern Bug empties into the Black Sea about 50 kilometres east of Odessa. It is mentioned again by Ovid at *Met* XV 285-86 'quid? non et Scythicis Hypanis de montibus ortus, / qui fuerat dulcis, salibus uitiatur amaris?' and Virgil *G* IV 370 'saxosumque sonans Hypanis'.

47. CALESQVE. Isaac Vossius made this correction for the manuscripts' CATESQVE (*I* has CHARESQVE) on the basis of 'Eustathio Scholiis in Periegeten'. Heinsius aptly cited a description of the occasionally violent flow of the river at Thucydides IV 75 2.

As indicated by this passage, the modern Alapli flows into the Black Sea near Ereğli, about 200 kilometres east of Istanbul.

48. CREBRO VERTICE TORTVS HALYS. An imitation of *Aen* VII 566-67 'fragosus / dat sonitum saxis et *torto uertice* torrens'. *Tortus* when used of water generally refers to the disturbance caused by rowing (*Fast* V 644; Catullus LXIV 13; *Aen* III 208).

48. HALYS. The modern Kizil Irmak flows into the Black Sea about 600 kilometres east of Istanbul. André compares Apollonius' description of the river (II 366-67) 'ῥοαὶ Ἅλυος ποταμοῖο / δεινὸν ἐρεύγονται'.

49-50. The three rivers mentioned in these lines are all named for their swiftness.

49. PARTHENIVSQVE RAPAX. The modern Bartin flows into the Black Sea about 280 kilometres east of Istanbul and about 240 kilometres west of Sinop. It is in fact a very calm river: this information was available to Ovid from Apollonius II 936-37 'Παρθενίοιο ῥοὰς ἁλιμυρήεντος, / πρηυτάτου ποταμοῦ' (cited by André).

49. VOLVENS SAXA. Similar phrasing at *Met* VIII 552-53 '[undae ...] ferre trabes solidas obliquaque *uoluere* magno / murmure *saxa* solent'.

49. CINAPSES *BC* CINAPSIS *L* TYNAPSES *H* CINASPES *FIT* NIPHATES *M*. Editors read CYNAPSES; but since the river is not otherwise known, restoration is dangerous. *M*'s reading looks like an interpolation from Lucan III 245 'Armeniusque tenens *uoluentem saxa* Niphaten' (cited by Micyllus).

50. NVLLO TARDIOR = *uelocior omni*; André mistranslates 'le plus lent des fleuves'. Compare *Tr* I v 1 'O mihi post nullos umquam [*uar* ullos numquam] memorande sodales' and *EP* I iii 65-66 'Zmyrna uirum tenuit, non Pontus et hostica tellus, / paene *minus nullo* Zmyrna petenda loco'.

50. TYRAS. The modern Dnestr flows into the Black Sea about fifty miles south of Odessa; near its mouth is the city of Ovidiopol. The river is briefly mentioned at Pliny *NH* IV 82 & 93, and at Mela II 7, where it is called the 'Tyra'; this however seems to be a scribal error induced by the following *separat*.

51. THERMODON. The modern Terme flows into the Black Sea about 100 kilometres southeast of the mouth of the Kizil Irmak (Halys). It was conventional to mention the Amazons in connection with the river (*Met* XII 611, *Aen* XI 659-60, Prop III xiv 13-14, Ammianus Marcellinus XXII 8 17). Professor E. Fantham suggests to me that Ovid may here be providing Albinovanus with material for the part of his *Theseid* dealing with Theseus' expedition against the Amazons.

Ovid also mentions the Thermodon at *Met* I 248-49 (the story of Phaethon) 'arsit et Euphrates Babylonius, arsit Orontes / Thermodonque citus Gangesque et Phasis et Hister'. As in the present distich, the Thermodon and Phasis, both prominent in mythology, are mentioned together.

51. TVRMAE *BCM* **TVRBAE** *FHILT*. There is a similar variation among the manuscripts at *AA* III 1-2 'Arma dedi Danais in Amazonas; arma supersunt / quae tibi dem et *turmae*, Penthesilea, tuae'. From other descriptions of the Amazons, the Auctor Electorum Etonensium aptly compares Val Fl IV 603 (*cateruas*) and 607 (*turma*); compare as well Statius *Sil* I vi 56 (*turmas*). It is possible that *turma* should be read at Prop III xiv 13-14 'qualis Amazonidum nudatis bellica mammis / Thermodontiacis *turba* lauatur aquis'; but this would make *bellica* redundant.

53. BORYSTHENIO ... AMNE = *Borȳsthĕnē*. The river is the modern Dnepr, which flows into the Black Sea about 120 kilometres east of Odessa, about 50 kilometres east of the mouth of the Bug (Hypanis). For the metrical device here employed, compare Prop II vii 17-18 'hinc etenim tantum meruit mea gloria nomen, / gloria ad hibernos lata *Borysthenidas*', Avienus *Descr Orb* 448 'inde *Borysthenii* uis sese *fluminis* effert' & 721 'ora *Borysthenii* qua *fluminis* in mare uergunt'.

53. LIQVIDISSIMVS is not found elsewhere in Ovid.

53. DIRAPSES. The river is not mentioned elsewhere.

54. MELANTHVS. The modern Melet Irmak flows into the Black Sea about 25 kilometres west of Trabzon (Trapezus). It is mentioned in passing at Pliny *NH* VI 11.

55-56. QVIQVE DVAS TERRAS, ASIAM CADMIQVE SOROREM, / SEPARAT ET CVRSVS INTER VTRAMQVE FACIT. The Tanais (Don) is named as the border between Europe and Asia by Pliny (*NH* IV 78) and Avienus (*Descr Orb* 28 & 861). Compare as well Lucan III 272-76 'qua uertice lapsus / Riphaeo Tanais diuersi nomina mundi / imposuit ripis Asiaeque et terminus idem / Europae, mediae dirimens

300

confinia terrae, / nunc hunc, nunc illum, qua flectitur, ampliat orbem'.

Vibius Sequester (*Geog Lat min* [Riese] p. 212) has an entry 'Hypanis Scythiae qui, ut ait Gallus "uno tellures diuidit amne duas": Asiam enim ab Europa separat'. The Hypanis cannot be the river Ovid is here referring to, for it has already been mentioned in 47; but, as Lenz saw, the line from Gallus could well have been in Ovid's mind as he wrote this passage. Professor R. J. Tarrant notes that the extraordinary *Cadmique sororem* could well be a borrowing from the earlier poet.

57-58. INTER MAXIMVS OMNES / CEDERE DANVVIVS SE TIBI, NILE, NEGAT. A similar conjunction at *Tr* III x 27-28 'ipse, papyrifero qui non angustior amne, / miscetur uasto multa per ora freto'. Herodotus compares the courses of the Nile and the Danube, concluding 'οὕτω τὸν Νεῖλον δοκέω διὰ πάσης τῆς Λιβύης διεξιόντα ἐξισοῦσθαι τῷ Ἴστρῳ' (II 34), referring to the length of the rivers, however, rather than their volume of discharge. At *NQ* III 22 Seneca mentions the belief of some that because of their large size and the fact that their sources were both unknown the Nile and the Danube must both have been formed at the creation of the world, unlike other rivers. At IV 1 1-2 he argues against those who equated the two rivers, pointing out that the source of the Danube was known to be in Germany, and that the two rivers flood at different times of the year.

59. COPIA TOT LATICVM QVAS AVGET ADVLTERAT AQVAS. The comparative freshness of the waters of the Black Sea was well known in antiquity. Besides the passages cited at 37-38, see Polybius IV 42 3 and Philostratus *Imag* I 13 7.

61-62. QVIN ETIAM, STAGNO SIMILIS PIGRAEQVE PALVDI, / CAERVLEVS VIX EST DILVITVRQVE COLOR. Ovid's drinking water was, on the other hand, rather brackish: 'est in aqua dulci non inuidiosa uoluptas: / aequoreo bibitur cum sale mixta palus' (*EP* II vii 73-74).

63. INNATAT VNDA FRETO DVLCIS. Similar wording at Macrobius *Sat* VII 12 32 'superficies maris, cui dulces aquae

innatant, congelascit'.

64. PONDVS *B¹CMFHT* NOMEN *ILB²*. Wakefield conjectured MOMEN on the basis of Lucretius VI 473-74 'quo magis ad nubis augendas multa uidentur / posse quoque e salso consurgere momine ponti'. But *pondus* seems appropriate to the context in a way that *momen* 'heaving' does not. *Nomen habe(n)t* is a frequent line-ending in Ovid, occurring some twenty-five times (once in *Her* XVI). *Proprium nomen* occurs in Ovid at *Fast* V 191-92 (Ovid is addressing Flora) 'ipsa doce quae sis. hominum sententia fallax: / optima tu *proprii nominis* auctor eris' and *EP* I viii 13-14 'Caspius Aegissos, de se si credimus ipsis, / condidit et *proprio nomine* dixit opus'. The phrase would have been very familiar to the scribes from grammatical treatises ('proper noun'). A combination of these circumstances no doubt induced the error.

Professor A. Dalzell suggests to me that *momen* is perhaps correct, the notion being that the salt water keeps moving, and so does not freeze. *Pondus* would then be a (mistaken) gloss that has displaced *momen* from the text; *nomen* would be a simple misreading of *momen*.

66. CERTIS ... MODIS. 'Metre'; compare *Fast* III 388 'ad *certos* uerba canenda *modos*', Tib II i 51-52 'agricola ... primum ... cantauit *certo* rustica uerba *pede*' and Manilius III 35 '*pedibus* ... iungere *certis*'.

67. DETINVI ... TEMPVS, CVRASQVE FEFELLI *excerpta Politiani* DETINVI ... TEMPVS CVRAMQVE FEFELLI *LT* DETINVI ... CVRAS TEMPVSQVE FEFELLI *BCMFHI*. *Tempus fallere* 'make time pass unnoticed' is perfectly acceptable Latin; compare *Tr* III iii 11-12 'non qui labentia tarde / *tempora* narrando *fallat* amicus adest', *Her* I 9-10 'nec mihi quaerenti spatiosam *fallere noctem* / lassaret uiduas pendula tela manus', *Met* VIII 651 'interea medias *fallunt* sermonibus *horas*', *Tr* IV x 112-14 'tristia ... carmine fata leuo. / quod quamuis nemo est cuius referatur ad aures, / sic tamen absumo *decipioque diem*', and *Her* XIX 37-38 'tortaque uersato ducentes stamina fuso / feminea tardas *fallimus* arte moras'. The difficulty with the manuscript reading in the

302

present passage is that *detinui curas* is without parallel. Heinsius therefore accepted Politian's reading, citing in its support *Met* I 682-83 'sedit Atlantiades et euntem multa loquendo / *detinuit* sermone *diem*'. The Auctor Electorum Etonensium objected that *detinui tempus* was inappropriate: 'poeta tempus detinere noluit, quod scilicet per se morari atque haerere uidebatur inuisum'. He conjectured DISTINVI CVRAS and Burman DIMINVI CVRAS, which he later found in one of his manuscripts. But *detinere* here can have the same meaning 'occupy, keep busy' as it has at the *Metamorphoses* passage, where A. G. Lee cites the present passage (with Politian's reading) and *Tr* V vii 39 '*detineo studiis animum* falloque dolores'.

The interchange of adjoining metrically and grammatically equivalent substantives is very common.

67-68. "DETINVI" DICAM "TEMPVS, CVRASQVE FEFELLI; / HVNC FRVCTVM PRAESENS ATTVLIT HORA MIHI". The thought of the passage also at ii 39-40 & 45 'quid nisi Pierides, solacia frigida, restant', *Tr* V i 33-34 'tot mala pertulimus, quorum medicina quiesque / nulla nisi in studio est Pieridumque mora', and *EP* I v 53-55 'magis utile nil est / artibus his, quae nil utilitatis habent. / consequor ex illis casus obliuia nostri'.

69. ABFVIMVS SOLITO ... DOLORE. Compare Cic *Fam* IV iii 2 'a multis et magnis molestiis abes'; I have found no parallel from verse.

71. CVM THESEA CARMINE LAVDES. See at 4 *Albinouane* (p 327).

71. THESEA. For Theseus as the type of loyalty, compare *Tr* I iii 66 'o mihi Thesea pectora iuncta fide!', I v 19-20, I ix 31-32, V iv 25-26 (Ovid's letter speaking) 'teque Menoetiaden, te qui comitatus Oresten, / te uocat *Aegiden* Euryalumque suum', and *EP* II iii 43, II vi 26 & III ii 33-34 'occidit et Theseus et qui comitauit Oresten; / sed tamen in laudes uiuit uterque suas'. From other authors, Otto *Theseus* cites Prop II i 37-38, Martial VII xxiv 3-4 & X xi 1-2, Claudian *Ruf* I 107, Ausonius *Epist* XXV 34, Apollinaris Sidonius *Ep* III xiii 10, *Carm* V 288 & *Carm* XXIV 29. Professor R. J. Tarrant notes that in Bion fr. 12 (Gow) there is a pairing of Theseus/Pirithous and Orestes/Pylades similar to what we find in Ovid.

72. TITVLOS. 'Claims to glory'; compare *Met* VII 448-49 (to Theseus) 'si *titulos* annosque tuos numerare uelimus, / facta prement annos' and *Met* XII 334 'uictori titulum ... Dictys Helopsque dederunt'.

73. VETAT ILLE PROFECTO. 'I am quite certain that he does not allow ...'

74. TRANQVILLI ... TEMPORIS implies *sed non temporis aduersi.*

75. CONDITVR A TE. Ovid does not elsewhere use a person as the object of *condere*, although at *Tr* II 335-36 he uses a person's achievements as object: 'diuitis ingenii est immania Caesaris acta / condere'.

76. TANTVS QVANTO *L* TANTO QVANTVS *B^{ac}CFHIT^{pc}* TANT<u>VS</u> QVANTVS *M^{2c}* TANTO QVANTO *B^{pc}T^{ac}* QVANTO TANTVS *fort legendum*. The transmitted reading, *tanto quantus*, can be construed: Professor E. Fantham translates 'a man so great as should have been sung with this mighty style'. This however subordinates Theseus to Albinovanus, while the purpose of the line is to emphasize Theseus' greatness. *Tanto quanto* is generally printed: it is acceptable enough (compare *EP* II ix 11-12 'regia, crede mihi, res est succurrere lapsis, / conuenit et *tanto, quantus* es ipse, uiro'), but is very weakly attested, and does not explain the transmitted reading. I have printed *L*'s *tantus quanto; quanto tantus* might also be read.

76. QVANTO ... ORE. For *os* 'grandness of utterance' Professor R. J. Tarrant compares *Am* II i 11-12 'ausus eram, memini, caelestia dicere bella ... et satis *oris* erat'.

78. INQVE FIDE THESEVS QVILIBET ESSE POTEST. For the use of mythological figures as character types, compare *RA* 589 'semper habe Pyladen aliquem qui curet Oresten' and Martial VI xi 9-10 'ut praestem Pyladen, aliquis mihi praestet Oresten. / hoc non fit uerbis, Marce: ut ameris, ama'.

79-82. Professor R. J. Tarrant points out to me how the example of Theseus balances the comparison with Ulysses at the start of the poem. Earlier Ovid argued against a difference of scale between his own case and the mythic figure's: here he insists on it.

79. HOSTES ... DOMANDI. For lists of these enemies, see *Her* II 69-70 'cum fuerit Sciron lectus toruusque Procrustes /

et Sinis' and the Athenians' hymn of praise to Theseus at *Met* VII 433-50.

79. CLAVAQVE. For Theseus' club see *Her* IV 115-16 (Phaedra to Hippolytus) 'ossa mei fratris *claua* perfracta trinodi / sparsit humi' and *Her* X 77 'me quoque, qua fratrem, mactasses, improbe, *claua*'. Ovid mentions the club of Hercules about a dozen times.

80. VIX ILLI. For *uix* 'with difficulty' *OLD uix* 1 cites *Fast* I 508 'uix est Euandri uixque retenta manu'.

Most editors print VIX VLLI (*BCT*), which is possible enough. *Vix illi* seems rather more forceful, however, as making the point that even Theseus was able to make the dangerous journey only with difficulty, and that before him the road was impassable. Compare *Met* VII 443-44 'tutus ad Alcathoen, Lelegeia moenia, limes / composito Scirone patet'.

81. OPEROSA. The word in the sense 'troublesome' seems confined to prose except for this passage and *Her* II 63-64 'fallere credentem non est *operosa* puellam / gloria; simplicitas digna fauore fuit'.

83. PERSTAS *IPF²ᵘˡ*. Compare *Tr* IV i 19-20 'me quoque Musa leuat Ponti loca iussa petentem: / sola comes nostrae *perstitit* illa fugae' and *Tr* V xiv 19-20 'quae ne quis possit temeraria dicere, persta [*uar* praesta] / et pariter serua meque piamque fidem'. PERSTAS, the reading of most manuscripts, would have no acceptable meaning in the present passage; it has no object, and the intransitive meaning, 'stand out', is clearly inappropriate. The error may have been induced by *Tr* IV v 23-24 'teque, quod est rarum, *praesta* constanter ad omne / indeclinatae munus amicitiae'; more probably, it is an aftereffect of *praestandus* in 81.

83. INDECLINATVS governs *amico*. The only other instance of the word in classical Latin seems to be *Tr* IV v 24, quoted at the end of the last note.

84. LINGVA QVERENTE. Ovid elsewhere uses persons as the subject of *queri*, except for similar uses of metonymy at xiv 26 '*littera* de uobis est mea *questa* nihil' and *Tr* V xi 1-2

'Quod te nescioquis per iurgia dixerit esse / exulis uxorem,
littera questa tua est'.

XI. To Gallio

The poem is a letter of condolence to the famous rhetor Junius Gallio, an old friend of Ovid (see at 1). Ovid starts the poem by saying that Gallio should certainly be mentioned in his poetry, because he helped Ovid at the time of his catastrophe (1-4). This one misfortune should have been enough for him, but now he has lost his wife (5-8). Ovid wept on receiving the news, but will not attempt to comfort him, since by now the grief is in the past, and he would risk renewing it (9-20). Also (and he hopes this will turn out to be the case), Gallio may already have remarried (21-22).

The poem is one of the shortest in Ovid's canon (*Am* II iii is shorter), and has few parallels with his other poems. The one that comes closest is *EP* I ix, addressed to Cotta Maximus, which describes Ovid's reaction on hearing of the death of Celsus. There are some verbal parallels as well with *EP* I iii, Ovid's answer to Rufinus' letter of consolation on his exile. In the commentary I cite passages from Ser. Sulpicius Rufus' famous letter to Cicero on the death of his daughter Tullia (*Fam* IV v) and from Seneca's treatises of consolation; Ovid was clearly making use of the common topics of the genre.

1. GALLIO. Junius Gallio[24], adoptive father of the younger Seneca's elder brother, is often cited by the elder Seneca, who considered him one of the four supreme orators of his time (*Contr* X praef. 13). At *Suas* III 6-8, Seneca discusses Gallio's fondness for the Virgilian phrase *plena deo* (which, oddly, is not found in our text of the poet), and quotes Gallio as saying that his friend Ovid was also very fond of the phrase. Quintilian and Tacitus did not share Seneca's high opinion of Gallio: Quintilian criticizes the lack of restraint in his style (IX ii 92), while at *Dial* 26 1 Tacitus has Messalla say how he prefers 'G. Gracchi impetum aut L. Crassi maturitatem quam calamistros ['curling irons' = 'excessive ornament'] Maecenatis aut tinnitus Gallionis'.

In AD 32 Gallio proposed in the Senate that ex-members of the Praetorian guard be permitted to use the theatre seats reserved for members of the equestrian order; this resulted in a bitter and sarcastic letter from Tiberius to the Senate attacking Gallio's presumption; he was first exiled, then brought back to custody in Rome after it was decided that Lesbos, chosen by him, was too pleasant a place of exile (Tac *Ann* VI 3; Dio LXVIII 18 4).

1. EXCVSABILE. The word is extremely rare, and is not found in verse outside the *Ex Ponto*: compare I vii 41-42 'quod nisi delicti pars *excusabilis* esset, / parua relegari poena futura fuit' and III ix 33-34 'nil tamen e scriptis magis *excusabile* nostris / quam sensus cunctis paene quod unus inest'.

2. HABVISSE could have the usual past sense of the perfect infinitive, but more probably is equivalent to *habere*: compare ix 20 'gauderem lateris non *habuisse* locum' and see at viii 82 *imposuisse* (p 282).

3-4. CAELESTI CVSPIDE FACTA ... VVLNERA. 'Wounds inflicted by no human weapon'. The *cuspis* is attributed to Mars at *Am* I i 11, to Neptune at *Met* XII 580, and to Athena at *Fast* VI 655. At Sen *Ag* 368-71 'tuque, o magni nata Tonantis / inclita Pallas, / quae Dardanias saepe petisti / cuspide terras', R. J. Tarrant cites *HF* 563 (Dis), *HF* 904 & *Phaed* 755 (Bacchus), *HO* 156 (Hercules), and Juvenal II 130 (Mars). Professor Tarrant points out to me that the *cuspis* does not seem to be attributed to Jupiter, no doubt because the *fulmen* was too firmly established as his weapon. Ovid is therefore not making his customary specific equation of Augustus with Jupiter.

4. FOVISTI. *Fouere* was a technical term in medicine for bathing something in a liquid (Cato *Agr* 157 4, Celsus IV 2 4, Columella VI 12 4). The word occurs in this sense in poetry: see *Met* II 338-39 'nomen ... in marmore lectum / perfudit lacrimis et aperto pectore *fouit*', *Met* VIII 654 (perhaps spurious; the passage is one where textual doublets occur), *Met* X 186-87 (Hyacinthus has just been struck by Apollo's discus) 'deus conlapsos ... excipit artus, / et modo te *refouet*, modo tristia uulnera siccat', *Met* XV 532 'et lacerum *foui* Phlegethontide corpus in unda', and *Aen* XII 420 *'fouit* ea uulnus lympha longaeuus Iapyx'.

5. RAPTI. The word could be taken to mean 'dead'; compare xvi 1 'Nasonis ... rapti', where the context shows this is the meaning, and *EP* I ix 1-2 (to Cotta Maximus) 'Quae mihi de *rapto* tua uenit epistula Celso, / protinus est lacrimis umida facta meis'. For the similarly ambiguous use of *ademptus*, see at vi 49 *qui me doluistis ademptum* (p 243).

6. QVOD QVERERERE. For the phrase, compare *Am* I iv 23-24 (Ovid is listing the signals his girl should use at the dinner-table) 'si quid erit de me tacita *quod* mente *queraris*, / pendeat extrema mollis ab aure manus', *Tr* V i 37 (of Fortune) *'quod querar*, illa mihi pleno de fonte ministrat', *Her* XIX 79, and *Her* XX 34 & 94.

7-8. PVDICA / CONIVGE. Being *pudica*, she deserved to survive—Professor E. Fantham points out to me here Ovid's use of what could be called the *quid profuit* topic.

The reference to Gallio's wife seems rather cool in tone. For some very warm descriptions of recently deceased wives, see Lattimore 275-80.

8. NON HABVERE NEFAS. This sense of *habere*, very common in prose, does not seem to occur elsewhere in Ovid; but Professor R. J. Tarrant cites *Aen* V 49-50 'dies ... adest quem semper acerbum, / semper honoratum ... *habebo'*.

9. LVCTVS = *causae luctus*. Other instances of this sense of *luctus*, which seems to be confined to poetical passages of great emotional content, at *Met* I 654-55 (Inachus to Io) 'tu non inuenta reperta / *luctus* eras leuior', *Met* IX 155, and *Aen* VI 868 (Aeneas has just seen Marcellus) 'o nate, ingentem *luctum* ne quaere tuorum'.

10. LECTAQVE CVM LACRIMIS SVNT TVA DAMNA MEIS. Compare *EP* I ix 1-2 (quoted above at 5 *rapti*) and *Fam* IV v 1 (Ser. Sulpicius Rufus to Cicero) 'Postea quam mihi renuntiatum est de obitu Tulliae, filiae tuae, sane quam pro eo ac debui grauiter molesteque tuli communemque eam calamitatem existimaui'.

10. TVA DAMNA. Compare *Fast* II 835-36 (Lucretia has just killed herself) 'ecce super corpus *communia damna* gementes / obliti decoris uirque paterque iacent' and *Tr* IV iii 35 'tu uero tua damna dole, mitissima coniunx'.

11. SED NEQVE SOLARI PRVDENTEM STVLTIOR AVSIM. Compare *Fam* IV v 6 'plura me ad te de hac re scribere pudet, ne uidear *prudentiae* tuae diffidere'. For the opposite reasoning, see Sen *Cons Marc* 1 1 'Nisi te, Marcia, scirem tam longe ab infirmitate muliebris animi quam a ceteris uitiis recessisse et mores tuos uelut aliquod antiquum exemplar aspici, non auderem obuiam ire dolori tuo'.

12. VERBAQVE DOCTORVM NOTA. Compare *EP* I iii 27-30 (to Rufinus, who has written him a letter of consolation on his exile) 'cum bene firmarunt animum *praecepta* iacentem, / sumptaque sunt nobis pectoris arma tui, / rursus amor patriae *ratione ualentior omni*, / quod tua fecerunt scripta retexit opus', and Sen *Cons Marc* 2 1 'scio a praeceptis incipere omnes qui monere aliquem uolunt, in exemplis desinere'.

13-14. FINITVMQVE TVVM ... DOLOREM / IPSA IAM PRIDEM SVSPICOR ESSE MORA. Compare *EP* I iii 25-26 'cura quoque interdum nulla medicabilis arte est— / aut, ut sit, longa est extenuanda mora', *Fam* IV v 6 'nullus dolor est quem non longinquitas temporis minuat ac molliat', and *Cons Marc* 8 1 'dolorem dies longa consumit'. For a variation of the theme, see *Cons Marc* 1 6 'illud ipsum naturale remedium temporis, quod maximas quoque aerumnas componit, in te una uim suam perdidit'.

The topic of time as the healer of pain is common in ancient literature from New Comedy on: see Tarrant on Sen *Ag* 130 'quod ratio non quiit, saepe sanauit mora', Otto *dies* 6, and Kassel 53.

13. SI NON RATIONE. *Ratio* similarly used to counter strong emotion (without success) at *EP* I iii 27-30 (quoted at 12), *Met* VII 10-11 (Medea falls in love with Jason) '*ratione* furorem / uincere non poterat', and *Met* XIV 701-2 (similar phrasing for Iphis' falling in love with Anaxarete).

14. IPSA ... MORA. 'By the mere passage of time'.

15-16. DVM TVA PERVENIENS, DVM LITTERA NOSTRA RECVRRENS / TOT MARIA AC TERRAS PERMEAT, ANNVS ABIT. Similar phrasing at *EP* III iv 59-60 'dum uenit huc rumor properataque carmina fiunt / factaque eunt ad uos, annus abisse potest'.

15. PERVENIENS is my correction for the manuscripts' *peruenit*. The perfect tense of *peruenit* conflicts with the following *permeat* and *abit*. It might be argued that the perfect is acceptable, since Ovid is speaking of a past event; but he would not have used the perfect of an action which took place over a considerable period of time. For *perueniens ... permeat* referring to a past event, compare Ovid's use of the present *uenit* in the very similar passage *EP* III iv 59-60 (quoted at the end of the last note).

The postponement of *permeat* to the following line made the corruption of *dum ... perueniens* to *dum ... peruenit* simple enough.

17. TEMPORIS OFFICIVM EST SOLACIA DICERE CERTI. Here Ovid says that words of comfort should not be offered too late; at *RA* 127-30 he says they should not be offered too early: 'quis matrem, nisi mentis inops, in funere nati / flere uetet? non hoc illa monenda loco est. / cum dederit lacrimas animumque impleuerit aegrum, / ille dolor uerbis emoderandus erit'.

For the same concern with time as in the present passage and medical imagery similar to that in 19-20, see *Cons Marc* 1 8 and *Cons Hel* 1 2 'dolori tuo, dum recens saeuiret, sciebam occurrendum non esse, ne illum ipsa solacia irritarent et accenderent; nam in morbis quoque nihil est perniciosius quam immatura medicina. expectabam itaque, dum ipse uires suas frangeret et ad sustinenda remedia mora mitigatus tangi se ac tractari pateretur'. See as well the passages cited at Kassel 52-53: from modern literature he quotes Sterne *Tristram Shandy* III 29 'Before an affliction is *digested* consolation ever comes too soon;—and after it is

312

digested—it comes too late: so that you see ... there is but a mark between those two, as fine almost as a hair, for a comforter to take aim at'.

18. DVM DOLOR IN CVRSV EST. Compare *RA* 119 *'dum furor in cursu est,* currenti cede furori' and *Met* XIII 508-10 (Hecuba speaking) *'in cursuque meus dolor est*: modo maxima rerum ... nunc trahor exul, inops, tumulis auulsa meorum'.

18. AEGER. The substantive *aeger* is quite common in both verse and prose, but always with the meaning 'physically ill'; even when used, as here, with a transferred meaning, the sense of metaphor is still present. Compare *RA* 313-14 'curabar propriis aeger Podalirius herbis, / et, fateor, medicus turpiter *aeger* eram', *EP* I iii 17 'non est in medico semper releuetur ut *aeger*', and *EP* III iv 7-8 'firma ualent per se, nullumque Machaona quaerunt; / ad medicam dubius confugit *aeger* opem'.

The adjective, however, is used by the poets from Ennius on (*Sc* 254 & 392 Vahlen[3]), particularly in the phrases *mens aegra* and *animus aeger*, to indicate a state of mental anguish. Compare, from Ovid, *Tr* III viii 33-34 'nec melius ualeo quam corpore mente, sed aegra est / utraque pars aeque', *Tr* IV iii 21, IV vi 43 & V ii 7, *EP* I iii 89-90 'uereor ne ... frustra ... iuuer admota perditus *aeger ope*', I v 18 & I vi 15 'tecum tunc aberant *aegrae solacia* mentis', and *Ibis* 115; from other poets, compare *Cons ad Liuiam* 395, Hor *Ep* I viii 8, and *Aen* I 208 & IV 35. The same use of the adjective is found occasionally in the historians (Sallust *Iug* 71 2, Livy II 3 5, etc).

19. LONGA DIES = *tempus.* Compare *Met* I 346, *Met* XIV 147-48 (the Sibyl to Aeneas) 'tempus erit cum de tanto me corpore paruam / *longa dies* faciet', and *Tr* I v 11-14 'spiritus et uacuas prius hic tenuandus in auras / ibit ... quam subeant animo meritorum obliuia nostro, / et *longa* pietas excidat ista *die*'.

19. VVLNERA MENTIS. Ovid is fond of this metaphorical sense of *uulnus*; see *Met* V 425-27 'Cyane ... inconsolabile *uulnus* / mente* gerit tacita', *Tr* IV iv 41-42 'neue retractando nondum coeuntia rumpam / *uulnera*: uix illis proderit ipsa quies', *EP* I iii 87-88 'nec tamen infitior, si possent nostra

313

coire / *uulnera*, praeceptis posse coire tuis', and *EP* I v 23 'parcendum est animo miserabile *uulnus* habenti'. To judge from Seneca, the metaphor was usual in treatises of consolation: 'antiqua mala in memoriam reduxi et, ut scires [*Schultess*: uis scire *codd*] hanc quoque plagam esse sanandam, ostendi tibi aeque magni *uulneris* cicatricem' (*Cons Marc* 1 5), 'itaque utcumque conabar manu super plagam meam imposita ad obliganda *uulnera* uestra reptare' (*Cons Hel* 1 1).

20. FOVET *Heinsius* MOVET *codd*. For the meaning of *fouet* see at 4 *fouisti* (p 361). *Mouet* here is to some extent supported by Ovid's use of such verbs as *tangere* and *tractare* in contexts like that of the present passage; compare *EP* I vi 21-22 'nec breue nec tutum peccati quae sit origo / scribere; *tractari uulnera* nostra timent', *EP* II vii 13, and *EP* III vii 25-26 'curando fieri quaedam maiora uidemus / uulnera, quae melius non *tetigisse* fuit'. But *tractare* and *tangere* are neutral in force, while *mouet* here would mean 'disturb', as at Hor *Carm* III xx 1-2 'Non uides quanto *moueas* periclo, / Pyrrhe, Gaetulae catulos leaenae?' and Lucan VIII 529-30 'bustum cineresque *mouere* / Thessalicos audes bellumque in regna uocare?'. As Professor R. J. Tarrant comments, if *mouet* were read in the present passage, *intempestiue* would lose the appropriateness it has when *fouet* is read: there is no proper time to "disturb" a wound.

20. NOVAT. Similar phrasing at *Tr* II 209 'nam non sum tanti *renouem* ut tua *uulnera*, Caesar' and *RA* 729-30 'admonitu refricatur amor, *uulnusque nouatum* / scinditur'.

21. ADDE QVOD. Professor E. Fantham points out to me how extraordinary the occurrence of this phrase in the last distich of the poem is. Of the twenty-five instances of the idiom in Ovid's poems[25], none except the present passage occur in the final distich of a poem or book. The other examples all occur in the middle of an argument, or lead into another distich containing a final injunction or proof of an argument. As Professor J. N. Grant suggests to me, this poem therefore furnishes another example of Ovid's favourite device of unexpectedly altering a poem's tone in the final distich, for a discussion of which see at xiv 61-62 (p

427).

21. MIHI *BF[1]* TIBI *MHILTF[2]* *om* C. As Burman saw, *mihi* must be the correct reading, the perfect subjunctive acting as a past optative: 'certe ego *mihi* praeferrem: utinam mihi, mentionem facienti noui tui coniugii, uerum illud omen uenerit, neque fallar, sed tu iam uxorem duxeris, ut ego uoueo'. *Tibi* is hardly possible, since an omen to Gallio indicating that he had remarried would be superfluous.

XII. To Tuticanus

Tuticanus[26] (known only from the *Ex Ponto*) seems from the testimony of the poem (19-30) to have been a close friend of Ovid; he is mentioned again at xiv 1-2 and xvi 27. It is reasonable to suppose that, like Sextus Pompeius, he had previously been unwilling to allow Ovid to mention him in his verse.

The poem opens with a discussion of the difficulty of fitting Tuticanus' name into elegiac verse: Ovid could split the name between verses, or alter the quantity of one or another of the name's syllables, but neither procedure would be acceptable to Ovid or to his readers (1-18). He has known Tuticanus since early youth; they assisted each other in their verse (19-30). He is quite certain that Tuticanus will not desert him (31-38). He should use his influence with Tiberius to assist Ovid; but Ovid is so confused after his hardships that he cannot suggest precisely what Tuticanus should do; he leaves this to Tuticanus' judgment (39-50).

The appeal for assistance is a constant theme of the poetry of exile; and the recalling of their assisting each other with their poetry is paralleled by *EP* II iv, in which Ovid recalls how he used to submit his verse to Atticus for criticism, and by *Tr* III vii, Ovid's letter to his stepdaughter Perilla, whom he assisted when she first began writing verse. The opening discussion of the metrical difficulty of Tuticanus' name finds parallels elsewhere in Latin and Greek literature (see at 1-2), but is remarkable for its fullness. The explanation for this fullness may well be Tuticanus' being a fellow poet: he would be amused by the use of his own name for the witty discussion of the handling of metrical difficulties with which he himself would be familiar enough.

1-2. QVOMINVS IN NOSTRIS PONARIS, AMICE, LIBELLIS, / NOMINIS EFFICITVR CONDICIONE TVI. A constant problem for the Latin poets was the impossibility of using words with cretic patterns (a long syllable, followed by a short syllable, followed by another long syllable) in hexameter or elegiac verse. The fact played an important part in determining Latin poetic vocabulary; for instance, such an ordinary word as *femina*, cretic in its oblique cases, is usually represented through metonymy by such words as *nurus* and *mater*. Proper names presented a special problem, which could however occasionally be solved through the use of special forms or circumlocutions; hence such lines as 'cumque *Borysthenio* liquidissimus *amne* [=Borysthēnē] Dirapses' (x 53) and '*Scipiadas* [=Scīpiŏnes], belli fulmen, Carthaginis horror' (Lucretius III 1034). Sometimes, as in the present passage, such avenues were not available, and the poet was simply unable to use the name he wanted. From Greek authors Marx, commenting on Lucilius 228-29, cites Critias fr. 5 'οὐ γὰρ πως ἦν τοὔνομα ἐφαρμόζειν ἐλεγείῳ' Archestratus fr. 29 (Brandt) 'ἰχθύος αὐξηθέντος ὃν ἐν μέτρῳ οὐ θέμις εἰπεῖν' and *Ep Gr* 616 (Kaibel) 'οὐ γὰρ ἐν ἑξαμέτροισιν ἥρμοσεν τοὔνομ' ἐμόν' In Latin, the best-known reference to this difficulty is Hor *Sat* I v 86-87 'quattuor hinc rapimur uiginti et milia raedis, / mansuri oppidulo, quod uersu dicere non est'. On the passage Porphyrion comments 'Aequum Tuticum significat [this is disputed by modern commentators, since the town's known location does not fit with Horace's indication; no certain candidate has been proposed], cuius nomen hexametro uersu compleri [*codd*: contineri *fort legendum*] non potest. hoc autem sub exemplo Lucili posuit. nam ille in sexto Saturarum [228-29 Marx] sic ait: "seruorum est festus dies hic, / quem plane hexametro uersu non dicere possis"'. In his comment on the passage from Horace, Lejay cites Martial IX xi 10-17 (Martial wanted to mention Flavius Ĕărĭnus, whose name starts with three consecutive short vowels) 'nomen nobile, molle, delicatum / uersu dicere non rudi uolebam: / sed tu, syllaba contumax, rebellas. / dicunt Eiarinon tamen poetae, / sed Graeci, quibus est nihil negatum, / et quos Ἄρες Ἄρες decet sonare: / nobis non licet esse tam disertis / qui Musas colimus seueriores', Rutilius Namatianus 419-22 (of Vŏlŭsĭanus [short 'o', 'u', and 'i'] Rufius) 'optarem uerum complecti carmine nomen, / sed quosdam refugit regula dura pedes. / cognomen uersu ueheris [*Préchac*: ueneris *uel* uenens *codd*], carissime Rufi; /

illo te dudum pagina nostra canit', and Apollinaris Sidonius *Carm* XXIII 485-86 'horum nomina cum referre uersu / affectus cupiat, metrum recusat'.

Professor C. P. Jones cites the discussion at Pliny *Ep* VIII iv 3-4. Pliny, writing to Caninius, who is composing a poem in Greek on the Dacian war, discusses the difficulty of using *barbara et fera nomina* in the poem: 'sed ... si datur Homero et mollia uocabula et Graeca ad leuitatem uersus contrahere extendere inflectere, cur tibi similis audentia, praesertim non delicata sed necessaria, non detur?'.

For a further discussion of the topic, see L. Radermacher, "Das Epigramm des Didius", *SAWW* 170,9 [1912] 1-31.

1. QVOMINVS is rare in Augustan verse; but compare *AA* II 720 'non obstet tangas quominus illa [*sc* loca] pudor'.

3. AVT *BC* AST *MFHILT*. The false reading was probably induced by a failure to understand the meaning of *aut* 'otherwise', for which compare iii 21 '*aut* age, dic aliquam quae te mutauerit iram', *Met* VII 699, *Met* X 50-52 'hanc [*sc* Eurydicen] simul et legem Rhodopeius accipit heros, / ne flectat retro sua lumina donec Auernas / exierit ualles; *aut* inrita dona futura', and *Tr* I viii 43-45 'quaeque tibi ... dedit nutrix ubera, tigris erat. / *aut* mala nostra minus quam nunc aliena putares'.

2. CONDICIONE. 'Nature'. Compare Lucretius II 300-1 'et quae consuerint gigni gignentur eadem / *condicione* et erunt et crescent uique ualebunt'.

4. SI MODO. 'If, that is ...' Compare 43-44 'quid mandem quaeris? peream nisi dicere uix est, / *si modo* qui periit ille perire potest'.

5. LEX PEDIS. 'The rules of metre'. *Lex* used similarly at Hor *Carm* IV ii 10-12 'per audaces noua dithyrambos / uerba deuoluit numerisque fertur / *lege* solutis', Cic *Or* 58 'uersibus est certa quaedam et definita *lex*', and Columella XI 1 1.

5. FORTVNAQVE. The sense of the word is difficult. It seems, as Professor R. J. Tarrant notes, to combine the idea of 'condition, state' (compare for example *Aen* II 350 'quae sit rebus *fortuna* uidetis') with that of 'unfortunate circumstances', giving the general sense 'the fact that you have the bad luck to possess a metrically impossible name'. Three lines before, Ovid used *nominis ... condicione tui*; and in the present line he seems to have been influenced by the common phrase *condicio et fortuna*, 'allotted circumstances of life', for which compare Cic *Off* I 41 'est autem infima *condicio et fortuna* seruorum', *Mil* 92 'in infimi generis hominum *condicione atque fortuna*'. At *II Verr* I 81 Cicero similarly adapts the expression to suit his context: 'Lampsacenis ... populi Romani *condicione* sociis, *fortuna* seruis, uoluntate supplicibus'.

7. NOMEN SCINDERE. That is, split the name so that the hexameter (*uersus prior*) would end in *Tŭtĭ-* and the following pentameter (*uersus minor*) begin with *-cānŭs*. Such word-divisions are not permissible in Augustan verse; from earlier poetry Professor C. P. Jones cites Ennius *Ann* 609 Vahlen[3] 'saxo *cere* comminuit *brum*'.

8. HOC = *nomine tuo*.

9-14. Ovid lists the three possible ways of scanning the name so as to remove the cretic: *Tŭtĭcānus, Tŭtĭcānus,* and *Tūtĭcānus*.

9. MORATVR = *longa est*. The *TLL* cites Velius Longus VII 55 5 Keil 'hanc ... naturam esse quarundam litterarum, ut *morentur* et enuntiatione sonum detineant'.

11. ET *BCHI^{ac}LT* NON *M* NEC *FI^{pc}*. *Nec*, printed by some editors, cannot by itself be correct, for there is no negative with the corresponding *producatur* in the following distich. A negative is implicitly supplied for *potes ... uenire* and *producatur* by 15-16 'his ego si uitiis ...', but Professor R. J. Tarrant is possibly right to suggest that *nec* should be read both here and (replacing *aut*) at the beginning of 13.

W. A. Camps (*CQ* n.s. IV [1954] 206-7) has pointed out that it is somewhat odd that 'The first two possibilities are introduced, in lines 7 and 9, in terms that disclaim them at once' and that 'the third and fourth possibilities are added without disclaimer ... in terms that would be quite appropriate to serious suggestions'. He suggests reading *at,* so that 11-12 represent an imaginary rejoinder to Ovid's rejection of the possibilities already suggested; Ovid's rejoinder is given at 15 'his ego si uitiis ...'. But *at potes* is difficult: Ovid could have written 'at, puto, potes', speaking in his own person to raise an objection he would then counter, or he could have represented Tuticanus as saying 'at ... possum'; but it is hard to see how he could have written 'at potes'.

13. PRODVCATVR *MHI* VT DVCATVR *LTB²F²ᵘˡ* VT DICATVR *B¹CF¹*. *Producere* is the correct technical term for 'lengthen'; compare Quintilian VII ix 13 '*productio* quoque in scripto et correptio in dubio relicta causa est ambiguitatis' & IX iii 69 'uoces ['words'] ... *productione* tantum uel correptione mutatae'. *Vt ducatur* is unlikely to be right. *Ducatur* could certainly stand for *producatur* (although this would destroy the balance with the following *correptius*), but the verb is clearly indicated as a potential subjunctive by the preceding *potes ... uenire*; and *ut* (which would in any case be taken as correlative with *ut* in line 12) cannot stand with this construction. *Vt dicatur*, Ehwald's preferred reading ('dicatur et sit secunda [syllaba] productâ morâ longa'—*KB* 68), is even less likely to be right, since *dicere* in this context could only mean 'pronounce', as at Cic *Or* 159 '"inclitus" dicimus breui prima littera, "insanus" producta'.

13. EXIT. *Exire* similarly used of words being uttered at *Her* VIII 115-16 (Hermione speaking) 'saepe Neoptolemi pro nomine nomen Orestae / *exit*, et errorem uocis ut omen amo'. *OLD exeo* 2d gives other instances from Cicero (*Brutus* 265), Seneca (*Ben* V 19 4), and Quintilian (XI iii 33), but from verse outside Ovid only Martial XII xi 3, where the word has a somewhat different meaning: 'cuius Pimpleo lyra clarior exit ab antro?'.

14. PORRECTA is equivalent to *longa*, and belongs to *secunda* (*sc* syllaba) by hypallage. Compare Quintilian I vi 32 'aut correptis aut *porrectis* ... litteris syllabisue' & I vii 14 'usque ad Accium et ultra *porrectas* syllabas geminis, ut dixi, uocalibus scripserunt [that is, they wrote *uiita* for *uita* and so on; such spellings occur sometimes in inscriptions]', and Rutilius Lupus I 3.

15. VITIIS. *Vitium* similarly used for faults of diction at *AA* III 295-96 'in *uitio* decor est: quaerunt male reddere uerba; / discunt posse minus quam potuere loqui', Cic *de Or* I 116, and Quintilian I v 17, a discussion of the shortening and lengthening of vowels; this he includes among the 'quae accidunt in dicendo *uitia*'. Ovid is probably combining this sense with that of 'poetic weakness', for which compare *Tr* I vii 39-40 'quicquid in his igitur *uitii* rude carmen habebit, / emendaturus, si licuisset, eram' and the use of *uitiosus* at xiii 17 and *Tr* IV i 1 and IV x 61.

16. MERITO PECTVS HABERE NEGER. 'People would quite rightly say that I was ignorant'. Compare *Met* XIII 290-91 & 295 (Ulysses is speaking of Ajax's claim to the arms of Achilles) 'artis opus tantae rudis et *sine pectore* miles / indueret? neque enim clipei caelamina nouit ... postulat ut capiat *quae non intellegit* arma!'.

17-18. MVNERIS ... QVOD MEVS ADIECTO FAENORE REDDET AMOR. *Adiecto faenore* = 'with interest added on'; Ovid will make up for his past negligence by sending Tuticanus more than one poem ('tibi *carmina* mittam'). It is clear from the opening distich of poem xiv that Ovid sent the poem to Tuticanus very soon after the composition of xii: 'Haec tibi mittuntur quem sum *modo* carmine questus / non aptum numeris nomen habere meis'.

A similar use of *faenus* at *EP* III i 79-81 'nec ... debetur meritis gratia nulla meis. / redditur illa quidem grandi cum *faenore* nobis'.

The variant AGER (*TM²I²*) for *amor* was clearly induced by such passages as Tib II vi 21-22 'spes sulcis credit aratis / semina quae magno *faenore* reddat *ager*', *RA* 173-74 'obrue uersata Cerealia semina terra, / quae tibi cum multo *faenore* reddat *ager*', and *EP* I v 25-26 'at, puto ... sata cum multo *faenore* reddit *ager*': these passages refer to the original meaning of *faenus* ('faenum appellatur naturalis terrae fetus; ob quam causam et nummorum fetus *faenus* est uocatum'— Festus 94 Muller, 83 Lindsay).

18. REDDET *GCMIT* REDDIT *BFHL*. Numerous instances of similar corruptions in Lucan and Juvenal given by Willis

(166-67), who remarks 'The general trend seems to be from other tenses to the present, and from other persons and numbers to the third person singular'.

19. QVACVMQVE NOTA. 'With whatever method of indicating your name is possible'. For the collocation of *nota* and *nomen*, see *Aen* III 443-44 'insanam uatem aspicies, quae rupe sub ima / fata canit foliisque *notas et nomina* mandat'.

Luck joins the phrase with the following *tibi carmina mittam*, but the construction seems somewhat cumbersome; it is probably better to retain the comma after *nota* and take the phrase with *teque canam*.

20-22. PVERO ... PVER ... FRATRI FRATER. For Ovid's use of polyptoton, see at viii 67 *uatis ... uates* (p 278).

23. DVXQVE COMESQVE. The same phrase at *Tr* III vii 18 (to his stepdaughter Perilla) 'utque pater natae *duxque comesque* fui' and *Tr* IV x 119-20 (to his Muse) 'tu *dux et comes* es, tu nos abducis ab Histro, / in medioque mihi das Helicone locum'.

24. FRENA NOVELLA. For the image, see at ii 23 *frena remisi* (p 169). *Nouellus* is a rare word in poetry. In prose, the word is often used of young plants or farm animals; and here *frena nouella* may well be a metonymy for *frena nouellorum equorum*. Alternatively, the word could be equivalent to *noua* 'new, unfamiliar', as at *Fast* III 455 'iamque indignanti *noua frena* receperat ore'. In either case, Ovid is clearly referring to the beginning of his poetic career.

25. SAEPE EGO CORREXI SVB TE CENSORE LIBELLOS. Compare *Tr* III vii 23-24 (to Perilla) 'dum licuit, tua saepe mihi, tibi nostra legebam; / saepe tui *iudex*, saepe magister eram'. *Censore* was probably still felt as a metaphor; the only precedent given at *OLD censor* 2b is Hor *Ep* II ii 109-10 'at qui legitimum cupiet fecisse poema / cum tabulis *animum censoris* sumet *honesti*', which is virtually a simile.

26. SAEPE TIBI ADMONITV FACTA LITVRA MEO EST. Similar phrasing in a similar context at *EP* II iv 17-18 (to Atticus) 'utque meus lima rasus liber esset amici, / *non semel admonitu facta litura tuo est*'.

27. DIGNAM MAEONIIS PHAEACIDA ... CHARTIS. 'A Phaeacid worthy of the Homeric original you were translating'. It is clear from xvi 27 that Tuticanus produced a translation rather than a new work in imitation of Homer: 'et qui Maeoniam Phaeacida *uertit*'.

27. MAEONIIS = 'Homeric', Homer being considered a native of Maeonia (Lydia). The same use at *RA* 373 'Maeonio ... pede', *EP* III iii 31-32 'Maeonio ... carmine', and Prop II xxviii 29 'Maeonias ... heroidas'; the word in this sense perhaps brought into standard poetic vocabulary by Horace (*Carm* I vi 2 'Maeonii carminis', *Carm* IV ix 5-6 'Maeonius ... Homerus').

27. CHARTIS = *carminibus*. Compare *AA* II 746 'uos eritis *chartae* proxima cura meae'. The metonymy is not found in Virgil or Propertius, but compare Lucretius IV 970 'patriis ... *chartis*' = 'Latinis uersibus' (I 137) and Hor *Carm* IV ix 30-31 'non ego te meis / *chartis* inornatum silebo' (where Kiessling-Heinze point out that *chartis* refers to the poem in its published state being transmitted to others, rather than to the poem at its moment of composition).

28. CVM TE PIERIAE PERDOCVERE DEAE. For the poet's being divinely taught, compare Prop II x 10 & IV i 133, *Her* XV 27-28 'at mihi Pegasides blandissima carmina dictant; / iam canitur toto nomen in orbe meum', and the disclaimers at Prop II i 3 and *AA* I 25-28 'non ego, Phoebe, datas a te mihi mentiar artes, / nec nos aeriae uoce monemur auis, / nec mihi sunt uisae Clio Cliusque sorores / seruanti pecudes uallibus, Ascra, tuis'. The topic is an important one in ancient literature, the most influential passages being the opening of Hesiod's *Theogony* (referred to in the passage just cited) and the beginning of Callimachus' *Aetia*.

29. TENOR. 'Course'; the same use at *Her* VII 111-12 (Dido speaking) 'durat in extremum uitaeque nouissima nostrae / prosequitur fati qui fuit ante *tenor*'.

29. VIRIDI ... IVVENTA. Ovid is perhaps imitating *Aen* V 295 'Euryalus forma insignis *uiridique iuuenta*'. Similar phrasing at *AA* III 557 'uiridemque iuuentam', *Tr* IV x 17 'frater ad eloquium *uiridi* tendebat ab aeuo', and *Tr* III i 7-8 'id

quoque quod *uiridi* quondam male lusit in aeuo / heu
nimium sero damnat et odit opus'; at the last passage Luck
aptly cites *Met* XV 201-3 'nam tener et lactens puerique
simillimus aeuo / uere nouo [*sc* annus] est; tunc *herba nitens*
et roboris expers turget'.

30. ALBENTES ... COMAS. For the synecdoche compare
Callimachus *Ep* LXIV (=*Anth Pal* V xxiii) 5-6 'ἡ πολιὴ δὲ /
αὐτίκ' ἀναμνήσει ταῦτά σε πάντα κόμη'.

Ovid would have been about sixty years of age at the time of
this poem, old by Roman standards; but his father lived to
ninety, and was survived by his wife (*Tr* IV x 77-80).

30. INLABEFACTA occurs in classical Latin only here and at
viii 9-10 'ius aliquod faciunt adfinia uincula nobis / (quae
semper maneant *inlabefacta* precor)'.

**31-32. QVAE NISI TE MOVEANT, DVRO TIBI PECTORA
FERRO / ESSE VEL INVICTO CLAVSA ADAMANTE
PVTEM.** Compare *Her* II 137 'duritia *ferrum* ut superes
adamantaque teque', *Her* X 109-10, and *Met* IX 614-15 (Byblis
on her brother) 'nec rigidas silices solidumue in pectore
ferrum / aut *adamanta* gerit'.

Professor R. J. Tarrant notes the unexpected shift in the
thought of the poem: earlier it was Ovid who was guilty of
delaying in sending Tuticanus any sign of his friendship.
Ovid might be postponing the real point of the letter for
reasons of tact: Tuticanus has acted as though his long
association with Ovid meant nothing to him, but Ovid does
not want to complain of this openly, and so stresses his own
failure to send Tuticanus a letter.

33-36. The set of *adynata* is remarkable for the way Ovid
makes each of them relate to his own hardships; even Boreas
and Notus have a specific connection, since Ovid complains
so often of the climate of Tomis.

35. TEPIDVS BOREAS ... SIT. A comparable inversion of
nature described at *Ibis* 34 'et tepidus gelido flabit ab axe
Notus' (before Ovid will forgive his enemy).

35. PRAEFRIGIDVS appears here for the first time in Latin;

it occurs later in Celsus and the elder Pliny. *Praegelidus*, however, is found at Livy XXI 54 7.

36. ET POSSIT FATVM MOLLIVS ESSE MEVM. The personal reference in the last element of the series of *adynata* is a clear break with the conventions of the topic. The last (and therefore greatest) curse in the *Ibis* has a similar personal reference: 'denique Sarmaticas inter Geticasque sagittas / his precor ut uiuas et moriare locis'.

37. LAPSO *FHILT* LASSO *BCM*. *Lapso ... sodali* seems to me the preferable reading, since it contrasts Ovid's former life in Rome with his disgrace and exile; but *lasso* is well attested and can be construed easily enough. Unfortunately, parallels from the poems of exile are of little use, since in most of them the one word could easily be read for the other: 'tu quoque magnorum laudes admitte uirorum, / ut facis, et lapso [*uar* lasso] quam potes adfer opem' (*EP* II iii 47-48), 'fac modo permaneas lasso [*uar* lapso], Graecine, fidelis, / duret et in longas impetus iste moras' (*EP* II vi 35-36), 'regia, crede mihi, res est succurrere lapsis [*uar* lassis], / conuenit et tanto, quantus es ipse, uiro' (*EP* II ix 11-12), 'digne uir hac serie, lapso [*uar* lasso] succurrere amico / conueniens istis moribus esse puta' (*EP* III ii 109). Professor R. J. Tarrant cites similar variants in the text of Seneca at *HF* 646 & 803 and *Thy* 616 & 658.

A clear decision can be made, however, for the phrase *res lassae*; it is certified as the correct term by the parallel phrase *res fessae*, for which see *Aen* III 145 'quam *fessis* finem *rebus* ferat' and *Aen* XI 335 'consulite in medium et *rebus* succurrite *fessis*', cited by Luck at *Tr* I v 35. For *res lassae* in Ovid, compare *Tr* I v 35 'quo magis, o pauci, *rebus* succurrite *lassis*', *Tr* V ii 41 'unde petam *lassis* solacia *rebus*?', *EP* II ii 47 'nunc tua pro *lassis* nitatur gratia *rebus*', and *EP* II iii 93 'respicis antiquum *lassis* in *rebus* amicum'; in each of these passages *lapsis* is found as a variant for *lassis*. Similarly, the sixth-century *codex Romanus* reads *lapsis* at Virgil *G* IV 449 'uenimus hinc *lassis* quaesitum oracula rebus'.

38. HIC CVMVLVS NOSTRIS ABSIT ABESTQVE MALIS. Festus defines *cumulus* as a heap added to an already full measure (s.u. *auctarium*, 14 Muller, 14 Lindsay). The transferred sense is common in Cicero (*Prou Cons* 26, *S Rosc* 8, *Att* XVI iii 3), and is found elsewhere in Ovid at *EP* II v 35-36 'hoc tibi facturo uel si non ipse rogarem / accedat cumulus gratia nostra leuis' and *Met* XI 205-6 'stabat opus: pretium rex infitiatur et addit, / perfidiae *cumulum*, falsis periuria uerbis'.

38. ABSIT ABESTQVE. The more natural *abest absitque* cannot be placed in a pentameter.

39. PER SVPEROS, QVORVM CERTISSIMVS ILLE EST. Similar line-endings at *Ibis* 23-24 'di melius! *quorum longe mihi maximus ille est,* / qui nostras inopes noluit esse uias' and *EP* I ii 97-98 'di faciant igitur, *quorum iustissimus ipse est,* / alma nihil maius Caesare terra ferat'.

40. QVO ... PRINCIPE. Professor R. J. Tarrant points out that Augustus must here be meant, since it appears from 20 that Ovid and Tuticanus were contemporaries: Tuticanus must by the time of the poem's writing have been in later middle age, rather late to be prospering only under Tiberius. T. P. Wiseman (268) has suggested that Ovid's Tuticanus might be the son of a Tuticanus Callus known to have been senator before 48 BC.

41-42. EFFICE ... NE SPERATA MEAM DESERAT AVRA RATEM. 'See to it that the breeze I hope for does not fail to come to my ship'. *Deserere* generally refers to something failing one that was originally operative: compare Cic *Att* VII vii 7 'nisi me lucerna desereret' ('if the lamp were not going out'—Shackleton Bailey), Plautus *Mer* 123 'genua hunc cursorem deserunt' and the other passages cited at *OLD desero* 2b. But *sperata* indicates that the breeze cannot yet be present; other instances of the same metaphor at viii 27-28 'quamlibet exigua si nos ea *iuuerit* aura, / obruta de mediis cumba resurget aquis', ix 73 'et si quae *dabit* aura sinum, laxate rudentes', and *Tr* IV v 19-20 'utque facis, remis ad opem luctare ferendam, / *dum ueniat* placido mollior aura deo',

43. QVID MANDEM QVAERIS. Similar wording at *EP* III i 33-34 (to his wife) '*quid facias quaeris?* quaeras hoc scilicet ipsa [*Riese*: ipsum *codd*]: / inuenies, uere si reperire uoles'.

Ovid's pretense of not knowing what to tell Tuticanus to do was an ingenious solution to his friends' complaint that he was constantly repeating the same instructions to them (*EP* III vii 1-6). Professor R. J. Tarrant points out the balance with the poem's start, where Ovid pretends not to know how to address Tuticanus.

43. PEREAM NISI DICERE VIX EST. Similar doubt expressed at *Tr* IV iii 31-32 'quid tamen ipse precer dubito, nec dicere possum / affectum quem te mentis habere uelim'. *Peream nisi,* which Ovid plays on in the next line, is colloquial and foreign to poetic diction: instances at *OLD pereo* 3b.

44. SI MODO QVI PERIIT ILLE PERIRE POTEST. Similar phrasing at *Tr* I iv 27-28 'uos animam saeuae fessam subducite morti, / *si modo qui periit non periisse potest*'.

45. NEC QVID NOLIMVE VELIMVE. Compare *Met* XI 492-93 *'nec* se ... fatetur / scire ratis [*codd*: satis *fort scribendum*] rector ... *quid iubeatue uetetue'* and *Tr* I ii 31-32 'rector in incerto est *nec quid fugiatue petatue /* inuenit'.

46. NEC SATIS VTILITAS EST MIHI NOTA MEA. 'And I am at a loss to know what is to my advantage'. *Satis* strengthens the sentence: compare Ter *Hec* 877 'ego istuc sati' scio', 'I know that very well'. For *utilitas*, see at ix 48 *publica ... utilitas* (p 300).

48. SENSVS here means 'judgement' or 'good sense', as at Prop II xii 3 'is primum uidit sine *sensu* uiuere amantes' and Val Max I vi ext 1 'si quod uestigium in uecordi pectore *sensus* fuisset'. Elsewhere in Ovid *sensus* carries the meaning 'awareness, consciousness'.

48. CVM RE *codd* CVM SPE *Heinsius*. *Cum re,* 'along with my fortune', seems somewhat out of place; but Burman pointed out that *consilium et res* seems to have been a Latin phrase, citing Sallust *Iug* 74 'neque illi *res neque consilium* aut quisquam hominum satis placebat' and Ter *Eun* 240-41 'itan parasti te ut spes nulla relicua in te siet tibi? / simul *consilium cum re* amisti?'.

50. QVAQVE VIA VENIAS AD MEA VOTA, VIDE. This is

a provisional restoration of the line. The manuscript reading which most closely approaches this text is that of *L* and *F³*, QVAQVE VIAM FACIAS AD MEA VOTA, VIDE; the other manuscripts have the same text, except that QVOQVE is found in some for *quaque*, while for *uide* there are the variants MODO, VADO, and VALE.

My restoration is based on 6 '*quaque* meos *adeas* est *uia* nulla modos' and *Fast* I 431-32 (Priapus approaches the sleeping nymph Lotis) 'a pedibus tracto uelamine *uota* / *ad sua felici coeperat ire uia*'.

Before Professor E. Fantham brought this passage to my attention, I had thought that *M*'s *quoque uiam facias ad mea uota modo* was correct. *Modo* is weak and does not fit well with the preceding *qua ... parte*, but at least is acceptable Latin; for *quo ... modo* compare *Med* 1-2 'Discite quae faciem commendet cura, puellae, / et *quo* sit uobis forma tuenda *modo*' and *Ibis* 55-56 'nunc *quo* Battiades inimicum deuouet Ibin, / *hoc* ego deuoueo teque tuosque *modo*'.

The image in *quoque ... uado* ['ford'] is rather strange, and for this sense of the word Ovid seems to have used the plural (*Met* III 19; *Met* IX 108). At *Fast* IV 300 'sedit limoso pressa carina *uado*', *uado* means 'river-bottom'.

Ovid does not end any one of his dozens of verse epistles with *uale*, so the reading of *FTI²ᵘˡ* must be discounted.

If my restoration is correct or nearly correct, the original corruptions would have been of *uia* to *uiam* and of *uenias* to *facias*; the latter corruption might have been a deliberate interpolation to procure a governing verb for *uiam*, or might have been a misreading of or conjectural restoration for a damaged archetype. The variant *quoque* for *quaque* and the different variants for *uide* would have been secondary corruptions, unless they also were the result of a damaged archetype.

50. VIDE. For *uide* at the end of the pentameter, compare *EP* II ii 55-56 'num tamen excuses erroris origine factum, / an nihil expediat tale mouere, uide'. It must however be said that *uide* is somewhat strange following the subjunctive *quaeras.*

———————————

XIII. To Carus

Nothing is known of the Carus to whom this poem is addressed beyond what Ovid tells us: that he wrote a poem on Hercules (11-12; xvi 7-8) and that he was teacher of the sons of Germanicus (47-48).

The poem begins with a pun on the meaning of Carus' name (1-2). This opening will in itself demonstrate to Carus who his correspondent is (3-6). Carus can himself be recognized through his style (7-12). Ovid does not claim that his poetry is excellent, only that it is individual; if his poetry is poor, it is because he is almost a Getic poet now (13-18). He has written a poem in Getic, which was well received (19-22). It was a description of the apotheosis of Augustus and a laudation of the members of the imperial family (23-32). When he finished reciting the poem, he was applauded; one person even suggested that his piety merited a recall (33-38). But it is now the sixth year of his exile, and poems will not assist him, since in the past they have done him harm. Carus should use his influence to secure Ovid's recall (39-50).

Certain elements of the poem, such as the flattering references to Carus' poetry and the request for his help, are commonplaces of the poetry of exile; the list of the members of the imperial family is similarly paralleled in Ovid's other poems (see at 25-32 [p 400]). Ovid nowhere else explicitly describes any of his Getic poems.

1. MEMORANDE *BMFHILT* NVMERANDE *C.* For *memorande* compare *Tr* I v 1 'O mihi post nullos umquam *memorande* sodales'. *Numerande* is in itself acceptable enough: see ix 35 'hic ego praesentes inter *numerarer* amicos'.

2. QVI QVOD ES, ID *BCFI* QVI QVOD ID ES *MH* QVIQVE QVOD ES *LT*. For the use of *id*, Ehwald (*KB* 47) cited *Fast* II 23-24 'quaeque capit lictor domibus purgamina uersis ['swept out'] / torrida cum mica farra, uocantur *idem* [*sc* februa]', Hor *Sat* II iii 139-41 (of Orestes) 'non Pyladen ferro uiolare aususue sororem / Electram, tantum male dicit utrique uocando / hanc Furiam, hunc *aliud*', Sen *Ben* I 3 10 'id quemque uocari iubent', and Tac *Germ* 6 'definitur et numerus: centeni ex singulis pagis sunt, *id*que ipsum inter suos uocantur' ['they are called "The Hundred"']'.

Quique quod es is, however, an attractive reading: compare *Tr* I v 1-2 'O mihi post nullos umquam memorande sodales, / *et cui* praecipue sors mea uisa sua est'. *Quique quod* is obviously prone to haplography; on the other hand, it could be a rewriting of *qui quod id es*, which is itself presumably a simple corruption through interchange of *qui quod es id*. I therefore print *qui quod es id*, although with some hesitation.

2. VERE. 'Justly'. For the same adverb used once again of names "properly" applied, see *Tr* V x 13-14 'quem tenet Euxini mendax cognomine litus, / et Scythici *uere* terra *sinistra* freti'.

2. CARE. Luck among others believes that Carus is also addressed at *Tr* III v 17-18 'sum quoque, *care*, tuis defensus uiribus absens / (scis "carum" ueri nominis esse loco)'; but it seems excessively ingenious to make Ovid say 'I call you *carus* instead of your real name, Carus'. Still, as Professor R. J. Tarrant points out to me, the passage is odd, in that Ovid elsewhere uses *care* only in conjunction with another vocative (compare viii 89 '*care* Suilli' and *Tr* III iv 1-2 '*care* quidem ... sed tempore duro / cognite'); *care* may have been used as a metrical equivalent to the suppressed name, in the way the "cover names" in elegy correspond to the shape of the alleged actual names of the women. Unlike *care*, *carissime* is often found by itself (*Tr* I v 3, III iii 27, III vi 1, IV vii 19 & V vii 5; *EP* II iv 21 & IV x 3).

2. AVE occurs in Ovid only here and at *RA* 639-40 'nec ueniat seruus, nec flens ancillula fictum / suppliciter dominae nomine dicat "aue!"', and is not common in writing. It was, however, frequent in everyday speech, as is clear from Sen *Ben* VI 34 3 'uulgare et publicum uerbum et promiscuum ignotis "aue"'.

3. SALVTERIS *MFT* SALVTARIS *BCHIL.* Ovid usually

employs the subjunctive in indirect questions; this is demonstrated by metre at such passages as *Fast* VI 385-86 'increpat illos / Iuppiter et sacro quid *uelit* ore docet', *Tr* II 294 '*sustulerit* quare quaeret Ericthonium', *Tr* II 297-98 'Isidis aede sedens cur hanc Saturnia quaeret / *egerit* Ionio Bosphorioque mari', *Tr* V xiv 1-2 'Quanta tibi *dederim* nostris monumenta libellis ... uides', *EP* I i 55-56 'talia caelestes fieri praeconia gaudent, / ut sua quid *ualeant* numina teste probent' and *EP* II vii 3 'subsequitur quid *agas* audire uoluntas'.

I have found two passages where metre demonstrates that Ovid used the indicative in an indirect question, *Met* X 637 'quid *facit* [*codd plerique*: quod facit *recc* quidque agat *Heinsius* quid factum *Merkel* quid uelit *Nick* quid facti *Rappold* dissidet *Korn* quid sciat *Slater*] ignorans amat et non sentit amorem' and *EP* I viii 25-26 'sed memor unde *abii* queror, o iucunde sodalis, / accedant nostris saeua quod arma malis'. But in the first passage *faciat* would have an ambiguous meaning, since it could represent either *quid facio* or *quid faciam*, and in the second *ăbĭĕrim* with its short 'a', 'i', and 'e', would be metrically intractable.

It is difficult to say whether the scribes were more prone to influence by the subjunctive normal in classical Latin prose, or by the indicative of the Romance languages and of ecclesiastical Latin. I print the subjunctive in view of Ovid's usual practice, and in particular because of *EP* I ii 5 'forsitan haec a quo *mittatur* epistula quaeras' and *EP* III v 1 'Quam legis unde tibi *mittatur* epistula quaeris?'. But Professor R. J. Tarrant notes that the need for a dependent subjunctive would be more strongly felt with *quaerere* in these two passages than with the *index* of the present passage.

Not all poets were as strict as Ovid in using the subjunctive in indirect questions. Propertius at III v 26-46 has the following verbs in a series of indirect questions: *temperet, uenit, deficit, redit, superant, captet, sit uentura, bibit, tremuere, luxerit* (from *lugere*), *coit, exeat, eat, sint* (uar *sunt*), *furit, custodit, descendit, potest*.

3. COLOR HIC. 'The style of this opening'. Ovid is presumably referring to its playful tone. Compare *Tr* I i 61 (to his poem) 'ut titulo careas, ipso noscere *colore*', at which

Luck cites Martial XII ii 17-18 'quid titulum poscis? uersus duo tresue legantur, / clamabunt omnes te, liber, esse meum'.

Color is not found in precisely this sense until Horace. For a discussion of its development, see Brink at Hor *AP* 86 *operumque colores*.

4. STRVCTVRA. This passage is the first instance cited by *OLD structura* 1b of *structura* in this transferred sense, which becomes common in Silver prose, particularly Quintilian (I x 23, VIII vi 67, IX iv 45). Lewis and Short point out that Cicero uses the word in similar contexts only as a simile: compare *Brut* 33 'ante hunc [*sc* Isocratem] enim uerborum *quasi structura* et quaedam ad numerum conclusio nulla erat', *Or* 149 *'quasi structura quaedam'*, and *Opt Gen* 5 'et uerborum est *structura quaedam'*.

There are two instances in Ovid of *struere* with a similar meaning, both from the *Ex Ponto*. One is from line 20 of this poem (*'structa ...* uerba'), while the other is at II v 19 *'structos* inter fera proelia uersus'.

5. MIRIFICA is a colloquialism. Common in the letters of Cicero, the word (according to *TLL* VIII 1060 52) is not found in Livy, Vitruvius, Celsus, Curtius, or Tacitus. The only poets apart from Terence and Ovid cited as using the word are Accius, Ausonius, and the author of the *Ciris* (although the passage where the word occurs, 12-13, is corrupt); see also Catullus LIII 2, LXXI 4, and LXXXIV 3. For a discussion of *mirificus*, see Axelson 61, and of the similarly colloquial *mirifice* Hofmann 78.

5. PVBLICA = 'usual, ordinary'. Compare *Am* III vii 11-12 'et mihi blanditias dixit dominumque uocauit, / et quae praeterea *publica* uerba iuuant', *AA* III 479-80 'munda, sed e medio consuetaque uerba, puellae, / scribite: sermonis *publica* forma placet', and Sen *Ben* VI 34 3 (quoted at 2 *aue*).

6. QVALIS ENIM CVMQVE EST. A common phrase in the poets when they speak of their own verse: compare Catullus I 8-9 'quare habe tibi quidquid hoc libelli / *qualecumque'*, Hor *Sat* I x 88-89 'quibus [*sc* amicis] haec, sunt *qualiacumque*, / arridere uelim, doliturus, si placent spe / deterius nostra' (at

333

which Bentley cited the present passage), Martial V lx 5 *'qualiscumque* legaris ut per orbem', and Statius *Sil* II praef 'haec *qualiacumque* sunt, Melior carissime, si tibi non displicuerint, a te publicum accipiant; sin minus, ad me reuertantur' (both passages cited by Munro, *Criticisms* 5).

7. VT TITVLVM CHARTAE DE FRONTE REVELLAS. The same hypothetical case at *Tr* I i 61-62 *'ut titulo careas*, ipso noscere *colore*; / dissimulare uelis, te liquet esse meum' and *EP* II ix 49-52 (to King Cotys) 'nec regum quisquam magis est instructus ab illis [*sc* the liberal arts] ... carmina testantur, quae *si tua nomina demas* / Threicium iuuenem composuisse negem'.

7. CHARTAE. See at xii 27 *chartis* (p 380).

7. REVELLAS 'tear away' is surprisingly strong in its overtones. It is found only here in the poems of exile, six times in the other elegies, and fifteen times in the *Metamorphoses*.

8. QVOD SIT OPVS VIDEOR DICERE POSSE TVVM. 'I think I could say which work was yours'. Heinsius' QVID SIT OPVS VIDEAR is a strange error: the interrogative adjective is acceptable enough, while the notion of the subjunctive must of course be contained in *posse*, not in the verb that governs it.

11. PRODENT AVCTOREM VIRES. 'His strength will reveal the poet's identity'. The same sense of *prodere* at *Met* II 433 'impedit amplexu nec se sine crimine *prodit*', *Met* XIV 740-41 'adapertaque ianua factum / *prodidit*', and *Am* I viii 109 'uox erat in cursu, cum me mea *prodidit* umbra'. *Vires* again used of poetic skill at *Tr* I vi 29 'ei mihi non magnas quod habent mea carmina *uires*', *Tr* IV ix 16 'Pierides *uires* et sua tela dabunt', *EP* III iii 34, and *EP* III iv 79.

13. DEPRENSA. *Deprendere* 'recognize, detect' is also found at *Met* II 93-94 'utinamque oculos in pectore posses / inserere et patrias intus *deprendere* curas' and *Met* VII 536-37 'strage canum primo uolucrumque ouiumque boumque / inque feris subiti *deprensa* potentia morbi', as well as at Livy XLII 17 7 (*uenenum*) and Celsus III 18 3 '[phrenetici ...] summam ...

speciem sanitatis in captandis malorum operum occasionibus praebent, sed exitu *deprenduntur*'. This seems to be a semi-medical sense; Professor R. J. Tarrant suggests that *colore* may bear the secondary meaning 'complexion' in this passage.

15. TAM MALA THERSITEN PROHIBEBAT FORMA LATERE. For Thersites' ugliness, see *Il* II 216-19 'αἴσχιστος δὲ ἀνὴρ ὑπὸ Ἴλιον ἦλθε· / φολκὸς ἔην, χωλὸς δ' ἕτερον πόδα· τὼ δέ οἱ ὤμω / κυρτώ, ἐπὶ στῆθος συνοχωκότε· αὐτὰρ ὕπερθε / φοξὸς ἔην κεφαλήν, ψεδνὴ δ' ἐπενήνοθε λάχνη'.

For the modern reader, Thersites' ugliness is hardly his leading characteristic; but at *EP* III ix 9-10 Ovid again refers to his appearance: 'auctor opus laudat: sic forsitan Agrius [his father] olim / Thersiten facie dixerit esse bona'. Other mentions of Thersites' ugliness at Lucian *Dial Mort* XXV (Thersites argues that he is now as handsome as Nireus) and Epictetus *Diss* II 23 32 (Thersites is contrasted with Achilles), to which Professor C. P. Jones adds from Greek epigram *Greek Inscr. Brit. Mus.* IV ii 1114; other citations from late Greek authors at PW V A,2 2457 18-38 & 2464 23-66 and Roscher V 670 23 ff.

16. NIREVS. For the beauty of Nireus, see *Il* II 671-74 'Νιρεὺς αὖ Σύμηθεν ἄγε τρεῖς νῆας ἐΐσας, / Νιρεὺς Ἀγλαΐης υἱὸς Χαρόποιό τ' ἄνακτος, / Νιρεύς, ὃς κάλλιστος ἀνὴρ ὑπὸ Ἴλιον ἦλθε / τῶν ἄλλων Δαναῶν μετ' ἀμύμονα Πηλεΐωνα'. This is the only mention of Nireus in the poem; but Demetrius (*Peri Hermeneias* 62; cited by Cope at Aristotle *Rhet* 1414a) remarks that because of Homer's use of epanaphora (the repetition of Nireus' name) and dialysis (asyndeton) 'σχεδὸν ἅπαξ τοῦ Νιρέως ὀνομασθέντος ἐν τῷ δράματι μεμνήμεθα οὐδὲν ἧττον ἢ τοῦ Ἀχιλλέως καὶ τοῦ Ὀδυσσέως'. Ovid mentions Nireus again at *AA* II 109-12 'sis licet antiquo Nireus adamatus Homero ... ingenii dotes corporis adde bonis'; see also Hor *Epod* XV 22 'forma ... uincas Nirea', Hor *Carm* III xx 15 (where Nireus is paired with Ganymede) and Prop III xviii 27 'Nirea non facies, non uis exemit Achillem'; from Greek epigram Professor C. P. Jones cites Peek *Griech. Versinschr.* 1728 (Merkelbach *ZPE* 25

[1977] 281).

16. CONSPICIENDVS. The word is metrically suited to the second half of the pentameter, before the disyllable: compare Tib I ii 70 & II iii 52, *Fast* V 118 & V 170, and *Tr* II 114.

17. MIRARI SI is a colloquialism: most of the passages from verse cited at *TLL* VIII 1067 14 are from Plautus and the hexameter poems of Horace; from Propertius compare II iii 33 'haec ego nunc *mirer si* flagret nostra iuuentus?' and from Ovid *Her* X 105 'non equidem *miror si* stat uictoria tecum' and *Tr* I ix 21 'saeua neque *admiror* metuunt *si* fulmina'.

19. A PVDET, ET GETICO SCRIPSI SERMONE LIBELLVM. The rest of the distich after *a pudet* explains the exclamation ('I have even written ...'), and so the punctuation should mark the break. The idiom is different from the *et pudet et* construction seen at xv 29 'et pudet et metuo ['I am both embarrassed and afraid'] semperque eademque precari' and *Tr* V vii 57-58 'et pudet et fateor ['I confess with embarrassment'], iam desuetudine longa / uix subeunt ipsi uerba Latina mihi'.

The only other instance of independent *a pudet* in Ovid is *AA* III 803-4 'quid iuuet et uoces et anhelitus arguat oris; / a pudet, arcanas pars habet ista notas', which, however, Professor R. J. Tarrant suspects is part of an interpolation.

19. GETICO ... SERMONE. Ovid repeatedly claims to have learned Getic and Sarmatian: compare *Tr* III xiv 47-48 'Threicio Scythicoque fere circumsonor ore, / et uideor Geticis scribere posse modis', *Tr* V vii 55-56 'ille ego Romanus uates—ignoscite, Musae!— / Sarmatico cogor plurima more loqui', *Tr* V xii 58 'nam didici Getice Sarmaticeque loqui', and *EP* III ii 40 (identical to *Tr* V xii 58).

It is of course not possible to prove that Ovid did or did not learn Getic and write poetry in that language. But in the absence of other evidence, it seems better to suppose that he did learn the language since (a) he claims to have do so, (b) Latin and Greek would hardly have been widely spoken in the region, and (c) a man with Ovid's linguistic facility would have had little difficulty in learning the languages of the region.

20. STRVCTAQVE ... VERBA. Compare Cic *de Or* III 171 'struere uerba', and see at 4 *structura* (p 393).

20. NOSTRIS ... MODIS. Ovid did not use native rhythms, but instead used Latin metres.

21. ET PLACVI. Luck compares *EP* I v 63-64 'forsitan audacter faciam, sed glorior Histrum / ingenio nullum maius habere meo', but it is clear enough from the context that Ovid was there speaking of his Latin poetry.

21. GRATARE. *Gratari* is extremely rare in Latin, being found only in the poets and historians; *grātŭlāri* was of course not available (except for *grātŭlŏr*) for use in dactylic verse. Other instances of the word in Ovid at ix 13 '*gratatusque* darem cum dulcibus oscula uerbis', *Her* VI 119 'nunc etiam peperi; *gratare* ambobus, Iason!', *Her* XI 65, *Met* I 578, VI 434, IX 244 & 312, and *Fast* III 418.

22. INTER INHVMANOS ... GETAS. The same phrase in the same metrical position at *EP* I v 65-66 'hoc ubi uiuendum est satis est si consequor aruo / *inter inhumanos* esse poeta *Getas*' and *EP* III v 27-28 'quem ... fatum ... *inter inhumanos* maluit esse *Getas*'.

23. LAVDES DE CAESARE DIXI. In 1896 J. Gilbert ingeniously proposed the punctuation 'laudes [potential subjunctive]: de Caesare dixi'. But *laus de* + ablative instead of the more usual objective genitive construction is supported by Tac *Ann* I 12 'addidit laudem de Augusto'. Nipperdey there explains *de* by equating *laus* with *oratio* and *sermo*, both of which take *de* as a normal construction; but it appears from the present passage that *laus de* may have been a special term for panegyric. Professor E. Fantham notes that Ovid may have been seeking a synonym for *laudātiō*.

24. ADIVTA EST NOVITAS NVMINE NOSTRA DEI. *Nouitas nostra* could mean either 'my novel attempt' (Wheeler, Lewis and Short) or 'my inexperience'; if the latter, *adiuta* would bear the uncommon but quite valid meaning 'compensated for'; *OLD adiuuo* 7 cites passages from Cicero (*Fam* V xiii 5 'ea quibus secundae res ornantur, aduersae adiuuantur'), Livy, and Ulpian.

25-32. Similar catalogues of the imperial family occur at *Met* XV 834-47, *Tr* II 161-68, *Tr* IV ii 7-12, *EP* II ii 69-74, and *EP* II viii 29-34; these passages are quoted from below.

25-26. NAM PATRIS AVGVSTI DOCVI MORTALE FVISSE / CORPUS, IN AETHERIAS NVMEN ABISSE DOMOS. Other mentions of the deified Augustus at vi 15-16 'coeperat Augustus detectae ignoscere culpae; / spem nostram terras deseruitque simul' and viii 63-64 'et modo, Caesar, auum, quem uirtus addidit astris, / sacrarunt aliqua carmina parte tuum'. Ovid had predicted Augustus' apotheosis: see *Met* XV 838-39 'nec nisi cum senior Pylios aequauerit annos, / aetherias sedes cognataque sidera tanget', *Tr* II 57-58 'optaui peteres caelestia sidera tarde, / parsque fui turbae parua precantis idem', and *Tr* V ii 51-52, V v 61-62, V viii 29-30 & V xi 25-26.

Augustus' apotheosis was similar to those of Hercules, Aeneas, Romulus, and Julius Caesar: compare the descriptions at *Met* IX 262-72 'interea quodcumque fuit populabile flammae / Mulciber abstulerat, nec ... quicquam ab imagine ductum / matris habet, tantumque Iouis uestigia seruat ... maiorque uideri / coepit et *augusta* fieri grauitate uerendus. / quem pater omnipotens inter caua nubila raptum / quadriiugo curru radiantibus intulit astris', *Met* XIV 603-4 'quicquid in Aenea fuerat mortale, repurgat [*sc* Numicius] / et respersit aquis; pars optima restitit illi', *Met* XIV 824-28 'abstulit [*sc* Mars] Iliaden: corpus mortale per auras / dilapsum tenues ... pulchra subit facies et puluinaribus altis / dignior', and *Met* XV 844-46 'Venus ... Caesaris eripuit membris neque in aera solui / passa recentem animam caelestibus intulit astris'.

25. PATRIS AVGVSTI. *Patris* to make it clear that Ovid is not speaking of Tiberius Caesar *Augustus*.

26. CORPVS ... NVMEN. Precisely the same distinction is found in Velleius' description of Augustus' apotheosis and the start of Tiberius' reign: 'post redditum caelo patrem et *corpus* eius humanis honoribus, *numen* diuinis honoratum, primum principalium eius operum fuit ordinatio comitiorum' (II 124 3).

27. PAREM VIRTVTE PATRI. Compare *EP* II viii 31-32 (to Augustus, about Tiberius) 'perque tibi *similem uirtutis imagine* natum, / moribus agnosci qui tuus esse potest'.

27-28. FRENA ... IMPERII. The same metaphor at *Tr* II 41-42 'nec te quisquam moderatius umquam / *imperii* potuit *frena* tenere sui', *EP* II ix 33 'Caesar ut *imperii* moderetur *frena* precamur', and *EP* II v 75 (of Germanicus) 'succedatque suis orbis moderator *habenis*'.

At *Fast* I 531-34 Ovid uses the same metaphor, as here, of Tiberius' accession to power: (Carmenta is prophesying Rome's future) 'et penes Augustos patriae tutela manebit: / hanc fas *imperii frena* tenere domum. / inde nepos natusque dei [Tiberius was the adopted son of Augustus, and therefore the grandson of Julius Caesar], licet ipse *recuset*, / pondera caelesti mente paterna feret'. In all of these passages Ovid may have had in mind *Aen* VII 600 (of Latinus) 'saepsit se tectis *rerumque* reliquit *habenas*'.

27-28. FRENA ... SAEPE RECVSATI ... IMPERII. At *Tr* V iv 15-16 Ovid had used *frena recusare* of a horse: 'fert tamen, ut debet, casus patienter amaros, / more nec indomiti *frena recusat* equi'. This perhaps influenced his choice of words here.

27. COACTVS *excerpta Scaligeri* ROGATVS *codd.* Ovid is referring to the second meeting of the Senate after the death of Augustus (the first meeting had been devoted to funeral arrangements); at this meeting there had been some confusion over Tiberius' intentions. *Rogatus* is awkward to construe, since Tiberius must already have been asked to accept power: otherwise he could not have refused the offer. The difficulty of *rogatus* is clearly shown by the description of the scene in Tacitus: 'et ille [*sc* Tiberius] uarie disserebat de magnitudine imperii sua modestia. solam diui Augusti mentem tantae molis capacem: se in partem curarum ab illo uocatum experiendo didicisse quam arduum, quam subiectum fortunae regendi cuncta onus, proinde in ciuitate tot inlustribus uiris subnixa non ad unum omnia deferrent: plures facilius munia rei publicae sociatis laboribus executuros ... senatu ad infimas obtestationes procumbente, dixit forte Tiberius se ut non toti rei publicae parem, ita quaecumque pars sibi mandaretur eius tutelam suscepturum ... fessus ... clamore omnium, expostulatione singulorum flexit paulatim, non ut fateretur suscipi a se imperium, sed ut negare et *rogari* desineret' (*Ann* I 11-13). Scaliger's conjecture is supported by (and is probably based on) the corresponding description at Suetonius *Tib* 24 'principatum ... diu ... recusauit ... tandem quasi *coactus* et querens miseram et onerosam iniungi sibi seruitutem, recepit imperium'.

Professor A. Dalzell notes, however, that Suetonius' description is an imperfect parallel, since *coactus* is there modified by *quasi*; he suggests to me that *rogatus* could be accepted, if it is taken closely with *recusati*—Tiberius finally accepted what he had many times been offered and had many times refused.

29. VESTAM. Ovid similarly equates Livia with Venus and Juno at *EP* III i 117-18 'quae Veneris formam, mores Iunonis habendo / sola est caelesti digna reperta toro', and implicitly equates her with Juno at *Fast* I 650 'sola toro magni digna reperta Iouis'. These appear to be instances of metaphor rather than true equations; but PW XIII,1 913-14 cites inscriptions indicating a cult of Livia-as-Juno.

29-30. LIVIA ... AMBIGVVM NATO DIGNIOR ANNE VIRO. Tiberius is mentioned by Ovid in connection with Livia at *Fast* I 649, a description of the rededication of the temple of Concordia in AD 10: 'hanc tua constituit genetrix et rebus et ara', but does not figure in Ovid's other mentions of Livia (*Fast* V 157-58, *Tr* II 161-62, *EP* II viii 29-30, and *EP* III i 117-18); these passages would have been written before Tiberius' assumption of power.

For the coupling of both Augustus and Tiberius with Livia, Professor C. P. Jones cites 'ἡ δοίους σκήπτροισι θεοὺς αὐχοῦσα Σεβαστή / Καίσαρας' from an epigram of Ovid's contemporary Honestus.[27]

30. AMBIGVVM. The same use of *ambiguum* (which may be an Ovidian peculiarity) at *Met* I 765-66 'ambiguum Clymene precibus Phaethontis an ira / mota magis' and *Met* XI 235-36 'est specus in medio, natura factus an arte / *ambiguum*, magis arte tamen'.

30. ANNE. The word is found at *Am* III xi 49-50 'quicquid eris, mea semper eris; tu selige tantum, / me quoque uelle uelis, *anne* coactus amem' and *Fast* VI 27-28 (Juno speaking) 'est aliquid nupsisse Ioui, Iouis esse sororem / fratre magis dubito glorier *anne* uiro'; the resemblances between this and the present passage are obvious. Bömer *ad loc* cites instances of *anne* from Plautus (*Amph* 173), Terence (*Eun* 556), Cicero (*Fin* IV 23, *Att* XII xiv 2), and Virgil (*G* I 32 & II 159, *Aen* VI 864).

31. DVOS IVVENES. Germanicus and Drusus. For other mentions of them, see *Tr* II 167 'tui, sidus iuuenale, nepotes', *Tr* IV ii 9 'et qui Caesareo iuuenes sub nomine crescunt', *EP* II ii 71-72 'praeterit ipse suos animo Germanicus annos, / nec uigor est Drusi nobilitate minor', and *EP* II viii 33-34.

31. ADIVMENTA. The word is rare in verse (but see Lucretius VI 1022 and Silius XI 605 & XVI 12), and Ovid here seems to be giving a version of the construction in which people are said to be *adiumento*, as at Cic *Att* XII xxxi 2 'magno etiam adiumento nobis Hermogenes potest esse in repraesentando ['in making cash payment'—Shackleton Bailey]', Varro *LL* V 90, and *Rhet Her* III 29. *TLL* I 704 1 cites "Caecil. *mort.* 18" for 'duo minores, qui sint adiumento', which resembles the present passage, but I do not understand the reference: "Caecil." does not appear in the table of authors.

33. NON PATRIA ... SCRIPTA CAMENA. 'Written in a poem that was not in Latin'. This is the only instance in Ovid of this sense of *Camena*, which seems to have been a Horatian idiom: see *Carm* II xvi 38 'spiritum Graiae tenuem Camenae', *Ep* I i 1-3 'Prima dicte mihi, summa dicende Camena ... Maecenas', and *AP* 275 'tragicae ... Camenae'. Professor R. J. Tarrant cites Martial XII xciv 5 'fila lyrae moui Calabris exculta Camenis', which possibly refers to Horace.

36. MVRMVR. The hum caused by the exchange of approving comments. Compare *Met* XIII 123-24 'finierat Telamone satus, uulgique secutum / ultima *murmur* erat'. Livy (XXXII 22 1) has a *murmur* of mingled praise and dissent following a speech: '*murmur* ortum aliorum cum adsensu, aliorum inclementer adsentientes increpantium'. Other

murmura are disapproving or anxious, as at *Met* I 206, VIII
431 & IX 421, and *Aen* XII 238-39.

The Latin *murmur* could be quite loud: Martial uses the
word of a lion's roar (VIII liii [lv] 1).

40. SEXTA ... BRVMA. The poem must have been written in
the winter of 14.

41. NOCVERVNT. *Nocere* again used of the *Ars Amatoria* at
xiv 20 'telaque adhuc demens quae *nocuere* sequor?' and *Tr* IV
1 35.

42. PRIMAQVE TAM MISERAE CAVSA FVERE FVGAE.
The second cause was of course Ovid's *error* (*EP* III iii 67-72).

43. STVDII COMMVNIA FOEDERA SACRI. Similar
references to shared poetic interests at viii 81 '*communia sacra*
tueri', *EP* II v 60 (to Salanus, a famous orator) 'seruat *studii
foedera* quisque sui', *EP* II ix 63-64 (to Cotys, king of Thrace,
who was a writer of verse) 'haec quoque res aliquid tecum
mihi *foederis* adfert; / eiusdem *sacri* cultor uterque sumus', *EP*
II x 17 'sunt tamen inter se *communia sacra* poetis', and *EP* III
iv 67 'sunt mihi uobiscum *communia sacra*, poetae'.

The *foedera* would carry the obligation of mutual assistance.

44. PER NON VILE TIBI NOMEN AMICITIAE. 'By the
name of friendship which is not cheap in your eyes'
(Wheeler). Professor R. J. Tarrant cites similar invocations at
Tr I viii 15 'illud *amicitiae* sanctum et uenerabile nomen', and
EP II iii 19-20 'illud *amicitiae* quondam uenerabile *nomen* /
prostat', III ii 43 & III ii 100.

44-46. AMICITIAE ... INGENIIS. For Ovid's use of
quadrisyllable endings for pentameters, see at ii 10 *Alcinoo* (p
164).

**45-46. SIC VINCTO LATIIS GERMANICVS HOSTE
CATENIS / MATERIAM VESTRIS ADFERAT INGENIIS.**
Compare *EP* II viii 39-40 'sic fera quam primum pauido
Germania uultu / ante triumphantes serua feratur equos'.
Germanicus celebrated his triumph in 17: see Tac *Ann* II 41.

Vestris is a true plural referring to Carus and other poets who might be inspired by Germanicus' exploits. For this use of *uester* to address one member of a collectivity, see Austin on *Aen* I 140 and Fordyce on Catullus XXIX 20.

45. VINCTO is my restoration for the manuscripts' CAPTO, which I am unable to construe with *catenis*. *Vincto* was first corrupted to *uicto*, which was then displaced by the gloss *capto*. For the picture compare *AA* I 215 'ibunt ante duces onerati colla catenis'; for *uincto* compare Livy VII 27 8 'eos *uinctos* consul ante currum triumphans egit', and for *uincto* ... *catenis* compare Caesar *BG* I 53 'trinis catenis uinctus'.

47. PVERI. The sons of Germanicus: Nero, Drusus III, and Gaius Caligula.

47. VOTVM COMMVNE DEORVM. Wheeler translates 'the source of universal prayers to the gods'. But it seems difficult to take *uotum* in this sense, and impossible to construe *deorum*. André translates 'c'est le voeu de tous les dieux', but it seems strange to have gods forming a *uotum*. Postgate placed a comma before *deorum*; but Germanicus and Agrippina were not gods. Heinsius conjectured SVORVM, but this seems rather forced. I suspect that *deorum* is correct, the sense of the passage being close to that of *Fast* II 63-64 'templorum positor, templorum sancte repostor, / sit superis opto mutua cura tui'; but what originally stood in place of *uotum* is not clear.

48. QVOS LAVS FORMANDOS EST TIBI MAGNA DATOS. 'Whose entrustment to you for education is an immense honour'. For the construction Ehwald (*KB* 68) cites *Aen* IX 92 (Cybebe asks that Aeneas' ships be rescued from fire) 'prosit nostris in montibus ortas', 'let it profit them that it was in my mountains that they had their origin' (Jackson Knight).

49. MOMENTA. 'Influence'. Compare Caesar *BC* III 70 2 'ita paruae res magnum in utramque partem *momentum* habuerunt', Livy I 47 6, Hor *Ep* I x 15-16 'ubi gratior aura / leniat et rabiem Canis et *momenta* Leonis', and Manilius II 901 (of the fifth temple) 'hic *momenta* manent nostrae plerumque salutis'.

49. MOMENTA *Vaticanus 1595 (saec xv), sicut coni Scaliger et Gronouius* MONIMENTA *BCMFHILT*. Similarly, most manuscripts have *monimenta* at *Met* XI 285-86 (Ceyx to Peleus) 'adicis huic animo ['my kindly nature'] *momenta* potentia, clarum / nomen auumque Iouem'.

49-50. SALVTI, / QVAE NISI MVTATO NVLLA FVTVRA LOCO EST. A similar qualification of *salus* at *Met* IX 530-31 'quam nisi tu dederis non est habitura salutem / hanc tibi mittit amans'; Bömer *ad loc* cites other word-plays with *salus* at *Her* IV 1, XVI 1 & XVIII 1, and at *Tr* III iii 87-88.

50. MVTATO ... LOCO. See at viii 86 *qui minus ... distet* (p 284).

XIV. To Tuticanus

In his first poem to Tuticanus, Ovid had promised that other poems would follow: 'teque canam quacumque nota, *tibi carmina mittam*' (xii 19). The present poem was written quite shortly after xii, perhaps in AD 16: 'Haec tibi mittuntur quem sum *modo* carmine questus / non aptum numeris nomen habere meis'.

The opening distich indicates that the poem is addressed to Tuticanus. The dedication is a perfunctory one, however, since he is not referred to at any other point of the letter: Ovid perhaps felt that he had fulfilled any obligations he had to Tuticanus with the highly personal earlier poem.

In 3-14 Ovid expresses at length his wish to be sent anywhere, even the Syrtes, Charybdis, or the Styx, as long as he can escape Tomis. Such complaints as these have caused the Tomitans to be angry with him (15-22). But he has been misunderstood: he was complaining not of the people but of the land. Hesiod criticized Ascra, Ulysses Ithaca, and Metrodorus Rome, all with impunity, but Ovid's verse has once more caused him trouble (23-44). The Tomitans have been as kind to him as the Paeligni would have been: they have even granted him immunity from taxation, and publicly crowned him (45-56). After this lengthy account of the Tomitans, he moves to an unexpectedly quick summing-up: Tomis is as dear to him as Delos is to Latona (57-60). This conclusion is immediately undercut by the final distich: his only wish is that Tomis were not subject to attack, and that it had a better climate. This type of undercutting is paralleled elsewhere in Ovid's verse: I discuss these passages at 61-62.

At ix 97-104 Ovid had mentioned the Tomitans' sympathy for him; but the present poem is unique for the praise Ovid bestows on them, and furnishes a striking contrast to the horrific picture of Tomis in, for instance, *Tr* V x. A primary purpose of Ovid's poetry from exile was to secure recall, and so he no doubt intentionally emphasized his hardships; it is clear enough from this poem that at the same time he was in fact reaching an accommodation with his new conditions of life.

3. VTCVMQVE. 'Somehow (in spite of my hardships)'. The word is used by Ovid only in the poetry of exile, and only in this sense: compare *Ibis* 9-10 'quisquis is est (nam nomen adhuc *utcumque* tacebo), / cogit inassuetas sumere tela manus' and *EP* III ix 53 'postmodo collectas [*sc* litteras] utcumque sine ordine iunxi'. This is a prose sense of *utcumque*, common in Livy; when the word is used in verse, it generally means 'whenever' (Hor *Epod* XVII 52, *Carm* I xvii 10, I xxxv 23, II xvii 11, III iv 29 & IV iv 35) or 'however' (*Aen* VI 822; the only instance of the word in Virgil).

4. TE *Berolinensis Diez. B. Sant. 1, saec xiii Bodleianus Rawlinson G 105^{ul}* ME *BCMFHILT. Me* seems unlikely to be right, for the phrase 'nil me praeterea quod iuuet inuenies' would not only be awkward in itself, but would also be in apparent contradiction with the following 'ipsa quoque est inuisa salus', where *salus* refers back to *utcumque ualemus*.

4. INVENIES. See at ii 10 *Alcinoo* (p 164).

5. VLTIMA VOTA. 'My utmost wish'. For this sense of *ultimus* compare Cic *Fin* III 30 'summum bonum, quod *ultimum* appello', Livy XXVII 10 11 'aurum ... quod ... ad *ultimos* casus ['the greatest emergencies'] seruabatur promi placuit', Hor *Carm* II vii 1-2 'O saepe mecum tempus in *ultimum* / deducte Bruto militiae duce' (*tempus* has the same meaning as *casus* in the passage from Livy), and Petronius 24 'non tenui ego diutius lacrimas ... ad *ultimam* perductus tristitiam'.

6. SCILICET seems difficult to explain in this context, and the translators ignore its presence. ILICET ('at once') should possibly be read: the corruption of the rarer word to the more common would be easy enough in view of the final *s* of the preceding *istis*.

7. MVTER *F^1 Bodleianus Canon. lat. 1, saec xiii Barberinus lat. 26, saec xiii. Muter* is so much choicer than the better attested

347

mittar that I have followed editors from Ciofanus to Merkel in printing it. Gronovius (*Obseruationes* III 1) made a strong case for *muter*, citing Virgil *G* II 50 (where however the meaning of *mutata* is disputed), Hor *Sat* II vii 63-64 'illa tamen se / non habitu *mutatue* loco peccatue superne', Claudian *Rap Pros* I 62 'rursus corporeos animae *mutantur* in artus' (where *mittuntur* is a variant reading, which Hall prints), and from Ovid *Tr* V ii 73-74 'hinc ego dum *muter*, uel me Zanclaea [*Politianus*: Panchea *codd*] Charybdis / deuoret aque [*Heinsius*: atque *codd*] suis ad Styga mittat aquis', and *EP* I i 79 'inque locum Scythico uacuum *mutabor* ab arcu'; compare as well Cic *Balb* 31 'ne quis inuitus ciuitate *mutetur*' and Livy V 46 11 'quod nec iniussu populi *mutari* finibus posset'.

11. SI QVID EA EST. See at i 17 *si quid ea est* (p 153).

11. BENE. 'Profitably'. Compare Tac *Ann* III 44 'miseram pacem uel bello *bene mutari*'. The word in this sense is generally used in describing good commercial investments: see Plautus *Cur* 679-80 'argentariis *male credi* qui aiunt, nugas praedicant, / nam et *bene* et male *credi* dico', Sen *Suas* VII v 'si *bene* illi pecunias *crediderunt* faeneratores', Cic *II Verr* V 56 'ut intellegerent Mamertini *bene* se apud istum tam multa pretia ac munera *conlocasse*', and Livy II 42 8.

11. COMMVTABITVR. *Commutare* was a commercial term: it is used of selling at Cic *Clu* 129 'ad perniciem innocentis fidem suam et religionem pecunia *commutarit*', Columella XII 26 2 'reliquum mustum ... aere *commutato*', *Dig* II xv 8 24 'si uinum pro oleo uel oleum pro uino uel quid aliud *commutauit*', and *CIL* I 585 27.

12. SI QVID ET INFERIVS QVAM STYGA MVNDVS HABET. Professor R. J. Tarrant notes another instance of the same idea at Sen *Thy* 1013-14 'si quid infra Tartara est / auosque nostros'.

13. GRAMINA. 'Weeds'. Compare *Met* V 485-86 'lolium tribulique fatigant / triticeas messes et inexpugnabile *gramen*' and *Tr* V xii 24 'nil nisi cum spinis *gramen* habebit ager'; *TLL* VI.2 2165 65 notes as well Columella IV 4 5 'omnesque herbas et praecipue *gramina* extirpare, quae nisi manu eleguntur ... reuiuiscunt'.

CARMINA, the reading of *C*, is a frequent corruption of *gramina*, occurring as a variant at *Met* II 841 & XIV 44 and *Fast* VI 749; it gives no obvious sense in this passage. Bentley's FLAMINA is ingenious but unattractive.

14. MARTICOLIS is possibly an Ovidian innovation, being found elsewhere only at *Tr* V iii 21-22 'adusque niuosum / Strymona uenisti Marticolamque Geten'.

14. NASO. The use of the third person adds to the emotive power of the tricolon 'ager ... hirundo ... Naso'.

15-16. TALIA SVSCENSENT PROPTER MIHI VERBA TOMITAE, / IRAQVE CARMINIBVS PVBLICA MOTA MEIS. For the similar omission of the *est* of a perfect passive, even in the presence of a parallel finite verb, see *Met* VII 517-18 'Aeacus ingemuit tristique ita uoce *locutus*: / "flebile principium melior fortuna secuta est"'.

15. SVSCENSENT. The word is foreign to high poetry. It occurs in Ovid only here and at *EP* III i 89-90 'nec mihi *suscense*, totiens si carmine nostro / quod facis ut facias teque imitere rogo'; the only instances from other poetry cited at *OLD suscenseo* are from *Her* XVI-XXI and Martial.

SVSCENSENT is the spelling of *C*; the other manuscripts have SVCCENSENT. I print *susc-* because that is the spelling given by the ninth-century Hamburg manuscript at *EP* III i 89 (cited above), where most manuscripts offer *succ-*. *Succ-* is, however, quite possibly correct, for although *susc-* is the spelling of the ancient manuscripts of Plautus and Terence (and of the older manuscripts of the *Heroides*), *succ-* is found at Livy XLII 46 8 in the fifth-century Vienna codex.

18. PLECTAR. Similar uses at *Tr* III v 49 'inscia quod crimen uiderunt lumina, *plector*' and *EP* III iii 64 (Ovid to Amor) 'meque loco *plecti* commodiore uelit'.

18. AB INGENIO is parallel to *per carmina* in the preceding line; for the idiom, see at x 46 *ab amne* (p 346).

20. TELAQVE ... QVAE NOCVERE SEQVOR. See at xiii 41

nocuerunt (p 406).

23. SED NIHIL ADMISI. 'But I have committed no crime'—
Wheeler. Compare *EP* III vi 13 'nec scelus *admittas* si
consoleris amicum'. *Admittere* in this sense belonged to daily
speech: *TLL* I 752 77 cites Plaut *Trin* 81, Ter *HT* 956 'quid ego
tantum sceleris *admisi* miser', Lucilius 690 Marx, and Hor *Ep*
I xvi 53.

25. EXCVTIAT. See at viii 17 *excutias* (p 263).

25. NOSTRI MONIMENTA LABORIS is rather grand,
perhaps because Ovid intended the poem to come near the
end of the collection. At *Tr* III iii 78 Ovid's *libelli* are called his
most lasting *monimenta*, and at *EP* III v 35 Ovid flatteringly
refers to Maximus Cotta's *monimenta laboris*.

26. LITTERA DE VOBIS EST MEA QVESTA NIHIL. This,
of course, is manifestly untrue. See *Tr* V x entire, and
compare for instance *Tr* V vii 45-46 'siue homines [*sc* specto],
uix sunt homines hoc nomine digni, / quamque lupi saeuae
plus feritatis habent'.

28. ET QVOD PVLSETVR MVRVS AB HOSTE QVEROR.
Compare *EP* III i 25 'adde metus *et quod murus pulsatur ab
hoste*'.

30. SOLVM *BCFILT* LOCVM *MH*. The interchange is very
common (examples at *Met* I 345 & VII 57); the reverse
corruption in some manuscripts at *EP* II ii 96 'sit tua
mutando gratia blanda *loco*'.

31-40. The argument Ovid here employs ("other have done
what I have done, and not suffered for it") is that used at *Tr*
II 361-538 to excuse the *Ars Amatoria*.

31-40. VITABILIS. A. G. Lee has ingeniously conjectured
VITIABILIS (*PCPhS* 181 [1950-51] 3). It would have the
sense *uitiosa*; Lee compares such words as *aerumnabilis*,
perniciabilis, and *lacrimabilis*. He argued that Hesiod nowhere
said that Ascra was 'always to be avoided' (although this is
a natural inference from *Op* 639-40) and that the variants
miserabilis, *mirabilis*, and *mutabilis* 'point to the conclusion
that the archetype was here difficult to make out'. For *uitium*

used of localities he cited *EP* III ix 37 'quid nisi de *uitio* scribam regionis amarae', and for the word *uitiabilis* (in the sense 'corruptible') Prudentius *Apoth* 1045 and *Ham* 215 (there is a variant *uitabilis* in a ninth-century manuscript of the *Hamartigenia*).

Lee's argument is a good one, but *uitabilis* does not seem in itself objectionable enough to be removed from the text. The variant readings he cites are from unnamed manuscripts of Burman, and are not safe evidence for the condition of the archetype. It can be said in Lee's favour that Heinsius and Bentley before him clearly found *uitabilis* somewhat strange: Heinsius considered the verse suspect, while Bentley conjectured VT ILLAVDABILIS.

31. ASCRA *MFILT.* I take ASCRE (*BCH*) to be a hypercorrect formation by the scribes; *Ascra* is metrically guaranteed at 34 'Ascra suo' and *AA* I 28 'Ascra tuis'. It is possible that *Ascre* is correct, although its use would be strange so close to *Ascra* in 34: Ovid certainly used both *nympha* and *nymphe* (*Her* IX 103; *Met* III 357).

32. AGRICOLAE ... SENIS. For Hesiod as an old man compare *AA* II 3-4 'laetus amans donat uiridi mea carmina palma, / praelata Ascraeo Maeonioque *seni*', Prop II xxxiv 77 'tu canis Ascraei *ueteris* praecepta poetae', and *Ecl* VI 69-70 'hos tibi dant calamos, en accipe, Musae, / Ascraeo quos ante *seni*'.

35. SOLLERTE ... VLIXE. *Sollerte* could represent either πολυμήχανος (*Il* II 173) or πολύτροπος (*Od* I 1). I believe that Ovid was translating πολύτροπος, since Livius Andronicus in translating *Od* I 1 had used *uersutus* to represent the adjective: 'Virum mihi, Camena, insece *uersutum*'. It is clear from Cic *Brut* 236 'genus ... acuminis ... quod erat in reprehendendis uerbis *uersutum et sollers*' that the Romans regarded the two adjectives as having much the same force.

At Hor *Sat* II v 3-5 πολυμήχανος is translated by *dolosus*: (Tiresias to Ulysses) 'iamne doloso / non satis est Ithacam reuehi patriosque penates / aspicere?'.

36. HOC TAMEN ASPERITAS INDICE DOCTA LOCI EST.
At *Od* IX 27 Ulysses describes Ithaca to Alcinous as 'τρηχεῖ'
[=*aspera*] ἀλλ' ἀγαθὴ κουροτρόφος'.

36. DOCTA (*B*; *C* has DOCTVS) seems clearly preferable to
DICTA, offered by most of the manuscripts, which cannot
be construed with *hoc ... indice*. The difficulty with *docta* is
that the passive of *docere* seems in general to have been used
of the person taught, not the thing; this is no doubt what
induced Riese to print NOTA, found in certain of Heinsius'
manuscripts. Still, the construction seems logical enough in
view of the double accusative construction of the verb in the
active.

38. SCEPSIVS. Metrodorus[28] of Scepsis (a town on the
Scamander, about 60 kilometres upstream from Troy) was
famous for his hatred of Rome; see Pliny *NH* XXXIV 34
'signa quoque Tuscanica per terras dispersa quin [*Detlefsen*:
quae *codd*] in Etruria factitata sint non est dubium. deorum
tantum putarem ea fuisse, ni Metrodorus Scepsius, cui
cognomen [Professor R. J. Tarrant suggests that
'Μισορωμαῖος' has fallen out of the text around this point] a
Romani nominis odio inditum est, propter MM statuarum
Volsinios expugnatos obiceret'. According to Plutarch
(*Lucullus* 22) and Strabo (*Geog* XIII 1 55), he was a close
confidant of Mithridates; apparently, when on a mission to
Tigranes, he privately advised him not to give Mithridates
the requested assistance against Rome. Tigranes reported
this to Mithridates; Metrodorus was either executed by
Mithridates, or died of natural causes while being sent back
to him. Cicero mentions Metrodorus and his phenomenal
memory at *de Or* II 360.

The present passage is more specific than any other
surviving reference to Metrodorus' anti-Roman sentiments;
Ovid had perhaps read the *scripta* in question.

As both Cicero and Pliny use the epithet 'Scepsius', Ovid's
reference would have been immediately understood:
Mētrŏdōrus could not be used in elegiac verse.

38. ACTAQVE ROMA REA EST. Similar verse-endings at
RA 387-88 'si mea materiae respondet Musa iocosae, /

uicimus, et falsi criminis *acta rea est'*, *Fast* IV 307-8 'casta quidem, sed non et credita: rumor iniquus / laeserat, et falsi criminis *acta rea est'*, and *Tr* IV i 26 'cum mecum iuncti criminis acta [*sc* Musa] rea est'; other instances of *reus agi* at *Her* XIV 120, *Met* XV 36, *Tr* I i 24, *Tr* I viii 46, and *Her* XX 91. See at xv 12 *nil opus est legum uiribus, ipse loquor* (p 434) for a full discussion of Ovid's use of legal terminology.

39. FALSA ... CONVICIA has a place in the rhetoric of Ovid's argument, balancing *uerissima crimina* at 29.

40. OBFVIT AVCTORI NEC FERA LINGVA SVO. *Obesse* is used of Ovid's own situation at *Tr* I i 55-56 'carmina nunc si non studiumque quod *obfuit* odi, / sit satis', IV i 25 'scilicet hoc ipso nunc aequa [*sc* Musa], quod *obfuit* ante', IV iv 39 'aut timor aut error nobis, prius *obfuit* error' & V i 65-68. Compare as well *Tr* II 443-44 'uertit Aristiden Sisenna, nec *obfuit* illi / historiae turpis inseruisse iocos'.

41. MALVS = *malignus*.

41. INTERPRES. The word probably combines the senses of 'translator' and 'interpreter'; that is, the person intentionally misconstrued the meaning of certain passages.

As André points out, Ovid's statement here that his Latin poems have caused him difficulty in Tomis indicates that Latin was not as completely unknown in the city as Ovid claims at, for example, *Tr* III xiv 47-48, V vii 53-54 'unus in hoc nemo est populo qui forte Latine / quamlibet [*Heinsius*: quaelibet *codd*] e medio reddere uerba queat' & V xii 53-54 'non liber hic ullus, non qui mihi commodet aurem, / uerbaque significent quid mea norit, adest'; compare as well *Tr* III xiv 39-40.

42. INQVE NOVVM CRIMEN CARMINA NOSTRA VOCAT. *In crimen uocare* was a normal idiom: compare Cic *Scaur* (e) 'custos ille rei publicae proditionis est *in crimen uocatus'* and *Fam* V xvii 2 'ego te, P. Sitti, et primis temporibus illis quibus in inuidiam absens et *in crimen uocabare* defendi'.

42. NOVVM CRIMEN. The *uetus crimen* was of course the accusation that the *Ars Amatoria* was immoral. Professor E.

Fantham suggests to me that *nouum* could have the meaning 'unprecedented', as at Cic *Lig* 1 '*Nouum crimen*, C. Caesar, et ante hunc diem non auditum propinquus meus ad te Q. Tubero detulit'. Ovid would therefore be saying that the kind of geographical *maiestas* the Tomitans were accusing him of did not constitute a proper charge.

43. PECTORE CANDIDVS. 'Kind of heart'. This sense of *candidus* is constantly misunderstood by modern commentators. The basic transferred sense of the word is 'kind' or 'generous towards others'. This can be clearly seen in such passages as *Tr* III vi 5-8 'isque erat usque adeo populo testatus, ut esset / paene magis quam tu quamque ego notus, amor; / quique est in caris animi [*codd*: animo *fort legendum*] tibi *candor* amicis— / cognita sunt ipsi quem colis ipse uiro', *Tr* IV x 130-32 'protinus ut moriar non ero, terra, tuus. / siue fauore tuli siue hanc ego carmine famam, / iure tibi grates, *candide* lector, ago', *Tr* V iii 53-54 'si uestrum merui *candore* fauorem, / nullaque iudicio littera laesa meo est', *EP* II v 5, *EP* III ii 21-22 'aut meus excusat caros ita *candor* amicos, / utque habeant de me crimina nulla fauet', and *EP* III iv 13 'uiribus infirmi uestro *candore* ualemus'.

For *pectore candidus* compare from other authors Hor *Epod* XI 11-12 'candidum / pauperis ingenium', Val Max VIII xiv praef 'candidis ... animis' and Scribonius Largus praef 5 26 'candidissimo animo'.

44. EXTAT ADHVC NEMO SAVCIVS ORE MEO. Ovid makes similar claims at *Tr* II 563-65 'non ego mordaci destrinxi carmine quemquam ... *candidus* a salibus suffusis felle refugi' and *Ibis* 1-8 'Tempus ad hoc, lustris bis iam mihi quinque peractis, / omne fuit Musae carmen inerme meae ... nec quemquam nostri nisi me laesere libelli ... unus ... perennem / *candoris* titulum non sinit esse mei'. André says of the present passage, 'C'est oublier le poème *Contre Ibis*', but Housman wrote 'Who was Ibis? Nobody. He was much too good to be true. If one's enemies are of flesh and blood, they do not carry complaisance so far as to chose the dies Alliensis for their birthday and the most ineligible spot in Africa for their birthplace. Such order and harmony exist only in worlds of our own creation, not in the jerry-built edifice of the demiurge ... And when I say that Ibis was nobody, I am repeating Ovid's own words. In the last book that he wrote, several years after the Ibis, he said, ex Pont. IV 14 44, "extat adhuc nemo saucius ore meo'" (1040). Housman is wrong to adduce this line as though it were a statement made under oath (compare the claim made in 26 'littera de uobis est mea questa nihil'). It is nonetheless true that in the extant poems of reproach Ovid does not identify the person he is addressing.

45. ADDE QVOD. See at xi 21 *adde quod* (p 368).

45. ILLYRICA ... PICE NIGRIOR. For the formula, Otto (*pix*) cites this passage and *Il* IV 275-77 'νέφος ... μελάντερον ἠύτε πίσσα' and from Latin poetry *AA* II 657-58 'nominibus mollire licet mala: fusca uocetur / *nigrior Illyrica* cui *pice* sanguis erit', *Met* XII 402-3 'totus *pice nigrior* atra, / candida cauda tamen', *EP* III iii 97 'sed neque mutatur [*uar* fuscatur] *nigra pice* lacteus umor', *Her* XVIII 7 'ipsa uides caelum *pice nigrius*', and Martial I cxv 4-5 'sed quandam uolo nocte *nigriorem*, / formica, *pice*, graculo, cicada'.

45. ILLYRICA ... PICE. A famous mineral pitch was produced near Apollonia; André cites Pliny *NH* XVI 59 'Theopompus scripsit in Apolloniatarum agro picem fossilem non deteriorem Macedonica inueniri', *NH* XXXV 178, and Dioscorides I 73.

45. NIGRIOR. The man who was *niger* had qualities opposite to those of the man who was *candidus*; that is, he habitually thought and spoke evil of others. This is illustrated by Hor *Sat* I iv 81-85 'absentem qui rodit amicum, / qui non defendit alio culpante, solutos / qui captat risus hominum famamque dicacis, / fingere qui non uisa potest, commissa tacere / qui nequit—hic *niger* est, hunc tu, Romane, caueto'. The same sense is seen at *Sat* I iv 91 & 100, and at Cic *Caec* 28 'argentarius Sex. Clodius cui cognomen est Phormio, nec minus *niger* nec minus confidens quam ille Terentianus est Phormio'. A similar sense of *ater* is seen at Hor *Epod* VI 15-16 'an si quis *atro* dente me petiuerit, / inultus ut flebo puer'; Lindsay Watson *ad loc* (in an unpublished University of Toronto dissertation) cites Hor *Ep* I xix 30 'nec socerum quaerit quem uersibus oblinat *atris*' for the same meaning.

A specific connection is often made between blackness and envy: compare *Met* II 760 (the home of *Inuidia* is *nigro squalentia tabo*) and Statius *Sil* IV viii 16-17 (*atra Inuidia*).

Catullus XCIII 2 'nec scire utrum sis albus an *ater* homo' and similar passages at Cic *Phil* II 41 and Apuleius *Apol* 16 are examples of an unrelated idiom meaning 'I know absolutely nothing about you'.

46. MORDENDA. For biting as an image of malice, Watson at Hor *Epod* VI 15 'atro dente' cites Cic *Balb* 57 'in conuiuiis rodunt, in circulis uellicant; non illo inimico, sed hoc malo dente carpunt', and Val Max IV 7 ext 2 'malignitatis dentes'; Professor R. J. Tarrant cites Hor *Sat* II i 77 and Martial V xxviii 7 'robiginosis cuncta dentibus rodit'. The image is of course used at times specifically of jealousy; Watson cites *Tr* IV x 123-24 'nec, qui detrectat praesentia Liuor iniquo / ullum de nostris dente momordit opus' and *EP* III iv 73-74 'scripta placent a morte fere, quia laedere uiuos / liuor et iniusto carpere dente solet', and Professor Tarrant cites Hor *Carm* IV iii 16 'et iam dente minus mordeor inuido' and Pindar *P* II 52-53 'ἐμὲ δὲ χρεὼν / φεύγειν δάκος ἀδινὸν κακαγοριᾶν'.

47. MEA SORS = *ego sortem grauem passus.*

48. GRAIOS. The more poetic *Graius* is more than four times as common in Ovid as *Graecus*, which, apart from *Her* III 2, is only found in the *Fasti* (I 330, IV 63 & V 196) and the *Tristia* (III xii 41, V ii 68 & V vii 11).

49. GENS MEA PAELIGNI REGIOQVE DOMESTICA SVLMO. This line is a type of hendiadys, the first half of the line being redefined by the second. The other cities of the Paeligni were Corfinium and Superaequum.

51-52. INCOLVMI ... SALVOQVE. The two words, equivalent in meaning, were used together as a common Latin phrase; see Caesar *BC* I 72 3 'mouebatur etiam misericordia ciuium ... quibus *saluis atque incolumibus* rem obtinere malebat' & II 32 12 '*saluum atque incolumem* exercitum', Cic *Fin* IV 19, *Diuin in Q Caec* 72, *Inuen* II 169, and

356

Livy XXIII 42 4 '*saluo atque incolumi* amico', XXIX 27 3 & XLI 28 9.

53. IMMVNIS is also used without a qualifying word or phrase at Plautus *Tr* 354, Sall *Iug* 89 4 'eius [*sc* oppidi] apud Iugurtham immunes', Cic *Off* III 49 'piratas *immunes*, socios uectigales habemus', Cic *Font* 17, Livy XXXIV 57 10 'urbes ... liberas et *immunes*' & XXXVII 55 7, and *CIL* XIV 4012 4. For a recent discussion of *immunitas*, see V. Nutton, "Two Notes on Immunitas: *Digest* 27,1,6,10 and 11", *JRS* 1971, 52-63.

54. EXCEPTIS SI QVI MVNERA LEGIS HABENT. The phrase is difficult. Perhaps legal magistrates enjoyed immunity from taxation; if this is what Ovid is saying, *munera legis* is related to such expressions as *consulatus munus* (Cic *Pis* 23) and *legationis munus* (*Phil* IX 3). *Munus* by itself of magistrates' duties is quite common.

Professor E. Fantham suggests to me, however, that *munera legis* is a reference to civic duties, or liturgies, that Greek cities imposed on certain of their citizens, and Ovid may be saying that citizens performing such liturgies at Tomis procured exemption from regular taxation.

Wheeler translates 'those only excepted who have the boon by law'. This seems difficult; but Professor A. Dalzell notes that the strangeness of the phrasing may be the results of Ovid's striving for a play on *munera/immunis*.

55. CORONA. Professor C. P. Jones notes that the *corona* indicates that Ovid was probably invested with a local priesthood.

57-58. DELIA TELLVS, / ERRANTI TVTVM QVAE DEDIT VNA LOCVM. Accounts of this at *Met* VI 186-91 (Niobe speaking) 'Latonam ... cui maxima quondam / exiguam sedem pariturae terra negauit! / nec caelo nec humo nec aquis dea uestra recepta est: / exul erat mundo, donec miserata uagantem / "hospita tu terris erras, ego" dixit "in undis" / instabilemque locum Delos dedit' and in the passages cited by Williams at *Aen* III 76 and Tarrant at Sen *Ag* 384f.

61-62. DI MODO FECISSENT PLACIDAE SPEM POSSET

HABERE / PACIS, ET A GELIDO LONGIVS AXE FORET.
In this final distich Ovid unexpectedly reverts from his
gratitude to the Tomitans to the subject of the first part of
the poem, the inhospitality of the region.

This passage provides an example of the technique pointed
out in the *Amores* by Douglass Parker ("The Ovidian Coda",
Arion 8 [1969]) whereby Ovid unexpectedly modifies a poem's
tone in the concluding distich. In *Am* I x Ovid rails against
his girl because she has asked him for a present: 'nec dare,
sed pretium posci dedignor et odi; / quod nego poscenti,
desine uelle, dabo!' (63-64). In *Am* II xiv Ovid scolds his girl
for having an abortion: 'di faciles, peccasse semel concedite
tuto, / et satis est; poenam culpa secunda ferat!' (43-44). In II
xv, Ovid imagines that he becomes the ring he is giving his
girl: 'inrita quid uoueo? paruum proficiscere munus; / illa
data tecum sentiat esse fide!' (27-28). *Am* I vii, I xiii, I xiv,
and II xiii are other examples of the device.

62. A GELIDO ... AXE. Compare XV 36 'dura iubet *gelido*
Parca *sub axe* mori' and *Her* VI 105-6 (Hypsipyle to Jason)
'non probat Alcimede mater tua—consule matrem— / non
pater, *a gelido* cui uenit *axe* nurus'.

XV. To Sextus Pompeius

The poem, the fourth and last in the book to be addressed to Pompeius, is an elaborate appeal to him to continue his assistance.

It starts with the assertion that Pompeius, after the Caesars, is principally responsible for Ovid's well-being (1-4). The favours Pompeius has done for Ovid are innumerable and extend throughout his life (5-10). Ovid will of his own volition declare that he is as much Pompeius' property as Pompeius' estates in Sicily and Macedonia, his house in Rome, or his country retreat in Campania; because of Ovid, Pompeius now has property in the Pontus (11-20). Ovid asks him to continue working on his behalf (21-24). He knows that he does not have to urge Pompeius, but he cannot help himself (27-34). No matter whether he is recalled or not, he will always remember Pompeius; all lands will hear that it is he who saved Ovid, and that Ovid belongs to him (35-42).

The poem effectively combines a number of commonplaces of the works of exile, subordinating them to the central theme of Ovid's indebtedness to Pompeius. The topic of Ovid as Pompeius' property is to a certain extent foreshadowed in *EP* I vii, throughout which Ovid refers to himself as a client of Messalinus' family: 'ecquis in extremo positus iacet orbe tuorum, / me tamen excepto, qui precor esse tuus?' (5-6); it is found explicitly at i 35-36 'sic ego sum rerum non ultima, Sexte, tuarum / tutelaeque feror munus opusque tuae'. Syme (*HO* 156) believes that the addressing of the first and penultimate letters to Pompeius constitutes a dedication of the book to Pompeius. However, as Syme recognizes, the abnormal length of the book indicates that it may be a posthumous collection (see page 4 of the introduction); if so, the arrangement of the poems is presumably by Ovid's literary executor.

The poem is remarkable for the cluster of legal terms at 11-

12. The passage is evidence for Ovid's expertise and interest in law. For other indications of this in his works, see at 12 (p 434).

1. SI QVIS ... EXTAT. Pompeius is kept in the third person through line 10; Ovid thereby indicates that he is making a public declaration.

1. EXTAT. As Riese pointed out, the choice in 1-2 is between *extat ... requirit* and *extet ... requirat*; the problem is that the manuscripts give *extat ... requirat, requirit* being found only in a few manuscripts of Heinsius, while *extet* is a conjecture of Guethling. Owen (1894) thought that the ending of *extat* caused *requirit* to be corrupted to *requirat*; on the other hand, the alteration of *extet* to *extat* would be all but automatic. There is a similar difficulty at *Tr* I i 17-18 'si quis ut in populo nostri non immemor illi [=*illic*], / si quis qui quid agam forte *requirat* erit', where most manuscripts have *requiret*. Both passages seem to involve the assimilation of *requirere* to the mood of the verb immediately following. I print *extat ... requirit* in consideration of *Tr* III x 1-2 'Si quis adhuc istic *meminit* Nasonis adempti, / et *superest* sine me nomen in urbe meum' (cited by Lenz), *Tr* III v 23-24 'si tamen interea quid in his ego perditus oris— / quod te credibile est quaerere—*quaeris*, agam' and *Tr* V vii 5 'scilicet ut semper quid agam, carissime, *quaeris*'.

3. CAESARIBVS = *Augusto et Tiberio*. Augustus is similarly given primary credit for Ovid's survival at v 31-32 'uiuit adhuc uitamque tibi debere fatetur, / quam prius a miti Caesare [=*Augusto*] munus habet'.

4. A SVPERIS ... PRIMVS. The same idiomatic use of *ab* 'after' at v 25-26 'tempus ab his uacuum Caesar Germanicus omne / auferet; *a magnis* hunc colit ille *deis*' and *Fast* III 93-94 (of the month of March) 'quintum Laurentes, bis quintum Aequiculus acer, / *a tribus* hunc *primum* turba Curensis habet'.

5. TEMPORA ... OMNIA. Compare i 23 '*numquam* pigra fuit nostris tua gratia rebus'.

5. COMPLECTAR. *Complecti* in the weak sense 'include, take in' is found in Ovid only here and at *Tr* I v 55 'non tamen idcirco *complecterer* omnia uerbis'. The usage is common in prose (*OLD complector* 8).

6. MERITIS. Compare i 21-22 'et leuis haec *meritis* referatur gratia tantis; / si minus, inuito te quoque gratus ero'.

7-10. QVAE NVMERO TOT SVNT. Ovid is very fond of using this type of catalogue to indicate great number. Compare *AA* I 57-59 ('tot habet tua Roma puellas'), *AA* II 517-19 ('tot sunt in amore dolores'), *AA* III 149-50 (the many ways women can ornament themselves), *Tr* V vi 37-40 (the number of Ovid's ills), and *EP* II vii 25-28 ('nostrorum ... summa laborum').

8. LENTO CORTICE. 'Tough skin'.

8. GRANA. Ovid does not use pomegranates in his similar catalogues elsewhere. Professor R. J. Tarrant points out to me how Ovid elaborates the novel item of comparison in a full distich with several picturesque details (*Punica, lento cortice, rubent*), then reviews familiar elements rather more quickly in 9-10, with geography the ordering principle.

9. AFRICA QVOT SEGETES. Compare *EP* II vii 25 'Cinyphiae segetis citius numerabis aristas' (the Cinyps was a river in Libya).

9. SEGETES ... RACEMOS. Compare *AA* I 57 'Gargara quot *segetes*, quot habet Methymna *racemos*'.

9. TMOLIA TERRA = *Lydia*. The adjective *Tmolius* (from *Tmolus*, a mountain in Lydia famous for its wines) occurs only here.

10. QVOT SICYON BACAS. Compare *AA* II 518 'caerula quot bacas Palladis arbor habet'. For Sicyonian *bacae* compare Virgil *G* II 519 'Sicyonia baca' and *Ibis* 317 'oliuifera ... Sicyone'.

10. QVOT PARIT HYBLA FAVOS. *Fauos* stands by a type of metonymy for *apes*; compare *AA* II 517 'quot apes pascuntur in Hybla', *AA* III 150 'nec quot apes Hybla nec quot in Alpe ferae', and *Tr* V vi 38 'florida quam multas Hybla tuetur apes'. For a similar metonymy, see *EP* II vii 26 'altaque quam multis floreat Hybla thymis'.

11. CONFITEOR; TESTERE LICET. 'I make a public deposition; you, Pompeius, may be a witness'. The deposition is to the effect that Ovid is now Pompeius' property by virtue of the many gifts Pompeius has made to him.

11. TESTERE ... SIGNATE. André cites *Dig* XXII v 22 'curent magistratus cuiusque loci *testari* uolentibus et se ipsos et alios testes uel *signatores* praebere'.

11. SIGNATE, QVIRITES. After addressing Pompeius directly (*testere licet*), Ovid addresses those witnessing the *mancipatio*. As Professor A. Dalzell points out, this was achieved *ex iure Quiritium*; there is a similar direct address to the witnessing *Quirites* in the formula for establishing a will (Gaius II 104).

Professor Dalzell also notes the abrupt change of audience; typical of Propertius, this is a very unusual procedure in Ovid.

For *signare* used without an object, compare Suet *Cl* 9 2 'etiam cognitio falsi testamenti recepta est, in quo et ipse *signauerat*' & *Nero* 17 'cautum ut testamentis primae duae cerae testatorum modo nomine inscripto uacuae *signaturis* ostenderentur'.

Ovid uses *testis* and *signare* in a similarly metaphorical sense at *EP* III ii 23-24 (he forgives those friends who deserted him in his disaster) 'sint hac [*M (Heinsius)*: hi *codd*] contenti uenia, *signentque* [*uarr* sientque; fugiantque] licebit / purgari factum me quoque *teste* suum'

12. NIL OPVS EST LEGVM VIRIBVS, IPSE LOQVOR. Ehwald (*KB* 52) aptly cites Quintilian V vii 9 'duo genera sunt testium, aut uoluntariorum aut eorum quibus in [in *add editio Aldina*] iudiciis publicis lege denuntiari solet ['or those who are summoned *sub poena* in trials']'.

The reference in this passage to a legal procedure is rather curious, as is the connected reference in 41-42. But it is clear from Ovid's verse that he had a solid practical expertise and interest in law. In his youth he had been one of the *tresuiri monetales* or *capitales* (*Tr* IV x 33-34), and had also served in the centumviral court (*Tr* II 93-94; *EP* III v 23-24). He must have been known for his knowledge of law as well as for his fairness in order to be selected as arbitrator in private cases: 'res quoque priuatas statui sine crimine iudex, / deque mea fassa est pars quoque uicta fide' (*Tr* II 95-96). E. J. Kenney has presented some interesting statistics concerning the frequent occurrence of legal terms in Ovid's poetry ("Ovid and the Law", *Yale Classical Studies* XXI [1969] 241-63) comparing the number of occurrences of certain legal terms in Ovid and in Lucretius, Catullus, Virgil, Propertius, Tibullus, and the *Odes* of Horace. *Ius* and *lex* are not much more common in Ovid than in the other poets (the proportions being 134:59 and 74:60 respectively for Ovid and the other poets combined); this is not surprising, since these common words could hardly be considered technical terms. *Arbiter* (7:4) and *lis* (23:10) are not much more common in Ovid than in the other poets. But it will be seen from the following list how fond Ovid was of legal terminology: *legitimus* (16:0), *iudex* (47:12), *iudicium* (39:7), *index* (26:1), *indicium* (36:8), *arbitrium* (23:6), *reus* (23:5), *uindex* (26:5), *uindicare* (16:6), *uindicta* (11:0), *asserere* (3:0), *assertor* (1:0). Compare as well the play on legal terminology at *AA* I 83-86 (with Hollis's notes), and the use of such terms as *addicere* (*Met* I 617), *fallere depositum* (*Met* V 480 & IX 120), *usus communis* (*Met* VI 349), *transcribere* (*Met* VII 173), *primus heres* (*Met* XIII 154), *rescindere* (*Met* XIV 784), *accensere* (*Met* XV 546), *subscribere* (*Tr* I ii 3), *sub condicione* (*Tr* I ii 109), and *acceptum referre* (*Tr* II 10).

13. OPES ... PATERNAS. Pompeius appears to have been very wealthy. Seneca speaks of the wealth of a Pompeius (presumably the son of Ovid's patron—so Syme *Ten Studies* 82, *HO* 162), who was murdered by Gaius Caligula (*Tranq* 11 10).

13. REM PARVAM *MHIT* PARVAM REM *BCFL*. Either reading is possible enough. On balance, I believe *paruam rem* to be an intentional scribal alteration to avoid the incidence of a spondaic word in the fourth foot of the hexameter; for a discussion of the phenomenon, see at i 11 *uellem cum* (p 150).

In an older poet, the alliteration of *paruam pone paternas* would be a strong argument for the reading (see page 15 of Munro's introduction to his commentary on Lucretius), but Ovid did not use the device in his poetry.

15. TRINACRIA = *Sicilia*, unusable because it begins with three consecutive short vowels; compare *Met* V 474-76 (of Ceres) 'terras tamen increpat omnes / ingratasque uocat nec frugum munere dignas, / *Trinacriam* ante alias'.

André avoids the literal meaning of the passage, joining *terra* with *Trinacria* as well as with *regnataque ... Philippo* and taking it to mean 'estate': 'ta terre de Trinacrie et celle où régna Philippe'. But this sense of *terra* is rare in Latin (Martial IX xx 2, Apuleius *Met* IX 35), it is difficult to see how *regnataque ... Philippo* could stand as an epithet in such a case, and it is clear enough that Ovid is imitating *Aen* III 13-14 '*terra* ... acri quondam *regnata Lycurgo*', as he does at *Her* X 69 'tellus iusto regnata parenti', *Met* VIII 623 'arua suo quondam regnata parenti', and *Met* XIII 720-21 'regnataque uati / Buthrotos Phrygio'. In these lines Ovid states that Pompeius owns Sicily, Macedonia, and Campania, and by the hyperbole indicates the size of Pompeius' holdings. Seneca similarly mentions how the Pompeius murdered by Gaius Caligula possessed 'tot flumina ... in suo orientia, in suo cadentia'.

16. QVAM DOMVS AVGVSTO CONTINVATA FORO. Compare v 9-10 'protinus inde domus uobis Pompeia petetur: / *non est Augusto iunctior ulla foro*'.

18. QVAEQVE RELICTA TIBI, SEXTE, VEL EMPTA TENES. The line seems rather prosaic. For the thought, compare Cic *Off* II 81 'multa *hereditatibus*, multa *emptionibus*, multa dotibus tenebantur sine iniuria'; for this sense of *relicta*, compare Nepos *Att* 13 2 'domum habuit ... ab auunculo hereditate *relictam*', Livy XXII 26 1 'pecunia a patre *relicta*', and Martial X xlvii 3 'res non parta labore, sed *relicta*'.

19. TAM TVVS EN EGO SVM. Professor A. Dalzell notes the play on the dual sense of *tuus* (devoted/belonging to you) which is probably the basis of the entire poem. For *tuus* 'devoted' compare *Tr* II 55-56 '[iuro ...] hunc animum fauisse tibi, uir maxime, meque, / qua sola potui, mente fuisse *tuum*' and the other passages cited at *OLD tuus* 6.

19. MVNERE. The word is difficult. 'Gift' seems strange in view of the stress placed on Pompeius' ownership of Ovid. Professor E. Fantham suggests to me that the phrase could mean 'by virtue of whose sad *service* you cannot say you own nothing in the Pontus', while Professor R. J. Tarrant suggests that *munere* could mean 'responsibility, charge', with *cuius* (=*mei*) as an objective genitive.

21. ATQVE VTINAM POSSIS, ET DETVR AMICIVS ARVVM. This elliptical use of *posse* seems to be colloquial. The only instance cited by *OLD possum* 2a from verse is Prop IV vii 74 'potuit [*uar* patuit], nec tibi auara fuit'; there as well the tone is that of lively speech.

21. AMICIVS ARVVM. The same phrase at *Met* XV 442-43 (Helenus to Aeneas) 'Pergama rapta feres, donec Troiaeque tibique / externum patrio contingat *amicius aruum*'. The use of the adjective *amicus* of things rather than person is in the main a poetic usage, but compare Cic *Quinct* 34 'breuitas postulatur, quae mihimet ipsi *amicissima* est', *ND* II 43 'fortunam, quae *amica* uarietati constantiam respuit', and *Att* XII xv 'nihil est mihi *amicius* solitudine'; other instances in the elder Pliny and Columella.

22. REMQVE TVAM PONAS IN MELIORE LOCO. Compare *EP* I iii 77-78 'liquit Agenorides Sidonia moenia Cadmus / poneret ut muros *in meliore loco*'.

24. NVMINA PERPETVA QVAE PIETATE COLIS. Tiberius and Germanicus are meant. For Pompeius' devotion to Germanicus, compare v 25-26 'tempus ab his uacuum Caesar Germanicus omne / auferet; a magnis hunc colit ille deis'.

25-26. ERRORIS NAM TV VIX EST DISCERNERE NOSTRI / SIS ARGVMENTVM MAIVS AN AVXILIVM. This distich does not belong in the text: it is in itself unintelligible, and interrupts a natural progression from 24 to 27. I am not certain that the distich is a simple interpolation, since there is nothing in the context to which it is an obvious gloss. Possibly it has been inserted from another letter from exile, in which its meaning would have been clear from context.

Argumentum is difficult. Wheeler translates, 'For 'tis hard to distinguish whether you are more the proof of my mistake or the relief', and notes 'Apparently Pompey could prove (*argumentum*) that "error" which Ovid regarded as the beginning of his woes'. But this seems a strange thing to say, for Ovid's *error* was hardly in need of demonstration.

Auxilium is used in its medical sense, *erroris* being equivalent to *morbi* or *uulneris*; compare *RA* 48 'uulneris auxilium' and the passages collected at *OLD remedium* 1.

25. DISCERNERE. Gronovius argued (*Obseruationes* III xiii) that DECERNERE (*MI*^{1}) should be read here, since *decernere* has the required sense 'uel decertare uel iudicare et certum statuere', whereas *discernere* means 'separare, dirimere, distinguere, diuidere'. On the evidence of the lexica, however, Gronovius' distinction breaks down, since *discernere* meaning 'decide, determine, make out' is common enough: compare Sallust *Cat* 25 3 'pecuniae an famae minus parceret haud facile *discerneres*', Cic *Rep* 2 6 'ne nota quidem ulla pacatus an hostis sit *discerni* ac iudicari potest', Varro *LL* VII 17 'quo *discernitur* homo mas an femina sit', and Livy XXII 61 10 'quid ueri sit *discernere*'. I therefore let *discernere* stand.

29-30. ET PVDET ET METVO SEMPERQVE EADEMQVE PRECARI / NE SVBEANT ANIMO TAEDIA IVSTA TVO. Compare *EP* III vii entire (an apology to his friends for the monotony of his verse), and especially the opening lines: 'Verba mihi desunt eadem tam saepe roganti, / iamque pudet uanas fine carere preces. / taedia consimili fieri de carmine uobis, / quidque petam cunctos edidicisse reor'.

30. SVBEANT ANIMO. *Subire animo* occurs also at *Tr* I v 13. Ovid uses *subire* with the dative several times in the poetry of exile (*Tr* I vii 9, II 147, III iii 14 & V vii 58; *EP* I ix 11, II x 43 & IV iv 47), but not beforehand; earlier he has the accusative (*Met* XII 472) or the simple verb (*Met* XV 307). The dative construction is taken up by the author of the later *Heroides* (XVI 99, XVIII 62).

31. RES IMMODERATA CVPIDO EST. *Cupido* similarly called *immoderata* at Apuleius *Plat* II 21; elsewhere qualified as *immodica* (Livy VI 35 6) and *immensa* (*Aen* VI 823, Tac *Ann* XII 7).

33. DELABOR. Cicero uses the word for moving from one subject to another (*OLD delabor* 5b); here the metaphorical sense 'fall' is still active.

34. IPSA LOCVM PER SE LITTERA NOSTRA ROGAT. This line as it stands is clearly corrupt. I do not understand Wheeler's 'my very letters of their own accord seek the opportunity'; André's 'c'est la lettre qui, d'elle-meme, demande le sujet' seems equally difficult, although *locus* can certainly have the meaning 'subject, topic of discussion' (*OLD locus* 24b).

The only parallel I have found is *Fast* II 861 'iure uenis, Gradiue: *locum tua tempora poscunt*'. If *littera* is retained in the present passage, this parallel is of little assistance, since *locum* there means 'a place within a larger work', and Ovid's poetry cannot ask for a *locus* in that sense. Taking the passage from the *Fasti* as a parallel, I once thought that Ovid wrote *ipsa locum pro se tristia nostra rogant* (or *petunt*); for the noun *triste* compare *Fast* VI 463 'scilicet interdum miscentur *tristia* laetis', *Ecl* III 80-81 '*triste* lupus stabulis, maturis frugibus imbres, / arboribus uenti, nobis Amaryllidis irae', and Hor *Carm* I xvi 25-26 'nunc ego mitibus / mutare quaero *tristia*'. I now consider this unlikely, since the personal adjective *nostra* with *tristia* seems unidiomatic; but I still believe that *littera* is the key to the corruption.

Professor R. J. Tarrant has tentatively suggested something like *inque locum ... redit*, but questions whether *in locum*, even just after *eodem*, can have the sense *in eundem locum*. Professor Tarrant also points out to me the possible relevance of *locus* in the sense *locus communis* (compare Sen *Suas* I 9 'dixit ... *locum* de uarietate fortunae'); Ovid might be saying that his poetry had made rather frequent use of the *locus de exilio*. In this case, *rogat* would require emendation.

367

One of Heinsius' manuscripts read *per se ... facit*, which is just possibly correct. Heinsius proposed *pro se ... facit*, which I do not understand.

35. HABITVRA is a good instance of the future participle used to express what is inevitably destined to happen (with *Parca* balancing in the pentameter); for the sense, see Tarrant on Sen *Ag* 43 'daturus coniugi iugulum suae'.

37. INOBLITA = *memori*. Apparently the only instance of the word in classical Latin.

39. CAELO ... SVB VLLO. Bentley oddly conjectured ILLO, the reading of M^{ac}, which gives the sense 'under the Tomitan sky'. This obviously contradicts the following *transit nostra feros si modo Musa Getas*.

41. SERVATOREM occurs in Ovid only here and at *Met* IV 737-38 (of Perseus) 'auxiliumque domus *seruatoremque* fatentur / Cassiope Cepheusque pater'. In prose it is several times used in a civic context (Cic *Pis* 34, *Planc* 102, Livy VI 20 16 & XLV 44 20; *CIL* IX 4852 in a dedication to *Ioui optimo maximo seruatori conseruatori ... ex uoto suscepto*). The solemn overtones of *seruatorem* must be part of what Ovid means for his own land and for the rest of the world to hear and know; the poem thus ends with an implied pronouncement to balance the public statement of the opening.

42. MEQVE TVVM LIBRA NORIT ET AERE MAGIS. This line clearly refers to *mancipatio*, the receiving of property (including slaves), which is described by Gaius as follows: 'adhibitis non minus quam [*Boeth.*: quod *cod*] quinque testibus ciuibus Romanis puberibus, et praeterea alio eiusdem condicionis qui libram aeneam teneat, qui appellatur libripens ['scale-holder'—de Zulueta], is qui mancipio accipit, aes [aes *add Boeth.*] tenens, ita dicit: "hunc ego hominem ex iure [*Boeth.*: iūst *cod*] Quiritium meum esse aio isque mihi emptus esto hoc aere aeneaque libra", deinde aere percutit libram, idque aes dat ei a quo mancipio accipit quasi pretii loco' (I 119).

MAGIS is found as a secondary reading in *F* and in the thirteenth-century *Barberinus lat. 26*; the reading of most manuscripts is MINVS, which seems to me impossible. Several explanations of *minus* have been advanced:

(i) Gronovius took the line to mean 'tuus sum, immo mancipium tuum, nisi quod sola libra et aes mea mancipatione abfuerunt'. This retention of *minus*, however, involves Ovid in a qualifying retraction just when he seems to be aiming for a ringing conclusion. As well, the instances of *minus* cited by Gronovius do not in fact illustrate this passage: among them are *EP* I vii 25-26 'uno / nempe salutaris quam prius ore minus', *Met* XII 554-55 'bis sex Herculeis ceciderunt me minus uno ['except for me alone'] / uiribus', and Manilius I 778 'Tarquinio ... minus reges', 'the kings, except for Tarquin'.

Gronovius seems to have realized that difficulties remained, and proposed to read NOVIT in 42 and make 41-42 a relative clause dependent on *tellus* in 38, so that the concluding lines of the poem would mean 'mea tellus, Sulmo, Roma, Italia, me tuum esse audiet. sed audiet idem etiam, quaecumque sub alia quauis caeli parte terra posita est, et te, meum seruatorem, meque, libra et aere tuum, minus nouit'. Once again, *minus* seems to weaken the poem fatally.

(ii) Ehwald (*KB* 71) followed Gronovius' second explanation, retaining the manuscripts' *norit*, and glossing 'tellus, quae sub ullo caelo posita est et te, meae salutis seruatorem, meque, libra et aere tuum, minus norit'.

(iii) Némethy followed Gronovius' first explanation, adding as an illustration *AA* I 643-44 'ludite, si sapitis, solas impune puellas: / hac *minus* [*Burman*: magis *codd*] est una fraude tuenda [*Naugerius ex codd suis*: pudenda *codd*] fides'. The citation does not strengthen the case for *minus*.

(iv) André wrote '*Minus* me paraît avoir le sens de *citra* "sans aller jusqu'à", i.e. "sans même avoir recours à la mancipation": "tu es mon maître de ma propre volonté, et non, comme tu l'es de tes autres propriétés, par achat."' But the meaning seems to weaken the force of the poem.

I have with reluctance adopted *libra ... et aere magis*, taking it in the sense *magis quam libra et aere* ('I am yours even more than I would be if I had been acquired through *mancipatio*'). The closest parallel I have found for this compressed use of the ablative is the idiom at v 7 'luce minus decima', 'before the tenth day'.

Of the other readings, F^1's *tuum ... datum* cannot itself be correct, although it may offer a clue to the truth. Heinsius' *tuum ... tuum* is grammatical enough, but (as Professor R. J. Tarrant points out to me) makes Ovid say that he is Pompeius' literally through *mancipatio*. As well, the repetition seems odd. Rappold's *tuae ... manus* cannot be right, since *manus* did not have the sense of *mancipium*, except for the limited meaning of a husband's authority over his wife. Still, Rappold's conjecture may be a step in the right direction, particularly in view of v 39-40 'pro quibus ut meritis referatur gratia, iurat / se fore *mancipii* tempus in omne *tui*'.

XVI. To a Detractor

The anonymous detractor to whom Ovid apparently addresses this poem is probably fictional; at 47 he substitutes *Liuor*, dropping the pretence of speaking to a single enemy.

Ovid begins the poem by asking his detractor why he criticizes Ovid's verse. A poet's fame increases after his death; Ovid's fame was great even while he was still alive (1-4). There were many poets contemporary with Ovid (5-38). There were also younger poets, not yet published, whom he will not name, with the necessary exception of Cotta Maximus (39-44). Even among such poets, he had a reputation. Envy should therefore cease to torment him; he has lost everything but life, which is left only so that he can continue to experience pain (45-50).

The poem is of particular interest because of the catalogue of the poets of the earlier part of the reign of Tiberius. It is a reminder of how much Latin verse has been lost, for of the poets listed only Grattius survives.

Similar catalogues of poets are found at Prop II xxxiv 61-92 and *Am* I xv 9-30, the poets listed being however not contemporaries but illustrious predecessors. *Tr* IV x 41-54 is complementary to the present poem, being a list of the leading Roman poets at the beginning of Ovid's career. All of these poems come last in their book, and it seems clear enough that the present poem was meant to close a published collection. Other links exist with the earlier poems: mention is similarly made in them of the poet's fame after his death (Prop II xxxiv 94, *Am* I xi 41-42, *Tr* IV x 129-30), and *Am* I xv (which Professor R. J. Tarrant suggests may have ended the original edition in five books of the *Amores*) is, like the present poem, addressed to *Liuor*.

1. INVIDE, QVID LACERAS NASONIS CARMINA RAPTI. Compare the question that opens *Am* I xv 'Quid mihi, Liuor edax, ignauos obicis annos, / ingeniique uocas carmen inertis opus'. For *inuide ... laceras* compare Cic *Brutus* 156 '*inuidia*, quae solet *lacerare* plerosque'.

1. LACERAS. *Lacerare* 'attack verbally' is a prose usage, found in Cicero, the historians, and the elder Seneca (*OLD lacero* 5; *TLL* VII.2 827 50).

The primary meaning of *lacerare* behind this usage is *mordere*; *lacerare* is found in this literal sense at Cic *De or* II 240 '*lacerat* lacertum Largi *mordax* Memmius', Phaedrus I xii 11 '*lacerari* coepit *morsibus* saeuis canum', and Sen *Clem* I 25 1.

For *mordere* in the same transferred sense, see at xiv 46 *mordenda* (p 424).

1. NASONIS ... RAPTI. 'Of Ovid, who is now dead'. For *rapti*, see at xi 5 *rapti* (p 362).

2. NON SOLET INGENIIS SVMMA NOCERE DIES. The same thought at *Am* I xv 39-40 'pascitur in uiuis Liuor; post fata quiescit, / cum suus ex merito quemque tuetur honos' and *EP* III iv 73-74 'scripta placent a morte fere, quia laedere uiuos / Liuor et iniusto carpere dente solet'.

3. CINERES = *mortem*. Bömer at *Met* VIII 539 *post cinerem* (where *cinerem*, as Bömer saw, means 'cremation'), cites among other passages Prop III i 35-36 'meque inter seros laudabit Roma nepotes: / illum *post cineres* auguror esse diem', Martial I i 2-6 'Martialis ... cui, lector studiose, quod dedisti / uiuenti decus atque sentienti, / rari *post cineres* habent poetae' and Martial VIII xxxviii 16 'hoc et *post cineres* erit tributum'.

3. AT is my correction for the manuscripts' ET. The point that Ovid was famous *even* while alive is made by *tum quoque* later in the verse; the only meaning that could therefore be given to *et mihi nomen* is 'even I had a name, even when I was alive', which is inappropriate, since in this poem Ovid is not belittling his poetic talent.

At seems to be the obvious solution, giving the sense 'poets usually become famous after they die; I, *however*, was famous even while alive'. Compare *Tr* IV x 121-22 (to his Muse) 'tu mihi, quod rarum est, uiuo sublime dedisti / nomen, ab exequiis quod dare fama solet' and Martial I i 2-6 (cited in the previous note). The more usual situation of obscurity during the poet's lifetime followed by posthumous fame is described at Prop III i 21-24.

Professor C. P. Jones points out to me that *et* can have an adversative sense (*OLD et* 14a). But the two instances there cited from Augustan verse are examples of *nec ... et* (*Fast* V 530; *Tr* V xii 63 'nec possum *et* cupio non nullos ducere uersus'). Where *et* alone carries the adversative sense, it is generally used to join two opposing verbs or verbal phrases: compare Cic *Tusc* I 6 'fieri ... potest ut recte quis sentiat *et* id quod sentit polite eloqui non possit' and Sen *NQ* II 18 'quare aliquando non fulgurat *et* tonat?'.

4. CVM VIVIS ADNVMERARER. For Ovid's considering himself already dead, compare *EP* I ix 56 'et nos extinctis adnumerare potest' and *EP* I vii 9-10 'nos satis est inter glaciem Scythicasque sagittas / uiuere, si uita est mortis habenda genus'.

Ovid is the first poet to use *adnumerare* in this sense ('reckon in with'), and only in his poems of exile; it is afterwards found at *Her* XVI 330 and Manilius V 438.

5-36. It is possible to discern a rough order in the catalogue of names; first come the writers of epic and Pindaric verse (5-28), then the dramatists (29-31), and finally the writers of lighter verse (32-36).

5. CVM FORET ET *FHT* CVMQVE FORET *BCMIL*. Clearly either *et* or *-que* was lost, and one or both inserted to restore the metre. *Cumque* would be a continuation of *at mihi nomen ...*, which seems an inelegant construction. *Cum foret et*, introducing a sentence of forty-two lines ending in 'dicere si fas est, claro mea nomine Musa / atque inter tantos quae legeretur erat' seems preferable; this very long sentence serves not as a continuation of the statement in 3-4, but as evidence for it.

5. MARSVS. Domitius Marsus[29] is often mentioned by Martial as a writer of epigram, sometimes being coupled with Catullus and Albinovanus Pedo (I praef, II lxxi 3 & lxxvii 5, V v 6, VII xcix 7). A friend of Maecenas, he wrote an epic poem on the Amazons (Martial IV xxix 8), and at least nine books of *fabellae* (Charisius I 72 Keil). Quintilian quotes from his treatise on *urbanitas* (VI iii 102 ff.); and he is cited as an authority by the elder Pliny (*NH* I 34).

The scholiasts and grammarians preserve seven fragments (Morel 110-11), the most interesting being the four lines on the death of Tibullus: 'Te quoque Vergilio comitem non aequa, Tibulle, / Mors iuuenem campos misit ad Elysios, / ne foret aut elegis molles qui fleret amores / aut caneret forti regia bella pede'.

5. MAGNIQVE RABIRIVS ORIS. Similar phrasing at Virgil *G* III 294 'magno nunc ore sonandum', Prop II x 12 'magni nunc erit oris opus', and *AA* I 206 (to Gaius) 'et magno nobis ore sonandus eris'. In the last two passages, as here, there is a specific reference to epic verse.

5. RABIRIVS. Velleius Paterculus (II 36 3) mentions Rabirius (Schanz-Hosius 267-68 [§ 316]; Bardon 73-74) alongside Virgil: 'paene stulta est inhaerentium oculis ingeniorum enumeratio, inter quae maxima nostri aeui eminent princeps carminum Vergilius Rabiriusque'. Quintilian speaks of him with rather less admiration: 'Rabirius ac Pedo non indigni cognitione, si uacet' (X i 90). Seneca (*Ben* VI 3 1) quotes a passage of his with Mark Antony speaking; presumably one of his poems dealt with the civil war.

Five short fragments of Rabirius survive (Morel 120-21).

6. ILIACVSQVE MACER. Pompeius Macer[30] was one of Ovid's closest friends; he is the addressee of *Am* II xviii and *EP* II x. The son of Theophanes of Mytilene, Pompey's confidant, he was intimate with Tiberius (Strabo XIII 2 3); under Augustus he had served as procurator of Asia and had been placed in charge of the libraries at Rome (Suet *Iul* 56 7). Two poems in the Greek Anthology are generally attributed to him (VII ccxix; IX xxviii).

Iliacus is explained by *Am* II xviii 1-3 'Carmen ad iratum dum tu perducis Achillem ['while you are writing a poem about the Trojan war up to the starting-point of the *Iliad*'] / primaque iuratis induis arma uiris, / nos, Macer, ignaua Veneris cessamus in umbra' and *EP* II x 13-14 'tu canis aeterno quicquid restabat Homero, / ne careant summa Troica bella manu'; Macer had written poems narrating those parts of the Trojan war not covered by the *Iliad*.

The Macer mentioned at Tr IV x 43-44 must be a different person, for he is described as already being *grandior aeuo* in Ovid's youth.

6. SIDEREVSQVE PEDO. On Albinovanus Pedo, see at x 4 *Albinouane* (p 327).

For *sidereus* ('divine' or 'resplendent'), Bardon aptly cited Columella X 434 (written in hexameters) '*siderei* uatis ... praecepta Maronis'.

7. ET, QVI IVNONEM LAESISSET IN HERCVLE, CARVS. This is the Carus to whom xiii is addressed: compare xiii 11-12 'prodent auctorem uires, quas Hercule dignas / nouimus atque illi quem canis ipse pares'.

As Jupiter's son by Alcmene, Hercules suffered from Juno's enmity until his deification.

8. IVNONIS SI IAM NON GENER ILLE FORET. Perhaps Carus' poem included Hercules' marriage to Hebe.

9. SEVERVS. On Severus, the addressee of poem ii, see the introduction to that poem; for *quique dedit Latio carmen regale*, see at ii 1 *uates magnorum maxime regum* (p 162).

10. SVBTILI ... NVMA. Numa is otherwise unknown. *Subtilis* means 'clean and elegant in style'; compare Cic *De or* I 180 'oratione maxime limatus atque *subtilis*' and *Brutus* 35 'tum fuit Lysias ... egregie *subtilis* scriptor atque elegans, quem iam prope audeas oratorem perfectum dicere'.

10. PRISCVS VTERQVE. Only one poet of this name is known, Clutorius (Tac *Ann* III 49-51) or C. Lutorius (Dio LVII 20 3) Priscus. All that is known of him is the manner of his death: in AD 21 he was put to death for composing and reciting a premature poem on the death of Drusus.

11. IMPARIBVS NVMERIS ... VEL AEQVIS. Like Ovid, Montanus wrote both elegiac and hexameter verse.

For *impar* used of elegiac verse, compare Hor *AP* 75 (the earliest instance) 'uersibus *impariter* iunctis', *Am* II xvii 21, *Am* III i 37, *AA* I 264, *Tr* II 220, *EP* II v 1 (*disparibus*), *EP* III iv 86 (*disparibus*), *EP* IV v 3 (*nec ... aequis*), and line 36 of the present poem.

11. MONTANE. Iulius Montanus is mentioned in passing at Sen *Cont* VII 1 27, where he is called *egregius poeta*; in Donatus' life of Virgil (29) his admiration of Virgil's manner of reciting is mentioned, on the authority of the elder Seneca. The younger Seneca, calling him 'tolerabilis poeta et amicitia Tiberi notus et frigore', tells some amusing anecdotes about the length of his recitations and his fondness for describing sunrises and sunsets (*Ep* CXXII 11-13). He quotes from him twice (Morel 120).

13-14. ET QVI PENELOPAE RESCRIBERE IVSSIT VLIXEM / ERRANTEM SAEVO PER DVO LVSTRA MARI. All that is known of Sabinus is what Ovid says here and in his list of Sabinus' poems at *Am* II xviii 27-34 'quam cito de toto rediit meus orbe Sabinus / scriptaque diuersis rettulit ille locis! / candida Penelope signum cognouit Vlixis; / legit ab Hippolyto scripta nouerca suo. / iam pius Aeneas miserae rescripsit Elissae, / quodque legat Phyllis, si modo uiuit, adest. / tristis ad Hypsipylen ab Iasone littera uenit; / det uotam Phoebo Lesbis amata lyram' (this line, like the letter of Sappho, has been considered suspect; see R. J. Tarrant, "The Authenticity of the Letter of Sappho to Phaon (*Heroides* XV)", *HSPh* 85 [1981] 133-53).

Since the letter of Ulysses is the first one mentioned in the list at *Am* II xviii 29, it was presumably the first poem in Sabinus' collection of epistles; hence Ovid's use of it here to indicate the entire collection.

Line 14 may be an echo of one of Sabinus' poems.

15. TRISOMEN C TRISOMEM B[1]. For the many other variants, see the apparatus. The word is clearly corrupt; correction is difficult in the absence of further information on Sabinus. TROEZENA (a conjecture reported by Micyllus) seems unattractive. Heinsius had difficulty with the passage: 'an *Tymelen*? opinor certe nomen puellae a Sabino decantatae hic latere'. TROESMIN, suggested by Ehwald (*JAW* CIX [1901] 187), is unlikely—why would Sabinus have wished to recount Vestalis' capture of the city?—but not, as claimed by Vollmer (PW I A,2 1598 34), unmetrical: lengthening is common enough before the main caesura (although I have found no example of lengthened -*in*). Bardon (61) wished to read TROEZEN (which is in fact the reading of *T*), apparently not realizing that an accusative form is required.

15-16. DIERVM ... OPVS. Sabinus apparently started work on a calendar-poem, which may have resembled the *Fasti*; compare *Fast* I 101 'uates operose *dierum*'.

16. CELERI = 'premature'.

17. INGENIIQVE SVI DICTVS COGNOMINE LARGVS. For the play on the name compare xiii 2 'qui quod es, id uere, Care, uocaris, aue'. Nothing is known of Largus beyond what Ovid here tells us.

18. GALLICA QVI PHRYGIVM DVXIT IN ARVA SENEM. Largus described Antenor's migration to Venetia and founding of Patavium, for which see *Aen* I 242-49 and Livy I 1.

18. GALLICA ... ARVA. Patavium was in Cisalpine Gaul.

18. PHRYGIVM ... SENEM. At *Il* III 149-50 Antenor is listed among the 'δημογέροντες ... γήραϊ δὴ πολέμοιο πεπαυμένοι' sitting on the Trojan wall who see Helen approach.

19. DOMITO ... AB HECTORE TROIAM. 'The story of Troy after the death of Hector'. *Gothanus II 121* has the interpolation DOMITAM ... AB HECTORE, which Korn printed.

19. CAMERINVS. Nothing is known of this poet.

20. SVA PHYLLIDE. Presumably Tuscus' equivalent of Gallus' Lycoris. However, as Professor A. Dalzell points out, the reference to love poetry is odd in a sequence of epic and didactic writers.

20. TVSCVS is not otherwise certainly known. Kiessling (*Coniectanea Propertiana*, Greifswald, 1875) proposed that he was the "Demophoon" addressed in Prop II xxii; this suggestion has won support from Birt [*RhM* XXXII [1877] 414), Bardon (61; I owe these references to him), and André, but does not seem extremely convincing, especially since Propertius had been writing some three decades earlier. Merkel, in his edition of the *Tristia* (p. 373), identifies him with the grammarian Clodius Tuscus, without offering a reason.

21. VELIVOLIQVE MARIS VATES. It is not known who this was, or what the precise subject of the poem might have been; perhaps it resembled the *Halieutica*. André mentions that Varro Atacinus has been proposed, but does not name the author of the suggestion, which seems rather fanciful; as he points out, Varro had died some fifty years previously. Luck in his edition has proposed Abronius Silo, of whom two hexameters survive (Sen *Suas* II 19 = Morel 120), but, as André remarks, the fact that he, like Ovid, was a follower of the rhetor Porcius Latro is hardly sufficient evidence for the identification.

For *ueliuolique* see at v 42 *ueliuolas* (p 224).

22. CAERVLEOS ... DEOS = 'the gods of the sea'. Compare *Met* II 8 '*caeruleos* habet unda deos'.

23. ACIES LIBYCAS ROMANAQVE PROELIA. The poem may have concerned the Jugurthine war, or Caesar's African campaign; compare *Fast* IV 379-80 'illa dies Libycis qua Caesar in oris / perfida magnanimi contudit arma Iubae'.

For the juxtaposition of opposing proper adjectives (*Libycas Romana*), see Tarrant on Sen *Ag* 613-13a *Dardana tecto / Dorici ... ignes*.

24. ET MARIVS SCRIPTI DEXTER IN OMNE GENVS. For the phrasing compare *Tr* II 381-82 '*omne genus scripti* grauitate tragoedia uincit: / haec quoque materiam semper amoris habet' and *Tr* II 517-18 'an *genus hoc scripti* faciunt sua pulpita ['stage'] tutum, / quodque licet, mimis scaena licere dedit?'. C's MARIVS SCRIPTOR and B's SCRIPTOR MARIVS were no doubt induced by the hyperbaton of *scripti ... genus*.

Marius is not otherwise known.

25. TRINACRIVSQVE ... AVCTOR. In view of the following *auctor ... Lupus*, *Trinacrius* should be taken as a proper name, and not as an adjective. The adjectival form of the name is, however, suspicious, and may be a corruption far removed from what Ovid wrote.

25. SVAE seems strange, and is probably corrupt. Wheeler translated 'Trinacrius who wrote of the *Perseid* he knew so well', while André ignored *suae* altogether: 'l'auteur trinacrien de la "Perséide"'.

25-26. AVCTOR / TANTALIDAE REDVCIS TYNDARIDOSQVE LVPVS. Lupus (otherwise unknown) apparently wrote of the return of Menelaus and Helen to Sparta.

Tantalides is used only here of Menelaus. Elsewhere in Latin verse it is used of Agamemnon, Atreus, and Pelops: see *OLD Tantalides*. Ovid is here using the diction of high poetry.

27. ET QVI MAEONIAM PHAEACIDA VERTIT. Tuticanus; his translation of the Phaeacian episode of the Odyssey is mentioned at xii 27-28. As that poem explains, his name could not be used in elegiac verse: hence the periphrasis in this passage.

27. ET VNE *HLB*[2] **ET VNE** *M*[2c] **ET VNA** *IT* **ET VNI** *B*[1]*C* **IN ANGVEM** *F*. *Vne* was liable to corruption because of the hyperbaton with *Rufe* in the next line, and because of the rarity of the vocative of *unus*. For *unus* in the sense 'unique, outstanding', compare Catullus XXXVII 17 'tu praeter omnes *une* de capillatis' ('you outstanding member of the long-haired set'—Quinn) and Prop II iii 29 'gloria Romanis *una* es tu nata puellis'.

27-28. VNE / PINDARICAE FIDICEN TV QVOQVE, RVFE, LYRAE. An imitation of Hor *Carm* IV iii 21-23 'totum muneris hoc tui est / quod monstror digito praetereuntium /

Romanae fidicen lyrae'.

28. RVFE. Otherwise unknown. André correctly points out that he is unlikely to be the Rufus addressed in *EP* II xi, 'dont Ovid n'aurait pas manqué alors de vanter le talent poétique'. Bardon (59) mentions that A. Reifferscheid ("Coniect. noua", *Ind. lect. Bresl.*, 1880/81, p. 7) identified this Rufus with the Pindaric poet Titius of Hor *Ep* I iii 9-10, thereby creating 'le très synthétique Titius Rufus'. But there is nothing very compelling about the identification.

29. MVSAVE TVRRANI. The poet is not otherwise certainly known. Bardon (48) reports the conjectures of Hirschfeld ("Annona", *Philologus*, 1870, p. 27) identifying him with C. Turranius, *praefectus annonae* at the time of Augustus' death (Tac *Ann* I 7) and of Munzer (*Beitr. zur Quellenkritik* 387-89), identifying him with the geographical writer Turranius Gracilis mentioned by the elder Pliny (*NH* III 3, IX 11).

29. INNIXA COTVRNIS. The *coturnus* was distinguished by its high sole; hence *innixa* ('supported by'). Compare *Am* III i 31 (of Tragedy) 'pictis *innixa coturnis*' and Hor *AP* 279-80 'Aeschylus ... docuit magnumque loqui *nitique coturno*'.

29. COTVRNIS. As Brink at Hor *AP* 80 points out, *coturnus* (not *cothurnus*) is the spelling favoured by the best manuscripts of Virgil and Horace.

30. ET TVA CVM SOCCO MVSA, MELISSE, LEVIS. *H* offers LEVI, also conjectured by Heinsius, which may be right: the epithet with *socco* would provide a pleasing balance with the preceding *tragicis ... coturnis*. On the other hand, Professor R. J. Tarrant in support of *leuis* cites *RA* 375-76 'grande sonant tragici, tragicos decet ira coturnos: / usibus e mediis *soccus* habendus erit' and Hor *AP* 80 '*socci ...* grandesque coturni'; in both passages *soccus* has no adjective.

Propertius uses *Musa leuis* of his verse (II xii 22); compare as well *Tr* II 354 'Musa iocosa' (Ovid's amatory verse), *EP* I v 69 'infelix Musa', Lucretius IV 589 & *Ecl* I 2 'siluestrem ... Musam', and Quintilian X i 55 'Musa ... rustica et pastoralis' (the poetry of Theocritus).

Leuis is used of comedy at *Fast* V 347-48 'scaena *leuis* decet hanc [*sc* Floram]: non est, mihi credite, non est / illa coturnatas inter habenda deas' and Hor *AP* 231 'effutire *leues* indigna Tragoedia uersus'.

30. MELISSE. Thanks principally to Suetonius *Gram* 21, we are comparatively well informed about Melissus (Schanz-Hosius 176-77 [§ 277]; Bardon 49-52). Brought up a slave (his father had disowned him at birth), he was given a good education by the man who accepted him, and was given to Maecenas, who manumitted him. He wrote one hundred and fifty books of *Ineptiae*. 'Fecit et nouum genus togatarum inscripsitque trabeatas'; it is no doubt these plays that Ovid is here referring to.

31. VARIVS. Possibly the famous author of the *Thyestes* and editor of the *Aeneid* (Schanz-Hosius 162-64 [§ 267]; Bardon 28-34; fragments at Morel 100-1 and Ribbeck 265). Riese objected to the identification on chronological grounds (the *Thyestes* was produced in 29 BC), but the date of his death is unknown, and he may have survived to the time of Ovid's exile.

31. GRACCHVSQVE. The manuscripts omit the aspirate, and Ehwald cites *CIL* VI 1 1505 for a mention of *Ti. Sempronius Graccus*, but in his discussion of the aspirate Quintilian makes it clear that *Graccus* was an obsolete spelling (I v 20).

Gracchus (Bardon 48-49) is mentioned by Priscian, Nonius, and the author of the *De dubiis nominibus*, who among them preserve four fragments and three titles (Ribbeck 266). One of the titles is a *Thyestes*; Professor R. J. Tarrant plausibly suggests that Ovid may here be alluding to the plays by Varius and Gracchus on the theme with his words *cum ... darent fera uerba tyrannis*, Atreus being the archetype of the tyrant in tragedy.

Nipperdey proposed that Ovid's Gracchus was the Sempronius Gracchus implicated in the disgrace of Julia (Vel Pat II 100 5); see Syme *HO* 196 and Furneaux on Tac *Ann* I 53 4. The identification is however far from certain.

32. CALLIMACHI PROCVLVS MOLLE TENERET ITER.

Proculus is otherwise unknown. Ehwald suggested (*JAW* 43 [1885] 141) that he was a dramatic poet like Varius and Gracchus, citing a mention of the 'σατυρικὰ δράματα, τραγῳδίαι, κωμῳδίαι' of Callimachus in the *Souda*. But Callimachus' primary reputation was hardly that of a tragedian; and *molle ... iter* must be a reference to *Aetia* 25-28: 'καὶ τόδ' ἄνωγα, τὰ μὴ πατέουσιν ἄμαξαι / τὰ στείβειν, ἑτέρων δ' ἴχνια μὴ καθ' ὁμά / [*Hunt:* δίφρον ἐλ]ᾶν μηδ' οἶμον ἀνὰ πλατύν, ἀλλὰ κελεύθους / [*Pfeiffer:* ἀτρίπτο]υς, εἰ καὶ στεινοτέρην ἐλάσεις'.

For *mollis* used specifically of elegy (the *Aetia* were in elegiac verse), see *EP* III iv 85 and Prop I vii 19 (cited by André); for the word in an overtly Callimachean context, see Prop III i 19 '*mollia*, Pegasides, date uestro serta poetae'.

Tenere here has the sense 'keep to', as at *Met* II 79 'ut ... uiam *teneas*' and Q Cic (?) *Pet* 55 'perge *tenere* istam uiam quam institisti [*Gruterus:* instituisti *codd*]'; Professor R. J. Tarrant rightly sees a suggestion of conscious artistic preference, and a faint allusion to the places where Augustan poets renounce the attractions of higher poetry.

33. TITYRON ANTIQVAS PASSERQVE REDIRET AD HERBAS B^1C.

For the many variants and emendations proposed, see the apparatus.

Housman has offered a defence of *B* and *C*'s version of this line (937-39). He accepted Riese's printing of *Passer* as a proper name ('M. Petronius Passer' is mentioned at Varro *RR* III 2 2), and took the passage to mean 'He wrote bucolics, or, as Ovid puts it, he went back to Tityrus and the pastures of old': the construction is 'cum Passer rediret ad Tityron antiquasque herbas'. In writing the line, Ovid resorted to three devices, 'each of them legitimate, but not perhaps elsewhere assembled in a single verse'. The first is the delay of the preposition *ad* after *Tityron*, which it governs; the second is the delay of *-que*, which properly belongs with *antiquas*; and the third is the placing of the verb between its two objects. For each of these devices Housman furnishes convincing parallels.

Housman's argument is ingenious and informative, but I do not believe that he is right in defending the line: the accumulation of difficulties is suspicious, and the divergence of the manuscripts is greater here than at any other point in the book. Heinsius wrote of the line, 'haec nec Latina sunt, nec satis intelligo quid sibi uelint'. Like Heinsius, I believe the line to be deeply corrupted and, in the absence of further evidence, impossible to correct.

34. APTAQVE VENANTI GRATTIVS ARMA DARET. Compare Grattius 23 'carmine et arma dabo et uenandi [*cod*: uenanti et *Vlitius*] persequar artis'.

34. GRATTIVS. The manuscripts have GRATIVS (*CFLT*) or GRACIVS (*BMHI*); and *Gratius* is what editors both of Ovid and Grattius printed until Buecheler pointed out (*RhM* 35 [1880] 407) that *Grattius* is the only form found in inscriptions, and is what is given in the oldest manuscript of Grattius, *Vindobonensis 277* (saec viii/ix), which predates the manuscripts of *EP* IV by at least four hundred years.

35. NAIADAS C. P. *Jones* NAIADAS A *HLI*^{2} NAYADES A *MT* NAIDAS A *BCFI*^{2}. Ovid elsewhere invariably uses the dative of agent with *amatus* (*Am* I v 12, II viii 12, III ix 55-56, *AA* II 80, *Tr* I vi 2, II 400, III i 42, IV x 40).

As Professor Jones notes, following the interpolation of *a*, the shorter form *Naidas* was introduced in *BCFI*^{1} to restore metre.

35-36. FONTANVS ... CAPELLA. Neither poet is otherwise known.

36. IMPARIBVS ... MODIS. See at 11 *imparibus numeris ... uel aequis* (p 453).

37-38. QVORVM MIHI CVNCTA REFERRE / NOMINA LONGA MORA EST. Similar phrasing at *Met* XIII 205-6 '*longa referre mora est* quae consilioque manuque / utiliter feci spatiosi tempore belli' and *Fast* V 311-12 (Flora speaking) '*longa referre mora est* correcta obliuia damnis; / me quoque Romani praeteriere patres'.

39-40. ESSENT ET IVVENES QVORVM, QVOD INEDITA CVRA EST, / APPELLANDORVM NIL MIHI IVRIS ADEST. All editors, misled no doubt by 37, mispunctuate this passage, placing a comma before *quorum* instead of after: this destroys the gerundive *quorum ... appellandorum*, leaving the pentameter without a construction.

Williams proposed excising this distich, the reasons being (1) the sudden change from *forent* to *essent*, (2) the use of *inedita*, which is not found elsewhere, (3) the use of *cura* in a sense, 'written work', that is found only in late Latin, and (4) the prose turn of *quorum ... appellandorum*. To which it can be replied that (1) *forent* and *essent* are equivalent, and metrical convenience alone could justify the change, (2) the use of negatived perfect participles such as *inedita*, *indeclinatus* (x 83), and *inoblita* (xv 37) is a hallmark of Ovid's style, (3) *cura* is used in this sense by Tacitus (*Dial* 3 3 & 6 5; *Ann* III 24 4 & IV 11 5); its earlier use in verse is not surprising, and (4) gerundives were allowed in Latin verse; here, as at ix 12 '*salutandi* munere functa *tui*', the hyperbaton compensates for any awkwardness.

39. CVRA *unus Thuaneus Heinsii* CAVSA *BCMFHILT*. The same error in some manuscripts at *Her* I 20 'Tlepolemi leto *cura* nouata mea est', and *Fast* I 55 'uindicat Ausonias Iunonis *cura* Kalendas'; the inverse corruption at *Am* II xii 17 and *Fast* IV 368.

In 1894 Owen printed *causa*. The word can certainly have the meaning he attributed to it ('ὑπόθεσις', 'theme'), as at Prop II i 12 'inuenio *causas* mille poeta nouas', but this does not seem appropriate to the context here. In his later edition Owen returned to the usual reading.

41. APPELLANDORVM. *Appellare* used with the same sense (*OLD appello*[2] 11) at III vi 6 'appellent ne te carmina nostra rogas'; *nōmĭnāre* was not available for Ovid's use.

41-44. COTTA ... MAXIME. M. Aurelius Cotta Maximus Messalinus[31] (*Forschungen in Ephesos* III 112 no. 22; cited by Syme *HO* 117) was the younger son of Messalla, the patron of Tibullus; he was the recipient of six of the *Epistulae ex Ponto* (I v, I ix, II iii, II viii, III ii & III v). He is undoubtedly the M. Aurelius or Aurelius Cotta recorded by Tacitus as consul for 20 (*Ann* III 2 3 & 17 4). He was born much later than his brother Messalinus (the addressee of *EP* I vii and II ii), who was consul in 3 BC; the chronology is confirmed by a mention of him as praetor in 17 (*Inscriptiones Italiae* XIII i p. 298; see Syme *Ten Studies* 52), and by Ovid's testimony that Cotta was born after Ovid had become acquainted with his family (*EP* II iii 69-80). Cotta was clearly a very close friend of Ovid; this can be seen particularly from *EP* II iii, in which Ovid recounts how Cotta sent the first letter of comfort after his catastrophe (67-68) and tells how he confessed his *error* to Cotta.] Tacitus gives some information on Cotta's public career. In AD 16, in the aftermath of the discovery of Libo's plot against Tiberius, Cotta proposed that Libo's image not be in his descendants' funeral processions (*Ann* II 32 1). In 20, as consul, he similarly proposed penalties against Piso's family (*Ann* III 17), and in 27 he is mentioned as attacking Agrippina so as to please Tiberius (*Ann* V 3). The most interesting mention of him is at *Ann* VI 5 (AD 32), where Tacitus tells of how Tiberius himself intervened in favour of Cotta after he had been charged with *maiestas*; the eventual result was that charges were laid against Cotta's chief accuser.

42. PIERIDVM LVMEN. At *EP* III v 29-36 Ovid asked Cotta to send him some of his poetry.

For the sense of *lumen* here ('ornament'), *OLD lumen* 11 cites among other passages Cic *Sul* 5 'haec ornamenta ac *lumina* rei publicae' and *Phil II* 54 (of Pompey) 'imperi populi Romani decus ac *lumen* fuit'.

42. PRAESIDIVMQVE FORI = 'defender of the law'. Compare vi 33-34 'cum tibi suscepta est *legis uindicta seuerae*, / uerba uelut taetrum singula uirus habent'.

43. MATERNOS COTTAS. This passage should be taken in conjunction with *EP* III ii 103-8 (to Cotta) 'adde quod est animus semper tibi mitis, et altae / indicium mores nobilitatis habent, / quos Volesus patrii cognoscat nominis auctor, / quos Numa maternus non neget esse suos, / adiectique probent genetiua ad nomina Cottae, / si tu non esses, interitura domus'. The simplest explanation of these

386

two passages is that Cotta had been adopted by a maternal uncle, the last surviving Aurelius Cotta.

The question of Cotta's maternal ancestry is a vexed one; for a full discussion see Syme *HO* 119-21.

The present passage was written with Prop IV xi 31-32 in mind: 'altera *maternos* exaequat turba *Libones*, / et domus est titulis utraque fulta suis'.

44. NOBILITAS INGEMINATA. In a famous study (*Kleine Schriften* I 1 ff.; trans. *The Roman Nobility* [1969]), Matthias Gelzer demonstrated that the usual meaning of *nobilis* was 'descended from a consul'. Cotta was descended from a consul on both sides.

At *Met* XIII 144-47 Ovid uses *nobilitas* to mean 'descent from a god': (Ulysses speaking) 'mihi Laertes pater est, Arcesius illi, / Iuppiter huic ... est quoque *per matrem* Cyllenius *addita* nobis / *altera nobilitas*: deus est in utroque parente!'.

44. INGEMINATA. A verbal echo of *EP* I ii 1-2 (to Fabius Maximus) 'Maxime, qui tanti mensuram nominis imples, / et *geminas* animi *nobilitate* genus'.

46. ATQVE INTER TANTOS QVAE LEGERETVR ERAT. This is the end of the sentence that began at 5.

46. INTER TANTOS. Compare *EP* III i 55-56 (Ovid has just compared himself to Capaneus, Amphiaraus, Ulysses, and Philoctetes) 'si locus est aliquis *tanta inter nomina* paruis, / nos quoque conspicuos nostra ruina facit'.

47. SVMMOTVM *codd* SVBMOTVM *edd*. The assimilated *summ-* is standard in the manuscripts of Virgil and Lucretius, and should not be altered.

47. PROSCINDERE = 'revile, defame'. This seems to be the first instance of the word in this sense; the other examples cited by *OLD proscindo* 3 are Val Max V iii 3, Val Max VIII 5 2 'C. Flauium eadem lege accusatum testis *proscidit*', Pliny *NH* XXXIII 6, and Suet *Cal* 30 2 'equestrem ordinem ut scaenae harenaeque deuotum assidue *proscidit*'. The word connects with *laceras* in the first line of the poem, and with *neu cineres* *sparge, cruente, meos* in 48.

49. OMNIA PERDIDIMVS. The same phrase at *Met* XIII 527-28 (Hecuba speaking) '*omnia perdidimus*: superest cur uiuere tempus / in breue sustineam proles gratissima matri'.

49. TANTVMMODO is a prose word. It occurs elsewhere in Ovid only at *Fast* III 361 'ortus erat summo *tantummodo* margine Phoebus' and at *Tr* III vii 29-30 'pone, Perilla, metum; *tantummodo* femina nulla / neue uir a scriptis discat amare tuis'. Being a colloquial term, it is found in satire (Hor *Sat* I ix 54) and comedy (Ter *Ph* 109).

50. SENSVM MATERIAMQVE MALI. 'An occasion for pain, and the ability to feel it'. For *sensum* compare *EP* I ii 29-30 'felicem Nioben ... quae posuit *sensum* saxea facta *mali* [*uar* malis]' and *EP* I ii 37 'uiuimus ut numquam *sensu* careamus amaro'. For *materiam* compare *Her* VII 34 'materiam curae praebeat ille meae!', *Met* X 133-34 'ut leuiter pro materiaque doleret / admonuit' and *EP* I x 23-24 'dolores, / quorum materiam dat locus ipse mihi'.

51-52. QVID IVVAT EXTINCTOS FERRVM DEMITTERE IN ARTVS? / NON HABET IN NOBIS IAM NOVA PLAGA LOCVM. I believe this distich is an interpolation for the following reasons:

(1) Lines 49-50 form an effective ending, which 51-52 weaken. In 49-50 Ovid says that life is all that is left to him; and in 52 it is stated that he is already wounded in every place possible. These statements are contradictory.

(2) The use of a weapon in 51 is at odds with the rending metaphor of *laceras* (1) and *proscindere* (47).

(3) There seems something peculiar about *ferrum demittere in artus*; the examples of *demittere* with this sense in the *Metamorphoses* involve *ilia* (IV 119, XII 441), *armi* (XII 491), and *iugulum* (XIII 436; similar phrasing at *Her* XIV 5).

The distich's fabrication was assisted by *EP* II vii 41-42 'sic ego continue Fortunae uulneror ictu, / *uixque habet in nobis iam noua plaga locum*'.

388

BIBLIOGRAPHY

1. Editions and commentaries

F. Puteolanus, *P. Ovidii Nasonis Opera Omnia*. Bologna, 1471.

J. Andreas de Buxis, *P. Ovidii Nasonis Opera Omnia*. Rome, 1471.

N. Heinsius, *P. Ovidii Nasonis Opera Omnia*. Amsterdam, 1652.

Electa minora ex Ovidio, Tibullo, et Propertio. London, 1705.

P. Burman, *P. Ovidii Nasonis Opera Omnia*. Amsterdam, 1727.

T. Harles, *Publii Ovidii Nasonis Tristium Libri V Ex Ponto Libri IIII*. Erlangen, 1772.

W. E. Weber, *Corpus Poetarum Latinorum*. Frankfurt, 1833.

R. Merkel, *P. Ovidius Naso*, vol. 3: *Tristia. Ibis. Ex Ponto Libri. Fasti. Halieutica*. Leipzig, 1853.

O. Korn, *P. Ovidii Nasonis Ex Ponto Libri Quattuor*. Leipzig, 1868.

A. Riese, *P. Ovidii Nasonis Carmina*, vol. 3: *Fasti. Tristia. Ibis. Ex Ponto. Halieutica. Fragmenta*. Leipzig, 1874.

W. H. Williams, *Ovid. The Pontic Epistles. Book IV*. London, 1881.

R. Merkel, *P. Ovidius Naso*, vol. 3: *Tristia. Ibis. Ex Ponto Libri. Fasti*. Leipzig, 1884, reprinted 1902.

S. G. Owen, in J. P. Postgate's *Corpus Poetarum Latinorum*, vol. 1. London, 1894.

S. G. Owen, *P. Ovidi Nasonis Tristium Libri Quinque Ibis Ex Ponto Libri Quattuor Halieutica Fragmenta*. Oxford, 1915, reprinted 1963.

G. Némethy, *Commentarius Exegeticus ad Ovidii Epistulas ex Ponto*. Budapest, 1915.

G. Némethy, *Supplementum Commentariorum ad Ovidii Amores, Tristia, et Epistulas ex Ponto*. Budapest, 1922.

R. Ehwald and F. W. Levy, *P. Ovidius Naso*, vol. 3: *Tristium Libri V. Ibis. Ex Ponto Libri IV*. Leipzig, 1922.

A. L. Wheeler, *Ovid. Tristia. Ex Ponto*. Cambridge (Massachusetts) and London, 1924, reprinted 1975.

F. W. Lenz, *P. Ovidi Nasonis Epistulae ex Ponto*. Turin, 1938.

G. Luck, *Publius Ovidius Naso. Briefe aus der Verbannung*, with a German translation by W. Willige. Zurich and Stuttgart, 1963.

F. della Corte, *Ovidio. I Pontica* [translation and commentary], 2 vols. Genoa, 1977.

J. André, *Ovide. Pontiques*. Paris, 1977.

2. Works cited

Austin, R. G., ed. *P. Vergili Maronis Aeneidos Liber Secundus*. Oxford, 1964; reprinted 1966.

Axelson, B., *Unpoetische Wörter. Ein Beitrag zur Kenntnis der lateinischen Dichtersprache*. Lund, 1945.

Bardon, H., *La littérature latine inconnue*. Tome II: *L'époque impériale*. Paris, 1956.

Bell, A. J., *The Latin Dual and Poetic Diction. Studies in Numbers and Figures*. London and Toronto, 1923.

Birt, T., "Animadversiones ad Ovidii heroidum epistulas", *RhM* 32 (1877), 386-432.

Bömer, F., *P. Ouidius Naso. Die Fasten*. 2 vols. Heidelberg, 1957-58.

Bömer, F., *P. Ouidius Naso. Metamorphosen. Kommentar*. Heidelberg, 1969-(in progress).

Bonner, S. F., *Education in Ancient Rome. From the elder Cato to the younger Pliny*. London, 1977.

Brink, C. O., ed. *Horace on Poetry. The 'Ars Poetica'*. Cambridge, 1971.

Buckland, W. W., *A Text-book of Roman Law from Augustus to Justinian*. Third edition, revised by Peter Stein. Cambridge, 1963; corrected reprint, 1975.

Chatelain, E., *Paléographie des classiques latins*. Paris, 1894-1900.

Cope, E. M., ed. *The Rhetoric of Aristotle*. London, 1877; reprint edition, New York, 1973.

Costa, C. D. N., ed. *Seneca. Medea*. Oxford, 1973.

Ehrenberg, V. and A. H. M. Jones, *Documents Illustrating the Reigns of Augustus and Tiberius*. Second edition. Oxford, 1955; reprinted 1963.

Ehwald, R., "Jahresbericht über Ovid von Mai 1894 bis Januar 1902", *JAW* 109 (1901), 162-302.

Ehwald, R., *Kritische Beiträge zu Ovids Epistulae ex Ponto*. Gotha, 1896.

Fordyce, C. J., *Catullus. A commentary*. Oxford, 1961; corrected reprint, 1968.

Gain, D. B., ed. *The Aratus ascribed to Germanicus Caesar*. London, 1976.

Getty, R. J., ed. *M. Annaei Lucani De Bello Ciuili Liber I*. Cambridge, 1940; reprint edition, New York, 1979.

Goold, G. P., "Amatoria Critica". *HSPh* 69 (1965), 1-107.

Gow, A. S. F., ed. *Theocritus*. 2 vols. Cambridge, 1950.

Gronovius, J. F., *Observationum Libri Quattuor*, ed. F. Platner, Leipzig, 1755; reprint edition, Leipzig, 1831. (*Observationum Libri Tres*, Leiden, 1639; second edition, 1662).

Haupt, M., *Opuscula*. Leipzig, 1875; reprint edition,

Hildesheim, 1967.

Hedicke, E., *Studia Bentleiana*. Part V: *Ovidius Bentleianus*. Freienwald, 1905.

Henderson, A. A. R., ed. *P. Ovidi Nasonis Remedia Amoris*. Edinburgh, 1979.

Hilberg, I., *Die Gesetze der Wortstellung im Pentameter des Ovid*. Leipzig, 1894.

Hofmann, J. B., *Lateinische Umgangsprache*. Third edition. Heidelberg, 1951.

Housman, A. E., *The Classical Papers of A. E. Housman*, edited by J. Diggle and F. R. D. Goodyear. 3 vols. Cambridge, 1972.

Kassel, R., *Untersuchungen zur griechischen und römischen Konsolationsliteratur*. Munich, 1958.

Kenney, E. J., "Nequitiae Poeta", in *Ovidiana*, pp. 201-9, ed. N. I. Herescu. Paris, 1958.

Kenney, E. J., "Ovid and the Law", *YClS* XXI (1969) 243-63.

Kenney, E. J., "Ouidius Prooemians", *PCPhS* 202, n.s. 22 (1976), 46-53.

Kiessling, A. G., *Coniectanea Propertiana*. Greifswald, 1876.

Kirfel, E.-A., *Untersuchungen zur Briefform der Heroides Ovids*. Bern and Stuttgart, 1969.

Korn, O., *De codicibus duobus carminum Ouidianorum ex Ponto datorum Monacensibus*. Breslau, 1874.

Lattimore, R. A., *Themes in Greek and Latin Epitaphs*. Urbana, 1962.

Lejay, P., ed. *Horace. Satires*. Paris, 1911; reprint edition, Hildesheim, 1966.

Lenz, F. W., "Die Wiedergewinnung der von Heinsius Benutzten Ovidhandschriften in den letzten fünfzig Jahren", *Eranos* 51 (1953) 66-88 & 61 (1963) 98-120.

Löfstedt, E., *Syntactica*. Vol. 2: *Syntaktisch-Stilistische*

Gesichtspunkte und Probleme. Lund, 1933; reprinted 1956.

Lowe, E. A., *Codices Latini Antiquiores*. 12 vols. Oxford, 1934-71.

Luck, G., ed. *P. Ovidius Naso. Tristia*. 2 vols. Heidelberg, 1967-77.

Madvig, J. N., *Adversaria Critica*. Vol 2: *Emendationes Latinae*. Copenhagen, 1873.

Martin, R. H., ed. *Terence. Adelphoe*. Cambridge, 1976.

Marx, F., ed. *C. Lucilii Carminum Reliquiae*. 2 vols. Leipzig, 1904; reprint edition, Amsterdam, 1963.

Merkel, R., ed. *P. Ovidii Nasonis Tristium libri quinque et Ibis*. Berlin, 1837.

Mommsen, T., *Römische Staatsrecht*. 3 vols. Third edition. Leipzig, 1887; reprint edition, Graz, 1952.

Morel, W., ed. *Fragmenta poetarum Latinorum epicorum et lyricorum praeter Ennium et Lucilium*. Leipzig, 1927.

Munari, F., *Catalogue of the MSS of Ovid's Metamorphoses*. London, 1957.

Munari, F., "Supplemento al catalogo dei manoscritti delle Metamorfosi ovidiane", *RFIC* 93 (1965) 288-97.

Munari, F., "Secondo supplemento al catalogo dei manoscritti delle Metamorfosi ovidiane", *Studia Florentina Alexandro Ronconi Sexagenario Oblata*, pp. 275-80, Rome, 1970.

Munro, H. A. J., *Criticisms and Elucidations of Catullus*. Cambridge, 1878; reprint edition, New York, 1938.

Munro, H. A. J., ed. *T. Lucreti Cari De Rerum Natura Libri Sex*. 3 vols. Fourth edition. London, 1886; reprinted 1908; reprint edition, New York, 1978.

Murgatroyd, P., *Tibullus I* [commentary]. Pietermaritzburg, 1980.

Nash, E., *Pictorial Dictionary of Ancient Rome*. 2 vols. London,

1961.

Nisbet, R. G. M. and M. Hubbard, *A Commentary on Horace: Odes Book 1*. Oxford, 1970.

Otto, A., *Die Sprichwörter und Sprichwörtlichen Redensarten der Römer*. Leipzig, 1898; reprint edition, Hildesheim, 1962.

Owen, S. G., ed. *P. Ovidi Nasonis Tristium liber secundus*. Oxford, 1924.

Palmer, A., ed. *P. Ovidi Nasonis Heroides*. Oxford, 1898.

Platnauer, M., *Latin Elegiac Verse. A study of the metrical usages of Tibullus, Propertius & Ovid*. Cambridge, 1951; reprint edition, Hamden (Connecticut), 1971.

Radermacher, L., "Das Epigramm des Didius", *SAWW* 170,9 (1912) 1-31.

Reeve, M. D., "Heinsius's Manuscripts of Ovid", *RhM* 117 (1974) 133-36 & 119 (1976) 65-78.

Ribbeck, O., ed. *Tragicorum Romanorum Fragmenta*. Leipzig, 1897.

Roscher, W. H., *Ausführliches Lexikon der Griechischen und Römischen Mythologie*. 6 vols. Leipzig, 1884-1937.

Sandys, J. E., *Latin Epigraphy*. Second edition. London, 1927; reprint edition, Chicago, 1974.

Schoenemann, C. P. C., *Bibliothecae Augustae sive notitiarum et excerptorum codicum Wolfenbuttelensium specimen*. Helmstadt, 1829.

Schwartz, J., "Pompeius Macer et la jeunesse d'Ovide", *RPh* 25 (1951) 182-94.

Scott, K., "Emperor Worship in Ovid", *TAPhA* 61 (1930), 43-69.

Shackleton Bailey, D. R., *Propertiana*. Cambridge, 1956.

Smith, K. F., ed. *The Elegies of Albius Tibullus*. New York, 1913; reprint edition, Darmstadt, 1978.

Syme, R., *History in Ovid*. Oxford, 1978.

Syme, R., *Tacitus*. 2 vols. Oxford, 1958.

Syme, R., *Ten Studies in Tacitus*. Oxford, 1970.

Tarrant, R. J., ed. *Seneca. Agamemnon*. Cambridge, 1976.

Tarrant, R. J., "The Authenticity of the Letter of Sappho to Phaon (*Heroides* XV)", *HSPh* 85 (1981) 133-53.

Tarrant, R. J., article on "Ovid", section on the *Ex Ponto, Texts and Transmission*, ed. L. D. Reynolds, Oxford, 1983, pp. 262-65.

Thibault, J. C., *The Mystery of Ovid's Exile*. Berkeley, 1964.

Wickham, E. C., ed. *Quinti Horati Flacci opera omnia*. 2 vols. Oxford, 1891.

Willis, J. *Latin Textual Criticism*. Urbana, 1972.

Woodcock, E. C., *A New Latin Syntax*. London, 1959; reprinted 1971.

INDEX OF TOPICS DISCUSSED

The scope of this index is described at pages vii-viii of the Preface.

Ehwald, Rudolf
  Kritische Beiträge zu Ovids Epistulae ex Ponto (1896), 45-46

ensis vs. *gladius*, 309-310

eques: Ovid's status as a member of the equestrian order, 263

Ex Ponto IV a work entirely separate from *EP* I-III; its structure, 4-5

Ex Ponto vs. *De Ponto*: correct title of the collection, 145

excidit = 'I forgot', 205

excutere = 'examine', 263

Fabius Maximus, 7

facie dative singular of *facies*, 343

fueram equivalent to imperfect, 230

Gallio, 7, 19-20

Gete ablative singular of *Getes*, 195-196

Giants' rebellion, Ovid's unfinished poem about, 272-273

Gracchus vs. *Graccus*, 461

Graecinus, 6-7, 16, 286

Graius vs. *Graecus*, 425

gratari used by the poets in place of the metrically difficult *gratulari*, 399

Harles, Theophilus
  edition of 1772; his discovery of manuscript *B* of the *Ex*

1963, 50-51

manuscripts of *Ex Ponto* IV, 23-34
    Antuerpiensis Musei Plantiniani Denucé 68 (*M*), 28-30
    fragmentum Guelferbytanum, Cod. Guelf. 13.11 Aug. 4°
(*G*), 23-24
    Francofurtanus Barth 110 (*F*), 30-31
    Hamburgensis scrin. 52 F (*A*), 23
    Holkhamicus 322 (*H*), 31
    Laurentianus 36 32 (*I*), 32
    Lipsiensis bibl. ciu. Rep. I 2° 7 (*L*), 32
    Monacensis latinus 384 (*B*), 25-28
    Monacensis latinus 19476 (*C*), 25-28
    Parisinus lat. 7993 (*P*), 33
    Turonensis 879 (*T*), 32-33
    vulgate manuscripts (*MFHILT*), 28-29

mare (ablative singular), 242

Merkel, Rudolf
    edition of 1853, 40
    edition of 1884, 45

Morrow, Rob, x

munus opusque = 'creation', 160

murmur, 406

nature of this edition, vii

Némethy, Geza
    commentary of 1915, 48

neque = *sed ... non*, 203

neque before vowel, vs. *nec*, 203

niger as a moral quality, 423-24

INDEX OF TEXTUAL EMENDATIONS

This is an index to those textual emendations first appearing in this edition.
Where a critic's name is not supplied, the emendation was proposed by the Editor.

FOOTNOTES:

[1] The evidence for Ovid's *error* and the many theories advanced to explain it are gathered and fully discussed in J. C. Thibault's *The Mystery of Ovid's Exile* (Berkeley: 1964).

[2] For these references I am indebted to page xxxv of A. L. Wheeler's excellent introduction to the Loeb edition of the *Tristia* and *Ex Ponto*. For the date of Tiberius' triumph, see Syme *History in Ovid* 40.

[3] Professor Tarrant notes however that unlike I-III the fourth book was not written within a very short time; if Ovid had collected what he thought worth publishing of his output over several years, it would not be surprising to find it longer than the preceding collections.

[4] Professor E. Fantham notes as well the central placement of poem ix, with its *laudes Augusti*.

[5] Full information on what is known of each of the addressees will be found in the introductions to the poems in the commentary.

[6] Ovid had used a similar technique in *Tr* I i, where he gives his book instructions for its voyage to Rome, including directions on how it should approach Augustus.

[7] Professor R. J. Tarrant points out to me in particular that lines 63-64 on the apotheosis of Augustus being in part accomplished through poetry are one of the few instances in the poetry of exile of Ovid's earlier mischievous irony towards Augustus—a sign of a return on Ovid's part to his earlier form.

[8] However, Albinovanus' poem on Germanicus' campaigns may have had a strong geographical element; as Professor E. Fantham notes, Ovid may here be appealing to this interest, or demonstrating competitive skill in handling the topic.

[9] The manuscripts were probably produced at the same German centre. Professor R. J. Tarrant has noted the presence of the *Ex Ponto* in book-lists of the eleventh and early twelfth centuries from Blaubeuern, Tegernsee, Bamberg, Egmond, and Cracow (*Texts and Transmission* 263); he suggests Tegernsee to me as a probable candidate for the production of *B* and *C*.

[10] G. P. Goold ("Amatoria Critica", *HSPh* 69 [1965] 10) has

an interesting discussion of the problems in establishing Ovid's orthography. For accusative plural endings in the third declension, he concludes that -*is* for Ovid can be neither established nor excluded.

[11] In recent years much progress has been made in identifying the manuscripts Heinsius used. See the monograph of Munari and the articles of Reeve and Lenz listed in the bibliography.

[12] *Electa minora ex Ovidio, Tibullo et Propertio*, London, 1705. The book was reprinted as late as 1860 (*Brit. Mus. Gen. Catalogue*, vol. 177, col. 470). I quote some of the notes on x in the commentary and apparatus.

[13] 'Diligenter autem et religiose tractaui codicem et singulas epistolas bis, et in locis uexatis saepius contuli. Neque tamen, quae hominum est imbecillitas, aciem oculorum quaedam effugisse, negabo' (xi-xii).

[14] A. Grafton has noted that Heinsius' publisher Elzevier seems to have been unwilling to alter the text as it already existed (*JRS* LXVII [1977], 173). I owe my knowledge of Heinsius' editorial practices as here described to Professor R. J. Tarrant, who has examined the Harvard copies of the 1664 edition of Heinsius' text (without notes), the 1670 Leiden edition of Bernard Cnippingius, which reproduces Heinsius' notes, and the 1663 reprint of Daniel Heinsius' edition.

[15] Consequently any statements I make on Heinsius' editorial practices are based on explicit statements in his notes.

[16] My knowledge of the manuscript is drawn from André's apparatus.

[17] He collated four other manuscripts, M, *Bernensis bibl. munic. 478, Diuionensis bibl. munic. 497,* and *British Library Burney 220,* but gives their readings only occasionally.

[18] These figures are taken from Platnauer 17 and from page vii of Riese's preface to his edition.

[19] A drinking-vessel holding one third of a *sextarius* (*OLD triens* 3).

[20] Compare Suet *Aug* 89 3 'componi tamen aliquid de se nisi et serio et a praestantissimis offendebatur, admonebatque praetores ne paterentur nomen suum commissionibus obsolefieri ['be cheapened in prize declamations'—Rolfe]'.

[21] *PIR*[1] A 343; *PIR*[2] A 479; PW 1,1 1314 21-40; Schanz-Hosius II 266 (§315); Bardon 69-73.

[22] Macrobius does include the explanation for the freezing-

over. In view of his fuller account, I believe that Macrobius drew his material from Gellius' source and not from Gellius. It is of course possible enough that Macrobius conflated Gellius with another source.

[23] This seems the best solution to the awkwardness of the line as currently printed. Gellius IX xiv 21 gives two examples of dative *facie* from Lucilius. Plautus regularly uses *fide* (*Aul* 667, *Pers* 193, *Poen* 890, *Trin* 117) and *die* (*Am* 546, *Capt* 464, *Trin* 843); dative *pube* is found at *Pseud* 126. Sallust and Caesar use *fide* (*Iug* 16 3; *BG* V 3 7); at the time of Germanicus, *fide* is found at Hor *Sat* I iii 94-95 'quid faciam si furtum fecerit, aut si / prodiderit commissa *fide* sponsumue negarit?', and *pernicie* at Livy V 13 5.

[24] *PIR*[1] I 493; *PIR*[2] I 756; PW X,1 1035 26; Schanz-Hosius 349 (§ 336)

[25] Instances at *Her* VI 99, *Am* I xiv 13 & II vii 23, *AA* II 675, III 81 & III 539, *Met* XIII 117, XIII 854 & XIV 684, *Fast* III 143, III 245 & VI 663, *Tr* I v 79, II 135, V x 43, V xii 21 & V xiv 15, *EP* I vii 31, II xi 23, III ii 103, III iv 45, III vi 35, IV x 45, the present passage, and IV xiv 45. (Ovid's imitator uses the expression at *Her* XVII 199.) The preponderance of this presumably colloquial expression in the poems of exile is noteworthy.

[26] *PIR*[1] T 314; PW VII A,2 1611 62; Schanz-Hosius 272 (§ 318 16)

[27] Honestus XXI 1-2 Gow-Page (*Garland of Philip*); discussed by Professor Jones at *HSCP* 74 (1970) 249-55.

[28] PW XV,2 1481 3; Jacoby *FGrH* no. 184.

[29] *PIR*[1] D 131; *PIR*[2] D 153; Schanz-Hosius 174-76 (§ 275-76); Bardon 52-57.

[30] *PIR*[1] P 473; Syme *HO* 73-74; Bardon 65-66; J. Schwartz, "Pompeius Macer et la jeunesse d'Ovide", *RPh* XXV (1951) 182-94. Macer is discussed in the section of Schanz-Hosius dealing with Ovid's catalogue of poets (269-72; § 318); I give references to Schanz-Hosius below only for poets dealt with outside this section.

[31] *PIR*[1] A 1236; *PIR*[2] A 1488; PW 11,2 2490 13

CPSIA information can be obtained
at www.ICGtesting.com
Printed in the USA
BVHW031342150419
545534BV00012B/2020/P